The Contemporary Law of Targeting

International Humanitarian Law Series

VOLUME 25

The International Humanitarian Law Series is a series of monographs and edited volumes which aims to promote scholarly analysis and discussion of both the theory and practice of the international legal regulation of armed conflict.
The series explores substantive issues of International Humanitarian Law including,

- protection for victims of armed conflict and regulation of the means and methods of warfare
- questions of application of the various legal regimes for the conduct of armed conflict
- issues relating to the implementation of International Humanitarian Law obligations
- national and international approaches to the enforcement of the law and
- the interactions between International Humanitarian Law and other related areas of international law such as Human Rights, Refugee Law, Arms Control and Disarmament Law, and International Criminal Law.

The titles in this series are listed at the end of this volume.

The Contemporary Law of Targeting

by

Ian Henderson

MARTINUS NIJHOFF PUBLISHERS

LEIDEN • BOSTON
2009

Cover photo printed with kind permission of the Royal Australian Air Force.

This book is printed on acid-free paper.

Library of Congress Cataloging-in-Publication Data

Henderson, Ian.
The contemporary law of targeting : military objectives, proportionality, and precautions in attack under additional protocol I / by Ian Henderson.
p. cm. – (International humanitarian law series)
Includes bibliographical references and index.
ISBN 978-90-04-17480-1 (hardback : alk. paper)
1. War (International law) 2. Military weapons–Law and legislation. 3. Humanitarian law. I. Title.

KZ5624.H46 2009
341.6–dc22

2009038519

ISSN 1389-6776
ISBN 978 90 04 17480 1

PRINTED IN THE NETHERLANDS

To my wife Nicki.

Table of Contents

Foreword

In February 2003, Australia deployed an array of forces as part of coalition operations against Saddam Hussein's Iraq. Royal Australian Air Force (RAAF) assets in the area of operations included C-130 Hercules transport aircraft, P3-C Orion maritime patrol aircraft and FA-18 Hornet fighter-bomber aircraft.

This was the most significant operational deployment for the RAAF since the Vietnam war. Australia had deployed transport, surveillance and fighter aircraft in operations since Vietnam, but this was the first time that combat aircraft had been employed in an air to ground bombing role. Australian aircraft had not dropped a bomb in combat since Canberra bombers of RAAF No. 2 Squadron dropped their final bombs of the Vietnam war on the 31st of May 1971. This deployment was a significant event for Australia, both politically and militarily.

Also deployed was a forward control element of specialist Air Force personnel, including aircrew from each of the aircraft types deployed, intelligence officers, imagery analysts, logistics and support personnel, and legal officers. As Commander of the air component of Australian forces, these specialist staff enabled me to integrate the Australian effort into the broader coalition air campaign. Collocated with the hub of the coalition air effort—the Combined Air Operations Centre—the role of the forward control element was to ensure that Australian air forces were employed effectively and in accordance with Australian law and government policy.

One of the central figures of my staff, helping to ensure that the RAAF forces met these obligations, was my senior legal officer, Wing Commander Ian Henderson. The Law of Armed Conflict (LOAC) was a pivotal factor in all of our thinking and planning. The nature of Saddam Hussein's totalitarian state apparatus did not lend itself to easy distinctions between combatants and civilians. Each of the coalition partners in the air campaign had different interpretations of, and obligations under, LOAC. Coalition partners also had differing rules of engagement and policies in relation to minimising the risk to civilians.

Wing Commander Henderson was instrumental in steering Australia through the law and policy maze. From reviewing potential targets against Australia's legal obligations, to providing the specialised air input to our rules of engagement, to liaising closely with our coalition partners to increase our mutual understanding, Wing Commander Henderson was a vital member of my staff. His mastery of his field of study was a significant contributing factor to the ultimate success of the Australian effort in the air campaign.

Wing Commander Henderson's ability to reduce complex legal concepts to practical guidance for war-fighters is one of the reasons that he was such a valuable member of my staff. That ability is on display in this work. The six-step process he describes for targeting decisions has applicability across all forms of warfare from aerial targeting to an infantryman with a rifle. It isolates the elements of a process that is at times intuitive and others seemingly complex, demonstrating that the same considerations apply in every case.

I congratulate Wing Commander Henderson on this excellent contribution to military thinking in this field and commend this work to military professionals everywhere.

Air Vice-Marshal Geoffrey Brown, AM
Deputy Chief of Air Force

Acknowledgements

This book was originally written as my doctoral thesis at the University of Melbourne. I would like to thank my supervisors, Professor Timothy McCormack and Doctor Andrew Mitchell. I am also indebted to my examiners for their comments—Professor Michael Schmitt and Mr William Fenrick. To all the legal officers of the Australian Defence Force and other militaries who were kind enough to listen to my half-expressed thoughts, I remain grateful. The black-letter of the law comes alive only in context. To all of the aircrew, intelligence officers and other members of the Australian Defence Force who patiently shared their technical knowledge and explained operations, thank you.

Chapter 7 deals with precautions in attack. In that chapter, I briefly mention that the standard for determining that an object is a military objective is one of 'reasonable belief'. I would like to acknowledge Maria Brick's assistance to helping me to refine my thinking on the issues presented in this work on the level of certainty required in determining whether an object is a military objective.

The material in chapter 9 has its origin in a series of questions and answers asked of me in my capacity as a Royal Australian Air Force legal officer in late 2002 and early 2003. After I had formulated the broad advice and a first draft of a targeting process, Pat Keane and the staff at the Australian Government Solicitor joined me in refining the final wording and the number of steps in the 6-step targeting process set out in chapter 9. Pat Keane has remained engaged in the issues ever since.

I would like to thank *The Age*, the *International Review of the Red Cross*, the *Yale Human Rights and Development Law Journal*, Professor Michael Schmitt, Major General (retired) Anthony Rogers, Mr Tom Allard and Mr Mark Forbes for their kind permission to reproduce certain quotes at various parts of this book. Copyright in the picture on the front cover remains with the Commonwealth of Australia.

While both my thesis and this book were written while I was serving as a legal officer in the Royal Australian Air Force, it was written in a personal capacity. All opinions and expressed thoughts are my own and may not reflect the position of the Air Force, Department of Defence or Commonwealth of Australia.

Finally, none of this would have been possible without the support and encouragement of my family, and my wife and her family.

Acknowledgements

Abbreviations

API	Protocol Additional to the Geneva Conventions of 12 August 1949, and relating to the Protection of Victims of International Armed Conflicts, opened for signature 12 December 1977, 1125 UNTS 3 (entered into force 7 December 1978)
APII	Protocol Additional to the Geneva Conventions of 12 August 1949, and relating to the Protection of Victims of Non-International Armed Conflicts, opened for signature 12 December 1977, 1125 UNTS 609 (entered into force 7 December 1978)
ATO	Air Task Order
C3	Command, Control and Communication
CE/1b	International Committee of the Red Cross, Conference of Government Experts on the Reaffirmation and Development of International Humanitarian Law Applicable in Armed Conflicts, Volume I, Introduction (1971)
CE/3b	International Committee of the Red Cross, Conference of Government Experts on the Reaffirmation and Development of International Humanitarian Law Applicable in Armed Conflicts, Volume III, Protection of the civilian population against dangers of hostilities (1971)
CE/4b	International Committee of the Red Cross, Conference of Government Experts on the Reaffirmation and Development of International Humanitarian Law Applicable in Armed Conflicts, Volume IV, Rules Relative to the Behaviour of Combatants (1971)

CE 1972 Report, Volume I	International Committee of the Red Cross, Conference of Government Experts on the Reaffirmation and Development of International Humanitarian Law Applicable in Armed Conflicts, Volume I, Report on the Work of the Conference (1972)
CE 1972 Report, Volume II	International Committee of the Red Cross, Conference of Government Experts on the Reaffirmation and Development of International Humanitarian Law Applicable in Armed Conflicts, Volume II, Report on the Work of the Conference (Annexes) (1972)
CDDH/III	International Committee of the Red Cross, Official Records of the Diplomatic Conference on the Reaffirmation and Development of International Humanitarian Law Applicable in Armed Conflicts, Volume III (1974–1977)
CDDH/VI	International Committee of the Red Cross, Official Records of the Diplomatic Conference on the Reaffirmation and Development of International Humanitarian Law Applicable in Armed Conflicts, Volume IV (1974–1977)
CDDH/XV	International Committee of the Red Cross, Official Records of the Diplomatic Conference on the Reaffirmation and Development of International Humanitarian Law Applicable in Armed Conflicts, Volume XV (1974–1977)
CEP	Circular Error Probable
ECHR	European Convention on Human Rights
FAC	Forward Air Controller
GCI	Geneva Convention for the Amelioration of the Condition of the Wounded and Sick in Armed Forces in the Field, opened for signature 12 August 1949, 75 UNTS 31 (entered into force 21 October 1950)
GCII	Geneva Convention for the Amelioration of the Condition of the Wounded, Sick and Shipwrecked Members of the Armed Forces at Sea, opened for signature 12 August 1949, 75 UNTS 85 (entered into force 21 October 1950)
GCIII	Geneva Convention Relative to the Treatment of Prisoners of War, opened for signature 12 August 1949, 75 UNTS 135 (entered into force 21 October 1950)

GCIV	Geneva Convention relative to the Protection of Civilian Persons in Time of War, opened for signature 12 August 1949, 75 UNTS 287 (entered into force 21 October 1950)
HAW	Hague Rules of Air Warfare 1923
HCP	Convention for the Protection of Cultural Property in the event of Armed Conflict, opened for signature 14 May 1954, 249 UNTS 240 (entered into force 7 August 1956)
HIV	Convention (IV) Respecting the Laws and Customs of War on Land, signed at The Hague 18 October 1907, 3 Martens Nouveau Recueil (ser. 3) 461 (entered into force 26 January 1910)
HIVR	Regulations Respecting the Laws and Customs of War on Land, annex to HIV, signed at The Hague 18 October 1907, 3 Martens Nouveau Recueil (ser. 3) 461 (entered into force 26 January 1910)
ICC	International Criminal Court
ICJ	International Court of Justice
ICRC	International Committee of the Red Cross
ICTR	International Criminal Tribunal for Rwanda
ICTY	International Criminal Tribunal for the Former Yugoslavia
IHL	International Humanitarian Law
IHRL	International Human Rights Law
Lieber Code	Instructions for the Government of Armies of the United States in the Field, prepared by Francis Lieber, promulgated as General Orders No. 100 by President Lincoln, 24 April 1863
OTP Report	Final Report to the Prosecutor by the Committee Established to Review the NATO Bombing Campaign Against the Federal Republic of Yugoslavia, published on 13 June 2000
PGM	Precision-guided munition
RAAF	Royal Australian Air Force
RTS	Radio Televizije Srbije (Radio Television Serbia)

UAV	Uninhabited aerial vehicle
UGM	Unguided munition
UN	United Nations
UNSCR	United Nations Security Council resolution
VCLT	Vienna Convention on the Law of Treaties, opened for signature on 23 May 1969, 1155 UNTS 331 (entered into force on 27 January 1980)

Glossary

Armed conflict	An international armed conflict unless explicitly stated otherwise.
Collateral damage	The incidental loss of civilian life, injury to civilians, damage to civilian objects, or a combination thereof as a result of attacking a legitimate military objective. Incidental is used in this context to mean both unintended and unwanted.
Hors de combat	Out of combat.
Military operations	While the term military operations covers the whole spectrum of activities of the military,[1] in this book military operations is defined to mean just armed conflict and UN peace enforcement operations under Chapter VII of the Charter of the United Nations.
Targeting	The deliberate process followed by a military commander in deciding against which objectives he or she will apply force and the means that will be used to apply force. To be distinguished from attacking a target, which is the actual application of force.
UN sanctioned operations	Operations conducted under UN command and control, and operations authorised by the UN but conducted under national command and control.

1 Eg., peaceful operations such as evacuation after floods or delivering relief supplies, more aggressive operations such as evacuating nationals in a 'collapsed State', through to anti-terrorist operations and then finally armed conflict.

Glossary

[illegible]

Chapter 1

Introduction

> The disputes arising among those who are held together by no common bond of civil laws to decide their dissensions ... all bear a relation to the circumstances of war or peace.[1]

This is a book about the law that applies when peace has failed and armed forces are engaged in conflict. It is fundamentally about the lawful use of force in an armed conflict, against whom and against what may force be used, and the precautions that must be taken in employing that force. Despite the 30th anniversary on 8 June 2007 of the adoption of the *Protocol Additional to the Geneva Conventions of 12 August 1949, and relating to the Protection of Victims of International Armed Conflicts*,[2] fundamental concepts of what is a military objective, the application of the rule of proportionality and other precautionary measures when launching an attack, and the allocation of legal responsibility for various targeting decisions are all still in need of significant clarification.

In March 2003 a senior Royal Australian Air Force officer deployed on operations to the Middle East. One of the commander's many jobs was to ensure that the Australian F/A-18 Hornets,[3] which were sent to the Middle East and were based out of an undisclosed air base in an undisclosed country, attacked targets that complied with the Australian Rules of Engagement and the Targeting Directive.[4] This

---

1 Hugo Grotius, *On the Law of War and Peace* (A. Campbell trans, 1814) [trans of: *De Jure Belli ac Pacis*] (available at <http://www.constitution.org/gro/djbp.htm> at 26 May 2006).

2 *Protocol Additional to the Geneva Conventions of 12 August 1949, and relating to the Protection of Victims of International Armed Conflicts*, opened for signature 12 December 1977, 1125 UNTS 3 (entered into force 7 December 1978) ('API').

3 The F/A-18 Hornets are fighter/attack aircraft that can engage in air-to-air missions (attacks on other aircraft with missiles and guns) and air-to-ground missions (dropping guided and unguided bombs).

4 "In this instance the coalition will be lead [sic] by the United States, but our forces are commandeered by Australians right from the ground through to Canberra. So the United States as leader of the coalition may task the Australian force but the task would have to be accepted by the Australian commander. And if it's outside of our rules of engagement or our targeting directive, then the commander would say no." (Radio 2BL, 'Senator the Hon. Robert Hill, Minister for Defence, Leader of the Government in the Senate, interview with Richard Glover' 18 March 2003 <http://www.minister.defence.gov.au/HillTranscripttpl.cfm?CurrentId=2442> at 5 March 2007) In the Australian context, a targeting directive is issued by the Chief of the Defence Force and will, among "other things - such as defining classes of legitimate targets and pro-

required the commander continually to make judgments that might be later commented on in the press on an almost daily basis and, in an extreme case, be judged in the International Criminal Court ('ICC').[5] At the same time, the commander was obliged to protect the lives of the pilots under his command and, as this was a coalition operation, the safety of aircrew in coalition forces also needed to be considered. The commander was legally obliged, as well as morally, to take precautions to protect the civilian population of Iraq. And, of course, there was a desire to win the war. Such was, and is, the role of a modern Air Force commander.

The commander's headquarters was made up of communications staff, logistics officers, administrative staff and many others. However, these staff were primarily there to keep the headquarters running and they did not directly assist in the decisions affecting the prosecution of the conflict.[6] For that, there were three primary groups to assist the commander. There were other aircrew like the commander (the operations staff), an intelligence staff (indeed, in a higher headquarters this group may be the most numerous), and legal officers. This book is aimed at the work of this last group and the legal issues on which they advised—and on which future lawyers will have to advise commanders. When the Rules of Engagement and Targeting Directive restrict allowable targets to 'military objectives', does this include television and radio transmission stations? If civilians cannot be targeted, how should human shields be dealt with? If the Rules of Engagement state that any expected incidental (ie, unintended) civilian losses are not to be excessive when compared to the military advantage anticipated to be gained from an attack, would an attack comply with those rules if the second-in-command of the enemy forces is having dinner at a local restaurant with possibly 10 civilians in the building where it is expected that the attack will kill all those present?

Our commander was aware that Australia was a State party to API, and the commander was also aware that not all of the coalition partners are parties to that treaty. If a coalition partner had assessed a target as lawful, could our commander rely upon this to comply with Australia's legal obligations? If the commander could not rely upon the assessment, could the commander rely on coalition intelligence sources when making a fresh assessment? If Australia had gone into the armed conflict to enforce United Nations Security Council Resolutions, would this change any of the above answers?

---

viding a process for determining possible unintended injury to civilians or damage to their property - the targeting directive will also include a number of steps outlining the requirements of the LOAC that apply to targeting decisions." (Air Marshal Angus Houston, 'The Law of Armed Conflict and Contemporary Air Operations—the ADF Approach' (Speech Delivered at the Solferino Seminar, Weston Creek, 11 May 2004) <http://www.defence.gov.au/raaf/corporate/leaders/Solferino%20Seminar.pdf> at 23 March 2006)

5 The ICC was created pursuant to the *Rome Statute of the International Criminal Court*, opened for signature 17 July 1998, 2187 UNTS 90, (entered into force 1 July 2002). See generally <http://www.icc-cpi.int/home.html&l=en>.

6 I write directly as their advice will affect almost every decision indirectly. Issues like availability of materiel, communication issues and personnel matters must constantly be considered when making war-fighting decisions.

These are just some of the issues discussed herein—issues that can be gathered together under the label of 'targeting law'.

1.1 Background

States have long recognised the existence of laws regulating the conduct of hostilities, which can be conveniently categorised as the *jus ad bellum* and the *jus in bello*. The *jus ad bellum* is the area of law that regulates the conditions under which a State may resort to war or to force in general. The *jus in bello* is the area of law that governs the conduct of belligerents during a war, and in a broader sense comprises the rights and obligations of neutral parties as well.[7] War has a significant and direct impact on the civilian population. One commentator has concluded that in the about 150 wars since 1945, four civilians have died for each of the seven million military personnel who have been killed.[8] The *jus in bello* is recognition of this fact and is, in part, an attempt to reduce the impact of war on civilians.

"There is no agreement on what to call jus in bello in everyday language."[9] So, while the international law comprising the *jus in bello* has in recent times generally been referred to as *international humanitarian law* ('IHL') by the International Committee of the Red Cross ('ICRC') and many writers,[10] military manuals and military (and some non-military) writers often use the terms *law(s) of armed conflict* or *laws of war*.[11] Whether the terms IHL, laws of war and law of armed conflict are synonymous is an interesting but largely academic debate.[12] While it is arguable

---

7 Robert Kolb, 'Origin of the twin terms jus ad bellum/jus in bello' (1997) 320 *International Review of the Red Cross*, fn 1 <http://www.icrc.org/Web/eng/siteengo.nsf/iwpList163/D9DAD4EE8533DAEFC1256B66005AFFEF> at 4 June 2006. While the legal concepts may have existed in some form or another for centuries or even millennia, the terms *jus ad bellum* and *jus in bello* are themselves of more recent origin. "The august solemnity of Latin confers on the terms *jus ad bellum* and *jus in bello* the misleading appearance of being centuries old. In fact, these expressions were only coined at the time of the League of Nations and were rarely used in doctrine or practice until after the Second world War, in the late 1940s to be precise." (Kolb, this note) (footnote omitted, italics in original). See also Karma Nabulsi, *Jus ad Bellum/Jus in Bello*, Crimes of War Project <http://www.crimesofwar.org/thebook/jus-ad-bellum.html> at 25 May 2006.

8 Walter Kendall III, 'Killing non-combatants in war: A critique of the justification and excuses' (2000) *Australian International Law Journal* 99, 99.

9 Nabulsi, above n 7 (chapter 1).

10 See for instance Marco Sassoli and Antoine Bouvier, *How Does Law Protect in War?* (1999) 67, where they state that IHL "can be defined as the branch of international law limiting the use of violence in armed conflict …".

11 Nabulsi, above n 7 (chapter 1); *What is international humanitarian law?* (2004) International Committee of the Red Cross <http://www.icrc.org/Web/eng/siteengo.nsf/htmlall/humanitarian-law-factsheet/$File/What_is_IHL.pdf> at 25 May 2006.

12 See, for example, an article by Shearer stating that traditionally the Law of Armed Conflict covers Hague Law and IHL deals with Geneva Law, while today the terms are interchangeable (Ivan Shearer, *Rules of Conduct during Humanitarian Interventions*, The University of North Carolina at Chapel Hill—American Diplomacy <http://www.unc.edu/depts/diplomat/archives_roll/2001_07-09/hum_intervention/hum_06_shearer.html> at 25 May 2006). The International Committee of the Red Cross considers the terms to be equivalent—*What is international humanitarian law?*, above n 11 (chapter 1).

that laws of war is synonymous with laws of armed conflict, and that both terms incorporate the distinct areas of IHL and the law of neutrality,[13] the more important issue is what actual law applies to a given situation and not the term for that law. In this case, I have chosen to use the term IHL; noting that IHL does not include the *jus ad bellum* (perhaps to emphasise that the *jus in bello* applies regardless of the *jus ad bellum*).[14]

Roberts and Guelff provide a brief history to the historical origins of the rules governing armed conflict, referring to rules many thousands of years old.[15] Nonetheless, as seems to be the nature of law, and international law in particular, the exact meanings of many of the various individual laws that make up IHL remain unclear. For instance, the issue of whether voluntary human shields have lost protection from attack, and therefore are also not counted when assessing the proportionality of an attack, remains unsettled. While some might be prepared to accept a high degree of ambiguity in the law, as has being clearly stated by Yves Sandoz: "Armed forces must know precisely what their own obligations are as well as those of their adversaries."[16]

Perhaps a higher level of uncertainty in the interpretation of IHL rules was acceptable when IHL was primarily concerned with the relations between States. However, since the end of World War II there has been an acceleration in developments towards categorising some parts of IHL as binding on individuals (rather than IHL being just a regulation between States). In particular, various parts of IHL can be equated to criminal law in that breaches of IHL can make an individual liable to prosecution and punishment. And, while they were not the first war crime tribunals to be held, nonetheless, the Nuremberg and Tokyo war crimes tribunals are a significant milestone—especially noting that in some cases the punishment awarded was execution. These tribunals are particularly significant for their attention, by the standards of the time, to detailed legal principle. The apportionment of individual criminal liability and the attention to fine legal points has continued, with significant developments since World War II including the two ad hoc tribunals arising out of the conflict in Rwanda (the International Criminal Tribunal for Rwanda ('ICTR'))[17] and the former Yugoslavia (the International Criminal Tribunal for the Former Yugoslavia ('ICTY')),[18] and the recent formation of the ICC. The modern expansion in international criminal law and domestic criminal

13 See *Legality of the Threat or Use of Nuclear Weapons (Advisory Opinion)* [1996] ICJ Rep 226, [51] ('*Nuclear Weapons Case*'). In other words, IHL is a subset of the laws or war or laws of armed conflict (International Committee of the Red Cross, *Conference of Government Experts on the Reaffirmation and Development of International Humanitarian Law Applicable in Armed Conflicts*, Volume I, *Introduction* (1971), 25–6 ('CE/1b').

14 Adam Roberts and Richard Guelff, *Documents on the Laws of War* (3rd ed, 2000) 1; UK Ministry of Defence, *The Manual of the Law of Armed Conflict* (2004) 1–2; Nabulsi, above n 7 (chapter 1); *What is international humanitarian law?*, above n 11 (chapter 1).

15 Roberts and Guelff, above n 14 (chapter 1), 3.

16 Yves Sandoz, 'Humanitarian Law: Priorities for the 1990s and Beyond' in William Maley (ed), *Shelters from the Storm: Developments in International Humanitarian Law* (1995) 11, 14.

17 See generally <http://www.un.org/ictr/>.

18 See generally <http://www.un.org/icty/>.

law based on war crimes makes it essential to clarify some of the most fundamental concepts in IHL.[19]

Of particular note for this book, two of the main concepts of IHL—what is a legitimate military objective[20] and the rule of proportionality[21]—have proved very elusive and the interpretation of these two concepts remain very much debated. Indeed, it was not until 1977 with the adoption of the API that:

(a) a treaty definition of *military objective* was widely adopted,[22] and
(b) the customary international law requirement of proportionality in the conduct of hostilities was first set out in treaty form.[23]

Despite the importance of IHL to the attainment of humanitarian principles during armed conflict, it is regrettable to observe that in an article discussing the training of IHL, Murphy was moved to comment that "[t]he language of the international instruments in question is often obtuse and unintelligible."[24] This is notwithstanding an exhortation at the 1972 *Conference of Government Experts on the Reaffirmation and Development of International Humanitarian Law Applicable in Armed Conflicts* of the "importance of succeeding in laying down … rules which were clear, precise, and easily understood and applicable by combatants and by civilians alike."[25] And

19 Alexandra Boivin, 'The Legal Regime Applicable to Targeting Military Objectives in the Context of Contemporary Warfare' (Research Paper Series No 2/2006, University Centre for International Humanitarian Law, 2006) i, <www.ucihl.org/research/legal_regime_applicable_to_targeting_military_objectives.pdf> at 24 May 2006. Interestingly, when the applicable IHL was to be found mainly in the orders of kings or other commanders, breach of the orders by an individual were punishable as such. For instance, King Gustavus II of Sweden (1594–1632) was asked by George William of Brandenburg what to do with some Swedish officers who had committed outrages. The King replied: "Has my brother-in-law no gallows in his country, or is he short of timber?" (Kenneth Ögren, 'Humanitarian law in the Articles of War decreed in 1621 by King Gustavus II Adolphus of Sweden' (1996) 313 *International Review of the Red Cross* 438) Clearly King Gustavus II thought that breaches of IHL by individual soldiers could result in direct punishment of the individuals involved!

20 Put simply, an object that it is lawful for one side in an armed conflict to attack (eg, a tank as opposed to a church). See, in particular, Chapter 3 below for a detailed discussion of 'military objective'.

21 Put crudely, the acceptable ratio of incidental civilian deaths, injury and property damage arising out of an attack on a legitimate military objective. See, in particular, Chapter 8 below for a detailed discussion of the proportionality principle.

22 See API, above n 2 (chapter 1), art 52(2). Earlier attempts had been made to define what is a military objective—see footnote 12.

23 Jacob Kellenberger, *International Humanitarian Law at the Beginning of the 21st Century* (2002) International Committee of the Red Cross <http://www.icrc.org.web.eng/siteengo.nsf/iwplist99/efc5a1c8d8dd70b9c1256c3600> at 25 May 2006.

24 Ray Murphy, 'International humanitarian law training for multinational peace support operations—lessons from experience' (2000) 840 *International Review of the Red Cross* <http://www.icrc.org/Web/eng/siteengo.nsf/iwpList180/C8F44398050AEB52C1256B66005F39DD> at 4 June 2006.

25 International Committee of the Red Cross, *Conference of Government Experts on the Reaffirmation and Development of International Humanitarian Law Applicable in Armed Conflicts, Volume I, Report on the Work of the Conference* (1972), 127 ('CE 1972 Report, vol I').

indeed, 25 years after the adoption of the text of API, the President of the ICRC has stated that the application of the rules in API "in practice is sometimes difficult due to the fact that the provisions are framed in rather abstract terms, thus leaving room for divergent interpretations."[26] Significantly for this book, two areas the President particularly refers to are the definition of military objectives and the rule of proportionality.[27]

1.2 Purpose and scope

The purpose of this book is to provide a contemporary and detailed analysis of the law concerning targeting that applies to Australia, and thereby to provide a solid foundation for decision making by military commanders confronted with complex targeting decisions. The scope of the study follows the issue raised by Kellenberger when he said: "One practical area where the law could be further clarified is with regard to targeting."[28] He went on to say that he did not see a need to modify the rules dealing with military objectives and the rule of proportionality, but rather "there might be a need to further clarify their proper interpretation and application."[29] It is my intention to analyse the relevant law from the perspective of a commander who might have to apply that law. This level and style of analysis is not available from the current literature and certainly is not available in one source.

In this study, I analyse the international law concerning target selection during international armed conflict. The focus of this book is on areas of current uncertainty in IHL. These areas, which have been attracting significant popular attention through the media, are the choice of targets for aerial or other forms of bombardment and the precautions to be taken when launching attacks on those targets. Due to my experience as a practising military lawyer, I also endeavour to address the "practical impact of the rules of humanitarian law on the conduct of military operations".[30] The law applicable to target selection during armed conflict is discussed in detail. In analysing the interpretation and application of that law, I adopted the view that one must always be conscious of the purpose behind the law.[31] The undisputed purpose behind IHL is "to mitigate and circumscribe the cruelty of war for humanitarian purposes"[32] based on the "overriding consideration of

---

26 Kellenberger, above n 23 (chapter 1).

27 Ibid. Similarly, a 2005 expert report states that the definition of military objectives is not controversial, but "[w]hat is controversial, however, is its interpretation and application." (*Expert Meeting: "Targeting Military Objectives"* (2005) University Centre for International Humanitarian Law, 2 <http://www.ucihl.org/research/military_objective_symposium_report.pdf> at 4 November 2007)

28 Kellenberger, above n 23 (chapter 1).

29 Ibid.

30 Sandoz, above n 16 (chapter 1), 16.

31 "A treaty shall be interpreted in good faith in accordance with the ordinary meaning to be given to the terms of the treaty in their context and *in the light of its object and purpose*." (*Vienna Convention on the Law of Treaties*, opened for signature on 23 May 1969, 1155 UNTS 331, art 31(1) (entered into force on 27 January 1980) ('VCLT') (emphasis added)).

32 *Nuclear Weapons Case* [1996] ICJ Rep 226, [86].

humanity".[33] The aim of this principle of humanity is to mitigate the effects of war on civilians and combatants alike.[34] It is also important to realise that the issues that IHL are intended to address are not mere philosophical debating points. As Judge Weeramantry has said:

> By their very nature, problems in humanitarian law are not abstract, intellectual inquiries which can be pursued in ivory-tower detachment from the sad realities which are their stuff and substance. Not being mere exercises in logic and black-letter law, they cannot be logically or intellectually disentangled from their terrible context. Distasteful though it be to contemplate the brutalities surrounding these legal questions, the legal questions can only be squarely addressed when those brutalities are brought into vivid focus.[35]

Chapter 2 is a review of the law relevant to targeting. The main treaties are briefly set out, followed by a discussion as to why customary international law is not a relevant consideration for the purpose of this work. The Martens Clause[36] is discussed at some length—in particular, possible interpretations are discussed along with an argument for a preferred interpretation. Chapter 2 includes a discussion on the continued relevance of human rights law during armed conflict and on how human rights law operates in conjunction with IHL. The chapter concludes with a discussion of one aspect of military necessity—namely, how an appeal to military necessity cannot be used to justify breaches of IHL.[37]

Having established the relevant law, Part I of this book addresses in detail the interpretation of that law concerning what or whom it is lawful to target. Part II then deals with the law that applies when attacking a lawful target. Chapter 3 focuses upon the interpretation of the test for when an object (ie, not a person) is a lawful military objective. In that chapter, I argue that there is a distinction between the political goals and military goals in a conflict; and for targets to be lawful, only the advantage that serves a military goal can be assessed when determining whether a target is subject to lawful attack. A further aspect of the above argument is that defending one's own combatants is a military advantage. I conclude that a test of general application is that the defensive range of activities that amount to a military advantage can be defined as those that preserve the capability to conduct military operations.

---

33 Ibid, [95].

34 Ibid, (Separate Opinion of Judge Koroma).

35 Ibid, (Separate Opinion of Judge Weeramantry).

36 The English translation of the original clause is: "Until a more complete code of the laws of war has been issued, the High Contracting parties deem it expedient to declare that, in cases not included in the Regulations adopted by them, the inhabitants and belligerents remain under the protection and the rule of the principles of the law of nations, as they result from the usages established among civilised peoples, from the laws of humanity, and the dictates of the public conscience." (Preamble to *Convention (IV) Respecting the Laws and Customs of War on Land*, signed at The Hague 18 October 1907, 3 Martens Nouveau Recueil (ser. 3) 461 (entered into force 26 January 1910) ('HIV').

37 The exception being where the relevant rule of IHL itself makes an exception for military necessity.

Chapter 4 deals with the targeting of humans. The basic rule is that combatants may be targeted and civilians may not be targeted. The main exception for when a combatant cannot be targeted is when the combatant is *hors de combat*.[38] I argue that *hors de combat* does not include when a combatant is merely outnumbered, overwhelmed or otherwise defenceless. In other words, there is no obligation to attempt to capture or otherwise use minimum force against an opposing combatant. And while there is an obligation not to attack a combatant who clearly expresses an intention to surrender,[39] there is no obligation to invite or offer an opportunity to surrender before launching an attack. The second part of chapter 4 deals with when it is lawful to attack civilians. I argue that unless a civilian has become a combatant, then the only time it is lawful to attack a civilian is when that civilian is taking a direct part in hostilities.[40] Taking a direct part in hostilities is more limited than contribution to the general war effort;[41] as a result, civilians who work in munitions factory and senior civilian politicians are not ipso facto targetable.

Traditional targeting theory focused on attrition—targets are progressively attacked with a view to cumulatively weakening the enemy's military forces.[42] However, there is now a theory known as effects-based operations ('EBO'). In EBO, targets are attacked for systematic effect.[43] In addition, attention is paid to not only direct effects but also indirect effects.[44] In chapter 5, I argue that while there is nothing inherently contrary to IHL in EBO, there is a risk that how EBO may be applied may raise IHL issues. I then discuss the lawfulness of targeting certain targets of contemporary interest—namely television and radio broadcasting stations, electrical power generation stations, economic targets, and (perhaps most controversially) a government's power base.

While considering the above points, another interesting and closely related issue arose. The generally accepted view is that the legality of the resort to force does not affect the IHL obligations of the parties to the conflict.[45] In other words, regardless of whether a State is an unlawful aggressor, a lawful aggressor, is defending itself against an unlawful attack, or is defending itself against a lawful attack, the State is bound by exactly the same IHL obligations. While I agree with this as a general proposition, it is a simplified view and, therefore, is not a completely accurate statement of the law. In chapter 6, I argue that where a State is acting pursuant to a UN Security Council resolution ('UNSCR') the IHL applicable to target selection, and even more particular still, the lawfulness of particular targets, may vary depending upon the terms of the UNSCR authorising the military action. For example, suppose that Australia invaded and occupied Rockall Island,

38 Out of combat—see API, above n 2 (chapter 1), art 41.

39 Ibid, art 41(2)(b).

40 Ibid, art 51(3).

41 CE 1972 Report, vol I, above n 25 (chapter 1), 143.

42 Michael Schmitt, 'Targeting and Humanitarian Law: Current Issues' (2004) 34 *Israel Yearbook on Human Rights* 59, 60.

43 Ibid.

44 Ibid, 62.

45 Christopher Greenwood, 'Historical Development and Legal Basis' in Dieter Fleck (ed), The *Handbook of Humanitarian Law in Armed Conflicts* (1995) 1, 7–8.

an island that forms part of the territory of the United Kingdom.[46] A UNSCR might authorise a coalition of countries to use all necessary means, including military force, to force the withdrawal of Australian forces from Rockall Island. In such circumstances, it would be difficult to envisage what military advantage could be gained from an attack by coalition forces on the recruiting office of the 12th/16th Hunter River Lancers, an Australian Army Reserve Light Armoured Regiment unit located in Tamworth, New South Wales, Australia.[47]

Part II of the book is the natural extension from Part I. Where Part I deals with what or who it is lawful to target, Part II is concerned with the law that applies when conducting the attack. With the exception of the rule of proportionality, chapter 7 analyses the law concerning the precautions to be taken when attacking a lawful target.[48] Due to size of the topic, the law relating to the rule of proportionality (which is just one aspect of the precautions to be taken when conducting an attack) is dealt with in its own chapter (chapter 8). Significantly for both chapters 7 and 8, I argue that the obligation to take precautionary measures when conducting an attack can, in appropriate circumstances, apply down to an individual soldier, fighter pilot etc—the obligation is not limited to just commanders and planners at the higher headquarter level. Perhaps one of the most important precautions to be taken when conducting an attack is to do everything feasible to verify that the target is a military objective subject to lawful attack.[49] What amounts to *everything feasible* and what level of certainty is implied by *verify* are very important issues. After reviewing the negotiating history of API, the various commentaries, recent case-law, and practical military requirements, I conclude that there is a requirement to take all practicable steps[50] to obtain information to enable the making of a good-faith assessment; and that when making the decision, the level of verification required will vary depending upon the likely adverse consequences of a wrong decision. Taking all of the above into consideration, a commander is then required to come to a *reasonable belief* about whether the object meets the criteria for being a military objective.[51]

Chapter 8 is an in-depth analysis of the codified rule stemming from the principle of proportionality. While the principle of proportionality takes different forms in IHL, as a codified rule in API it prohibits attacks where the attack "may be expected to cause incidental loss of civilian life, injury to civilians, damage to civilian objects, or a combination thereof, which would be excessive in relation

46 Rockall Island is a rather desolate rock in the North Atlantic about 461 kilometres from mainland Scotland. The island is the tip of an extinct volcano, and it is about 25 metres wide and 22 metres high. Accordingly, the island is not suited to the use of armoured vehicles or other manoeuvre warfare.

47 *12th/16th Hunter River Lancers*, Department of Defence <http://www.defence.gov.au/army/12_16hrl/index.htm> at 3 December 2006.

48 See API, above n 2 (chapter 1), art 57.

49 Ibid, art 57(2)(a)(i).

50 What steps are considered practical will depend upon the difficulty in obtaining the necessary information.

51 *Prosecutor v Galic, (Trial Chamber)* Case No IT-98-29-T (5 December 2003) [51]. See also Boivin, above n 19 (chapter 1), 20.

to the concrete and direct military advantage anticipated [from the attack]".[52] This codified rule requires the comparing of anticipated military advantage with the expected collateral damage. Clearly, therefore, exactly what can be considered as a military advantage and what must be assessed as collateral damage are very important issues. I argue that the security of the attacking force is one aspect of the military advantage anticipated from an attack. However, that does not mean that the security of the attacking force can be given primacy over the risk to civilians and civilian objects. The security of the attacking force is but one factor in determining whether an attack can proceed. When determining the military advantage anticipated from an attack, an attacker is not required to consider the military advantage from the attack in complete in isolation. At the other extreme end, an attacker cannot consider the advantage to be gained from the entire conflict. I argue that an attack must be viewed as a whole but only to the extent of the particular operation of which the attack forms a part. This applies in particular where an attack is against part of a system where an advantage accrues only where multiple parts of the system are attacked.[53]

When considering what must be assessed as collateral damage, a very important point is that only civilians and civilian objects are counted. This is because both articles 51(5)(b) and 57(2)(a)(iii) API refer to only "incidental loss of *civilian* life, injury to *civilians*, damage to *civilian* objects, or a combination thereof".[54] Some consequences of this are that combatants who are *hors de combat* and military medical facilities are not collateral damage per se. When assessing military advantage, only *direct* military advantage may be assessed.[55] No similar words of limitation appear in relation to the expected collateral damage. It is my view that API is less than clear on whether indirect injury, deaths and property damage as the result of an attack are counted as part of the proportionality equation; and if they are counted at all, to what extent are they counted.[56] It is my suggestion that there is a need to distinguish between deaths that are inevitable as the result of the attack and deaths that result not only from the attack but also from a lack of possible remedial action. My conclusion is that the better view of the law is that there is a need to distinguish between collateral damage that, in the ordinary course of events, can be expected[57] (and, therefore, must be counted as part of the proportionality equation)

52 API, above n 2 (chapter 1), art 57(2)(a)(iii). See also the combination of API, above n 2 (chapter 1), arts 51(4) and 51(5)(b). For ease of expression, from now on I use 'collateral damage' as short-hand for 'incidental loss of civilian life, injury to civilians, damage to civilian objects, or a combination thereof'.

53 For example, redundant communication nodes. See Air Force Pamphlet 14-210 Intelligence, 'USAF Intelligence Targeting Guide' (1998) [A4.2.2.1] <http://www.e-publishing.af.mil/pubfiles/af/14/afpam14-210/afpam14-210.pdf> at 1 March 2005.

54 API, above n 2 (chapter 1) (emphases added).

55 See ibid, arts 51(5)(b) and 57(2)(a)(iii).

56 Matthew Waxman, *International Law and the Politics of Urban Air Operations* (2000) RAND Corporation, 21 (fn 44) <http://www.rand.org/publications/MR/MR1175> at 28 February 2005.

57 Recalling that the opening words of API, above n 2 (chapter 1), art 57(2)(a)(iii) are "refrain from deciding to launch any attack which may be *expected* to cause incidental loss of civilian life" (emphasis added).

and collateral damage that one would expect might be avoided (and, accordingly, is not counted as part of the proportionality equation).

Both voluntary and involuntary human shields are an unfortunate aspect of warfare. The status of voluntary human shields in particular is a topic of recent debate. Are voluntary human shields liable to direct attack or, as a minimum, not counted as collateral damage when considering the proportionality of an attack?[58] Alternatively, despite voluntarily acting as human shields, do they remain civilians and as such are entitled to all the protection that entails?[59] In my view, there is not one simple answer. Rather, I argue for a distinction between human shields who actually impede the progress of an attack (eg, by physically blocking a route of advance) and those human shields who are merely providing what I term a 'moral pause' to an attacker.[60] The former would be subject to direct attack and also would not count as collateral damage in an attack on the shielded military objective, whereas the latter are not subject to attack and are counted as collateral damage.

The final substantive chapter of this book concerns the allocation of responsibility for the individual targeting decisions and the execution of the attack. It is not uncommon for targeting scenarios to involve a number of discrete actors. For example, the person who collects the information about a target might be separate from the person who decides whether that target meets the legal test for being a military objective. This second person, or even a third person, might have the responsibility to make a decision about whether the collateral damage that is expected will be excessive when compared to the military advantage anticipated from the attack. Yet another person again might be responsible for the execution of the attack (eg, the pilot of a strike aircraft). In chapter 9, the applicable law is reviewed with a view to setting out a targeting process that facilitates determining and allocating responsibility for the discrete legal obligations that arise in a targeting scenario. An *IHL 6-step targeting process* is set out, where the first four steps constitute the planning phase of an attack, and the last two steps comprise the attack phase. The intent behind this IHL 6-step targeting process is not to set out additional obligations to those already found in IHL, but rather the process is meant as a way of conveniently expressing some of those obligations. Chapter 9 concludes with applying the IHL 6-step targeting process to some case studies and an explanation of how the process can be reduced to a useful aide-memoire for use in combat.

In a book of this length, only certain matters can be covered. This book deals with only international armed conflict,[61] and accordingly a reference to an armed conflict is a reference to an international armed conflict unless expressly stated oth-

58 See Michael Schmitt, '"Direct participation in hostilities" and 21st century armed conflict' (2004) 522 <http://www.michaelschmitt.org/images/ Directparticipationpageproo fs.pdf> at 12 June 2005.

59 *Civilians Must Not Be Used to Shield Homes Against Military Attacks* (2006) Human Rights Watch <http://hrw.org/english/docs/2006/11/22/isrlpa14652_txt.htm> at 16 December 2006.

60 I explain what I mean by a 'moral pause' in section 8.3.3. Briefly, I mean a situation where the physical presence of the human shield will not practically impede the conduct of an attack.

61 In other words, a conflict to which API applies and not the *Protocol Additional to the Geneva Conventions of 12 August 1949, and relating to the Protection of Victims of Non-*

erwise. On this occasion, the law during non-international armed conflicts is not considered. As the basic definitions of issues like lawful objectives, combatants[62] vis-à-vis civilians etc are not well defined in the law applying to non-international armed conflict, significant space would need to be devoted to just establishing what law applies; whereas the purpose of my study was to review and refine the *interpretation* of the law applicable to targeting.

The law applicable to weapon selection (eg, whether cluster bombs are lawful) is not covered for two reasons. First, is a discrete area of the law that I think it best addressed separately. Second, it will generally be the case at the operational and tactical level of armed conflict that the weapons available have already been assessed as lawful,[63] and the issue, therefore, is how to use those weapons lawfully.[64] In addition, only traditional attacks on targets are considered. By traditional, I mean the kinetic attack on a target by use of force (eg the dropping of bombs) and not 'information operations' or other forms of attack not involving the overt use of force.[65] Again, this is primarily due to space constraints. Non-kinetic attacks can

---

International Armed Conflicts, opened for signature 12 December 1977, 1125 UNTS 609 (entered into force 7 December 1978) ('APII').

62 Arguably, there are no combatants per se in a non-international armed conflict; however, there is still a need to use a term to distinguish between civilians who take no part in hostilities from organized resistance groups and armed government forces.

63 Of course, this assessment may be disputed.

64 Weapons generally fall into three classes. First, weapons that are lawful in all circumstances (noting that a lawful weapon might be used to achieve an unlawful purpose). For example, a rifle using lawful bullets can be used for any lawful purpose in an armed conflict. If used to shoot an unarmed civilian, it is the act itself that is unlawful and not the weapon (in other words, the act itself cannot become lawful by using a different weapon). Second, some weapons are unlawful per se regardless of how they are used. For example, there is a complete ban on the use, under any circumstances, of non-command detonated anti-personnel mines by States that are a party to the *Convention on the Prohibition of the Use, Stockpiling, Production and Transfer of Anti-Personnel Mines*, opened for signature 3 December 1997, 2056 UNTS 211 (entered into force 1 March 1999). Finally, there is a category of weapons that are lawful for some uses and unlawful for others. For example, the use of exploding bullets against human targets is prohibited but there is no prohibition on the use of exploding bullets against enemy materiel—see the *Declaration Renouncing the Use, in Time of War, of Explosive Projectiles Under 400 Grammes Weight*, 18 Martens Nouveau Recueil (ser. 1) 474, 138 Consol. TS 297 (entered into force 11 December 1868 (29 November 1868 by the Julian calendar)) ('*St Petersburg Declaration*'), and the commentary on the similar customary international law rule in Jean-Marie Henckaerts and Louise Doswald-Beck (eds), *Customary International Humanitarian Law* (2005) vol I, 272–3. Henckaerts and Doswald-Beck argue, and I agree, that while the *St Petersburg Declaration* appears on its face to impose a complete ban, the better interpretation (based on the purpose behind the ban of preventing unnecessary suffering, and as supported by subsequent State practice) is that the ban on exploding bullets is limited to not using such bullets in an anti-personnel role.

65 An interesting example of information operations occurred during the 1991 Gulf War. "Several weeks before the Baghdad was bombed on January 17th, 1991, U.S. intelligence agents successfully inserted a computer virus into Iraq's military computers. It was designed to disable much of Baghdad's air-defense system." (*Gulf War* (2003) <http://www.cryan.com/war/> at 3 July 2005) A good introduction to the legal regime covering the non-kinetic use of force, and cyber attacks in particular, is in Michael Schmitt,

raise significant issues in addition to those considered in this study. For example, if a computer virus causes financial loss to a civilian, is such economic loss a civilian object? If data is routed through a network that goes through a neutral State, is that a violation of the laws of neutrality? Importantly though, unless a particular weapon or means of warfare is specifically banned by a treaty or under customary international law, it is now generally considered irrelevant what means are used when conducting an attack. Rather, the determining factor is the consequences of the attack and not the means or methods employed.[66] Accordingly, if a non-kinetic attack were to be conducted, the legal analysis in this study would still apply to the extent of the issues covered in this study.[67] What would then be required is a consideration of the *additional* issues raised by non-kinetic attacks.

This book is limited to attacks on land-based objects.[68] The first reason for this limitation is that the primary focus of my study was on API, and the main articles in API dealing with targeting issues apply only to attacks against objectives on land or to attacks that may affect civilians or civilian objects on land.[69] Accordingly, attacks on naval targets[70] and airborne targets[71] are not considered. My further reasoning for this limitation is that it would appear that this is where most of the current controversy lies, and certainly it is the area that would appear to have the greatest impact on civilians.

'The Sixteenth Waldemar A. Solf Lecture in International Law' (2003) 176 *Military Law Review* 365, 416–20.

66 *Direct Participation in Hostilities under International Humanitarian Law* (2003) International Committee of the Red Cross <http://www.icrc.org/Web/Eng/siteengo.nsf/iwpList74/459B0FF70176F4E5C1256DDE00572DAA> at 10 April 2006. As an interesting side issue, note that the obligation imposed by API, above n 2 (chapter 1), art 36 to conduct a legal review for compliance with IHL applies to a "new weapon, means or method of warfare" and not just to weapons per se. See generally *A Guide to the Legal Review of New Weapons, Means and Methods of Warfare: Measures to Implement Article 36 of Additional Protocol I of 1977* (2006) International Committee of the Red Cross <http://www.icrc.org/web/eng/siteengo.nsf/html/new-weapons-publication-190106> at 5 May 2007.

67 For example, "[i]t may be argued that computer network attacks are attacks in the meaning of API because … [API, art 52(2)] does not only apply to the destruction of a target but also to its neutralization, which may be more relevant for computer networks." (*Expert Meeting: "Targeting Military Objectives"*, above n 27 (chapter 1), 5, fn 19)

68 In this context, *land* also covers "rivers, canals and lakes." (Yves Sandoz, Christophe Swinarski, and Bruno Zimmerman (eds), *Commentary on the Additional Protocols of 8 June 1977 to the Geneva Conventions of 12 August 1949* (1987) ('*ICRC Commentary*'), [1898])

69 API, above n 2 (chapter 1), art 49(3).

70 This is a specialised area of the law deserving of its own detailed treatment and many such works have been written. See generally *San Remo Manual on International Law Applicable to Armed Conflicts at Sea* (1994) International Committee of the Red Cross <http://www.icrc.org/Web/Eng/siteengo.nsf/iwpList375/966627225C719EDCC1256B6600598E0> at 25 May 2006 ('*San Remo Manual*').

71 A research initiative is underway to provide an "informal contemporary restatement of customary international law governing air and missile warfare"—*IHL in Air and Missile Warfare*, International Humanitarian Law Research Initiative <http://www.ihlresearch.org/amw/> at 6 March 2007.

Attacks on or that affect the environment are not specifically considered, nor is there detailed discussion on attacks that affect cultural property. This is because these areas are specific subsets of targeting and are significant and complex enough to require separate treatment. However, it is worth noting that the discussion in this book applies to those topics. What is required is further and additional consideration if issues concerning the environment or cultural property arise.

The international law applicable to Australia is adopted as the frame of reference for this study.[72] Consistent with the purpose of this study to make a contribution to national decision making in Australia, adopting Australia's legal obligations as the frame of reference allows for each chapter to be focussed in its conclusions and recommendations on the preferable interpretation of IHL rules. While there would be some minor benefit in the Australia context to set out what might be the obligations for third parties, as the applicable rules of IHL vary for each State,[73] it is not possible in the space available to consider all of the various permutations to the level of detail and analysis required for such a task to be truly useful. Having adopted Australia's legal obligations as the frame of reference, this is carried over into the fictitious examples. So, for the purpose of examples, it is assumed that all other Parties have the same international law obligations as Australia. In particular, it is assumed that API applies to all parties; and where Australia has made a declaration or reservation to API, that declaration or reservation is applied on a reciprocal basis.[74]

As the purpose of this work is to analyse IHL,[75] there is no discussion of whether armed conflict should be banned or ways of preventing armed conflict; nor is there discussion of the means for the (laudable aim of the) prevention of armed conflict.[76] In addition, except where relevant to understanding the current law, I do

---

72 Australian domestic law is not discussed. A useful introduction to how domestic law can also regulate a belligerent's conduct is provided in Duncan Blake, *Coalition Bombardment: Legal problems arising from aerial bombardment in a coalition context* (Masters Paper, University of Melbourne, 2004) 29–47.

73 See CE/1b, above n 13 (chapter 1), 26.

74 These qualifications are necessary as a number of treaty obligations apply only on a reciprocal basis. See, for instance, API, above n 2 (chapter 1), art 96. By reciprocal, I mean that the other belligerent in the armed conflict is a party to the relevant treaty. State A remains bound as long as State B is formally bound, even if State B is, in fact, not complying with its treaty obligations. Also, as the majority of IHL is applicable on a reciprocal basis, this extends to the reciprocal application of declarations of understanding and similar other statements—see Christopher Greenwood 'The twilight of the law of belligerent reprisals' (1989) 20 *Netherlands Year Book of International Law* 35, 60. Customary international law is, by its very nature, universally applicable—with the exceptions of States not bound as persistent objectors or when the custom is regional custom. Note that some treaties impose unilateral obligations (see, for example, the *Convention on the Prohibition of the Use, Stockpiling, Production and Transfer of Anti-Personnel Mines and on Their Destruction*, opened for signature on 3 December 1997, 2056 UNTS 211 (entered into force 1 March 1999)).

75 See section 1.1 for what I mean by this term.

76 For an argument for banning armed conflict and a proposal to achieve this, see Robert Kehl, *The Time is Ripe for a More Effective International Law* <http://users.westnet.gr/~cgian/rkehl.htm> at 25 May 2006.

not look at the history of IHL;[77] nor do I argue for the desirability of complying with IHL[78] or amendment of those rules.[79] Instead, I accept the existence of current international legal obligations as a given and I focus upon an analysis of military compliance when using military force consistent with those rules.

1.3 Literature review

The current literature in the area can be divided into five main groups. The first group is composed of the military manuals of specific States; or in the case of the United States, the various arms of its naval and military forces. The various manuals from the United States are available on the internet, as is Canada's. Interestingly, the United Kingdom's manual has recently been published as a book.[80] Regrettably, particularly in the context of this work, Australia's military manual of IHL is not publicly available. However, the manual specific to the Royal Australian Air Force, *Operations Law for RAAF Commanders* (2nd edition, 2004), is publicly available.[81] Somewhat like the textbooks described next, military manuals on IHL are broad ranging in the coverage of topics. They also have the advantage of being specific to a particular State. The law tends to be grouped according to topics like military objectives, weapons, law of the air etc. Interestingly, the manuals often do not have a very in-depth analysis. This may be because a State would not want to commit itself to an interpretation of the law that it might later dissent from, noting that in the meantime that interpretation might have been used as an expression of *opinio juris*. While most manuals will refer to a particularly treaty article or the like to support a proposition, rarely are cases (except sometimes historical cases), learned works or other sources cited in support of propositions. It is also often the case that supporting argument is not provided. While this is quite understandable in the context of a military manual, it does have obvious drawbacks when the manual is being read critically. Cleary the overseas military manuals are only of peripheral assistance to an Australian military commander. As the Australian military manual on IHL is not publicly available, I am limited in the comments I can make

77 Readers interested in this area are referred to the following short but interesting article—V S Mani, 'International humanitarian law: an Indo-Asian perspective' (2001) 841 *International Review of the Red Cross* <http://www.icrc.org/Web/eng/siteengo.nsf/iwpList182/FD9E38D48A5BAE3DC1256B66005FA894> at 4 June 2006).

78 For an interesting paper which argues that in asymmetric warfare (eg, between a superpower and a less powerful enemy) an enemy that is prepared to sustain and manipulate civilian casualties will often have "tremendous incentives to do so" see Waxman, above n 56 (chapter 1).

79 For an argument on why and how the current rules on what are lawful targets should be amended to allow for choosing targets on the legal basis that attacking those targets is intended to undermine the will of the enemy civilian populace, see Charles Dunlap, Jr, 'The End of Innocence: Rethinking Noncombatancy in the Post-Kosovo Era' (2000) Vol XXXVIII:3 *Strategic Review* 9.

80 UK Ministry of Defence, above n 14 (chapter 1).

81 Air Power Development Centre, Royal Australian Air Force AAP 1003, *Operations Law for RAAF Commanders* (2nd edition, 2004).

on its content. However, by way of example, the 'Law of Aerial Targeting' is covered in *Operations Law for RAAF Commanders* in just ten pages.[82]

The second group comprises books on IHL. These works tend to be general in nature, and the level of detail dedicated to questions concerning targeting varies from work to work. Compare, for instance, the approximately 20 pages on targeting related issues in *The Contemporary Law of Armed Conflict*[83] with the well over 100 pages in *Law on the Battlefield*[84] on the same topic. Like military manuals, the law is usually grouped functionally. Such works are very useful as an introduction to the issues discussed in this book and also help to place targeting law in overall context. However, due to their breadth, they often do not have a deep level of analysis and, therefore, they often do not offer much assistance with resolving other than straightforward issues. Generally speaking, they also are not limited to the law that applies to a particular State; and this means that the books can be either non-specific, or require the reader to be able to determine which parts of the book or which comments would apply to the State of interest. There are no books written from an Australian perspective or by authors familiar with Australian military capabilities and practice. One book deserves special mention, and that is *The Handbook of Humanitarian Law in Armed Conflicts*.[85] This book is unique, as it is both a published version of the manual for the German armed forces, followed by significant academic commentary on the various statements of the rules set out in the manual. It is a very good resource.

The third group, which is best exemplified by the *ICRC Commentary*,[86] is an article-by-article analysis of API. The other main work in this area is *New Rules for Victims of Armed Conflicts: Commentary on the two 1977 Protocols Additional to the Geneva Conventions of 1949*.[87] As this book is concerned with the targeting law applicable to Australia, and as that law is primarily to be found in API, these works are very valuable resources. However, their very specificity is also a problem. Each article of API is worked through sequentially and not functionally. To a greater or lesser extent, articles can be looked at in isolation; and the interrelationship between the various parts of API is not always clearly set out, and particularly not how the various articles might affect a targeting decision. Additionally, other areas of the law that affect targeting are not addressed. Finally, there has not been a current restatement of these works to take into account subsequent State practice or case law.

The fourth group is the significant number of journal articles available dealing with various aspects of targeting law. The journal articles come in many different forms. Some look at a particular conflict or even an event in that conflict. Others will deal with a specific topic—eg, proportionality. Alternatively, some articles look

82 Ibid, 63–72.

83 Leslie Green, *The Contemporary Law of Armed Conflict* (2nd ed, 2000).

84 Anthony Rogers, *Law on the Battlefield* (2nd ed, 2004).

85 Fleck, Dieter (ed), *The Handbook of Humanitarian Law in Armed Conflicts* (1995).

86 Sandoz, Swinarski and Zimmerman (eds), above n 68 (chapter 1).

87 Michael Bothe, Karl Partsch, and Waldemar Solf, *New Rules for Victims of Armed Conflicts: Commentary on the two 1977 Protocols Additional to the Geneva Conventions of 1949* (1982).

at an issue—eg, human shields—and review the applicable law. Each of these types of articles have their own strengths and weaknesses in the context of this work. Articles that comment on a particular conflict or an aspect thereof are very useful for providing a contextual analysis of the law. However, they are generally limited in the number of issues addressed. Articles that deal with a particular legal topic tend to provide the most in-depth analysis of that issue but usually at the expense of breadth of analysis. Articles that look at the law that applies to a particular subject often have general breadth and depth of analysis but are less useful when considering other topics. Also, interrelationships and consequences for other scenarios may not be addressed.

The final group of interest are reports prepared by the likes of Amnesty International and Human Rights Watch. These reports are similar to journal articles that deal with a specific conflict[88] or an aspect of a specific conflict.[89] Due to this similarity, similar comments apply. However, these reports tend to be longer, often much longer, than a journal article. The reports will usually dedicate much more space than a journal article would to setting out the factual context for the commentary. This is useful when determining whether any particular statement of the lawfulness or otherwise for a particular event is correct, as often the point in issue might be the facts and not the law. At the same time, this often results in the analysis being fact specific and conclusions may not always be easily translatable to other scenarios. While not a perfect fit, best grouped within this class is the *Final Report to the Prosecutor by the Committee Established to Review the NATO Bombing Campaign Against the Federal Republic of Yugoslavia*.[90] The particularly interesting aspect of this report is that it analyses particular fact scenarios but does so from the point of view of whether there is a sufficient basis for prosecution of individuals involved in those scenarios. It is particularly interesting for the areas of law considered by the authors of the report to be incomplete or not sufficiently precise enough to support a prosecution. By their nature, these works are useful for research purposes but are not directly useful to a commander when planning a future military campaign.

This book is loosely modelled on a military manual, in that it looks at the law functionally and from the point of view of one particular State—Australia. In particular, the law is considered in the approximate chronological sequence that a commander would have to consider when making a targeting decision. However, unlike for military manuals, the law is analysed in some depth and arguments are supported with citation. While particular scenarios from actual conflicts are referred to, this is only by way of example. This study does not address whether any historical scenarios were or were not lawful.

---

88 See, for example, *Civilian Deaths in the NATO Air Campaign* (2000) Human Rights Watch <http://www.hrw.org/reports/2000/nato> at 25 May 2006.

89 See, for example, *Amnesty International's initial comments on the review by the International Criminal Tribunal for the Former Yugoslavia of NATO's Operation Allied Force* (2000) Amnesty International <http://web.amnesty.org/library/index/ENGEUR700302000> at 26 May 2006.

90 *Final Report to the Prosecutor by the Committee Established to Review the NATO Bombing Campaign Against the Federal Republic of Yugoslavia* (2000) <http://www.un.org/icty/pressreal/nato061300.htm> at 2 April 2006 ('*OTP Report*').

1.4 Methodology

The methodology for this study was consistent with a typical legal analysis to determine the law on a particular subject. As it was not the intention to conduct a jurisprudential style critique of the areas of international law applicable to targeting but rather to highlight and, where possible, resolve areas of uncertainty in that law, a relatively traditional legal approach was adopted. I have undertaken a comprehensive literature review of the relevant conventions, cases and learned commentary on the conventions. This review then enabled me to analyse carefully the literature to enable the articulation of the current law.

There exists very little disagreement as to which conventions, and even which particular articles of the conventions, are applicable to targeting issues. Therefore, the most important step was identifying areas of uncertainty in the law. This was achieved by both a direct reading of the applicable conventions, which revealed areas of uncertainty, and by reviewing the body of literature that already exists in the area. From there, I endeavoured to identify either a preferred interpretation of a legal point; or where that was not possible, to argue why certain interpretations should not be preferred. In doing so, I was conscious of three main principles. First, that the essential purpose of IHL is humanitarian. Second, that the "laws of armed conflict are not designed to be applied *ex post facto* by international lawyers but in the heat of combat by non-lawyers."[91] Third, as "[i]nternational humanitarian law in armed conflicts is a *compromise* between military and humanitarian requirements"[92] and "[i]ts rules *comply with both* military necessity and the dictates of humanity",[93] neither military necessity nor the dictates of humanity can be given undue prominence when endeavouring to resolve a difficult area of interpretation. Although noting that this last principle needs to be balanced against the first principle I quoted—that the purpose of IHL is humanitarian. As IHL can be considered a special regime of international law,[94] the interpretation of its norms should reflect the object and purpose of the special regime.[95]

In the previous section, I quoted the President of the ICRC as stating that the application of the rules in API "in practice is sometimes difficult due to the fact that the provisions are framed in rather abstract terms, thus leaving room for divergent interpretations."[96] While it may not be possible to remove all ambiguity,

91 Hilaire McCoubrey, 'Jurisprudential Aspects of the Modern Law of Armed Conflicts' in Michael Meyer (ed), *Armed Conflict and the New Law: Aspects of the 1977 Geneva Protocols and the 1981 Weapons Convention* (1989) 23, 40.

92 Greenwood, 'Historical Development and Legal Basis', above n 45 (chapter 1), 32 (emphasis added).

93 Ibid (emphasis added).

94 A special regime is a branch of international law with a "group of rules and principles concerned with a particular subject matter"—see Chapter XII 'Fragmentation of International Law: Difficulties Arising From the Diversification and Expansion of International Law' of the *Report on the work of its fifty-eighth session*, International Law Commission, [251(11)] UN Doc A/61/10 (2006) (available at <http://untreaty.un.org/ilc/reports/2006/2006report.htm> at 11 January 2007).

95 Ibid, [251(13)].

96 Kellenberger, above n 23 (chapter 1).

by the methodology outlined, I hope at least to reduce that ambiguity or room for divergent interpretations. In some cases it will be possible to argue for a preferred interpretation, while in others it will at least be possible to argue why certain interpretations should not be accepted.

Numerous examples appear in this book. Some are obviously fictitious and nothing further need be said about those examples. Some, however, are from actual international or internal armed conflicts. The examples are used to help illustrate a point; they are not meant to be allegations of what actually occurred. As this work is meant as a general analysis of the law, and not a review of the legality of actions in a particular armed conflict, I was less concerned with whether any given example was an accurate and factual representation of history. I remained conscious that the "truth is not only the first casualty of war; it is often the first casualty of efforts to learn lessons from a given conflict."[97] Indeed, some would say that "postmodernism, amongst other things, challenges the concept of objective, rationally discoverable truth."[98] Whether or not this is true, most examples will be cited with only one reference and no meaningful attempt to research whether the facts asserted in the referenced work are true, half-truths, or just plain fictitious as the examples cited are being used to help illustrate a point and not to make legal statements about historical occurrences.

There is often dispute about the applicability of IHL to certain conflicts. In some cases, one or more of the parties may deny that the conflict is an armed conflict of any sort. In other cases, there may be a dispute as to whether the conflict is an international or non-international armed conflict. For the purpose of this book, where examples are drawn from either an internal armed conflict or a conflict to which the application of IHL is not clear or is otherwise debated, the example is being used to illustrate a point as though the IHL applicable to international armed conflicts applied to the example cited.

1.5 Definitions and abbreviations

A number of the terms used in book are either terms of art amongst military members (military lawyers in particular) or are not terms of art and can have various meanings. A glossary is included at the start of the book to define how certain words are used in the book.[99] Also included is a list of commonly used abbreviations. The first time an abbreviation is used, the phrase is set out in full with the abbreviation following in brackets. Thereafter, just the abbreviation is used.

One particular word deserves special mention, because the meaning of the word substantially sets the parameters of this book. The term *targeting* is used to describe the deliberate process followed by a military commander in deciding against which

97 Anthony Cordesman, *The Lessons and Non-Lessons of the air and Missile Campaign in Kosovo* (2003) Center for Strategic and International Studies, 1 <http://www.csis.org/media/csis/pubs/kosovolessons-full.pdf> at 25 May 2006.

98 Justice Peter Heerey, 'Storytelling: Postmodernism and the law' (2000) 74 *Australian Law Journal* 681, 683.

99 Of course, Mas'd Zavazadeh is attributed with having once "dismissed a critic because of his 'unproblematic prose and clarity of his presentation, which are the conceptual tools of conservatism'"—Heerey, above n 98 (chapter 1), 681.

objectives he or she will apply force. This is distinguished from attacking a target, which is the actual application of force. There is a middle step, which receives particular attention in an air force context, called weaponeering. Weaponeering is the process whereby weapons (and often the method for delivering those weapons) are assigned to targets. This process involves considering such factors as the required amount of damage to be achieved, available weapons delivery platforms (ie, aircraft, ships etc), available weapons and their projected usage and resupply, and what would be the expected collateral damage in any given scenario.

When discussing targeting, the term *attacker* is used to describe the party conducting the tactical attack, and *defender* to describe the party whose combatants or objects are being attacked. The terms are not used or influenced by who may or may not have started the armed conflict or in whose territory the attack may be occurring.

1.6 ICRC Commentary on API

As it is referred to extensively in this book, and most other detailed works on IHL, the status of the *ICRC Commentary* on API deserves particular mention. The *ICRC Commentary* is often attributed a special authority. Indeed, sometimes this is extended to not just the *ICRC Commentary* but to the ICRC itself. For example, in a report by Human Rights Watch, comments by the ICRC are introduced with the words "[t]he International Committee of the Red Cross ..., the principal authority on the interpretation of international humanitarian law".[100] It is important to distinguish between a work that can be referred to as an authority on a particular point and something that is authorative on the point. A work that is an authority is a work that is to be taken seriously. An authorative work is a work that is determinative of the issue. When analysed in these terms, the *ICRC Commentary* is an authority but is not authoritative on the interpretation of IHL. Were it otherwise, where would this place decisions not in strict accordance with the *ICRC Commentary* by such courts as the ICTR, the ICTY, and indeed the International Court of Justice ('ICJ')? That the *ICRC Commentary* cannot be considered as authoritative on issues relating to interpretation of the conventions is made clear by Judge Kooijmans, who when discussing the interpretation of common article 1 of the 1949 Geneva Conventions,[101] states that "the ICRC in its (non-authoritative) commentaries on the 1949 Convention ...".[102] I should add that, to the best of my knowledge, the ICRC does not claim authoritative status for itself.[103] The preceding comments

100 *Civilian Deaths in the NATO Air Campaign*, above n 88 (chapter 1).

101 See footnotes 5 to 8 for the full citations of the four 1949 *Geneva Conventions*.

102 *Legal Consequences of the Construction of a Wall in the Occupied Palestinian Territory* [2004] ICJ Rep 131, [48] (Separate Opinion of Judge Kooijmans) ('*Palestinian Wall Case*').

103 Rather, the ICRC "is an impartial, neutral and independent organization whose exclusively humanitarian mission is to protect the lives and dignity of victims of war and internal violence and to provide them with assistance." (*The ICRC's Mission Statement* (2005) International Committee of the Red Cross <http://www.icrc.org/Web/Eng/siteengo.nsf/htmlall/68EE39?OpenDocument> at 3 December 2006) Based on my discussions with representatives of the Australian Committee of the Red Cross, it is probably most accurate to say that the ICRC's role is to assist in the development, dis-

also apply to the other learned works referred to in this book. Therefore, where Robertson refers to the book by Bothe, Partsch and Solf[104] as providing the "authoritative interpretation of Article 52(2)" API,[105] I would once again demur.

semination and compliance with IHL. Of course, the lines are not always clear-cut. For example, Smyth in his article on the 1991 Gulf War writes: "The U.S.-led coalition commander, Gen. Norman Schwarzkopf, frequently consulted with law of war experts, including members of the … [ICRC], to ensure that specific military operations would not be seen later as violations. In fact, Schwarzkopf's aides requested so much guidance from the ICRC that its representatives eventually stopped providing it, protesting that they were not legal counsel for the coalition." (Frank Smyth, *Gulf War*, Crimes of War Project <http://www.crimesofwar.org/thebook/gulf-war.html> at 25 May 2006)

104 Bothe, Partsch and Solf, above n 87 (chapter 1).

105 Horace Robertson Jr, 'The Principle of the Military Objective in the Law of Armed Conflict' (1997–98) 8 *United States Air Force Journal of Legal Studies* 35, 50.

Chapter 2

What is the law applicable to targeting?

> My guiding maxim has always been that every injury inflicted, even though it may be within the rules, is excusable only insofar as it is absolutely necessary; anything beyond that is simply criminal.[1]

In this chapter, the IHL relevant to targeting in an international armed conflict is identified and explained. This background is a preliminary to the further chapters that provide a contemporary and detailed analysis of the law concerning targeting that applies to Australia military commanders when confronted with complex targeting decisions.

First, the main treaties that affect targeting decisions are briefly set out, along with a short discussion on the Hague *Rules of Air Warfare* ('HAW'). I then discuss what relevance customary international law may have where API is de jure applicable. I conclude that while customary international law is concurrently applicable, nonetheless it is not a relevant consideration for targeting issues by Australian military commanders. This is because when considering targeting issues, there is no rule of customary international law that is more stringent than the relevant treaty rule. As a natural next step on from discussing customary international law, the role and possible interpretations of the Martens Clause[2] are discussed. I conclude that while the Martens Clause has independent normative effect, the scope of that effect is unsettled. Chapter 2 includes a discussion of the continued relevance of human rights law during armed conflict. After arguing how human rights law operates in conjunction with IHL, I discuss how the two areas of law do not operate independently but may in fact interact. I conclude with the observation that IHRL will be the de jure standard where IHL is applied not as matter of law but only as a matter of policy.

The last two sections of chapter 2 concern broad concepts that are relevant to the application of IHL. Section 2.6 is a discussion of one aspect of military necessity—namely, how an appeal to military necessity generally cannot be used to justify breaches of IHL. The exception to this general principle is where the relevant rule of IHL itself states that the rule does not apply in cases of military necessity. Chapter 2 concludes with a brief discussion on the nature of IHL itself. I explain

1 A translation of a quote by Napoleon Bonaparte in Geoffrey Best, 'The Restraint of War in Historical and Philosophical Perspective', in Astrid Delissen and Gerard Tanja (eds), *Humanitarian law of armed conflict: Challenges ahead: Essays in honour of Frits Kalshoven* (1991) 3, 15.

2 See above n 36 (chapter 1).

that IHL is inherently a set of prohibitions on what is otherwise a legal landscape where all means and methods of warfare are legally permitted.[3] However, I then argue that due to the Martens Clause and other general rules of IHL that contain broad prohibitions it is often useful to identify rules of IHL that permit, explicitly or implicitly, a desired course of action.

2.1 Relevant treaties

It is reasonably uncontroversial that the "sources of international law are generally considered to be exhaustively listed in Article 38 of the Statue of the International Court of Justice".[4] For present purposes, these sources can be summarised as treaties, customary international law, the general principles of law recognised by civilised nations and, as a subsidiary means, judicial decisions and the writings of the most highly qualified publicists. Accordingly, the task is to determine from those sources the subset of international law applicable to targeting.

A review of the literature reveals that the treaties that may affect targeting include:

(a) the four Geneva Conventions of 1949, being:
   i. *Geneva Convention for the Amelioration of the Condition of the Wounded and Sick in Armed Forces in the Field;*[5]
   ii. *Geneva Convention for the Amelioration of the Condition of the Wounded, Sick and Shipwrecked Members of the Armed Forces at Sea;*[6]
   iii. *Geneva Convention Relative to the Treatment of Prisoners of War;*[7] and
   iv. *Geneva Convention Relative to the Protection of Civilian Persons in Time of War;*[8]

---

3 "Means and methods" is a regularly used term in IHL. "'[M]eans of combat' or 'means of warfare' … generally refers to the weapons being used, while the expression 'methods of combat' generally refers to the way in which such weapons are used." (Sandoz, Swinarski and Zimmerman (eds), above n 68 (chapter 1), [1957])

4 *Prosecutor v Erdemovic, (Appeals Chamber)* Case No IT-96-22 (7 October 1997) [40] (Joint Separate Opinion of Judge McDonald and Judge Vohrah); see Ian Brownlie, *Principles of Public International Law* (6th ed, 2003) 5. There are some commentators, however, who either criticise this list, or consider it to be incomplete (see William Slomanson, *Fundamental Perspectives on International Law* (5th ed, 2007) 10–11). For example, Cassese writes that there "are other sources to which that provision [*Statute of the International Court of Justice* art 38] makes no reference, but which are nonetheless envisaged by international law and applied by the ICJ itself: unilateral acts of States creating rules, general principles of international law, and binding decisions of international organizations." (Antonio Cassese, *International Law* (2001) 149)

5 *Geneva Convention for the Amelioration of the Condition of the Wounded and Sick in Armed Forces in the Field*, opened for signature 12 August 1949, 75 UNTS 31 (entered into force 21 October 1950) ('GCI').

6 *Geneva Convention for the Amelioration of the Condition of the Wounded, Sick and Shipwrecked Members of the Armed Forces at Sea*, opened for signature 12 August 1949, 75 UNTS 85 (entered into force 21 October 1950) ('GCII').

7 *Geneva Convention Relative to the Treatment of Prisoners of War*, opened for signature 12 August 1949, 75 UNTS 287 (entered into force 21 October 1950) ('GCIII').

8 *Geneva Convention relative to the Protection of Civilian Persons in Time of War*, opened for signature 12 August 1949, 75 UNTS 135 (entered into force 21 October 1950) ('GCIV').

(b) API,[9]
(c) the Hague *Convention (IV) Respecting the Laws and Customs of War on Land* of 1907,[10] and
(d) the Hague *Convention for the Protection of Cultural Property in the Event of Armed Conflict* of 1954.[11]

I introduced the list with the word 'include', as some would argue that while the above lists are the 'standard' list, the list does not include human rights law treaties. I deal with that issue at section 2.5 below.

Of course, not every article in the above treaties is relevant to a targeting issue. In addition, as I have previously stated, I do not consider the HCP in detail in this work. Nor will I be further discussing HIVR. This is because while it is still in force—indeed, it is also considered to represent customary international law—it is my opinion that API has superseded HIVR. To take one example, article 25 HIVR provides protection for undefended towns, villages etc from attack or bombardment. However, an undefended town, village etc would not meet the definition of military objective in article 52(2) API; and therefore would be a civilian object for the purposes of article 52(1) API; and therefore would be protected from attack in accordance with article 52(1) API.[12] Accordingly, article 52 API provides the same protection for undefended towns, villages etc as article 25 HIVR and accordingly there is no need to consider separately article 25 HIVR when considering the lawfulness of an attack.[13]

---

9 As the scope of this book is limited to international armed conflicts, APII, above n 61 (chapter 1), is not considered.

10 HIV, above n 36 (chapter 1). The actual prohibitions are set out in the annex to HIV, known as the *Regulations Respecting the Laws and Customs of War on Land*, signed at The Hague 18 October 1907, 3 Martens Nouveau Recueil (ser. 3) 461 (entered into force 26 January 1910) ('HIVR').

11 *Convention for the Protection of Cultural Property in the Event of Armed Conflict*, opened for signature 14 May 1954, 249 UNTS 240 (entered into force 7 August 1956) ('HCP').

12 My approach reflects VCLT, above n 31 (chapter 1), art 30 and the concept of *lex posterior derogat legi priori* ("later law supersedes earlier law"—see Chapter XII 'Fragmentation of International Law: Difficulties Arising From the Diversification and Expansion of International Law' of the *Report on the work of its fifty-eighth session*, above n 94 (chapter 1)). Art 30(1) VCLT provides: "When all the parties to the earlier treaty are parties also to the later treaty but the earlier treaty is not terminated or suspended in operation under article 59, the earlier treaty applies only to the extent that its provisions are compatible with those of the later treaty."

13 It has been suggested that 'undefended' to the early drafters meant a place subject to immediate occupation by advancing ground troops. So, while a place might be undefended from the air, if it is well behind the front lines and thus protected from immediate occupation by the enemy, the place would not meet the criteria of 'undefended' for the purposes of HIVR, above n 10 (chapter 2), art 25—Hamilton DeSaussure, 'Belligerent Air Operations and the 1977 Geneva Protocol I' in Nicolas Matte (ed), *Annals of Air and Space Law*, Volume 4, (1979) 459, 473. This is not a point that needs to be settled for the purpose of this study, as regardless of whether a restricted or liberal interpretation of 'undefended' is adopted, in either event API, above n 2 (chapter 1), art 52 would limit an attack to military objectives.

Before moving on, and noting the importance that aircraft have in targeting operations, it is appropriate to make a few brief comments on the only treaty ever drafted with the goal of specifically regulating military aircraft operations.

2.2 Hague Rules of Air Warfare

At the instigation of the ICRC in 1920, the HAW were drafted by a Commission of Jurists at The Hague and adopted by them in 1923.[14] Experts from France, Italy, Japan, the Netherlands, the United Kingdom and the United States attended.[15] While never set out in a treaty or in any other way officially endorsed as international law, it is suggested by some that the HAW are generally recognised as constituting customary international law.[16] However, as Rogers points out, as the HAW was never adopted in treaty form, each individual rule "would have to be tested against customary law and state practice".[17] Notwithstanding what might be the status of other draft rules in the HAW, subsequent custom or treaty law has superseded the few HAW rules that deal with targeting. The relevant rules from HAW dealing with targeting, and the reasons why I believe they have been superseded, are:

(a) Article XXII, which prohibits aerial bombardment for the purpose of terrorising the civilian population, of destroying or damaging private property not of a military character, or of injuring non-combatants. Article 48 API sets out the principle of distinction and states that operations shall be directed only against military objectives. Further, article 51(2) API prohibits acts or threats of violence the primary purpose of which is to spread terror among the civilian population. Admittedly, article 51(2) refers to the 'primary' purpose of the attack whereas article XXII HAW merely refers to 'purpose'. Therefore, it is arguable that it is not a breach of article 51(2) API if an attack has as a secondary purpose the intent of spreading terror among the civilian population.[18]
(b) Article XXIV, which states that aerial bombardment is legitimate only when directed at a military objective, provides an exhaustive list of legitimate objectives and prohibits indiscriminate bombardment. Articles 48 and 52(2) API deal with attacking only military objectives, and articles 51(4) and (5) API prohibit and define indiscriminate attacks. With respect to providing an exhaustive list of military objectives, this approach has been abandoned and replaced with a more general definition at article 52(2) API. However, article XXIV(2)

14 Reprinted in Roberts and Guelff, above n 14 (chapter 1), 139–49.

15 Sandoz, Swinarski and Zimmerman (eds), above n 68 (chapter 1), [1997], (fn 2).

16 Green, above n 83 (chapter 1), 181; Roberts and Guelff, above n 14 (chapter 1), 139. See also Sandoz, Swinarski and Zimmerman (eds), above n 68 (chapter 1), [1637], fn 13. The HAW are referred to by the ICTY as being "considered to be an authorative interpretation of the law." (*Prosecutor v Galic, (Trial Chamber)* Case No IT-98-29-T (5 December 2003) fn 103) For a short but interesting article on the development of the HAW, and discussions as to why the HAW were never adopted, see Richard Wyman, 'The First Rules of Air Warfare' (1984) *Air & Space Power Chronicles* <http://www.airpower.au.af.mil/airchronicles/aureview/1984/mar-apr/wyman.html> at 19 November 2005.

17 Rogers, *Law on the Battlefield*, above n 84 (chapter 1), 61.

18 This issue is further discussed at Chapter 4 below.

HAW could be used to assist when deciding what objects amount to military objectives as article XXIV(2) HAW provides an example of what was considered by the experts of the time to constitute military objectives. Article XXIV(4) HAW, which states a proportionality rule, has been replaced by the more stringent proportionality requirements of article 57(2) API. Finally, while article XXV(5) HAW has been replaced by article 91 API, article XXV(5) HAW could be used as an aid to interpreting article 91 API. In particular, article XXV(5) HAW makes it clear that compensation can be payable to individuals and not just States.

(c) Article XXV, which deals with the protection of hospitals, places of worship and what would now be called cultural objects. Article 27 HIVR affords similar protection to the objects listed in article XXV HAW.[19] The protection of medical units and hospital zones is now covered by Chapter III of GCI and article 12 API.[20] The protection of cultural objects is extensively dealt with in HCP, and cultural objects and places of worship "which constitute the cultural or spiritual heritage of peoples" are afforded protection by article 53 API. Other cultural objects and places of worship that do not meet the criterion of constituting 'the cultural or spiritual heritage of peoples' would normally be afforded protection as civilian objects by, inter alia, article 52 API.

(d) Article XXVI, which deals with establishing zones for the protection of important historic monuments. This is perhaps the one article that has not been so obviously replaced by latter treaties. However, it is nonetheless superseded by the law just discussed in paragraph c above; and where specific areas of article XXVI HAW have not been repeated in subsequent treaty law, they are now inapplicable and do not represent customary international law (eg, the 500-metre in width buffer zone mentioned in article XXVI(3) HAW).

2.3 Customary international law

Customary international law remains relevant to parties (along with non-parties) to API. There are various reasons for this. First, API does not purport to be a complete codification of the relevant law (as evidenced by the contemporary restatement of the Martens Clause in article 1(2) API). Second, it is explicitly stated that the rules in articles 48–67 API are additional to, inter alia, "other rules of international law relating to the protection of civilians and civilian objects on land … against the effects of hostilities."[21] That said, nonetheless, there is no relevant customary international law concerning targeting decisions where a State is a party to all of the 1949 Geneva Conventions, HCP and API.[22] This conclusion is based on a review of the

19 I suggest little turns on the use of the words "buildings dedicated to religion" in HIVR, above n 10 (chapter 2), and "buildings dedicated to public worship" in HAW.

20 Particularly with respect to the protection of civilian hospitals.

21 API, above n 2 (chapter 1), art 49(4). See also Bothe, Partsch and Solf, above n 87 (chapter 1), 291 and 300.

22 For a general introduction to customary international law and IHL, see Theodor Meron, *Customary Law*, Crimes of War Project <http://www.crimesofwar.org/thebook/customary-law.html> at 25 May 2006.

literature and case law, where in no case was it suggested that there were customary laws that provide greater restrictions than those found in the treaties mentioned in the previous sentence. In particular, a review of the recent work titled *Customary International Humanitarian Law*,[23] which provides a comprehensive review of contemporary customary international law applicable in armed conflicts, revealed that none of the suggested customary international law rules applicable to targeting are more restrictive than the aforementioned treaties.[24]

This conclusion does not apply for non-parties to API, as many articles of API are considered to reflect customary international law;[25] therefore, there is significant customary international law regulation for non-parties to API. In fact, it appears as though there is little customary IHL applicable to targeting that has not been codified in or drawn from some treaty. Accordingly, most commentators discuss whether certain articles from treaties have become custom—and therefore binding on non-parties—as opposed to identifying customary international law that does not appear in a treaty article somewhere.[26]

2.4 Martens Clause

The Martens Clause is referred to in almost all works dealing with IHL. There is a very good reason for this—the Martens Clause continues to have significance over one hundred years after it was first introduced. The Martens Clause is based upon a declaration read by de Martens, the Russian delegate, to the 1899 Hague Peace Conference. The declaration was introduced after delegates at the conference failed to agree on the issue of the status of civilians who took up arms against an occupying force.[27] It is said that de Martens introduced the clause with a desire to break the deadlock and keep the Peace Conference alive. Allegedly, Martens's proposal was greeted by applause from the delegates.[28] Slightly different versions of the Martens Clause now appear in most of the major IHL treaties; however, as discussed below, the intent remains the same throughout. The English translation of the original Martens Clause is:

> Until a more complete code of the laws of war has been issued, the High Contracting parties deem it expedient to declare that, in cases not included in the Regulations adopted by them, the inhabitants and belligerents remain under the

23 Henckaerts and Doswald-Beck (eds), *Customary International Humanitarian Law*, vol I, above n 64 (chapter 1).

24 See also Stefan Oeter, 'Methods and Means of Combat' in Dieter Fleck (ed), The *Handbook of Humanitarian Law in Armed Conflicts* (1995) 105, 109–111.

25 See ibid; Sassoli and Bouvier, above n 10 (chapter 1), 109; Meron, above n 22 (chapter 2).

26 See, for instance, an excerpt of the *Report of the Swedish International Humanitarian Law Committee Stockholm*, in Sassoli and Bouvier, above n 10 (chapter 1), 597–602.

27 Roberts and Guelff, above n 14 (chapter 1), 9.

28 Vladimir Pustogarov, 'Fyodor Fyodorovich Martens (1845–1909)—a humanist of modern times' (1996) 312 *International Review of the Red Cross* <http://www.icrc.org/Web/eng/siteengo.nsf/iwpList153/80D55047E77CCE46C1256B66005A0861> at 4 June 2006.

> protection and the rule of the principles of the law of nations, as they result from the usages established among civilised peoples, from the laws of humanity, and the dictates of the public conscience.[29]

In the preamble to the HIV, the immediately following sentence is: "They declare that it is in this sense especially that Articles 1 and 2 of the Regulations adopted must be understood."[30]

The regulations referred to are the HIVR. Regulations 1 and 2 of HIVR deal with the issue of who can be lawful combatants, particularly militias, volunteer corps and *levee en masse*. It has been argued, therefore, that the Martens Clause is often quoted out of context.[31] However, the above quoted sentence from the preamble does not impose a strict limitation on the operation of the Martens Clause. Also, no explicit or implicit limitation attaches to the contemporary restatement of the Martens Clause in article 1(2) API. Accordingly, the better view is that the ambit of the Martens Clause is not limited to the particular issue of civilians taking up arms against an occupying force.[32] That said, there is no accepted interpretation of just what the Martens Clause does mean.[33] Perhaps one of the best references to the Martens Clause is: "The Martens Clause bears the marks of its period; it is not easy of interpretation."[34] In the same vein, it has been described as "*ambiguous* and *evasive*".[35] Notwithstanding its wording and "multiplicity of often conflicting interpretations", due to its frequent reliance in international dealings, restatement in treaties, citation in courts and general invocation, it has also been described as "one of the *legal myths* of the international community."[36]

So, what normative effect does the Martens Clause have? At a minimum, the narrow or restrictive interpretation is that the Clause serves as a reminder that customary international law continues to apply after the adoption of a treaty norm. Cassese, in particular, dismisses this interpretation, emphasising that such an interpretation is redundant. The continued applicability of, for instance, customary international law, was and is so well established that Martens and the other

---

29 Preamble to HIV, above n 36 (chapter 1). For a more contemporary restatement (eg, replacing "inhabitants and belligerents" with "civilians and combatants" and "principles of the law of nations, as they result from the usages established among civilised peoples" with "principles of international law derived from established custom"), see API, above n 2 (chapter 1), art 1(2). A shorter version appears in the preamble to APII, above n 61 (chapter 1). See generally Sassoli and Bouvier, above n 10 (chapter 1), 113.

30 Preamble to HIV, above n 36 (chapter 1).

31 Antonio Cassese, 'The Martens Clause: Half a Loaf or simply Pie in the Sky' (2000) 11 *European Journal of International Law* 187, 188.

32 Rupert Ticehurst, 'The Martens Clause and the Laws of Armed Conflict' (1997) 317 *International Review of the Red Cross* <http://www.icrc.org/Web/eng/siteengo.nsf/iwpList160/32AEA038821EA35EC1256B66005A747C> at 4 June 2006.

33 Ibid.

34 *Nuclear Weapons Case* [1996] ICJ Rep 226, (Separate Opinion of Judge Shahabuddeen).

35 Cassese, 'The Martens Clause: Half a Loaf or simply Pie in the Sky', above n 31 (chapter 2), 189 (original emphasis).

36 Ibid, 188 (emphasis in original).

delegates could have hardly thought a Martens Clause to this effect was required.[37] The widest interpretation is that the laws of armed conflict include not only treaties and custom but also the principles of international law derived from the other sources mentioned in the Martens Clause.[38] A middle ground interpretation is that the Martens Clause reminds us that something that is not explicitly prohibited in a treaty is not ipso facto permitted.[39] It has been suggested that the correct interpretation to be placed on the Martens Clause also appears to be affected by positivist versus natural law theories.[40]

On a plain reading of the words of the Martens Clause, I find it hard to adopt anything other than an expansive interpretation. This interpretation is also consistent with article 38(1) of the *Statute of the International Court of Justice*. Of course, this does not equate to carte blanche to introduce mere morality or other desired rules into IHL. My opinion on the correct interpretation of the Martens Clause notwithstanding, it is also correct to say that there is no authoritative decision of a higher court providing a decisive interpretation. Indeed, in the *Nuclear Weapons Case*, while the ICJ did find that the Clause is part of customary international law,[41] and arguably does have an independent normative status,[42] nevertheless the Court adopted no single interpretation of the Clause.[43] Indeed, "beyond mere general statements such as those in the *Krupp* case, no international or national court has ever found that a principle or rule had emerged in the international community as a result of 'the laws of humanity' or the 'dictates of public conscience'."[44]

The *Krupp* case, more formally *United States of America v Krupp von Bohlen und Halbach*, was a trial by a United States Military Tribunal sitting at Nuremberg post World War II with the judgment handed down on 30 June 1948.[45] In that case, the Martens Clause was described as:

---

37 See ibid, 192–3.

38 Recalling that this clause pre-dates the *Statute of the International Court of Justice*, and in particular, article 38(1) of that *Statute*.

39 Ticehurst, above n 32 (chapter 2).

40 Ibid.

41 *Nuclear Weapons Case* [1996] ICJ Rep 226 [84]; John McNeil, 'The International Court of Justice Advisory Opinion in the Nuclear Weapons Case—A first appraisal' (1997) 316 *International Review of the Red Cross* <http://www.icrc.org/Web/eng/siteengo.nsf/iwpList159/177FA9E94321B0DFC1256B66005A6346> at 4 June 2006. At least one commentator suggests that the Martens Clause "must be elevated to the position of *jus cogens*"—Mani, above n 77 (chapter 1).

42 Vincent Chetail, 'The contribution of the International Court of Justice to international humanitarian law' (2003) 850 *International Review of the Red Cross* 235, 257.

43 *Nuclear Weapons Case* [1996] ICJ Rep 226. See in particular paragraphs [78], [84] and [87]; and 20–5 (Separate Opinion of Judge Shahabuddeen).

44 Cassese, 'The Martens Clause: Half a Loaf or simply Pie in the Sky', above n 31 (chapter 2), 208.

45 *United States of America v Krupp von Bohlen und Halbach* ('*Krupp*') in Hersch Lauterpacht (ed), *Annual Digest and Reports of Public International Law Cases: Being a Selection from the Decisions of International Courts and Tribunals and Military Courts given during the year 1948* (1953), 620. In the *Krupp* judgment, the clause is unfortunately referred to as the "Mertens Clause", and is attributed to the Belgian delegate to the Hague Peace

> much more than a pious declaration. It is a general clause, making the usages established among civilized nations, the laws of humanity and the dictates of public conscience into the legal yardstick to be applied if and when the specific provisions of the Convention and the Regulations annexed to it do not cover specific cases occurring in warfare, or concomitant to warfare.[46]

The above quote from the *Krupp* case is referred to with apparent approval by two judges in the *Nuclear Weapons Case*.[47] Interestingly, the Russian submission to the ICJ in the *Nuclear Weapons Case* went so far as to say that as the Martens Clause was predicated upon the issuing of a more complete code of the laws of war, and as since 1907 a more complete code has been issued in the form of the *Geneva Conventions of 1949* and the *Additional Protocols of 1977* thereto, the Clause nowadays "may formally be considered inapplicable".[48] Arguably, this is going too far as this submission is based upon the premise that the *Geneva Conventions* and the *Additional Protocols* form a complete code, which, it would seem, is the very argument the Martens Clause is meant to reject given that variations of the Clause have been restated in the *Geneva Conventions* and the *Additional Protocols*.[49]

As to whether the Martens Clause has any actual efficacy, at least one commentator has written that it "has generally been viewed as ineffectual."[50] However, for the purpose of this work, we are only interested in the scope of the Martens Clause with respect to targeting issues. In this respect, and whilst noting that the intent and sentiment of the Martens Clause is admirable, and noting that it may well have had greater scope for operation in 1899 and the years immediately thereafter (when the number of IHL treaties and the detail therein was significantly less than today), the rule set out in the Clause will have little or no relevance to targeting questions today for States that are parties to the main IHL treaties including API. This is because it is hard to argue that the Geneva Conventions, the Hague law and particularly API do not amount to a more complete code with respect to *targeting issues* or that there are targeting issues that are "not covered by this Protocol or by other international agreements".[51] In support of this argument, for targeting questions that are to be considered under API obligations, none of the material in the bibliography to this book refers to a rule that is derived because of the Martens Clause or customary or other law beyond what can be found in existing treaty law.

Conference of 1899. However, from the context it is clear that it is the Martens Clause introduced by the Russian delegate that is under consideration.

46 Ibid, 622.

47 *Nuclear Weapons Case* [1996] ICJ Rep 226, (Separate Opinion of Judge Shahabuddeen), (Separate Opinion of Judge Weeramantry).

48 Ibid, (Separate Opinion of Judge Weeramantry).

49 See above n 29 (chapter 2).

50 Bernard Brown, 'The Proportionality Principle in the Humanitarian Law of Warfare: Recent Efforts at Codification' (1976) 10 *Cornell International Law Journal* 134, 136.

51 API, above n 2 (chapter 1), art 1(2). Note that this paragraph is restricted to targeting issues, whereas the previous paragraph where I disagreed with the Russian submission to the ICJ was dealing with the entirety of issues that may arise in or out of an armed conflict.

In summary, the Martens Clause does have normative effect; however, for the purpose of this work, the Martens Clause can be put to one side as its normative effect is spent as far as the applicable IHL concerning targeting operations by Australia is concerned.

2.5 Human rights law

The above treaties, along with HAW and the Martens Clause, all come from that branch of the law known as IHL. However, what about International Human Rights Law ('IHRL')? Is it also relevant to targeting decisions?

For many years, a number of lawyers would most likely have answered 'no', along with an initially puzzled look as they tried to work out how the question was even relevant. For example, when the Secretary General of the UN was asked to submit reports to the General Assembly from 1969 onwards on *Human Rights in Armed Conflicts*, some writers questioned whether the right terms were being used.[52] However, this is no longer the case or at least is no longer the case to the extent of asking the question about whether IHRL is relevant during an armed conflict. There is now "general agreement … as regards the continued applicability of human rights law in situations of both international and non-international armed conflict."[53] So, for example, de Lupis has a section in her book *The Law of War* titled 'Operation of human rights in war',[54] and Fleck has a similar chapter in his book *The Handbook of Humanitarian Law in Armed Conflicts*.[55] Interestingly though, both books seem to do little more than say that IHRL is not irrelevant but then do not refer to IHRL under the substantive issues in the books. Equally interesting, while Roberts and Guelff state in their book *Documents on the Laws of War* that "the human rights stream of law merges at many points with the laws of war, and is often relevant to situations of armed conflict", this appears under the heading of *Documents Omitted* from the book![56] There are some exceptions, with perhaps the recent book by Peter

52 Ingrid de Lupis, *The Law of War* (1987) 130.

53 *Third Expert Meeting on the Notion of Direct Participation in Hostilities: Summary Report* (2005) International Committee of the Red Cross <http://www.icrc.org/Web/eng/siteengo.nsf/htmlall/participation-hostilities-ihl-311205/$File/Direct_participation_in_hostilities_2005_eng.pdf> at 20 December 2006, 51. A draft clause that stated that "fundamental human rights continue to apply in all situations of armed conflicts" was proposed by the experts from Norway at the 1972 *Conference of Government Experts on the Reaffirmation and Development of International Humanitarian Law Applicable in Armed Conflicts*, but for unknown reason not adopted—International Committee of the Red Cross, *Conference of Government Experts on the Reaffirmation and Development of International Humanitarian Law Applicable in Armed Conflicts*, Volume II, *Report on the Work of the Conference (Annexes)* (1972), 71 ('CE 1972 Report, vol II'); and CE 1972 Report, vol I, above n 25 (chapter 1), 143.

54 de Lupis, above n 52 (chapter 2), 131.

55 See section titled *Humanitarian Law and the Law of Human Rights*, in Greenwood, 'Historical Development and Legal Basis', above n 45 (chapter 1), 9. The relationship between IHL and IHRL is also briefly discussed in CE/1b, above n 13 (chapter 1), 26–32.

56 Roberts and Guelff, above n 14 (chapter 1), 35 and 38.

Rowe being the most notable.[57] However, even in a book dedicated to the subject of human rights law and armed forces, only about three pages deal with targeting issues.[58] While Rene Provost has an interesting book titled *International Human Rights and Humanitarian Law*, this book more compares and contrasts how IHL and IHRL respectively deal with similar issues.[59] And while a book by Stuart Kaye and Ryszard Piotrowicz does deal with human rights law in an Australian context, and while there is a whole Part on IHL, the book does not address in detail the operation of particular norms of IHRL in a targeting context.[60] Rather, it more looks at how IHL norms reflect some IHRL principles.

Therefore, what are we to make of this apparent willingness by some authors to recognise the applicability of IHRL during armed conflict but then subsequently not to refer to it? While there may just be an aspect of one scholarly discipline acting in isolation of another,[61] it could also be because in most cases it is IHL that provides the tests against which violations of human rights are to be judged. In other words, IHL is the *lex specialis*.[62] This view is supported by the decision in the *Nuclear Weapons Case*. In that case, the ICJ held:

> The Court observes that the protection of the International Covenant of Civil and Political Rights does not cease in times of war, except by operation of Article 4 of the Covenant whereby certain provisions may be derogated from in a time of national emergency. Respect for the right to life is not, however, such a provision. In principle, the right not arbitrarily to be deprived of one's life applies also in hostilities. The test of what is an arbitrary deprivation of life, however, then falls to be determined by the applicable *lex specialis*, namely, the law applicable in armed conflict which is designed to regulate the conduct of hostilities. Thus whether a particular loss of life, through the use of a certain weapon in warfare, is to be considered an arbitrary deprivation of life contrary to Article 6 of the Covenant, can only be decided by reference to the law applicable in armed conflict and not deduced from the terms of the Covenant itself.[63]

---

57 Peter Rowe, *The Impact of Human Rights Law on Armed Forces* (2006).

58 This is in no way meant as a criticism. It is just that a significant part of Rowe's book deals with the human rights of civilians and military members of a State vis-à-vis their own armed force, with further issues such as detention, torture and fair trials occupying a good part of the book. Rowe's work is also heavily influenced by the *Convention for the Protection of Human Rights and Fundamental Freedoms*, opened for signature on 4 November 1950, 213 UNTS 222, entered into force 3 September 1953 (also known as the *European Convention on Human Rights*). The court decisions in relation to this convention are only indirectly relevant to Australian military commanders as Australia is subject to a different legal regime.

59 Rene Provost, *International Human Rights and Humanitarian Law* (2002).

60 Stuart Kaye and Ryszard Piotrowicz, *Human Rights in International and Australian Law* (2000).

61 Noting that, in the reverse, Prof Shearer has written that IHL "has tended to be ignored, especially by scholars of human rights, as though by way of wishing the whole distasteful subject of war away." (Ibid, foreword)

62 *Third Expert Meeting on the Notion of Direct Participation in Hostilities: Summary Report*, above n 53 (chapter 2), 51.

63 *Nuclear Weapons Case* [1996] ICJ Rep 226, [25].

The ICJ has effectively repeated this assertion in a case concerning the *Legal Consequences of the Construction of a Wall in the Occupied Palestinian Territory*.[64]

To summarise the position, during an armed conflict both IHL and IHRL are applicable,[65] noting that in certain circumstances the general propositions of IHRL will be interpreted through the applicable rules of IHL. In addition, IHRL may fill any normative gaps in IHL and the provisions of human rights treaties may provide for more sophisticated enforcement mechanisms.[66] Finally, IHRL may provide "direction for the interpretation and application of [IHL]".[67]

A further point worth noting is that if IHL is not applicable in a given situation, IHRL may well still apply.[68] This can be important if, as would usually be the case, the relevant rule of IHRL is more restrictive than the (non-applicable) permissive rule of IHL. For example, IHL permits the detention of persons (eg, as prisoners of war) in circumstances that may not be permitted under IHRL. Equally, IHL permits the lawful destruction of property in circumstances that may not be permitted by IHRL. And at the extreme end, IHL permits the lawful killing of persons (eg, combatants) in situations that would be prohibited under IHRL. Accordingly, where IHL is not de jure applicable certain acts may be impermissible due to IHRL. This issue becomes important as many States, and even the UN, will talk of voluntarily applying IHL or at least the spirit and principles of IHL. The problem is that although a State can always voluntarily assume *obligations* (or restrictions), it cannot assume *rights* (or authorisations or permissions). This is the difficulty I have with Hays Parks's article on the applicability of IHL during operations other than war.[69] Hays Parks focuses on the fact that an army, and more particularly a soldier, will execute operations as they have been trained. In my view, it is accurate to summarise his article as arguing that if soldiers have been well trained in IHL they will comply with IHL during all types of operations; and therefore breaches will not occur. It would appear that Hays Parks overlooks the fact that if

---

64 *Palestinian Wall Case* [2004] ICJ Rep 131, [106].

65 Subject, of course, to any reservations or derogations and only to the extent and limit of the jurisdiction set out in a relevant treaty (Rowe, *The Impact of Human Rights Law on Armed Forces*, above n 57 (chapter 2)).

66 Chetail, above n 42 (chapter 2), 241–2 (footnotes omitted). See also Hans-Joachim Heintze, 'On the relationship between human rights law protection and international humanitarian law' (2004) 856 *International Review of the Red Cross* 789; Yoram Dinstein, *The Conduct of Hostilities under the Law of International Armed Conflict* (2004) 20–5.

67 Chapter XII 'Fragmentation of International Law: Difficulties Arising from the Diversification and Expansion of International Law' of the *Report on the work of its fifty-eighth session*, above n 94 (chapter 1).

68 Alexandre Faite and Jeremie Grenier (eds), *Report of the Expert Meeting on Multinational Peace Operations: Issues Relating to the Application of International Law* (2004) International Committee of the Red Cross <http://www.icrc.org/web/eng/siteengo.nsf/htmlall/5upd5e?opendocument> at 28 January 2007, i. This report is an interesting, contemporary discussion on the application of IHL and IHRL to UN-mandated forces.

69 W. Hays Parks, 'Rules of Conduct during Operations Other Than War: The Law of War Does Apply' (2001) The University of North Carolina at Chapel Hill—American Diplomacy <http://www.unc.edu/depts/diplomat/archives_roll/2001_07-09/hum_intervention/hum_08_parks.html> at 28 February 2005.

IHL is not applicable de jure, then actions that comply with IHL may nonetheless breach the law—and in particular IHRL—unless some other legal basis for the action can be found.

In conclusion, for the purposes of this work we can restrict our discussion on the law applicable to targeting issues to the relevant IHL treaty law and in particular to API.

2.6 Military necessity and IHL

Military necessity is a fundamental principle in IHL. "Military necessity permits a belligerent, subject to the laws of war, to apply any amount and kind of force to compel the complete submission of the enemy with the least possible expenditure of time, life and money."[70] At its most basic, the principle of military necessity is what allows combatants to *lawfully* kill and injure other persons and to damage and destroy property. Military necessity is sometimes also expressed as the principle that combatants may use the minimum amount of force necessary to achieve a legitimate military objective.[71]

Another aspect of military necessity is that it sometimes allows non-compliance with a particular rule of IHL. This occurs when the rule itself allows for non-compliance in the event of military necessity.[72] However, there is also a fourth use of the term military necessity. As per some examples in the following pages, military necessity is also sometimes used when discussing whether IHL in general (ie, not just certain specific rules that allow for non-compliance in the event of military necessity) can be disregarded or breached in extreme necessity.[73] The following discussion concerns this latter use of the term.

It is not unusual to see or hear the argument that where the very survival of a State is threatened, then laws, and in particular IHL, cannot limit the actions the State can use to defend itself. For example, Barber writes:

---

70 *United States of America v List ('Hostages Trial')*, in Lauterpacht (ed), above n 45 (chapter 2), 632, 646.

71 See generally Air Power Development Centre, above n 81 (chapter 1), 49. Note, in this context 'military objective' is not being used in the API, art 52(2) sense; but rather is more akin to 'military goal'.

72 For example, HCP, above n 11 (chapter 2), art 4(1) requires parties to respect cultural property. However, HCP, art 4(2) states that the "obligations mentioned in paragraph 1 of the present Article may be waived only in cases where *military necessity* imperatively requires such a waiver." (emphasis added) Similarly, API, above n 2 (chapter 1), art 54(2) provides that objects indispensable to the survival of the civilian population shall be protected from attack etc. However, API, art 54(5) provides that in "recognition of the vital requirements of any Party to the conflict in the defence of its national territory against invasion, derogation from the prohibitions contained in paragraph 2 may be made by a Party to the conflict within such territory under its own control where required by imperative *military necessity*." (emphasis added)

73 While this can conceivably occur at the individual level or at the State level, the discussion usually deals only with the State level. The following discussion in this book likewise looks at the issue at the State level. At the individual level, the question might arise whether a soldier could use a weapon otherwise prohibited under IHL in defence against a lawful attack where the attack would without use of the prohibited weapon be likely to cause serious death or injury to the soldier.

> Because SCUD attacks appear so clearly to be violations, it must then be asked if the rules operate to the distinct disadvantage of the underdeveloped countries. Arguably, the SCUDs represented one of the few methods Iraq had to defend itself when facing insuperable odds. ... A hypothetical situation might suggest an answer. If SCUDs were Kuwait's only means of resisting the Iraqi invasion, it would be hard to imagine universal condemnation or punishment under Protocol I if they fired missiles at Baghdad in the honest belief they could forestall or stop the invasion.[74]

This type of argument in IHL is known as the concept of *kreigsraison*,[75] which can be stated as "the demands of military necessity should always override the obligations of international law."[76] Rather emphatically, the *ICRC Commentary* states:

> 'Kreigsraison' was condemned at Nuremberg, and this condemnation has been confirmed by legal writings. One can and should consider this theory discredited. It is totally incompatible with the wording of Article 35, paragraph 1, and with the very existence of the Protocol.[77]

The other standard responses are that "[t]he notion of 'military necessity' cannot be invoked against rules which already make allowance for it",[78] and "military necessity cannot justify violation of the other rules of IHL."[79] A similar view of the law

---

74 Peter Barber, 'Scuds, Shelters and Retreating soldiers: The Laws of Aerial Bombardment and the Gulf War' (1993) XXXI No.4 *Alberta Law Review* 662, 687.

75 'Kreigsraison geht vor Kriegsmanier' ('the necessities of war take precedence over the rules of war')—Sandoz, Swinarski and Zimmerman (eds), above n 68 (chapter 1), [1386].

76 Chris af Jochnick and Roger Normand, 'The Legitimation of Violence: A Critical History of the Laws of War' (1994) 35 *Harvard International Law Journal* 49, 63. Footnote 53 to their article explains that the term [*kreigsraison*] derives from the German phrase 'kreigsraison gehs vor kreigsmanier', which translates as 'the necessities of war are prior to the customs of war'. Note, the citations are not meant to suggest that the authors support the concept *kreigsraison*.

77 Sandoz, Swinarski and Zimmerman (eds), above n 68 (chapter 1), [1386]. See also International Committee of the Red Cross, *Conference of Government Experts on the Reaffirmation and Development of International Humanitarian Law Applicable in Armed Conflicts*, Volume IV, *Protection of the civilian population against dangers of hostilities* (1971) ('CE/4b'), 6. But see the statement of Italy at *Diplomatic Conference on the Reaffirmation and Development of International Humanitarian Law Applicable in Armed Conflicts*—International Committee of the Red Cross, *Official Records of the Diplomatic Conference on the Reaffirmation and Development of International Humanitarian Law Applicable in Armed Conflicts* (1974–1977) vol VI, 232 ('CDDH/VI').

78 Hans Blix, 'Means and Methods of Combat', in Henry Dunant Institute and UNESCO (eds), *International Dimensions of Humanitarian Law* (1988) 135, 137.

79 Francoise Hampson, *Military Necessity*, Crimes of War Project <http://www.crimesofwar.org/thebook/military-necessity.html> at 25 May 2006. See also Christopher Greenwood, 'International law and the United States' air operation against Libya' (1987) 89 *West Virginia Law Review* 933, 957; Rogers, *Law on the Battlefield*, above n 84 (chapter 1), 4–5.

is espoused by the United Kingdom's Ministry of Defence.[80] However, some commentators are concerned that the ICJ may have backed away from this strong rejection of the concept of *kreigsraison* in the *Nuclear Weapons Case*.[81] In that case, the court held, by seven votes to seven, by the President's casting vote, that:

> It follows from the above-mentioned requirements that the threat or use of nuclear weapons would generally be contrary to the rules of international law applicable in armed conflict, and in particular the principles and rules of humanitarian law;
>
> However, in view of the current state of international law, and of the elements of fact at its disposal, the Court cannot conclude definitively whether the threat or use of nuclear weapons would be lawful or unlawful in an extreme circumstance of self-defence, in which the very survival of a State would be at stake[.][82]

The wording of this part of the judgment is rather unfortunate. It is hard not to conclude that the court was saying that IHL can be disregarded in extreme circumstances. The most favourable interpretation that can be offered is that the court was actually saying that in an extreme enough circumstance the military advantage to be gained from the use of a nuclear weapon might be just large enough so that IHL would still be complied with notwithstanding the no doubt extensive collateral damage, environmental damage etc. Of course, it is not clear that this is what the court was saying. However, the court, no doubt aware of the extensive criticism of this aspect of its decision, has clarified the matter in its subsequent decision in the *Palestinian Wall Case*.[83] In that case, the ICJ reaffirmed the absolute requirement for compliance with IHL in all circumstances. Noting that both the Israelis and Palestinians often state that their very survival as States or peoples is at stake, the court observed:

> The Court would emphasize that both Israel and Palestine are under an obligation scrupulously to observe the rules of international humanitarian law, one of the paramount purposes of which is to protect civilian life.[84]

The rationale behind rejecting a plea to broad military necessity to support non-compliance with IHL was well set out in the *Krupp* case:

> the contention that the rules and customs of warfare can be violated if either party is hard pressed must be rejected … War is by definition a risky and haz-

80 UK Ministry of Defence, above n 14 (chapter 1), [2.3].

81 Issue 316 of the International Review of the Red Cross is a thematic issue on the *Nuclear Weapons Case* [1996] ICJ Rep 226, and it is a very good starting point for readers interested in comments on the case—see <http://www.icrc.org/Web/eng/siteengo.nsf/html/section_review_1997_316?OpenDocument>.

82 *Nuclear Weapons Case* [1996] ICJ Rep 226, [105]. This line of argument was foreshadowed, but not supported, in the *ICRC Commentary*—Sandoz, Swinarski and Zimmerman (eds), above n 68 (chapter 1), [1387–89 and 1857–9]).

83 *Palestinian Wall Case* [2004] ICJ Rep 131.

84 Ibid, [162].

> ardous business. That is one of the reasons that the outcome of war, once started, is unforeseeable and that, therefore, war is a basically unrational means of 'settling' conflicts—why right-thinking people all over the world repudiate and abhor aggressive war. It is an essence of war that one or the other side must lose and the experienced generals and statesmen knew this when they drafted the rules and customs of land warfare. In short, these rules and customs of warfare are designed specifically for all phases of war. They comprise the law for such emergency. To claim that they can be wantonly—and at the sole discretion of any one belligerent—disregarded when he considers his own situation to be critical, means nothing more or less than to abrogate the laws and customs of war entirely.[85]

To conclude, the concept of *kreigsraison* is not good law. Despite the consequences for a belligerent in a battle or the armed conflict as a whole, then except and only to the extent specifically provided for in a particular rule,[86] military necessity does not permit a breach of IHL.[87]

2.7 Is IHL prohibitory or permissive?

One further introductory point is required before turning to the body of the work. International humanitarian law rules are often expressed in prohibitive language—ie, the rules state what is not allowed. No doubt partly because of this, it is sometimes asked, particularly in military circles, whether IHL is prohibitory or permissive in character.[88] I personally find the terms unhelpful as a short answer in the affirmative or in the negative to either term usually does little to clarify understanding or to achieve assured agreement or understanding between the person asking the question and the person giving the answer.[89] However, the question itself is helpful. The point of the question is to try to determine whether all actions in armed con-

85 *Krupp*, Lauterpacht (ed), above n 45 (chapter 2), 628.

86 See above n 72 (chapter 2).

87 Dinstein, *The Conduct of Hostilities under the Law of International Armed Conflict*, above n 66 (chapter 2), 18–9.

88 A similar question can come up when considering military orders; and in particular, rules of engagement. Tactical level commanders will often want to know what they are prohibited from doing, and from there it is assumed that everything else is permitted. Strategic level commanders may prefer the opposite approach and prefer to tell subordinate commanders only what they are permitted to do. Not only can this assist with the principle of command responsibility, it means that higher command does not have to consider every eventuality and set out a large list of prohibitions. In a limited conflict and a complex strategic and political environment, higher command may have a desire to keep subordinate commanders on a tight rein. Of course, the problem with this approach is that it might overly restrict flexibility and ingenuity at the tactical level; and it can lead to a long list of permissions. One need be asked only once whether the use of hand-held torches has been permitted to realize that neither approach to interpretation can be applied absolutely.

89 It is somewhat like being asked: 'You did not do that, did you?' Does an answer of 'yes' mean the person did not do the thing alleged or that the person did do the thing alleged?

flict are permitted unless prohibited by law, or alternatively are all actions in armed conflict prohibited unless permitted by law.

It has been suggested that the reason why IHL treaties generally set out prohibitions rather than permissions is "the belief of humanitarian scholars that a humanitarian instrument should provide what is to be spared, and not explicitly authorize violence."[90] However, this is surely only part of the point. Arguably treaties are also written in this way because States initially feel unconstrained in how they wage war; therefore, the prohibitory rules of IHL, be those rules customary or treaty based, are the most essential. Whether this is the case or not, nonetheless it would appear that the better legal answer is that all means and methods of warfare in armed conflict are permitted (ie, are lawful) unless prohibited by IHL.[91] In other words, the correct legal question is to look to see if a particular practice of warfare has been prohibited.[92] The prohibitions may be in customary international law or in treaty law. Some treaty law prohibitions are very specific, while others—for example article 35 API[93]—provide general prohibitions. However, in the absence of a relevant treaty article or customary international law rule there is no prohibition on what is permitted in armed conflict if called for by military necessity.[94] Having arrived at this conclusion, it must be remembered that some IHL rules provide very broad prohibitions. In particular, and as argued in section 2.4, the Martens Clause is of itself a source of prohibitory rules. See, for example, Judge Weeramantry's decision in the *Nuclear Weapons Case* where his honour stated that there need not be a specific treaty prohibition on nuclear weapons for the use of such weapons to be banned as the general principles of customary international law or the Martens Clause provided the relevant prohibition.[95] Consequently, it is often practically helpful and legally useful to look for a relevant authorisation in IHL for a desired action. These authorisations or permissions can be thought of as exceptions from the prohibitory rules. Such authorisations might be explicit or implicit. For example, it is possible to think of IHL as explicitly authorising attacks on military objectives,[96] or as implicitly permitting the use of force (including lethal force) against persons who meet certain criteria (eg, the criteria for being a combatant).[97] Two advantages of this approach are that it sits neatly with a military mind-set of

---

90 Waldemar Solf, 'Protection of Civilians Against the Effects of Hostilities under Customary International Law and under Protocol I' (1986) 1 *American University Journal of International Law and Policy* 117, 121 (footnote omitted). See also Sandoz, Swinarski and Zimmerman (eds), above n 68 (chapter 1), [2015].

91 McNeil, above n 41 (chapter 2); Sandoz, Swinarski and Zimmerman (eds), above n 68 (chapter 1), [1389].

92 *Hostages Trial*, Lauterpacht (ed), above n 45 (chapter 2), 645.

93 API, above n 2 (chapter 1), art 35(2) prohibits means and methods of warfare that by their nature cause superfluous injury or unnecessary suffering.

94 Dinstein, *The Conduct of Hostilities under the Law of International Armed Conflict*, above n 66 (chapter 2), 18.

95 *Nuclear Weapons Case* [1996] ICJ Rep 226, (Separate Opinion of Judge Weeramantry).

96 See API, above n 2 (chapter 1), art 52(2).

97 See API, above n 2 (chapter 1), arts 37(1), 41(1) and 48. A prohibition on killing an adversary by means of perfidy implies that it is lawful in some other circumstances to kill an adversary by a non-perfidious means. Similarly, a prohibition on attacking a

command and control,[98] and it facilitates an analysis as to why certain acts that would otherwise be unlawful under domestic law are not unlawful when conducted during an armed conflict. When trying to determine the lawfulness of an action, it is always preferable to be to able to find the authority for the act under review rather than having to exclude all possible prohibitions for the act.

In conclusion, it is my view that all means and methods of warfare are legally permitted unless prohibited under IHL; but the Martens Clause and other general rules of IHL need to be considered before concluding that no relevant prohibition exists. Due to the broad prohibitions, it is often useful to identify rules of IHL that permit, explicitly or implicitly, a desired course of action.

The remainder of this book is split into two Parts. In Part I, I look at the law that applies when *determining* whether an object or a person is a lawful target. Part II then deals with the law that applies when *executing* an attack against a lawful target.

person who is *hors de combat* implies that it is lawful in some other circumstances to kill a person who is not *hors de combat*.

98 It is much easier for a senior commander to retain control where subordinates are acting in accordance with a range of permissions than merely refraining from certain acts based on prohibitions.

Part I

The Law Concerning What Are Lawful Targets

Chapter 3

Lawful non-human targets

Part I of this book is a detailed analysis of the interpretation of the law concerning what or who it is lawful to target. It is a fundamental rule of IHL that it is lawful to target only military objectives.[1] Military objectives can be both human and non-human (ie, objects), although human targets are not clearly mentioned (perhaps deliberately) in API. Different rules apply to each group for determining whether someone or something is a lawful target. The law dealing with human targets is discussed in chapter 4. The second class of targets, which are discussed in this chapter, are all other objects (both inanimate such as buildings and living non-human objects).[2]

As an introductory point it is worth noting that while the specific rules for the lawfulness of targeting objects or humans are different, in each case those rules are governed by the general principle of military necessity. In the context of targeting, this principle is expressed in the preamble to the *St Petersburg Declaration*: "The only legitimate object which States should endeavour to accomplish during war is to weaken the military forces of the enemy".[3] Reference back to this guiding principle is useful when trying to resolve disputed interpretations of specific rules concerning lawful targets.

The focus of Chapter 3 is upon the interpretation of the test for when an object is a lawful military objective. This is essentially a matter of interpreting the various parts of article 52(2) API. Therefore, this chapters looks at the meaning of "effective contribution to military action" (and in particular, the words 'nature', 'location', 'purpose' and 'use') and 'military advantage'. In this chapter, I argue that there is a distinction between the political goals and military goals in a conflict; and for targets to be lawful, only the advantage that serves a military goal can be assessed when determining whether a target is subject to lawful attack. As a result, it is my argument that an object becomes a military objective only where the attack will directly or indirectly weaken the military capability of the enemy; and an object cannot be attacked just because damaging or destroying that object will contribute to the political or strategic goals of the armed conflict.

---

1 First sentence of API, above n 2 (chapter 1), art 52(2).

2 For example, a cavalry horse or even a bottlenose dolphin that has been trained to detect sea mines (John Pickrell, *Dolphins Deployed as Undersea Agents in Iraq* (2003) National Geographic News <http://news.nationalgeographic.com/news/2003/03/0328_030328_wardolphins.html> at 7 August 2005).

3 *St Petersburg Declaration*, above n 64 (chapter 1).

3.1 Basic rule—military necessity and distinction

In section 2.6 above, the principle of military necessity was introduced. That section was primarily concerned with arguing how, as a general principle, an appeal to military necessity cannot be used as a reason to disregard positive rules of IHL. However, it was also noted that military necessity has other meanings. This section deals with the concept of military necessity in perhaps its most used meaning as a general principle of IHL that permits the use of force to achieve military goals.

Military necessity is a fundamental principle in IHL that "permits a belligerent, subject to the laws of war, to apply any amount and kind of force to compel the complete submission of the enemy with the least possible expenditure of time, life and money."[4] At its most basic, the principle of military necessity is what allows combatants to *lawfully* kill and injure other persons and to damage and destroy property. However, in any general discussion on targeting, it is always worth recalling that there are only certain targets that it is lawful to attack. While often considered as a permissive aspect of IHL (ie, military necessity is what authorises military action), the very concept of military necessity is also a *limit* on military action. Rogers points out that military necessity is "encapsulated in the preamble to the St Petersburg Declaration".[5] The preamble includes the statement: "The *only* legitimate object which States should endeavour to accomplish during war is to weaken the military forces of the enemy and for this purpose it is sufficient to disable the greatest possible number of men".[6] So, the very concept of military necessity as expressed in the preamble includes a limitation on the extent of permissible military action.[7]

That only the weakening of the *military* potential of an enemy is acceptable in armed conflict has been described as an "axiom that is the very foundation of international humanitarian law".[8] It is a principle that will regularly reappear in this work to assist in the interpretation of the substantive rules of IHL. A basic understanding of this rule is essential to any discussion on what *are* lawful targets.[9] When it is recognised that the principle of military necessity is both an authorisation to conduct military operations and also an inherent limit on the scope of those operations, it can be seen that military necessity is intrinsically linked to the related principle of distinction. The current general rule expressing the principle of distinction is explicitly set out in article 48 API as follows:

> In order to ensure respect for and protection of the civilian population and civilian objects, the Parties to the conflict shall at all times distinguish between the civilian

---

4 *Hostages Trial*, Lauterpacht (ed), above n 45 (chapter 2), 646.

5 Rogers, *Law on the Battlefield*, above n 84 (chapter 1), 4.

6 *St Petersburg Declaration*, above n 64 (chapter 1).

7 Rogers, *Law on the Battlefield*, above n 84 (chapter 1), 6–7.

8 Chetail, above n 42 (chapter 2), 253.

9 For the purposes of this study, I put to one side discussions on what *should be* lawful targets. For an introduction to the discussion of different theories of target selection, like utility targeting compared to axiological targeting, see Paul Kan, 'What Should We Bomb? Axiological Targeting and the Abiding Limits of Airpower Theory' (2004) XVIII:1 *Air & Space Power Journal* 25.

> population and combatants and between civilian objects and military objectives and accordingly shall direct their operations only against military objectives.[10]

It can be seen that article 48 API is still a general rule. While article 48 API sets out a principle of distinction and impliedly the concept of lawful targets, it does not define essential concepts such as the civilian population, combatants, civilian objects and military objectives. Therefore, to know what objects are lawful targets, we need to discuss what are military objectives. Yet, as recently as 2002, the President of the ICRC had occasion to state that "[s]pecific challenges arising in modern conflicts relate to the definition of military objectives."[11]

3.2 Military objectives

Additional Protocol I is the first IHL treaty to provide a working definition of all non-human military objectives.[12] Military objectives are defined in API to mean:

> In so far as objects are concerned, military objectives are limited to those objects which by their nature, location, purpose or use make an effective contribution to military action and whose total or partial destruction, capture or neutralization, in the circumstances ruling at the time, offers a definite military advantage.[13]

While the 1949 Geneva Conventions repeatedly refer to military objectives, no definition appears in any of those conventions. Accordingly, while API is 'additional' to the 1949 Geneva Conventions, there is no need to refer to the previous conventions when interpreting article 52(2) API.

A very significant aspect of the article 52(2) API definition is that while it provides a test for determining whether something is a military objective, in no case does it provide that an object is ipso facto a military objective. Both approaches have been advanced over the years. Indeed, article XXIV HAW is an example of both approaches being used at once. Article XXIV(1) HAW is clearly a forerunner to article 52(2) API, in that it sets out a test for determining whether an object can be classified as a military objective.[14] But interestingly, article XXIV(2) HAW then goes on to state that bombardment of such military objectives is legitimate only when the object is also part of an exclusive list.[15] It is very important to read articles XXIV(1) and (2) HAW carefully, as the effect of the articles is that an object that:

10 API, above n 2 (chapter 1), art 48 (emphases added).

11 Kellenberger, above n 23 (chapter 1).

12 A useful review of the history of the codification of the definition of a military objective can be found in Boivin, above n 19 (chapter 1), 8–15.

13 Second sentence API, above n 2 (chapter 1), art 52(2).

14 HAW, art 24(1) provides that: "Aerial bombardment is legitimate only when directed at a military objective, that is to say, an object of which the destruction or injury would constitute a distinct military advantage to the belligerent."

15 HAW, art XXIV(2) provides that: "Such bombardment is legitimate only when directed exclusively at the following objectives: military forces; military works; military establishments or depots; factories constituting important and well-known centres engaged

(a) satisfies the test in article XXIV(1) HAW and is listed in article XXIV(2) HAW is a legitimate object of attack;
(b) satisfies the test in article XXIV(1) HAW but is not listed in article XXIV(2) HAW is not a legitimate object of attack; and
(c) is listed in article XXIV(2) HAW is not, by the very fact of being listed, a legitimate object of attack.

Of course, it would be very unusual to find that an object that was listed in article XXIV(2) HAW would not concurrently satisfy the test set out in article XXIV(1) HAW for being a military objective. Nonetheless, if article XXIV HAW were the applicable law, a belligerent would be obliged to ensure that a potential target came within both articles.

A similar approach to that used in the HAW was adopted in 1956 when the ICRC put forward a test for legitimate military objectives in article 7 of its *Draft Rules for the Limitation of Dangers incurred by the Civilian Population in Time of War.*[16] The list was drawn up by the ICRC with the help of military experts and was presented as a model, subject to modification.[17] Article 7 provided, relevantly, that:
(a) attacks may only be directed against military objectives;
(b) only objectives belonging to the categories of objective which, in view of their essential characteristics, are generally acknowledged to be of military importance, may be considered as military objectives;
(c) those categories are listed in an annex to the present rules; and
(d) even if they belong to one of those categories, objectives cannot be considered as a military objective where their total or partial destruction, in the circumstances ruling at the time, offers no military advantage.

By the time the ICRC drew up the draft of API in 1970–1, it had abandoned the draft list in favour of a more abstract definition of military objectives similar to that found in article 52(2) API today.[18] It has been suggested that the "draft from 1956 can only be considered of historical interest today."[19] This, however, is overstating the case. While dated, a list drawn up by the ICRC and military experts must clearly be of assistance, albeit not determinative, when trying to decide what does and does not come within the article 52(2) API test. Indeed, attempts to list likely military objectives continue to this day. The important point to note, however, is

---

in the manufacture of arms, ammunition, or distinctively military supplies; lines of communication or transportation used for military purposes."

16 Reproduced in Sandoz, Swinarski and Zimmerman (eds), above n 68 (chapter 1), [2002]. A copy of the entire *Draft Rules*, but without the annex, is available at *Draft Rules for the Limitation of the Dangers incurred by the Civilian Population in Time of War* (2005) International Committee of the Red Cross <http://www.icrc.org/ihl.nsf/FULL/420?OpenDocument> at 24 May 2006.

17 Sandoz, Swinarski and Zimmerman (eds), above n 68 (chapter 1), [2002], fn 3.

18 Ibid, [2004]. There were still delegates at the 1974–77 *Diplomatic Conference* who would have wished for a list—ibid, [2035]. See also CE 1972 Report, vol I, above n 25 (chapter 1), 147.

19 Andreas Laursen, 'NATO, the War Over Kosovo, and the ICTY Investigation' (2002) 17 *American University International Law Review* 765, 782.

that such lists are merely lists of objects that the authors consider as being likely to be military objectives, which while clearly useful when trying to focus intelligence and planning resources are not a substitute for applying the article 52(2) API test. In this respect, Fenrick refers to a tentative list of military objectives list drawn up by Major General Rogers, the then British Director of Army Legal Services, using the API definition of military objective and Rogers's own review of state practice. Fenrick concludes with:

> The list was not intended to be exhaustive. It remains a requirement that both elements of the definition must be met before a target can be properly considered an appropriate military objective.[20]

While this point may seem straight forward, it is not always reflected in State practice. For example, the *USAF Intelligence Targeting Guide* states:

> Controversy exists over whether, and under what circumstances, other objects such as civilian transportation and communications systems, dams, and dikes can properly be classified as military objectives. Modern transportation and communications systems are *deemed* military objectives because they are used heavily for military purposes in intense conflicts.[21]

The use of the word 'deemed' in the last sentence is interesting. Some commentators also write that "[s]ome objects, 'by their nature,' are military objectives and remain so at all times, regardless of their location or use."[22] Accordingly, it is worth repeating that the correct legal position is that each potential target must be assessed

20 William Fenrick, 'Attacking the Enemy Civilian as a Punishable Offense' (1997) 7:2 *Duke Journal of Comparative and International Law* 539, 543–4 (footnotes omitted). The list was:

> military facilities, military equipment, including military vehicles, weapons, munitions and stores of fuel, military works, including defensive works and fortifications, military depots and establishments, including War and Supply Ministries, works producing or developing military supplies and other supplies of military value, including metallurgical, engineering and chemical industries supporting the war effort; areas of land of military significance such as hills, defiles and bridgeheads; railways, ports, airfields, bridges, main roads as well as tunnels and canals; oil and other power installations; communications installations, including broadcasting and television stations and telephone and telegraph stations used for military communications.

21 Air Force Pamphlet 14-210 Intelligence, above n 53 (chapter 1), [A4.2.2.1] (emphasis added). While the USA is not a party to API, paragraph A4.2.2 adopts almost word for word the definition in API, above n 2 (chapter 1), art 52(2) of a military objective.

22 Robertson Jr, above n 105 (chapter 1), 49.

against the article 52(2) API test, as it "is not possible to have a class of target."[23] So, for example, "bridges are not, as such, military objectives."[24] Put another way:

> It is true that in traditional conflicts, traffic infrastructure and lines of communication are generally considered to be military targets. But as the report rightly points out, tradition is not enough.[25]

By way of an example to illustrate this point, imagine a bridge that crosses a river. Further, that river forms the border with a neutral country. Finally, the border between the two countries is the bank of the river on the side of the neutral country. Now, if the laws of neutrality are being complied with, there are very few occasions when a military advantage could accrue from attacking the bridge even though the bridge is wholly within the territory of the enemy.[26]

Just in case there is any doubt that this might not have been the intended result of the article 52(2) API test, it is worth noting that the drafting history. It was recognised at the 1971 *Conference of Government Experts on the Reaffirmation and Development of International Humanitarian Law Applicable in Armed Conflicts* that an:

> object which, buy its normal purpose, constitutes a military objective, may become a non-military object if its function changes (for example, the barracks abandoned by troops and transformed into a hospital[)].[27]

Subsequently, the draft of what was to become article 52(2) API that was considered at the 1972 *Conference of Government Experts on the Reaffirmation and Development*

---

23 Francoise Hampson, 'Proportionality and Necessity in the Gulf Conflict', in ASIL Proceedings, *Implementing Limitations on the Use of Force: The Doctrine of Proportionality and Necessity* (1992) 45, 49. See also the section titled 'Target Lists are not an Option' in *Expert Meeting: "Targeting Military Objectives"*, above n 27 (chapter 1), 8.

24 Ibid.

25 Michael Bothe, 'The Protection of the Civilian Population and NATO Bombing on Yugoslavia: Comments on a Report to the Prosecutor of the ICTY' (2001) Vol 12 No 3 *European Journal of International Law* 531, 534 (footnote omitted). The reference to the report is to the *OTP Report*—see above n 90 (chapter 1).

26 One such occasion would be if enemy troops were using the bridge as a firing point. But, the point of this example is to reinforce the test in API, above n 2 (chapter 1), art 52(2). While the bridge in question could not be deemed a military objective, it could potentially become a military objective under the test in art 52(2). *Ya Libnan* reports an attack by Israel on the Mdairej bridge in Lebanon during the 2006 conflict, and states that the bridge was:

> not used by Hezbollah since it lies in a mountain resort area of Mount Lebanon, far away from the south of Lebanon. Hence it has no strategic value for Israeli fight against Hezbollah. (*Israel destroys the highest bridge in Lebanon* (2006) Ya Libnan <http://yalibnan.com/site/archives/2006/07/israel_destroys.php> at 6 November 2007)

27 International Committee of the Red Cross, *Conference of Government Experts on the Reaffirmation and Development of International Humanitarian Law Applicable in Armed Conflicts*, Volume III, *Protection of the civilian population against dangers of hostilities* (1971) 56 ('CE/3b').

of International Humanitarian Law Applicable in Armed Conflicts was in the following terms:

> Only those objectives which, by their nature or use, contribute effectively and directly to the military effort of the adversary, *or which are of a generally recognized military interest*, are considered as military objectives.[28]

If this test had have been adopted, then certain targets would have been able to be considered as deemed to be military objectives.

While there is a requirement for there to be a military advantage from an attack on a particular target, determining what was the anticipated military advantage from an attack is not always evident without a good knowledge of the planning behind the attack. To take an example from the 1991 Persian Gulf War:

> On 27 January, eight bridges were dropped or substantially damaged. These strikes not only caused traffic backups, which themselves became lucrative targets, but also further degraded Iraqi C3 because some bridges carried communications cables.[29]

Neither the potential for the traffic back ups nor the existence of the communication cables may have been evident to the lay observer.

Generally speaking, the requirement to identify a definite military advantage associated with attacking a particular target arises most often with respect to potential dual-use objects like bridges and communication facilities.[30] However, the definition of military objectives leads to an interesting legal conclusion—not all enemy military objects are ipso facto military objectives. Put another way, nothing, including a military object, can a priori be classed as a military objective. Rather, everything (including military vehicles, weapons barracks and headquarters) must be assessed against the test in API.[31] Now, it is certainly hard to envisage a situation in which an enemy tank will not be of at least some small benefit to the enemy and

28 CE 1972 Report, vol I, above n 25 (chapter 1), 146 (emphasis added). A slightly differently worded clause, but one with similar effect, was unsuccessfully proposed by Canada at the 1974–77 *Diplomatic Conference on the Reaffirmation and Development of International Humanitarian Law Applicable in Armed Conflicts* (International Committee of the Red Cross, *Official Records of the Diplomatic Conference on the Reaffirmation and Development of International Humanitarian Law Applicable in Armed Conflicts* (1974–1977) vol III, 212 ('CDDH/III')).

29 US Department of Defense, *Conduct of the Persian Gulf War: Final Report to Congress* (1992) National Defense University <http://www.ndu.edu/library/epubs/cpgw.pdf> at 25 May 2006, 184. References to page numbers are references to the page numbers of the PDF file available at <http://www.ndu.edu/library/epubs/cpgw.pdf>. 'C3' stands for 'Command, Control and Communication'.

30 The term *dual-use target* is not strictly a legal term, but is often used to describe "a target with both civilian and military functions, such as a factory that makes both civilian and military products or an airfield from which both civilian and military aircraft fly"—Michael Schmitt, *Precision Attack and International Humanitarian Law* (2005) 859 International Review of the Red Cross 445, 453 (fn 28).

31 UK Ministry of Defence, above n 14 (chapter 1), [5.4.5].

its destruction will not offer at least some small benefit to the attacker. However, this does not detract from the conclusion that the attacker must apply the article 52(2) API test. Therefore, a consequence of the article 52(2) API definition is that the mere nature of an object (ie, the fact that it is a military barracks) does not lead by that very fact alone to that object being a military objective. Rather, there has to be a line of reasoning that can show:

(a) how the object does or will contribute to the enemy's military action; and
(b) how attacking that object will, in the current circumstances, benefit the attacker.

While military necessity allows a belligerent to attack targets, not otherwise protected by IHL, to achieve military victory, military necessity does not allow wanton destruction. And wanton destruction includes attacking military targets of no value in the current phase of the campaign plan (ie, it is not lawful to attack a target the destruction of which does not contribute towards achieving a military victory). I am not suggesting that there *are* military targets of no military value. I do not know whether this is the case or not. Rather, what I am arguing is that it cannot be *assumed* that all military targets at all times and in all conceivable circumstances have a military value. Contrary to my view, Robertson offers the example of stocks of ammunition as being something that is always a military objective. But, how can an attack on a stock of the enemy's air-to-air missiles meet the test set out in article 52(2) API if, for example, all of the enemy's aircraft have been destroyed (with the result that it would be very unlikely for the enemy to be able to launch air-to-air missiles)? Once again, I am not saying that I am certain that such missiles would have no military value. My argument is that the correct test is not for the side asserting that a military object was not a military objective to have an onus to show that the object had no conceivable military value. Rather, the correct test is that it is for the attacker to show how the object made an effective contribution to military action and to identify the military advantage to be gained from targeting the object in the circumstances ruling at the time.

While this book is about what the law is, rather than what it should be, it is interesting to note in conclusion that there remains a debate over whether military objectives should be defined by a *test* or by a *list*. For example, after stating that "[t]he United States has consistently adhered to the position that the best thing to do is to not have a binding list of legitimate targets for aerial attack",[32] Dinstein goes on to argue that whilst this theoretically gives the greatest operational latitude and allows for changing means and methods of warfare, in fact it has led to a decreasing target set. Dinstein suggests that "the best thing for the United States"[33]

32 Yoram Dinstein, 'The Thirteenth Waldemar A. Solf Lecture in International Law' (2000) 166 *Military Law Review* 93, 104. Dinstein is discussing air warfare at this point, which I suggest is why he used the word *aerial* and why I believe he did not thereby intend to indicate that binding lists of military objectives should be used for other (non-aerial) modes of attack.

33 It is not clear if Dinstein was suggesting this course was best for the United States due to its massive aerial bombardment power, or whether he directed the comments at the United States merely because he was making his comments at the Judge Advocate General's School of the US Army. However, he restates his view that it would be better

would be to have an open-ended list to let everyone know what targets are permissible and impermissible.[34]

In the next section, the individual components of the article 52(2) API test are discussed.

3.3 A two-pronged test

There are two main points to determine whether an object is a military objective. First, whether the object is something that makes an 'effective contribution to military action' on behalf of the defending party;[35] and second, whether an attack on the object 'offers a definite military advantage' to the attacking party.[36] This is often referred to as a "two-pronged test",[37] and the double nature of the test is often emphasised by italicising the *and* or using words like *must also* (again in italics) between the *effective contribution* and *military advantage* part of article 52(2) API.[38] As Hampson puts it, "it is not enough that the object makes an effective contribution to military action; its destruction or other debilitation must offer a definite military advantage."[39] It is clear, therefore, that it must always be borne in mind that there are two separate criteria that have to be met separately.[40] But, what else can be said about the criteria?

It is incorrect to argue that once an attacker can show that it would gain a military advantage from an attack on a particular object, then, ipso facto, the object must be contributing to the military action of the defending party.[41] This line of reasoning in effect reduces the test to a single criterion and not a two-pronged test. While it would be unusual for the two aspects of the test not to go hand in hand,[42] nonetheless, the test is a two-part test. Accordingly, an attacker must be able to demonstrate how both aspects are present. It is not acceptable to deem one present due to the existence of the other.[43] By demonstrating how both parts of the test are

---

to have a general test (an 'abstract statement') with a non-exhaustive list in a subsequent work, and he does not on that occasion limit his comments to the United States—Dinstein, *The Conduct of Hostilities under the Law of International Armed Conflict*, above n 66 (chapter 2), 84.

34 Dinstein, 'The Thirteenth Waldemar A. Solf Lecture in International Law', above n 32 (chapter 3), 107.

35 API, above n 2 (chapter 1), art 52(2).

36 Ibid.

37 Robertson Jr, above n 105 (chapter 1), 48.

38 See, for example, *Needless Deaths in the Gulf War: Civilian Casualties During the Air Campaign and Violations of the Laws of War* (1991) Human Rights Watch <http://www.hrw.org/reports/1991/gulfwar/> at 2 March 2005.

39 Hampson, 'Proportionality and Necessity in the Gulf Conflict', above n 23 (chapter 3), 49. See also Bothe, above n 25 (chapter 3), 533.

40 *Expert Meeting: "Targeting Military Objectives"*, above n 27 (chapter 1), 2. This interpretation is supported by the drafting history—see CE/3b, above n 27 (chapter 3), 57–8.

41 See generally *Expert Meeting: "Targeting Military Objectives"*, above n 27 (chapter 1), 2–3.

42 See Sassoli and Bouvier, above n 10 (chapter 1), 161 (fn 140).

43 Boivin, above n 19 (chapter 1), 15–16.

satisfied, an attacker would then be able to argue not only how there was a military advantage to the attack (the second part of the test), but also how the attack met the requirement of military necessity (as reflected in the first part of the test).

Oeter refers to the:

(a) first part of the test being an "'objective' element (concerning the capacity to contribute effectively to military operations)";[44] and
(b) second part of the test being a "'subjective criterion which refers to the military operations of the acting state."[45]

These are useful points and help to emphasise the dual nature of the test. Care must be taken, however, when introducing words like *objective* and *subjective*. It appears as though Oeter is using these words to show how one aspect of the test (the objective aspect) concerns conditions outside of the attacker's control (namely, how the target affects the defender's military actions), while the other aspect of test (the subjective aspect) concerns assessing how attacking the target might assist the attacker. However, these terms are also used to describe whether a given state of affairs is assessed based on what a particular person believed (a subjective test), or what a *reasonable person* would have believed in the same circumstances (an objective test). This point is considered further at section 3.5.3 below.

While the wording of article 52(2) API makes it clear that the two criteria must both be fulfilled, the article is not clear on *when* the criteria must be fulfilled. The *ICRC Commentary* on article 52 API states: "Whenever these two elements are *simultaneously* present, there is a military objective in the sense of the Protocol."[46] In a more recent work, Sassoli merely states that "an object must cumulatively fulfil two criteria to be a military objective."[47] Cleary the *ICRC Commentary* has a temporal aspect while Sassoli's work does not. As an expert in the field, it can be assumed that Sassoli was well aware of the *ICRC Commentary*. Yet Sassoli chose to use the word *cumulative* and not the word *simultaneously*. This issue is not directly discussed in Bothe, Partsch and Solf, but I note that the example they use of an deceptive attack by the Allies in the *Pas de Calais* seems to support Sassoli's view.[48]

It is my view that mere cumulative fulfilment is enough and simultaneous fulfilment is not required. Take, for example, an attack on a computer system that is used to support the long term planning of military operations.[49] While such a computer system clearly would make an effective contribution to the enemy's military

44 Oeter, above n 24 (chapter 2), 157.

45 Ibid.

46 Sandoz, Swinarski and Zimmerman (eds), above n 68 (chapter 1), [2018] (emphasis added).

47 Marco Sassoli, Legitimate Targets of Attacks under International Humanitarian Law (2003) *Harvard Program on Humanitarian Policy and Conflict Research* <http://www.ihl-research.org/ihl/pdfs/Session1.pdf> at 2 March 2005, 2.

48 Bothe, Partsch and Solf, above n 87 (chapter 1), 325. This example is discussed in slightly more detail below.

49 For ease of the argument, suppose the computer system is a stand-alone system that is used solely for planning purposes. In reality, such a system actually might be isolated. Reasons for isolation include unique hardware, to reduce the risk of data access, or to minimise the risk of attack by viruses and other malware.

action, it is arguable that damaging or destroying the system would be of benefit only in the longer term—as arguably the enemy's current operations and even short term plans would continue. Of course, some might suggest this is partly a question of semantics, as one could also argue that an immediate military advantage has accrued from the attack, namely the degrading of the enemy's planning capability. However one frames the argument, the correct conclusion is that military advantage can substantively accrue in the future.[50]

The military advantage gained from the attack need not directly relate to or flow from the damage or destruction of the target.[51] In other words, while an object must contribute to the military action of the defending party, and while the attacker must gain a military advantage from an attack on that object, the military advantage gained need not be limited to the reduction in military action suffered by the defending party as a direct result of the damage caused to the attacked object. An example of this point is provided by the allied attacks on the *Pas de Calais* area of France prior to the Normandy invasion of 1944. "The military advantage was not the reduction of German military strength in that area but rather to deceive the Germans as to where the invasion would take place."[52] This is also a good example as to why the military advantage gained need not be immediate. Meyer also uses this example when arguing that an overly restrictive interpretation is being placed on article 52(2) API, and concludes that whilst consistent with prior state practice and customary international law, the above ruse would not be lawful based on some of the current interpretations of the test for a military objective.[53] I disagree. Article 52(2) API does not require that the military advantage gained come from the direct or immediate disadvantage caused to the enemy.[54] Rather, what article 52(2) API does do is limit the types of targets that can be attacked as a ruse to what would otherwise be lawful targets. So, it would be lawful to feint an attack on a fortified military position as a distraction for another military operation; however, it would not be lawful to bombard an undefended civilian town as a feint.

3.4 Effective contribution to military action

We have seen above that the first part of the test is that the target must be making an effective contribution of the military action of the attacked Party. In determining whether this will exist, the assessment is made by looking at the object's "nature, location, purpose or use".[55] The words used to describe what can be considered when

50 See the 'Report on United States practice' in Henckaerts and Doswald-Beck (eds), *Customary International Humanitarian Law*, vol II, above n 64 (chapter 1), 188.

51 Bothe, Partsch and Solf, above n 87 (chapter 1), 325; quoted with approval in Robertson Jr, above n 105 (chapter 1), 52 (footnote omitted).

52 Robertson Jr, above n 105 (chapter 1), 67, footnote 71. For a more detailed description, see Bothe, Partsch and Solf, above n 87 (chapter 1), 325. Dinstein refers to this example with apparent approval in Dinstein, *The Conduct of Hostilities under the Law of International Armed Conflict*, above n 66 (chapter 2), 86.

53 Jeanne Meyer, 'Tearing down the facade: A critical look at the current law on targeting the will of the enemy and air force doctrine' (2001) 51 *Air Force Law Review* 143, 173.

54 See footnotes 51 and 52 (chapter 3).

55 API, above n 2 (chapter 1), art 52(2).

determining whether an object is making an effective contribution would appear to be exhaustive. However, in my view the words 'nature, location, purpose or use' should not be considered as words of limitation but rather as a way of providing a *test* for determining what is a military objective (rather than setting out a list of military objectives).[56] If it could be shown that an object truly did provide a military[57] advantage but somehow (and I confess I currently cannot see how) that military advantage arose other than through the object's 'nature, location, purpose or use', what would be the objection to an attack on that target? In other words, the true issue is whether an object is making an effective contribution to military action and it should be considered far less important to be able to pigeonhole how that contribution arises under one of the words 'nature, location, purpose or use'.

It is permissible to look at more than one category for a single object when determining whether that object is a military objective. For example, a tank is, usually, of more effectiveness when closer to a battle than if a 1,000 miles away.[58] Therefore, both its nature and location are relevant to determining whether the tank is contributing to the military effectiveness of the defending belligerent. This could be important when determining whether an attack will offer a *definite* military advantage.

The following sections look at the individual words *nature*, *location*, *purpose* and *use*. While it is useful to look at these words individually, it is essential to note that the definition of military objectives in article 52(2) API is qualified by the words 'in the circumstances ruling at the time'. What is meant by this qualification is extremely important and is discussed at length in section 3.6 below. Therefore, it should be kept in mind that if in the immediately following sections it is written that a tank is by its nature a military objective, this merely means that the tank meets the criterion of nature and this does not thereby indicate that the tank, without further analysis, also meets all the other requirements of the test for a military objective set out in article 52(2) API.

3.4.1 Nature

The category of objects that by their nature are military objectives includes the materiel and buildings that are usually owned or controlled by the military for use by the military. The *ICRC Commentary* refers to this category as being objects directly used by the armed forces.[59] Without saying so explicitly, the examples used in the *ICRC Commentary* make it clear that it is dealing with objects that are *usually* controlled and used by the military as opposed to objects that while being directly

56 Compare, for example, the definition of "works or installations containing dangerous forces" in API, above n 2 (chapter 1), art 56(1), which clearly is meant to be limited to just dams, dykes and nuclear electrical generating stations and not any other facility that may contain dangerous forces (eg, a petrochemical plant).

57 I emphasise in this context the word *military*.

58 There is subsequent discussion in this book on how the additional qualification of 'in the circumstances ruling at the time' can mean that an object that prima facie appears to be a military objective may, nonetheless, not be in a particular case.

59 Sandoz, Swinarski and Zimmerman (eds), above n 68 (chapter 1), [2020].

used are only under *temporary* military control (eg, a temporarily occupied civilian house).[60]

Perhaps the most important legal point about this category is that the word used for the category is potentially misleading. This is because another usual interpretation of the word *nature* is the native or inherent character of a thing.[61] Using this interpretation, one might conclude that an armoury of rifles is a military objective. However, this would be incorrect. For instance, a civilian rifle club might own the rifles. In such a case, and without more information, it could not be concluded that the rifles by their nature make an effective contribution to military action. It is important not to read the first half of the second sentence of article 52(2) API as meaning that any object that falls within one of the categories of 'nature, location, purpose or use' thereby automatically make an effective contribution to military action. Indeed, it is arguable that article 52(2) API would be easier to interpret and more logically consistent if the words 'nature, location, purpose or use' were deleted. The result would be that the test would merely be whether an object makes an effective contribution to military action without artificially trying to see whether it is making that contribution via its 'nature, location, purpose or use'.

Following on from the above point and the introductory commentary in the *ICRC Commentary*, the category of objects covered by *nature* are all military objects owned or usually controlled by the military.[62] So, a military transport vehicle would fall within this category, while a civilian vehicle commandeered by the military would, as we shall see below, come within the category of *use*.

An important point about military equipment and buildings is that there is no such thing as *hors de combat* for military objects. For instance, during the 1990–91 Gulf War between the coalition forces and Iraq, Iraq positioned two fighter aircraft adjacent to the ancient temple of Ur.[63] In this example, the aircraft retained their general military value; they were just not of immediate use to Iraq. So, while the "positioning of the aircraft adjacent to Ur (without servicing equipment or a runway nearby) effectively had placed each out of action, thereby limiting the value of their destruction by Coalition air forces when weighed against the risk of damage to the temple",[64] the aircraft remained legitimate military objectives but with only small military value. Another example is that during operation Iraqi Freedom, the United States of America decided not to target abandoned Iraqi military vehicles—principally so the vehicles could be used by a post occupation Iraqi army. However, the abandoned vehicles were re-occupied by the Iraqi military during the course of the

60 See ibid.

61 *Macquarie Dictionary* (3rd revised ed, 2001) 1276.

62 Subject, of course, to those objects contributing to military action. For example, a trophy or painting owned by the military would be unlikely to contribute to military action.

63 US Department of Defense, *Conduct of the Persian Gulf War: Final Report to Congress*, above n 29 (chapter 3), 701.

64 Ibid, 702.

conflict.[65] It can be seen from this example how in certain circumstances even abandoned military vehicles can remain military objectives.

The legal position, therefore, is that a fighter aircraft (for example) will usually remain a military object whether it is operational or disabled as even a disabled fighter aircraft can either be repaired or scavenged for spare parts. However, obviously a disabled fighter aircraft is of less military benefit to its owner and, therefore, causing it further damage or destruction is of less military benefit to an attacking armed force.[66] A military object is unlikely to be a military objective when the object is no longer capable of making any form of effective contribution to military action. The simple concept of the object's current serviceability is not a definitive test for whether this has occurred. While it would be very rare for a military object to lose so completely its usefulness as to no longer be a military objective, it is at least theoretically possible. However, there will be many situations where a military object is not bereft of military value but is most certainly of less military value than it once was or could be again.

3.4.2 Location

The category of objects that by their *location* can be classified as military objectives includes objects such as bridges as well as areas of land with strategic importance.[67] The *ICRC Commentary* states that an area of land designated as a military target must be of limited size, with which I agree, and that the area must be in the combat area.[68] I disagree with this second point. The *ICRC Commentary* does not cite any authority for the proposition, nor can any support be found in a review of the drafting history (as the issue was not discussed).[69] Neither this limitation nor similar appears in any of the State practice referred to in section of *Customary International Humanitarian Law* dealing with the definition of military objectives and areas of land.[70] Interestingly, in the context of barrage fire to deny an enemy the use of an area, the *ICRC Commentary* refers to "narrow passages, bridgeheads or strategic points such as hills or mountain passes" as being military objectives in certain circumstances in an earlier part of the *Commentary* but does not state at that point that such areas must be in the combat area.[71] Contextually, and as a matter of interpretation, there seems to be no reason to read down 'location' as only applying in the combat area when such a limitation is not applied to 'nature, purpose or use'. Finally, an example might help to show why such a limitation should not be read into the text. Suppose that a body of troops or supplies appears to be moving from a

65 *News Letter*, No. 03-27 (2003) Center for Army Lessons Learned <http://call.army.mil> at 15 May 2003.

66 With respect to collateral damage, a damaged fighter aircraft has a lower value in a proportionality equation than the equivalent functioning fighter aircraft.

67 Sandoz, Swinarski and Zimmerman (eds), above n 68 (chapter 1), [1955] and [2021].

68 Ibid, [2026].

69 As noted in the *ICRC Commentary*—see ibid.

70 Henckaerts and Doswald-Beck (eds), *Customary International Humanitarian Law*, vol II, above n 64 (chapter 1), 224–5.

71 Ibid, [1955].

rear area towards the front line along a route through a narrow pass in a mountain range. It would make military sense to attempt to close that pass, which might be many hundreds of kilometres from the front line, by way of causing an avalanche or rockslide.

Additionally, an object may be attacked due to its location to further subsequent military operations. For example:

> In tactical operations ... it might be necessary to destroy a particular facility or dwelling, though not used for military purposes, to provide a line of fire, or to neutralize it so as to deny the enemy the use of it.[72]

Robertson uses a similar example when he writes that an object may become a military objective due to its location if it "obstructs[s] the field of fire for attack on another valid military objective."[73] I agree with these points, with two main qualifications and an additional point. First, I would add that the destruction of the object could not be too speculative in the temporal sense. So, it would not be permissible to destroy a large building merely because there is a possibility in the future that it might impede military operations. My argument in support of this point is that such an action would not offer a *definite* military advantage as required by article 52(2) API. See also the discussion in section 3.4.4 below on the meaning of *purpose* in article 52(2) API and how the mere possibility of future use of an object by an enemy is insufficient to convert that object into a military objective.

Second, the number or extent of objects destroyed cannot be too speculative. So, it would not be permissible to destroy a large number of buildings merely because there is a possibility that one or more of the buildings in the immediate future might impede military operations subject to variables such as in which direction an urban battle proceeds. Again, the argument in support of this point is that such an action would not offer a *definite* military advantage as required by article 52(2) API.

The additional point I would add is that targeting is not the only lawful basis for destruction of civilian property. For example, article 53 GCIV and article 23(g) HIVR provide alternative legal bases for destruction of civilian property;[74] however, such issues are outside the scope of a book on targeting.[75]

The next two categories of *purpose* and *use* are perhaps two of the most important, as they include a large variety of prima facie civilian objects. Contrary to the

---

72 DeSaussure, 'Belligerent Air Operations and the 1977 Geneva Protocol I', above n 13 (chapter 2), 459 (fn 48).

73 Robertson Jr, above n 105 (chapter 1), 49.

74 For a famous example of this area of IHL, see the scorched earth policy adopted by the Germans, under the command of General Rendulic, in their retreat from the Russians in Finnmark, Norway in October-November 1944. A brief description of the event, and a copy of a proclamation to the civilian population, is at *Nazi Conspiracy and Aggression Volume IV—Document No. 1800-PS* (2005) The Avalon Project <http://www.yale.edu/lawweb/avalon/imt/document/nca_vol4/1800-ps.htm> at 10 September 2005.

75 See also Bothe, Partsch and Solf, above n 87 (chapter 1), 320–1; *Expert Meeting: "Targeting Military Objectives"*, above n 27 (chapter 1), 11–12.

order adopted in article 52(2) API, it is helpful to deal with *use* before *purpose* as an aid to understanding the distinction between the two categories.

3.4.3 *Use*

The *ICRC Commentary* states that *use* refers to present function.[76] Put another way, *use* refers to the current employment of an object. Accordingly, if a civilian object is being utilized by the military then at that moment it is potentially a military objective. The corollary of this is that under this category once the military ceases using the object it regains its protected status. For instance, if a group of soldiers are using a tall building (perhaps a lighthouse) as an observation post it would be permissible to attack the building to prevent its continued use. The important point is that this is not a case of the building being acceptable collateral damage when attacking the soldiers but rather the building itself becoming a military objective. However, in most cases, when the soldiers move on the building regains its protected status and cannot be attacked on the off chance that it might be used again.

Of course, a certain level of common sense must be applied when determining whether something is being used or not. For example, where a small group of soldiers have commandeered a civilian vehicle, and where they have been using it for a number of days, but the soldiers are currently outside the vehicle (perhaps in a bivouac), then the soldiers would still be using that vehicle within the meaning of *use* in article 52(2) API.

The category of *use* can also be applied to factories and the like that are currently producing military materiel. For example, a ball bearing factory is not inherently a military objective; but if those ball bearings are being used in military aircraft, then the factory may become a military objective. This is a point that Benvenuti seems not to consider when he comments on an example from the *OTP Report*. To illustrate the concept of proportionality, the *OTP Report* uses the example of an attack on a refugee camp where the people inside the camp are knitting socks for soldiers.[77] Benvenuti refers to this example as 'nonsense' and states that "[S]uch a case is not a problem of proportionality at all: a refugee camp is not per se a military objective".[78] Benvenuti is correct in that a refugee camp is not 'per se a military objective'. However, if a sufficiently large enough part of the camp is turned over to knitting socks for soldiers, then the camp itself becomes a military objective in the same way that a factory might become a military objective.[79] By its current use, the camp

76 Sandoz, Swinarski and Zimmerman (eds), above n 68 (chapter 1), [2022].

77 *OTP Report*, above n 90 (chapter 1), [48].

78 Paolo Benvenuti, 'The ICTY Prosecutor and the Review of the NATO Bombing Campaign against the Federal Republic of Yugoslavia' (2001) Vol 12 No 3 *European Journal of International Law* 503, 517.

79 Compare this to Tokyo during World War II, where the cottage industries might have been significant in number but not so numerous as to turn the entire city into a military objective. While I am arguing that the camp has become a military objective in the same way that a factory that was producing tanks would be a military objective, as will become apparent in chapter 4, I am not suggesting that the individual sock knitters have compromised their civilian status by taking a 'direct part in hostilities'—see API, above n 2 (chapter 1), art 51(3).

has become a military objective. However, and this is where I agree with the *OTP Report*, the camp would almost certainly be of so low military value as to make an attack on it very likely to be disproportionate in the sense that the expected loss of civilian life would be excessive relative to the concrete and direct military advantage anticipated.

In summary, *use* refers to objects currently being used by the military or being used to provide a benefit to the military. The next section deals with the category of objects that are not currently contributing to military action but are of potential military value.

3.4.4 Purpose

The *ICRC Commentary* states that *purpose* refers to intended future use.[80] Clearly, *purpose* overlaps with *nature* when it comes to military materiel. For instance, the *purpose* of a tank will generally make that tank a military objective as will its *nature* (ie, the fact that it is owned or controlled by the military). Like the category covered by *use*, the main area of legal interest with *purpose* is civilian objects. There is an important distinction between *purpose* and *use*. As I argued above, if a civilian object is being used by the military then at that moment it is a military objective; however, once it ceases being used it regains its protected status when assessed against *use*. However, a civilian object can be targeted not only while not being used by the military but even prior to its initial use due to the *purpose* to which the object may be put. Accordingly, I believe Benvenuti is partly mistaken when, in commenting on a part of the *OTP Report* concerning whether industrial infrastructure, media, ministries and refineries are military objectives, he writes that the aforementioned objects:

> are not per se military objectives, they are under the protection of the principle of distinction; they lose protection only if they are actually (not potential) used at the time for military purposes.[81]

I agree with one of Benvenuti's points and disagree with the other, which I believe is his main point. As I have previously written, I am of the view that no objects, not even military materiel, are per se military objectives. However, I disagree if Benvenuti was saying that an object becomes a military objective only if it is being used for a military purpose at the actual time of the attack. This is the difference between *use* and *purpose*. However, there are limitations to what can be included under the category of *purpose*.

The NATO attacks on electrical power grids in Yugoslavia are discussed in a 1999 newsletter jointly produced by the International & Operational Law Branch in the Headquarters of the United States Marine Corps and the United States

80 Sandoz, Swinarski and Zimmerman (eds), above n 68 (chapter 1), [2022].

81 Benvenuti, above n 78 (chapter 3), 516. The reference to 'time' is presumably to at the time of the attack.

Marine Corps Representative to CLAMO.[82] After paraphrasing the article 52(2) API definition of military objectives, the newsletter then states: "nor is it an issue of present use; it is its *potential* military use that governs."[83] As argued more fully below, this is an incorrect statement of the law. If it were a correct statement of the law, any building, vehicle etc could be targeted on the basis that it merely might be used by a belligerent in the future. To that extent, I would agree with Benvenuti as quoted above, and mere potential for future use is not enough—purpose means something more than potential (or mere objective *possibility* of use).[84]

Another interesting example on the issue of potential use versus purpose is provided in the asserted military reasoning behind the attack by the United States of America on television and radio broadcasting stations during the 1991 Persian Gulf War. The April 1992 *Final Report to Congress* on the conduct of that war states that civil TV and radio facilities were attacked on the basis that they "*could* be used easily for C3 backup for military purposes."[85] If the API test for military objective were applied, the justification provided for the attack would have been legally insufficient. The mere fact that an enemy could use an object is not sufficient; rather, as the *ICRC Commentary* states, there must be an *intention* on behalf of a belligerent to use an object before it can be targeted based on purpose.

What amounts to intention to use? Intention means a determination "upon some action or result; a purpose or design."[86] The intended use of an object would normally be the use for which the object was designed (ie, its *nature*) but it might also be a declared future use. Declared future use is clearly the more relevant consideration when considering the category of *purpose*. In the current context, an intention might manifest itself only in certain circumstances. For instance, say a car-manufacturing factory is also used to produce armoured personnel carriers. But, the factory does not produce both civilian vehicles and armoured personnel carriers at the same time. Rather, the factory produces them alternatively. In such a case, although on any particular day the factory might be producing civilian cars, the intended purpose of the factory includes the manufacture of armoured personnel carriers; therefore, the factory could be a legitimate military objective even on the days when the factory is producing cars. However, in another example, say a car-manufacturing factory is capable of being used to produce armoured personnel carriers. Additionally, the relevant belligerent has rehearsed this capability during exercises, which involved, amongst other things, the notional destruction of the sole primary armoured personnel carrier manufacturing plant. But the car-manufacturing factory so far in the conflict has not been used to produce armoured personnel carriers as the primary armoured personnel carrier manufacturing plant has sufficient

82 CLAMO is the Center for Law and Military Operations at the Judge Advocate General's School in Charlottesville, Virginia USA.

83 *Marine Judge Advocate Newsletter*, Volume IV, Issue 6, (June 1999) Staff Judge Advocate to the Commandant of the Marine Corps <http://sja.hqmc.usmc.mil/newsletter/1999/6_99/june.htm> at 25 May 2006 (emphasis added).

84 *Expert Meeting: "Targeting Military Objectives"*, above n 27 (chapter 1), 7 (footnote omitted, emphasis in original).

85 US Department of Defense, *Conduct of the Persian Gulf War: Final Report to Congress*, above n 29 (chapter 3), 149 (emphasis added).

86 *Macquarie Dictionary*, above n 61 (chapter 3), 985.

capacity. In such circumstances, it would be more accurate to say that the intention of the belligerent was a determination to use the car-manufacturing factory to produce armoured personnel carriers in the event that the primary armoured personnel carrier manufacturing plant was disabled or (perhaps) *in the event* that extra capacity were required. This could be described as a conditional intention; and, being a conditional intention, the object could not be considered as fulfilling the test for *purpose* unless the condition had been met. While a similar conclusion could also be reached by applying "in the circumstances ruling at the time",[87] the point is that the conditional limitation is inherent to the word *purpose*.

What is the test—or the standard of proof—for whether the condition has been met? It has been suggested that "all that is required is a 'reasonable belief' as to the future use of the object."[88] Unfortunately, no authority was cited for this statement. On the face of it though, it does seem like an attractive and probably correct view of the law. It is supported in a later work by Boivin,[89] and is also consistent with the overall test for whether an object has met the test for being a military objective.[90]

To summarise, *purpose* means the intended future use of an object; but *purpose* does not include the mere potential for use by a belligerent. The standard of proof is whether there is a 'reasonable belief' as to the future use. That concludes the discussion on what are the characteristics of an object that may be considered when determining whether that object makes an effective contribution to military action. The next section covers the second part of the article 52(2) API test.

3.5 What is a meant by 'military advantage'?

Perhaps the two most important words in article 52(2) API are 'military advantage'. While it is important to consider the terms 'direct', 'in the circumstances ruling at the time', and 'nature, location, purpose or use' when determining whether an object is a military objective, these terms do not help to define what is a 'military advantage' for the purposes of the second part of the article 52(2) API test. It is fundamental to IHL that attacks may be conducted against objects only where an attack against that object will offer a *military* advantage.

One of the best ways to determine what is a military advantage is to go back to the preamble of the *St Petersburg Declaration*: "The only legitimate object which States should endeavour to accomplish during war is to weaken the military forces of the enemy".[91] Consistent with this declaration in the preamble, the *ICRC Commentary* states that a "military advantage can only consist in ground gained and in annihilating or weakening the enemy armed forces."[92] I agree with this analysis, with one explanatory point. For there to be a military advantage, the action must logically relate, either directly or indirectly, to weakening the military forces of the enemy. The important point here is the word indirectly. Not only is it permissible

87 See API, above n 2 (chapter 1), art 52(2).

88 *Expert Meeting: "Targeting Military Objectives"*, above n 27 (chapter 1), 7.

89 Boivin, above n 19 (chapter 1), 19.

90 *Prosecutor v Galic, (Trial Chamber)* Case No IT-98-29-T (5 December 2003) [51].

91 *St Petersburg Declaration*, above n 64 (chapter 1).

92 Sandoz, Swinarski and Zimmerman (eds), above n 68 (chapter 1), [2218].

to attack enemy combatants directly, but it is also permissible to attack objects with a sufficient link to weakening the fighting or defending capability of those military forces. In other words, weakening the military forces of the enemy is not limited only to directly causing a physical weakening of enemy personnel but includes weakening the enemy's war fighting and defending capability. Accordingly, in the right circumstances permitted attacks would include attacks on military aircraft runways or ammunition depots. Another example would be attacking a factory that produces helmets for use by the enemy soldiers. This does not directly weaken the enemy military forces but does weaken them indirectly. The relevant test for determining whether destruction of property is consistent with military necessity, as expressed in the preamble to the *St Petersburg Declaration*, is whether there is a "reasonable connection between the destruction of property and the overcoming of the enemy forces."[93]

A further aspect of the above argument is that defending one's own combatants is a military advantage.[94] Not only is this logical, but arguably it can be said to still be related to weakening the enemy as it is not possible to fight the enemy if all of one's own combatants are disabled first. The same argument applies not just to protecting one's own combatants but would also apply to protecting—for instance—military equipment from destruction. These statements can be turned into a test of general application stated as follows: the defensive range of activities that amount to a military advantage can be defined as those that preserve the capability to conduct military operations.

Based on the above argument that attacking an object—as opposed to just combatants—may offer a military advantage, then if he was quoted in context, I would have to disagree with Blix who is quoted as saying that "the sole legitimate function of a weapon was to put an enemy *hors de combat*."[95] Rather, I would agree with those who challenged his view. The correct view is "that the 'military necessity' concept include[s] other elements besides putting an enemy *hors de combat*, such as the destruction or neutralisation of enemy material, restrictions of movement, weakening of resources and enhancement of the security of friendly forces."[96] As Human Rights Watch state, the "requirement that military objectives effectively contribute to military action does not necessarily require a direct connection with combat operations."[97]

I have argued that the relationship between the attack and weakening the enemy forces need not be direct, so the important point now becomes—just how indirect can the link be? For a start, clearly it cannot be so distant or speculative as

---

93 *Hostages Trial*, Lauterpacht (ed), above n 45 (chapter 2), 646.

94 See Anthony Rogers, 'Zero-casualty warfare' (2000) 837 *International Review of the Red Cross* <http://www.icrc.org/Web/eng/siteengo.nsf/iwpList177/A41F49D9F3CE3756C1256B66005E3594> at 4 June 2006; *Expert Meeting: "Targeting Military Objectives"*, above n 27 (chapter 1), 19.

95 Hans Blix, quoted in Marie Jacobsson, 'Weapons and Humanitarian Norms' in William Maley (ed), *Shelters from the Storm: Developments in International Humanitarian Law* (1995) 121, 126.

96 Ibid, 127; see also Bothe, Partsch and Solf, above n 87 (chapter 1), 196.

97 *Needless Deaths in the Gulf War: Civilian Casualties During the Air Campaign and Violations of the Laws of War*, above n 38 (chapter 3).

to affect only the enemy forces by a barely perceptible chain of events—the relationship must be one of sufficient proximity to avoid allowing the attack on an excessive and indeterminate range of objects. This concept is reinforced by the use of the word 'definite' in article 52(2) API.

As to the meaning of *definite*, at the 1974–77 *Diplomatic Conference on the Reaffirmation and Development of International Humanitarian Law Applicable in Armed Conflicts*:

> Extensive discussion took place before agreement was reached on the word "definite" in the phrase "definite military advantage". Among the words considered and rejected were "distinct", "direct", "clear", "immediate", "obvious", "specific", and "substantial".[98]

The Rapporteur stated he was "unable to draw any clear significance from this choice."[99]

After making a similar reference to the report of the 1974–77 *Diplomatic Conference*, Bothe, Partsch and Solf write that *definite* "is a word of limitation denoting in this context a concrete and perceptible military advantage rather than a hypothetical and speculative one."[100] Israel, who accept the definition of 'military objective' in article 52(2) API as representing customary international law, use the word 'clear' to explain what is meant by *definite*.[101] Perhaps the best explanation is that a commander should "be able to articulate how the attack affects military operations that he or she controls."[102]

Much depends upon context. For example, in a report to Congress on the conduct of the 1991 Gulf War, the United States Department of Defence stated:

> "Military advantage" is not restricted to tactical gains, but is linked to the full context of a war strategy, in this instance, the execution of the Coalition war plan for liberation of Kuwait.[103]

---

98 International Committee of the Red Cross, *Official Records of the Diplomatic Conference on the Reaffirmation and Development of International Humanitarian Law Applicable in Armed Conflicts* (1974–1977) vol XV, 277 ('CDDH/XV'). See also *Needless Deaths in the Gulf War: Civilian Casualties During the Air Campaign and Violations of the Laws of War*, above n 38 (chapter 3), 332.

99 *Needless Deaths in the Gulf War: Civilian Casualties During the Air Campaign and Violations of the Laws of War*, above n 38 (chapter 3), 332.

100 Bothe, Partsch and Solf, above n 87 (chapter 1), 326.

101 *Preserving Humanitarian Principles While Combating Terrorism: Israel's Struggle with Hizbullah in the Lebanon War* (2007) Israel Ministry of Foreign Affairs <http://www.mfa.gov.il/NR/rdonlyres/74D04C9D-FA73-4A54-8CBA-DBCB1152C82E/0/DiplomaticNotes01.pdf> at 4 November 2007, 10; quoting from the Israel Defense Force's 'Law of War on the Battlefield'.

102 *Expert Meeting: "Targeting Military Objectives"*, above n 27 (chapter 1), 8.

103 US Department of Defense, *Conduct of the Persian Gulf War: Final Report to Congress*, above n 29 (chapter 3), 699.

As long as this statement is read carefully and not too broadly, it is clearly correct. For example, it is very likely that a military officer training academy would be a lawful military objective yet only in a very few cases would there be any tactical gain from an attack on such an academy. However, in a protracted campaign clearly it would be a feasible strategy to degrade the enemy's officer corp. It is only where the war plan or strategy includes means other than degrading the war fighting capability of the enemy that targets cannot be selected on the basis that contributing to achieving the war plan equals military advantage.

The next important point to consider is at what point the advantage sought goes from being a *military* advantage to some other sort of advantage. Hampson poses the question directly when she writes:

> Moreover, the action in question has to be in furtherance of a military, not a political, goal. This poses obvious problems of characterization. Is persuading the enemy to surrender a military or political goal? Is "persuading" the enemy to surrender by aerial bombardment a military or political goal?[104]

While she did not clearly answer her own question in the Crimes of War article, she has previously said: "Furthermore, it must be a military advantage. The ultimate advantage—the end of the war—appears to have too remote a connection with the attack."[105] This is the main legal problem with so-called axiological targeting.[106] The aim of axiological targeting is to force a behaviour shift in the belligerent leadership. It does not focus on elements that an adversary uses to mount a military campaign. At the extreme end, instead of attacking a military objective with a view to forcing surrender, axiological targeting advocates that if an attack on a target will contribute to persuading an adversary to surrender then that target should be classed as a military objective. As such, axiological targeting stands in contradistinction to the current theory and practice of utility targeting.[107]

By moving away from attacks on targets that affect an enemy's military capability, significant problems of predicting human behaviour arise. As Kan has noted:

> throughout the history of airpower's use in warfare, human behavior has remained difficult to predict. In many cases, bombing elicited the opposite of the desired response—instead of inciting rebellion, it strengthened enemy resolve; instead of crippling an economy, it led to the streamlining of industry.[108]

Some of the problems associated with axiological targeting can be overcome by refocusing the 'target set' on objects that assist the enemy's war fighting capability. Once this is done, as long as there is a strong enough chain of reasoning between

---

104 Hampson, *Military Necessity*, above n 79 (chapter 2).

105 Hampson, 'Proportionality and Necessity in the Gulf Conflict', above n 23 (chapter 3), 47.

106 Another term appears to be 'compellance operations'—see, *Expert Meeting: "Targeting Military Objectives"*, above n 27 (chapter 1), 9.

107 See Kan, above n 9 (chapter 3).

108 Ibid, 28–9.

the target choice and the likelihood of attacking that target actually causing a re-think of the enemy's desire to continue the armed conflict, axiological targeting becomes legally sustainable as long as two limitations are observed. First, when assessing whether a target is a military objective, the test in article 52(2) API must be strictly applied. In particular, the desired behavioural change is not a factor that can be considered when applying the test. Second, if any collateral damage is expected, the desired behavioural change is not a factor that can be considered when calculating the concrete and direct military advantage anticipated from the attack. Put another way, the 'real' goal of the attack cannot be used to justify an attack that would not otherwise be lawful; but at the same time, the 'real' goal does not make an otherwise lawful attack an unlawful attack.

Some might argue, however, as "war is merely the continuation of policy by other means",[109] should not targeting be concerned with achieving the real purposes of the conflict and not with the killing of soldiers and winning a battle?[110] As this is a book about the law as it is, rather than the law as it should be, it is appropriate to re-phrase the question and look at whether this can be legally done under the law as it currently stands.

3.5.1 Can targets be selected to achieve the political goals of the conflict?

As I will argue in this section, the answer to the question posed in the title must be a clear no—targets cannot be selected to achieve the political goals of the conflict. While an armed conflict might be started for many reasons, IHL is not an absolute or unfettered license to pursue political or diplomatic goals by military force. Some might find this a difficult concept, as (hopefully) "the destruction of the enemy's military apparatus is … never an end in itself."[111] However, as I will show in this section, to argue that targets can be selected to obtain directly political goals without reference to weakening an enemy's military forces is in effect to argue that military force may legally be used to achieve political goals. As this is no longer the case under the *jus ad bellum*,[112] clearly it cannot be the case under the *jus in bello*.

As a starting point, I note that the report on a 2005 meeting of experts states that all the "experts agreed that while the aim of a conflict was always political, it may only be pursued by affecting the military assets of the enemy".[113] So, how does this translate into the realities of an armed conflict?

Solf directly contrasts "national-strategic planning"[114] and the planning of a field commander. He writes that national-strategic planning is focused on the "attain-

109 Carl von Clausewitz, *On War* (8th revised ed, 1984) 87.

110 Assuming, of course, that the purpose of the conflict is not just merely to kill enemy soldiers.

111 CE/4b, above n 77 (chapter 2), 5; Oeter, above n 24 (chapter 2), 157.

112 See Yoram Dinstein, *War, Aggression and Self-Defence* (4th ed, 2005) 82 and 87. Query whether a State may use force to achieve goals that are consistent with the purposes of the UN (see Christine Gray, *International Law and the Use of Force* (2nd ed, 2004) 29).

113 *Expert Meeting: "Targeting Military Objectives"*, above n 27 (chapter 1), 3.

114 Solf, above n 90 (chapter 2), 128.

ment of the object for which the armed conflict is waged",[115] whereas, under API, the field commander's viewpoint is the "attainment of a definite military advantage."[116] Accordingly, in target selection[117] it is important not to confuse seeking the ultimate surrender of the enemy[118] with political or national goals. The former is the goal of the military, the latter the goal of the State. A field commander quite rightly seeks the defeat of the enemy, including through surrender. Axiological targeting aimed at influencing the enemy to surrender, when limited as I have described above, is legally permissible. However, following Solf's reasoning, it is my view that axiological targeting aimed at achieving national-strategic planning goals is impermissible. To restate the argument, this is because the achievement of national-strategic goals are not a military advantage and under article 52(2) API an attack on an object must offer a military advantage for that object to be a lawful military objective. As Dinstein states, "the advantage gained must be military and not, say, purely political".[119] A target cannot be selected purely to force a change in negotiating attitude.[120] But, an attack on an otherwise lawful military objective can be given a higher military priority to achieve this desired outcome.

An excellent case in point is the NATO bombing campaign in Kosovo.

> NATO's objectives for the conflict in Kosovo were set out in the Statement issued at the Extraordinary Meeting of the North Atlantic Council held at NATO on 12 April 1999 and were reaffirmed by Heads of State and Government in Washington on 23 April 1999. They included,
>
> – A verifiable stop to all military action and the immediate ending of violence and repression;
> – The withdrawal from Kosovo of the military, police and paramilitary forces;
> – The stationing in Kosovo of an international military presence;
> – The unconditional and safe return of all refugees and displaced persons and unhindered access to them by humanitarian aid organizations; and
> – The establishment of a political framework agreement for Kosovo on the basis of the Rambouillet Accords, in conformity with international law and the Charter of the United Nations.[121]

Interestingly, these objectives were not set until April yet the "NATO air and missile campaign in Kosovo began at 1400 EST (1900 GMT) on March 24th."[122] These objectives are what Solf would describe as national-strategic objectives. Accordingly,

---

115 Ibid.

116 Ibid.

117 And for that matter, whenever else concepts like 'military advantage' and 'military necessity' need to be considered.

118 Or any other form of cessation of hostilities such as an armistice or compliance with a UN Security Council Resolution.

119 Dinstein, *The Conduct of Hostilities under the Law of International Armed Conflict*, above n 66 (chapter 2), 86.

120 Ibid.

121 Cordesman, above n 97 (chapter 1), 23–4.

122 Ibid, 16.

targets could not be selected purely on the basis that attacking the targets would assist in achieving NATO's objectives. To attack such a target, there would also have to be a military advantage to the attack.

What is and is not permissible under IHL can become confusing if the distinction that Solf makes between national-strategic objectives and the objectives of a field commander is not adhered to. For example, at a joint press conference with the NATO Secretary-General, General Clark said:

> The military mission ... is to attack Yugoslav military and security forces and associated facilities with sufficient effect to degrade its capacity to continue repression of the civilian population and to deter further military actions against its own people.[123]

The mission described is a national-strategic objective. Accordingly, targets could not be selected purely on the basis that attacking those targets would assist in the achievement of that mission. Of course, the priority for attacking the targets can be based on the national-strategic objectives.

Oeter states the point succinctly when he writes that prohibited attacks include "attacks of a purely political purpose, whether to demonstrate military strength, or to intimidate the political leadership of the adversary."[124] I agree with this statement, as long as the proper emphasis is placed on the word *purely*. For example, it would be permissible to launch a forceful attack on otherwise lawful military objectives to convince other enemy military units to surrender. In this circumstance, the attack would not have been for a 'purely political purpose'. Also, see the comments on axiological targeting above where it was argued that secondary purposes in target selection (for example, convincing the civilian government of the adversary to surrender) are legitimate but only to a limited extent and such secondary purposes cannot be counted as a military advantage.

Armed conflict inevitably involves killing people and destroying property. What is sometimes forgotten is that while IHL permits this to occur in circumstances when, but for a state of armed conflict, such actions would generally be illegal and punishable as such, this legalising of the otherwise illegal is premised on the military actions being *necessary* and not merely convenient or even preferable. And, as recognised in the *St Petersburg Declaration*, the only *necessary* thing to win is to weaken the enemy.[125] As Kalshoven notes, "a situation of armed conflict does not provide a 'licence to kill'".[126]

The limitations just discussed on lawful targets appear not to have been considered by Cordesman when he writes: "For at least some civilians and diplomats, it is far more politically and morally easy to attack conscripts in uniform than the

123 Wesley Clark, Waging Modern War: Bosnia, Kosovo, and the Future of Combat (2001) 203.

124 Oeter, above n 24 (chapter 2), 158.

125 Preamble of the *St Petersburg Declaration*, above n 64 (chapter 1).

126 Frits Kalshoven, 'Remarks' in ASIL Proceedings, *Implementing Limitations on the Use of Force: The Doctrine of Proportionality and Necessity* (1992) 41, 43.

power base of the civilian leadership that sends them to war".[127] However, as the power base of the civilian leadership is not a lawful target set, the choices available to the attacker include attacking the conscripts, not attacking the conscripts and pursuing victory by attacking other lawful targets, not entering the armed conflict in the first place, or ending the armed conflict. So, while the choices enjoyed by a State are not binary but usually (possibly always) numerous, those choices would usually not extend to attacks on a civilian government's powerbase or other political-goal oriented targets.

Having determined in general terms what is and what is not a military advantage, the following concerns some issues dealing with the assessment of military advantage.

3.5.2 Case by case approach or cumulative basis?

Brown points out that military advantage:

> can be construed either on a 'case-by-case' or on a 'cumulative' basis; the former refers to the specific tactical objective of a particular action, whereas the latter refers to the manner in which the action will contribute to the belligerent's overall strategic goals.[128]

After discussing some historical examples, the discussions at the Diplomatic Conference for the negotiation of API and the consequences of adopting a cumulative approach, Brown concludes that "both policy factors and the language of the [Diplomatic] Conference's articles support a 'case-by-case' interpretation of military advantage."[129] Notably, Brown did not discuss any of the declarations[130] made by States on becoming a party to API. For example, Australia made a declaration of understanding to the effect that military advantage in articles 51 and 57 API means "the advantage anticipated from the attack considered as a whole and not from isolated or particular parts of the attack".[131] A similar declaration was

127 Cordesman, above n 97 (chapter 1), 151.

128 Bernard Brown, above n 50 (chapter 2), 141 (footnote omitted). It is apparent from the context of the quote that Brown is using the word *strategic* in a military sense rather than a political sense.

129 Ibid, 142.

130 A reservation or declaration is a "unilateral statement, however phrased or named, made by a State when ratifying, acceding or succeeding to a treaty, whereby it purports to exclude or to modify the legal effect of certain provisions of the treaty in their application to that State (provided that such reservations are not incompatible with the object and purpose of the treaty)." (*States party to the Geneva Conventions and their Additional Protocols* (2005) International Committee of the Red Cross, 1 <http://www.icrc.org/Web/eng/siteeng0.nsf/htmlall/party_gc/$File/Conventions%20de%20Geneve%20et%20Protocoles%20additionnels%20ENG.pdf> at 28 August 2005)

131 Roberts and Guelff, above n 14 (chapter 1), 500.

made by Canada,[132] the Federal Republic of Germany,[133] Italy,[134] Netherlands,[135] New Zealand,[136] Spain,[137] the United Kingdom,[138] and the United States of America.[139] Belgium's declaration is subtly different in that it declared that military advantage meant the advantage "expected from an attack considered in its totality."[140] Somewhat peculiarly, only the statement of understanding by Canada refers to military advantage in, inter alia, article 52(2) API. All the others refer to only articles 51 and 57 API. Subsequent State practice of Australia, Belgium, Canada, Germany, New Zealand and Spain, along with Nigeria and the United States of America, is consistent with the above declarations.[141]

Interestingly, after a review of the negotiating history like Brown, Fenrick concludes—unlike Brown—that the assessment is not based on a single strike, while at the same time military advantage is not to be assessed too broadly (eg, one cannot look at the benefit derived from the whole strategic bombing offensive against Germany in World War II). Fenrick states:

> Whether a definite military advantage would result from an attack must be judged in the context of the military advantage anticipated from the specific military operation of which the attack is a part considered as a whole, and not only from isolated or particular parts of that operation.[142]

The most important words in the preceding sentence are *context* and *specific*. Consistent with Fenrick's view, it is my view that the military advantage to be

---

132 Ibid, 503. Canada made a similar statement at the 1974–77 *Diplomatic Conference on the Reaffirmation and Development of International Humanitarian Law Applicable in Armed Conflicts*—CDDH/VI, above n 77 (chapter 2), 179.

133 Roberts and Guelff, above n 14 (chapter 1), 505. The Federal Republic of Germany made a similar statement at the 1974–77 *Diplomatic Conference on the Reaffirmation and Development of International Humanitarian Law Applicable in Armed Conflicts*—CDDH/VI, above n 77 (chapter 2), 226.

134 Roberts and Guelff, above n 14 (chapter 1), 507. Italy made a similar statement at the 1974–77 *Diplomatic Conference on the Reaffirmation and Development of International Humanitarian Law Applicable in Armed Conflicts*—CDDH/VI, above n 77 (chapter 2), 231.

135 Roberts and Guelff, above n 14 (chapter 1), 508.

136 Ibid.

137 Ibid, 509.

138 Ibid, 511. The United Kingdom made a similar statement at the 1974–77 *Diplomatic Conference on the Reaffirmation and Development of International Humanitarian Law Applicable in Armed Conflicts*—CDDH/VI, above n 77 (chapter 2), 164.

139 Roberts and Guelff, above n 14 (chapter 1), 512. The United States of America made a similar statement at the 1974–77 *Diplomatic Conference on the Reaffirmation and Development of International Humanitarian Law Applicable in Armed Conflicts*—CDDH/VI, above n 77 (chapter 2), 241.

140 Ibid, 501.

141 Henckaerts and Doswald-Beck (eds), *Customary International Humanitarian Law*, vol II, above n 64 (chapter 1), 328.

142 Bothe, Partsch and Solf, above n 87 (chapter 1), 324–5; quoted with approval in Robertson Jr, above n 105 (chapter 1), 52.

gained from an attack on a target cannot be considered in isolation;[143] but at the same time, the anticipated military advantage cannot be achieving the end of the armed conflict (except, perhaps, for the rarest of targets). This analysis is consistent with the various State declarations and also makes military sense. To take a simple example, an attack on one part of a communication system that has redundancy arguably provides no, or at least very limited, military advantage. However, when combined with attacks on other parts of the system a military advantage is gained. Attacks will often be planned in such a way to produce cumulative effects, where "the overall impact of various attacks is greater than the sum of the individual attacks themselves; the attacks operate synergistically."[144]

A further aspect of this argument is that while the military advantage to be assessed must be concrete and direct, it need not occur immediately. In an article that discusses the history of the development of the definition of a military objective, Horace Robertson, Jr refers to a resolution adopted by the Institute of International Law at Edinburgh in 1969.[145] That resolution defined military objectives as only those objects:

> which, by their very nature or purpose or use, make an effective contribution to military action, or exhibit a generally recognized military significance, such that their total or partial destruction in the actual circumstances gives a substantial, specific and *immediate* military advantage to those who are in a position to destroy them.[146]

While this formulation clearly influenced the definition of military objective adopted in article 52(2) API,[147] article 52(2) API does not use the word *immediate* or any synonym thereof. Further, logic indicates that the attack on a number of military objectives that are regularly considered uncontroversial will only manifest a military advantage at some later time. For example, an attack on a military fuel dump does not cause military vehicles immediately to cease operations.[148] Even more tellingly, the very definition of military objective includes objects that by their *purpose* contribute to military action, and *purpose* means intended future use.[149] It must be remembered, however, that other factors will impose limits on how far the claimed military advantage can be temporally removed from the attack. Issues like foreseeability, the military advantage being concrete and direct and the military

143 Bothe, Partsch and Solf, above n 87 (chapter 1), 311.

144 Schmitt, 'Targeting and Humanitarian Law: Current Issues', above n 42 (chapter 1), 62.

145 Robertson Jr, above n 105 (chapter 1), 35.

146 Ibid, 39 (footnote omitted) (emphasis added). The *ICRC Commentary* on API, art 52 refers to the 1969 definition but does not clearly indicate how it influenced the drafting and negotiating of API, art 52(2)—Sandoz, Swinarski and Zimmerman (eds), above n 68 (chapter 1), [2003]).

147 Robertson Jr, above n 105 (chapter 1), 40.

148 Contrast an attack on a power station that may, subject to whether there is a power distribution grid or back up power supply, cause near instantaneous power cuts and immediate cessation of equipment that runs on electrical power.

149 See section 3.4.4.

advantage being attributable to the actual attack (when considered as a whole) will in effect impose restrictions on the claimed military advantage being able to accrue too far into the future.

In summary, while the anticipated military advantage must be concrete and direct, it may nonetheless include more than the immediate tactical gain from the attack looked at in isolation, it may be calculated in light of other related actions, and it may arise in the future.

3.5.3 *Who assesses 'definite military advantage'?*

In section 3.3, I referred to how Oeter had classified the first part of the test in article 52(2) API as being objective and the second part as being subjective. I then noted that objective and subjective can be used in different ways, and, in my opinion, Oeter was not referring to the issue that is about to be covered—namely whether military advantage is assessed against what the attacking commander believed or, alternatively, on what a reasonable commander would have believed in the same circumstances.

Whether an attack on a target will offer a military advantage is a crucial question in IHL. If the answer to the question is yes, then the target may be the subject of a *lawful* attack. The problem is that determining what is a military advantage, and whether such advantage exists in any given case, is not a mathematical science. While the various rules and principles of IHL can determine what may be considered, and equally importantly prohibit certain factors from being considered, when determining whether a military advantage exists, IHL still does not provide a neat equation from which an unequivocal answer of whether a military advantage will exist or not can be deduced. Indeed, an interesting concern was raised in the report of a workshop titled *Understanding Collateral Damage*.

> Many representatives of human rights groups expressed a fundamental unease with their ability to interpret or define certain military concepts articulated in international humanitarian law (IHL). … For example, some feel ill equipped to define 'military advantage,' a concept with central relevance to many other aspects of IHL.[150]

Indeed, it is not always easy for military commanders to agree. For example, the difficulty in determining the actual military advantage is indicated by the following quote in relation to the NATO bombing campaign in Kosovo: "Clark and Short never reached mutual agreement during the campaign over the relative priority of strikes on Serbian ground forces versus strategic targets in Belgrade and Serbia proper".[151] General Wesley Clark was the NATO Supreme Allied Commander in Europe. Lieutenant General Michael Short was NATO's Joint Force Air Component Commander for the campaign. It would appear from this example

150 *Understanding collateral damage workshop* (2002) Carr Center for Human Rights Policy—Project on the Means of Intervention, 9–10 <http://www.ksg.harvard.edu/cchrp/Web%20Working%20Papers/WebJuneReport.pdf> at 15 May 2005.

151 Cordesman, above n 97 (chapter 1), 20.

that while there was agreement on the existence of some military advantage in each case, there was disagreement as to the relative priorities. Therefore, arguably, there was a disagreement over the quantum of military advantage anticipated from attacking one target compared to another target. Accordingly, ipso facto, there would have to be disagreement over the assessment of proportionality in the event that any given attack was expected to cause collateral damage. This last point shows how determining who decides on the existence and extent of the anticipated military advantage for a planned attack is a very important issue. The decision on the amount of military advantage to be gained from attacking a particular target will affect not just whether a target is a military objective (ie, does a military advantage exist at all) but also what level of collateral damage would be proportional based on what quantum of military advantage is anticipated from the attack.

Without clearly stating so, it would appear that the *ICRC Commentary* on article 52(2) API favours a subjective interpretation. The Commentary states that "it remains the case that the text adopted by the Diplomatic Conference largely relies on the judgment of soldiers who will have to apply these provisions."[152] In addition, that the test is subjective is supported by Solf when he writes that the provisions of API "remain to a large extent general principles which require subjective judgement in specific situations."[153] He goes on to write that this is one of the reasons why the Diplomatic Conference that led to API "developed specific provisions regulating attacks on particular objects and specific areas."[154]

Reference to article 7 of the 1956 ICRC *Draft Rules for the Limitation of Dangers incurred by the Civilian Population in Time of War*[155] is useful when considering this issue. Article 7 refers to categories of objectives that "are generally acknowledged to be of military importance". The importance of these words is that these words mean that the test that was proposed in article 7 would have been an objective test. Of course, as the article went on to provide an exclusive list of military objectives, the test could be none other than objective. However, it is possible to have an objective test without providing a list. Accordingly, it is interesting to observe that similar words to 'generally acknowledged' are not repeated in article 52(2) API. The absence of such words is even more important as the original Draft Protocol that was prepared by the ICRC in 1970–1 read as follows: "Attacks shall be strictly limited to military objectives, namely, to those objectives which are, by their nature, purpose or use, *recognized* to be of military interest".[156] This would clearly have added an objective aspect to the test. Therefore, the drafting history of article 52(2) API indicates a move from an objective test to a subjective test and this provides added support for interpreting the test as being subjective. And while a proposal at the 1972 *Conference of Government Experts on the Reaffirmation and Development of International Humanitarian Law Applicable in Armed Conflicts* to add the words "in

152 Sandoz, Swinarski and Zimmerman (eds), above n 68 (chapter 1), [2037].

153 Solf, above n 90 (chapter 2), 132.

154 Ibid.

155 See above n 16 (chapter 3).

156 Draft art 47(1), reproduced in Sandoz, Swinarski and Zimmerman (eds), above n 68 (chapter 1), 633 (emphasis added).

the opinion of the operational commander"[157] to the test for whether an object was a military objective was not successful, it would seem that the comprise was to set out a test that provided objective criteria to which "the military commander would, in practice, refer."[158]

So, it would appear that the assessment of military advantage is a subjective test. This means that whether or not a military advantage exists, and to what degree, is to be judged by what the commander authorising or conducting the attack thought; not by what a hypothetical commander would have thought if presented with the same information. Therefore, it is the actual belief of the commander at the time that is relevant. The effect of this is two-fold. First, an attack is not unlawful where a reasonable commander would have concluded that attacking the target would not produce a military advantage as long as the commander who ordered the attack believed that there was a military advantage to be gained from attacking the target. Second, an attack is not legal merely because a reasonable commander would have concluded that attacking the target would produce a military advantage. Instead, one must determine that the commander who ordered the attack did in fact believe that there was a military advantage to be gained from attacking the target.[159]

Once the subjective nature of the test is appreciated, an interesting point follows. Not only is it the commander who makes the decision on whether a military advantage exists, it is only the commander. While a commander may be assisted by various staff officers, ultimately those officers only advise and it is a commander who decides. Being aware of the above also helps to understand the role that lawyers, be they military or civilian, should have in the targeting process. For example, it is stated that during the Kosovo campaign, "[i]t was British law that targets struck by aircraft based in the United Kingdom had to be approved by their lawyers".[160] Unfortunately, more information on the exact process is not available; however, I query what is meant by 'approve'. Traditionally, a lawyer's role is to advise a client and not to make determinations. However, and quite correctly, this is not always the case for in-house lawyers.[161] Consistent with what is written above, the proper role of a lawyer in the targeting process would not be to determine whether and to what extent a military advantage existed or whether a given level of collateral damage would be proportional. Rather, the proper role would be to confirm that the appropriate legal and policy steps have been taken, that the correct legal interpretations had been applied when assessing a target, and so on. This is consistent with the practice of the United States of America, or at least United States practice during the 1991 Gulf War, as can be seen from the following quote:

157 CE 1972 Report, vol I, above n 25 (chapter 1), 147.

158 Ibid.

159 See also the discussion at section 7.2.

160 Clark, above n 123 (chapter 3), 224.

161 Realising, of course, that while being involved in the actual decision-making would, inter alia, compromise claims for legal professional privilege, there may be good reasons for policy and governance reasons for preferring a more active role for an in-house lawyer over an ability to claim legal professional privilege.

> In addition, military judge advocates and civilian attorneys with international law expertise provided advice on the law of war and other legal issues at every level of command in all phases of Operations Desert Shield and Desert Storm. Particular attention was given to the review of target lists to ensure the consistency of targets selected for attack with United States law of war obligations.[162]

However, a lawyer should not be tasked to substitute there own view on the advisability of the attack. The risk is that compliance with the law may be jeopardised when a commander, and perhaps even the lawyer, is in doubt as to whether the advice being provided is that the attack is contrary to IHL, or is merely contrary to what the lawyer would do if the lawyer was the commander. In this context, it is interesting to read Hampson, who writes "[m]ore might be achieved by reminding military commanders of the limited function of the law. The mere fact that an attack would be lawful does not mean that it is required or even advisable."[163] Hampson seems to confuse the role of the lawyer. How can a lawyer advise that an attack is lawful unless a commander has determined (or will determine) that a military advantage exists? And if such an advantage exists, why would an attack not be advisable? Who would advise on the 'advisability' of the attack that is otherwise legal except for the commander or operational staff?[164]

Interestingly, in a newspaper article discussing Australia's involvement in the 2003 Iraq conflict, it was noted that Australia had "sent about six military lawyers to the Gulf to advise troops and F/A-18 Hornet pilots on what they can attack."[165] This was followed two paragraphs later by the comment: "Legal advisers had to decide if the military advantage gained by a strike justified the civilian loss of life."[166] This is incorrect, or at least it is an incorrect statement of the law. Such lawyers would have assisted the commander with advice but would not have true legal responsibility for making the decision. The rationale for this is nicely expressed by one Australian army infantry officer who commented, "[i]t is worth recalling that no practising legal advisers were hanged after Nuremberg, only commanders."[167] I suggest Dunlap expresses the role better when he states that a "good [lawyer] asks the

---

162 US Department of Defense, *Conduct of the Persian Gulf War: Final Report to Congress*, above n 29 (chapter 3), 692.

163 Hampson, 'Proportionality and Necessity in the Gulf Conflict', above n 23 (chapter 3), 54.

164 While not this author's personal experience, Dunlap notes that "there remains an underlying resentment if not hostility among many in the armed forces to the growing presence and, more specifically, the influence of lawyers in the conduct of modern conflict." (Charles Dunlap, Jr, 'The Revolution in Military Legal Affairs: Air Force Legal Professionals in 21st Century Conflicts' (2001) 51 *Air Force Law Review* 293, 294) Such a problem could only be exacerbated if the respective roles of lawyer and commander get confused.

165 Mark Forbes, 'Saddam a Legal Target for our Troops', *The Age* (Melbourne), 22 March 2003.

166 Ibid.

167 Colonel David Hurley, 'An Application of the Laws of Armed Conflict: Operation Solace' in Hugh Smith (ed), *The Force of Law: International Law and the Land Commander* (1994) 179, 186.

hard questions, plays devils advocate, and demands the best of intelligence assets and operational processes."[168]

A final issue that follows from the above is that it is not appropriate for civilian governments officials (eg, Prime Ministers, cabinets etc) to make the decision on whether something is a military objective. So, when we read that "[t]he final decision on attacking controversial targets will be made by Prime Minister John Howard and his cabinet",[169] or "[s]everal target categories were subject to Australian Ministerial approval before they could be engaged",[170] these comments should be understood to mean that the Prime Minister has the right to veto an attack on an objective that the military has assessed as being a military objective. These comments should not be understood to mean that the Prime Minister made an affirmative decision about whether something was a military objective in the first place. This point is consistent with State practice. For example, the following quote comes from the Kosovo bombing campaign:

> Press reports indicate that France's President Chirac was not fully aware of the scale of the NATO attacks until he saw live television coverage of their effects on April 3rd, and he then asked for the ability to review targets, including all strikes in Montenegro.[171]

Not unsurprisingly, "France was not the only nation seeking a *veto* power. Prime Minister Blair is reported to have asked for a *veto* on all B-52 strikes taking off from Britain."[172] A veto, or approval process, might also be imposed under domestic law, government direction or military policy. For example, in a post 2003 Gulf War report, Lieutenant General Mosley, the Combined Force Air Component Commander, is attributed with saying that air commanders were obliged to obtain Rumsfeld's personal approval to undertake any air strike that could likely result in the deaths of 30 or more Iraqi civilians.[173] This is an example of where the military have undertaken the necessary IHL steps (eg, assessing the target as being a military objective and the attack as being legally proportional) and where political responsibility is also being exercised for accepting the non-legal consequences of the attack.

It is worth concluding this section by noting that where there is any subsequent investigation of the targeting decision, the decision is to be considered against the information available to the commander at the time the commander made the decision and not assessed with the benefit of hindsight. This statement is not generally

168 Charles Dunlap, Jr, *Law and Military Interventions: Preserving Humanitarian Values in 21st Conflicts* (2001) Duke University, 10 <http://www.duke.edu/~pfeaver/dunlap.pdf> at 27 November 2007.

169 Forbes, above n 165 (chapter 3).

170 *The War in Iraq: ADF Operations in the Middle East in 2003* (2004) Department of Defence, 13 <http://www.defence.gov.au/publications/lessons.pdf> at 27 March 2005.

171 Cordesman, above n 97 (chapter 1), 63 (footnote omitted).

172 Ibid, 64 (emphasis added).

173 Rebecca Grant, *Gulf War II: Air and Space Power Led the Way* (2003) Air Force Association, 14–5 <http://www.afa.org/media/reports/GulfWar.pdf> at 1 May 2005.

considered to be controversial and is supported by the fact that Australia (along with many other states) made a declaration of understanding that "commanders and others responsible for planning, deciding upon, or executing attacks, necessarily have to reach their decisions on the basis of their assessment of the information from all sources, which is available to them at the relevant time."[174] Not only have many other States made similar or identical declarations, it would appear that these declarations have not been challenged by other State parties.

Having now discussed both what is meant by military advantage and who determines whether and to what extent military advantage would exist from an attack, the next extremely important aspect of article 52(2) API is that the military advantage must exist in the circumstances ruling at the time.

3.6 Circumstances ruling at the time

When assessing whether an object is a military objective for the purposes of article 52(2) API, the determination that the attack on the target will offer a definite military advantage must be made "in the circumstances ruling at the time".[175] This aspect of article 52(2) API has a significant effect on targeting decisions. Simply stated, the effect of these words is that an object cannot be assessed as being a military objective once and for all; rather, the attack object must be tested against the second prong of the test in article 52(2) API whenever it is proposed to target the object. Human Rights Watch adopts this approach in their report on the 1991 Gulf War:

> The *New Rules* states in this regard: "This element emphasizes that in the dynamic circumstances of armed conflict, objects which may have been military objectives yesterday, may no longer be such today and vice versa. Thus, timely and reliable information of the military situation is an important element in the selection of targets for attack."
> A leading authority on the laws of war, who was present at the drafting of Protocol I, endorses these interpretations, stating:
> [T]he "definite military advantage" required under the definition must be present "in the circumstances ruling at the time". This element in the definition effectively precludes military commanders from relying exclusively on abstract categorizations in the determination of whether specific objects constitute military objectives ("a bridge is a military objective"; "an object located in the zone of combat is a military objective", etc.). Instead, they will have to determine whether, say, the destruction of a particular bridge, which would have been militarily important yesterday, does, in the circumstances ruling today, still offer a "definite military

---

174 Roberts and Guelff, above n 14 (chapter 1), 500. See the declarations and the practice of many States referred to in Henckaerts and Doswald-Beck (eds), *Customary International Humanitarian Law*, vol II, above n 64 (chapter 1), 331–3.

175 API, above n 2 (chapter 1), art 52(2).

advantage": if not, the bridge no longer constitutes a military objective and, thus, may not be destroyed.[176]

I agree with the above statement.

After noting that certain railway lines, bridges etc may undoubtedly be of fundamental military importance and as such be legitimate military objectives, Oeter writes that the defending belligerent "will be able to compensate for the destruction of "strategically important" lines of communication by switching to railway lines or roads which had previously been totally unimportant."[177] He then poses the question: "But does that not lead to the conclusion that such objects or lines which for the present seem 'unimportant' may be perceived as militarily important from the beginning, and may accordingly constitute relevant military objectives ab initio?"[178] The answer to this question in a particular circumstance will come from applying the test of 'in the circumstances ruling at the time' when determining whether an attack on the object offers a definite military advantage to the attacking party. For instance, most, if not all, civilian airfields could also be used by at least one or more types of military aircraft. A civilian airfield could be used either as an auxiliary airfield or as alternative airfield in the event of destruction of the military airfield. However, without more information, this does not make a civilian airfield a military objective. For that to occur, an intention to use the airfield must be present.[179] In coming to a conclusion about the enemy's intentions, an attacker would have to have a reasonable belief about the other party's intention.[180] Ways that this intention could be evidenced include past practice, the use of the airfield in military exercises,[181] or an intention to use civilian airfields as auxiliary or alternative airfields expressed in the military doctrine or plans of the defending State.

Even if the attacker does have the necessary intelligence about the intentions of the defending party, this is not of itself sufficient to make an attack on a civilian airfield lawful. The attack must still offer a definite military advantage in the circumstances ruling at the time. Accordingly, the circumstances in which the defending State has the intention to use the civilian airfield must also be present. For example, the defending party may have an intention to use the civilian airfield only in the event of damage to the nearby military airfield. While the military airfield is operational, the defending party's intention could be described as inchoate. The intention only manifests itself once the military airfield is damaged. For an attack on the civilian airfield to offer a definite military advantage in the circumstances ruling at the time, there would need to be existing damage to the military airfield or—argu-

176 *Needless Deaths in the Gulf War: Civilian Casualties During the Air Campaign and Violations of the Laws of War*, above n 38 (chapter 3).

177 Oeter, above n 24 (chapter 2), 160–1 (footnote omitted).

178 Ibid.

179 See the discussion at section 3.4.4.

180 Boivin, above n 19 (chapter 1), 19.

181 For example, "the use of the Autobahn in Germany as an airstrip for U.S. Air Force F-16 Falcon fighters and C-130 Hercules transport aircraft during NATO exercises"—W. Hays Parks, 'Air War and the Law of War' (1990) 32 *Air Force Law Review* 1, 140 (fn 413).

ably—the concurrent attack on the military airfield. It would not be permissible to attack the civilian airfield first with the expectation that the military airfield is going to be attacked the next day as, for various reasons, the subsequent attack may not occur. A further example where a definite military advantage would exist in the present circumstances would be where intelligence indicates an impending relocation of belligerent military aircraft to the civilian airfield because, for example, the civilian airfield is in a more favourable location for the conduct of the desired military aircraft sorties.

In summary, the words *in the circumstances ruling at the time* have the effect of limiting the classification of objects as military objectives to objects whose total or partial destruction, capture or neutralization will produce a military advantage to the attacker based on an assessment of the *circumstances* existing at the time of the attack. While the assessment must be made based on the circumstances existing at the time of the attack, in some cases that military advantage may not *materialise* until sometime in the future. One example of this is what Schmitt refers to as cascading effect.

> Cascading effects are "indirect effects [that] ripple through an adversary target system, often influencing other target systems as well". Typically, they occur when striking targets at a higher level of conflict. For instance, damaging a national level command and control net will influence lower levels of the conflict as the ability to receive intelligence and direction from above, and to coordinate operations with other units, diminishes.[182]

The existence of a military advantage to attacking a national level command and control net is clear, even though the effect on tactical level operations does not materialise instantaneously.

That concludes the discussion of *what* it is lawful to attack. The next chapter deals with the law concerning *who* it is lawful to attack.

---

182 Schmitt, 'Targeting and Humanitarian Law: Current Issues', above n 42 (chapter 1), 62 (footnote omitted).

Chapter 4

Lawful human targets

> The determination of combatant status is a necessity of civilised warfare on land, on sea, or in the air. The distinction between the combatant and the non-combatant elements of a community is the essential condition precedent of the humanising of warfare.[1]

Following on from chapter 3, which dealt with the targeting of objects, this chapter deals with the law that applies to targeting people. The basic and uncontroversial rule is that combatants may be targeted and civilians may not be targeted. So, the main issues in this chapter are when is a combatant not subject to attack and when does a civilian lose protection from attack.

The main exception for when a combatant cannot be targeted is when the combatant is *hors de combat*. I argue that other than when *hors de combat*, a combatant is subject to lawful attack at all times; this is regardless of whether the combatant at that time is posing a threat to the attacker or other belligerents associated with the attacker. Accordingly, what amounts to *hors de combat* is a very important issue. For example, it might be argued that an unarmed combatant is de facto *hors de combat*, or at least there is no military necessity present to justify the use of lethal force against that combatant. I review the negotiating history of API, various commentaries and examples from actual conflicts with a view to determining whether *hors de combat* includes when a combatant is merely outnumbered, overwhelmed or otherwise defenceless. In other words, is there an obligation to attempt to capture or otherwise use minimum force against an opposing combatant? The related issue of whether there is an obligation to invite or offer an opportunity to surrender before launching an attack is also addressed.

The second part of chapter 4 deals with when it is lawful to attack civilians. According to article 51(3) API, it is lawful to attack a civilian for such time as that civilian is taking a direct part in hostilities. I argue that taking a direct part in hostilities is more limited than contribution to the general war effort;[2] as a result, civilians who work in munitions factory and senior civilian politicians are not ipso facto targetable. As it is lawful to attack a civilian only "for such time"[3] as that civilian is taking a direct part in hostilities, there is an issue known as the "revolving door".[4]

---

1 J.M. Spaight, *Air Power and War Rights* (1924) 59.

2 CE 1972 Report, vol I, above n 25 (chapter 1), 143.

3 API, above n 2 (chapter 1), art 51(3).

4 Schmitt, '"Direct participation in hostilities" and 21st century armed conflict', above n 58 (chapter 1), 510.

The issue is how to categorise a civilian who regularly starts and stops taking a direct part in hostilities. In resolving this issue, I argue for a distinction between a civilian who is acting independently and one who has become a member of an organised armed group.

4.1 Combatants

As one would expect, it is lawful to target combatants;[5] although this is not obvious from reading the conventions.[6] Indeed, if one was to read article 48 API and the definition of military objectives in article 52 API, you might conclude that the military personnel of the enemy are not lawful targets. This is not the case. Combatant status "implies … being considered a legitimate military objective",[7] and combatants can be "harm[ed] due to their status as combatants".[8] The interesting question, therefore, is who is a combatant?

Combatants are defined under IHL as members of:

(a) the armed forces of a Party to the conflict, including members of militias or volunteer corps forming part of such armed forces,[9] other than:
  i. medical personnel and chaplains covered by article 33 GCIII;[10] and
  ii. members of the armed forces assigned to civil defence organizations acting in compliance with article 67 API;[11]

(b) other[12] militias and volunteer corps, who fulfil the following conditions:
  i. being commanded by a person responsible for his subordinates,
  ii. having a fixed distinctive sign recognizable at a distance,
  iii. carrying their arms openly, and

---

5 Sandoz, Swinarski and Zimmerman (eds), above n 68 (chapter 1), [2017]; see also Rogers, *Law on the Battlefield*, above n 84 (chapter 1), 8; *Why They Died: Civilian Casualties in Lebanon during the 2006 War*, above n 3 (chapter 2), 33.

6 It is suggested that this is because during the diplomatic conferences for the negotiation of API, there was shared by some delegates a "sentiment that affirmatively suggesting violence even against combatants is not appropriate in a humanitarian instrument"—Bothe, Partsch and Solf, above n 87 (chapter 1), 285 (fn 17).

7 *Prosecutor v Galic, (Trial Chamber)* Case No IT-98-29-T (5 December 2003) fn 88.

8 *The Public Committee against Torture in Israel v The Government of Israel*, HCJ 769/02 (13 December 2006) [29] (Barak P (emeritus), Rivlin V-P and Beinisch P concurring) (available at <http://elyon1.court.gov.il/Files_ENG/02/690/007/a34/02007690.a34.pdf> at 09 January 2007). See the consistent State practice on this point at Henckaerts and Doswald-Beck (eds), *Customary International Humanitarian Law*, vol II, above n 64 (chapter 1), 190–3. Dinstein argues that combatants come within the meaning of 'military objective' in the first sentence of API, art 52(2)—Dinstein, *The Conduct of Hostilities under the Law of International Armed Conflict*, above n 66 (chapter 2), 84–5.

9 API, above n 2 (chapter 1), art 43(1); GCI, above n 5 (chapter 2), art 13(1); and GCIII, above n 7 (chapter 2), art 4(A)(1). The definitions of combatant in HIVR, above n 10 (chapter 2), art 1, whilst technically still in force, have been repeated and expanded upon in GCI; accordingly, no further reference to HIVR, art 1 is made.

10 API, above n 2 (chapter 1), art 43(2).

11 The non-combatant status of this group is often overlooked; however, see the State practice of Russia quoted in Henckaerts and Doswald-Beck (eds), *Customary International Humanitarian Law*, vol II, above n 64 (chapter 1), 84.

12 'Other' refers back to other than in sub-paragraph a.

iv. conducting their operations in accordance with the laws and customs of war;[13]

(c) regular armed forces who profess allegiance to a Government or an authority not recognized by the Detaining Power (or, for the purposes of this section, the attacking party);[14] and

(d) a *levee en masse*.[15]

Subject to the exceptions for medical and religious personnel and those members of the armed forces assigned exclusively to civil defence tasks, all members of the armed forces are combatants—be they infantry soldiers or Air Force legal officers.[16] This is the case whether they are actually armed as part of their day-to-day duties or not. The important point is that they have the right to shoot the enemy (and they can be shot by the enemy).[17]

For the purposes of targeting, in cases of doubt about a person's status the person shall be considered a civilian.[18] A person shall not be made the object of attack as a combatant unless it was "reasonable to believe, in the circumstances of the person contemplating the attack, including the information available to the latter, that the potential target [was] a combatant".[19] Factors that may be useful in helping to resolve a person's status as a civilian or a combatant include the person's location, clothing, activities, age and sex.[20]

The four conditions set out in article 13(2)(b) GCI apply to certain militia and other volunteer corps. Do they also apply to members of the armed forces? The better view is yes, as the conditions are implicit to the meaning of being in an armed

---

13 GCI, above n 5 (chapter 2), art 13(2) and GCIII, above n 7 (chapter 2), art 4(A)(2).

14 GCI, above n 5 (chapter 2), art 13(3) and GCIII, above n 7 (chapter 2), art 4(A)(3).

15 GCI, above n 5 (chapter 2), art 13(6) and GCIII, above n 7 (chapter 2), art 4(A)(6). It is convenient to include members of a *levee en masse* in the definition of combatants. While API, above n 2 (chapter 1), art 43 provides a more limited definition of combatants, art 43 does not purport to be the sole definition of combatant. And importantly, API, art 50(1) excludes from the definition of civilians a member of a *levee en masse*.

16 Although it is sometimes suggested, quite unfairly, that by the time an Air Force legal officer has to raise a weapon the battle has been—or very soon will be—lost!

17 Sandoz, Swinarski and Zimmerman (eds), above n 68 (chapter 1), [1677].

18 API, above n 2 (chapter 1), art 50(1).

19 *Prosecutor v Galic, (Trial Chamber)* Case No IT-98-29-T (5 December 2003) [50].

20 Ibid; Bothe, Partsch and Solf, above n 87 (chapter 1), 296.

force.[21] This view is supported by the decision in *United States v Lindh*,[22] where it was held that:

> the four criteria [in article 1 HIVR] have long been understood under customary international law to be the defining characteristics of any lawful armed force. … Thus, all armed forces or militias, regular and irregular, must meet the four criteria if their members are to receive combatant immunity. Were this not so, the anomalous result that would follow is that members of an armed force that met none of the criteria could still claim lawful combatant immunity merely on the basis that the organization calls itself a "regular armed force." It would indeed be absurd for members of a so-called "regular armed force" to enjoy lawful combatant immunity even though the force had no established command structure and its members wore no recognizable symbol or insignia, concealed their weapons, and did not abide by the customary laws of war. Simply put, the label "regular armed force" cannot be used to mask unlawful combatant status.[23]

Of course, a person remains a member of an armed force while out of uniform (eg, while in bed). What is important is that as a general rule the person in question meets the four criteria while on duty. Article 44(3) API[24] would not make much sense if the requirement to wear a uniform did not apply to regular military forces.[25] Also, that combatants "must distinguish themselves from the civilian population while they are engaged in an attack or in a military operation preparatory to an attack" is considered to reflect customary international law.[26]

---

21 Bothe, Partsch and Solf, above n 87 (chapter 1), 234–5; Michael Schmitt, 'Humanitarian Law and Direct Participation in Hostilities by Private Contractors or Civilian Employees' (2004) 5 *Chicago Journal of International Law* 511, 525–6; Joseph Bialke, 'Al-Qaeda & Taliban unlawful combatant detainees, unlawful belligerency, and the international laws of armed conflict' (2004) 55 *Air Force Law Review* 1, 20; Dinstein, *The Conduct of Hostilities under the Law of International Armed Conflict*, above n 66 (chapter 2), 36. See also Sandoz, Swinarski and Zimmerman (eds), above n 68 (chapter 1), [1692–3 and 1695]. See generally the State practice listed in Henckaerts and Doswald-Beck (eds), *Customary International Humanitarian Law*, vol II, above n 64 (chapter 1), 88–93 and 2538–2542. Some of the State practice listed requires all four conditions while some requires just being under responsible command, compliance with IHL and carrying arms openly. See also the statement of Israel on respect for the rules of IHL and distinction at CDDH/VI, above n 77 (chapter 2), 122. But see Bothe, Partsch and Solf, above n 87 (chapter 1), 234–5 (fn 6). See also Julius Stone, *Legal Controls of International Conflict: A Treatise on the Dynamics of Disputes and War Law* (1954) 549.

22 *United States v Lindh*, 212 F Supp 2d 541 (ED Va, 2002).

23 Ibid, fn 35.

24 The requirement for combatants to distinguish themselves from the civilian population while engaged in an attack on military operations preparatory to an attack.

25 See generally Sandoz, Swinarski and Zimmerman (eds), above n 68 (chapter 1), [1672].

26 Henckaerts and Doswald-Beck (eds), *Customary International Humanitarian Law*, vol I, above n 64 (chapter 1), 384. Interestingly, after quoting the codified version of this rule in API, art 44, Human Rights Watch state that "article 44 is not considered reflective of customary international law." (*Why They Died: Civilian Casualties in Lebanon during the 2006 War*, above n 3 (chapter 2), 17, fn 18) I suggest this might have been a misunderstanding on Human Rights Watch's behalf. That aspect of API, art 44 that attracts the

Article 44(3) API has relaxed the criteria in article 13(2)(b) GCI.[27] Pursuant to article 44(3) API, it is permissible, in some situations, for a combatant not to wear a distinctive sign (eg, a uniform) and thereby not distinguish him or herself from the civilian population, noting that in some cases it "is the practice for such fighters to resume their everyday life in between engagements with the enemy."[28] Best has written that the effect of API is that guerrillas off combatant duty are civilians.[29] Along with Sandoz, Swinarski and Zimmerman, I disagree. A person can only go from being a civilian to a combatant and vice versa through incorporation into the military, a militia etc and then through permanent demobilisation.[30] A soldier on leave and out of uniform is still a soldier. Equally, a guerrilla fighter is a full-time combatant and, therefore, a lawful target at all times. The carrying arms openly etc requirements of article 44(3) API are relevant only to whether or not that person has committed a breach of IHL and not to whether he or she is a combatant at other times (and therefore a legitimate target). Article 44 API "does not recognize combatant status 'on demand'."[31] As for the civilian who regularly takes part in hostile actions without being a guerrilla fighter, see section 4.2.1.

It is worth noting that it would seem that the provisions of article 44(3) API could also apply to regular armed forces, "but only under the same exceptional circumstances as for members of so-called guerrilla forces."[32]

While the general rule is that combatants are lawful targets, there are some limitations to this general rule.

4.1.1 Is hors de combat the only limitation on attacking combatants?

It is unlawful to attack a combatant when that person is *hors de combat*. A combatant is *hors de combat* if the person:

---

most controversy and is generally considered not to reflect customary international law is not the requirement for combatants to distinguish themselves, but rather the second part of art 44(3) that *relaxes* the requirement of distinguishment to allow persons not wearing a uniform to retain combatant status so long as they carry their arms openly during each military engagement and in the preparatory phases thereto while visible to the adversary.

27 For a short critique of the undesirability of this relaxation, see Dinstein, *The Conduct of Hostilities under the Law of International Armed Conflict*, above n 66 (chapter 2), 44–7.

28 Judith Gardam, *Non-combatant Immunity as a Norm of International Humanitarian Law* (1993) 103.

29 Best, above n 1 (chapter 2), 25.

30 Sandoz, Swinarski and Zimmerman (eds), above n 68 (chapter 1), [1677–8].

31 Ibid, [1678]

32 Ibid, [1703]. But see the statement of Egypt that "[t]he right to disguise was confined to the combatants of liberation movements; regular combatants were not released by the article from the obligation to wear uniform during military operations"—CDDH/VI, above n 77 (chapter 2), 145; and again at CDDH/XV, above n 98 (chapter 3), 160. See also the statement of Iran (CDDH/VI, above n 77 (chapter 2), 152) and Australia (CDDH/XV, above n 98 (chapter 3), 164). While the statements of Egypt, Iran and Australia might reflect, at least in part, the original motivation for the article, as there is no such limitation in the wording of the article, the statements are contrary to the accepted principle that IHL applies equally between the parties (see section 4.1 below).

(a) is in the power of an adverse Party;
(b) clearly expresses an intention to surrender; or
(c) has been rendered unconscious or is otherwise incapacitated by wounds or sickness, and therefore is incapable of defense;

provided that in any of these cases the person abstains from any hostile act and does not attempt to escape.[33] The reasons behind the *hors de combat* exception to a combatant being a lawful target would appear to be a combination of military necessity and humanity. As Barber explains:

> This definition [of *hors de combat*] gives substance to the idea that necessity does not require harming a person who is no longer a threat. It provides protection during the difficult interim period between when a person is an active combatant and when he gets the full protection accorded prisoners of war.[34]

If it is partly because of the application of the principle of military necessity that a combatant who is *hors do combat* is exempt from attack, then (aside from the other specific cases mentioned later in this section) are there any other general circumstances when due to a lack of military necessity a combatant may not be attacked (eg, when defenceless, asleep or on leave)?

In addition to the above treaty definition of *hors de combat*, Bothe, Partsch and Solf suggest that the customary international law definition of *hors de combat* includes when a combatant is no longer capable of resistance due to having been overpowered or being weaponless.[35] However, a rule to this effect was considered but not adopted during the drafting of API. The draft rule was put in terms of being an elaboration or supplementation to existing rules.[36] Also, the recent comprehensive work on customary IHL law by Henckaerts and Doswald-Beck does not state this to be a rule of customary international law.[37] With due respect to Bothe, Partsch and Solf, while the principle of humanity may dictate that where feasible a defenceless combatant should be captured rather than killed, this is not a strict

---

33 API, above n 2 (chapter 1), art 41(2). Hostile acts include not just combat actions but also destroying installations or military equipment—Sandoz, Swinarski and Zimmerman (eds), above n 68 (chapter 1), [1622]. Note, the *and* between "the person abstains from any hostile act and does not attempt to escape" is better understand as being an *or*—see statement by Venezuela at the *Diplomatic Conference on the Reaffirmation and Development of International Humanitarian Law Applicable in Armed Conflicts* (CDDH/XV, above n 98 (chapter 3), 87).

34 Barber, above n 74 (chapter 2), 679.

35 Bothe, Partsch and Solf, above n 87 (chapter 1), 220. See also Sandoz, Swinarski and Zimmerman (eds), above n 68 (chapter 1), [1366].

36 See CE/4b, above n 77 (chapter 2), annex II, 10. See also the unsuccessful amendment proposed by Brazil (CDDH/III, above n 28 (chapter 3), 169).

37 Henckaerts and Doswald-Beck (eds), *Customary International Humanitarian Law*, vol I, above n 64 (chapter 1). In particular, see 164–70. None of the military manuals reviewed impose such a requirement (see ibid, vol II, 917–20), but the penal codes of Ethiopia and Lithuania do seem to make it a criminal offence to kill an unarmed combatant (ibid, vol II, 921–2).

rule of IHL. Accordingly, a combatant is not *hors de combat* merely due to being no longer capable of offering effective resistance.

It is also suggested that in certain cases the overwhelmed and/or unarmed might actually be *hors de combat*. For example, it has been argued that the meaning of "in the power of an adverse Party" at article 41(2)(a) API is broader than the meaning of "fallen into the power of the enemy" as used in article 4(1) GCIII to define prisoners of war.[38] The argument is that article 41(2)(a) API applies to persons other than just prisoners of war, with an overwhelmed enemy and unarmed combatants being given as examples.[39] As argued above, this is over-stretching the natural meaning of the words used in the article. It is particularly notable that the 1972 draft of an article defined any "disarmed combatant unable to defend himself"[40] as having "fallen into the power of an enemy".[41] This definition is not reflected in API. It is not appropriate to re-write back into a treaty by way of interpretation a position that was discussed and not adopted. Reference should also be made to the relevant rule in HIVR, which states that it is forbidden to "kill or wound an enemy who … having no longer any means of defence, *has surrendered at discretion*".[42] This rule clearly states that it is still incumbent upon a defenceless adversary to actually surrender; surrender is not inferred for the mere fact of defencelessness. The State practice referred to in *Customary International Humanitarian Law* on this point varies slightly, but the majority of State practice is consistent with this interpretation.[43]

Kalshoven doubts, but does not express a concluded view, on whether it is lawful to attack a combatant in all circumstances. After noting that defenceless soldiers are not thereby *hors de combat*, he asks: "But what if they are in fact utterly defenseless; could it not be argued that for want of any military necessity to attack them, they cease to be military objectives?"[44] Alternatively, Hampson states: "The destruction of the opposing armed forces, however, does not appear to require the justification of military necessity. It is lawful by virtue of the existence of a state of war."[45] And further, when discussing an attack on retreating Iraqi soldiers during the 1991 Gulf war, Hampson states: "The coalition forces, legally speaking, need not prove the necessity of the attacks. The attacks were lawful."[46] Similarly, Human Rights Watch state that "international humanitarian law does not prohibit soldiers from killing enemy combatants—even if the opposing fighters are

38 Sandoz, Swinarski and Zimmerman (eds), above n 68 (chapter 1), [1612].

39 Ibid. The argument is partly predicated on the basis that "the rules of some armies purely and simply prohibit any form of surrender, even when all means of defence have been exhausted."

40 CE 1972 Report, vol I, above n 25 (chapter 1), 132.

41 Ibid.

42 HIVR, above n 10 (chapter 2), art 23(c) (emphasis added).

43 Henckaerts and Doswald-Beck (eds), *Customary International Humanitarian Law*, vol II, above n 64 (chapter 1), 942–54.

44 Kalshoven, 'Remarks', above n 126 (chapter 3), 42.

45 Hampson, 'Proportionality and Necessity in the Gulf Conflict', above n 23 (chapter 3), 53.

46 Ibid, 54.

in retreat—so long as they are not wounded, captured, or otherwise out of combat (hors de combat)."[47] I agree with Hampson and Human Rights Watch. This conclusion is not contradicted by any of the State practice referred to in Henckaerts and Doswald-Beck (eds), *Customary International Humanitarian Law*, vol II, and is specifically supported by the cited State practice of Israel and the Netherlands.[48] To conclude, combatants are lawful targets except where they are afforded protection from attack under article 41 API.[49]

Perhaps Kalshoven's concerns arise because when referring to military necessity in IHL, it is necessary to distinguish between the different uses of the term military necessity in different contexts. The first context is where military necessity is used in a particular article of a treaty or in the formulation of a rule of customary international law. For example, article 4(1) HCP provides that parties shall respect cultural property and refrain from, inter alia, using such property in a way that is likely to expose the property to destruction or damage from the armed conflict. However, the requirements of article 4(1) HCP may be waived where "military necessity imperatively requires such a waiver."[50] In this context, military necessity must be assessed on a case-by-case basis.

The second context in which military necessity is used in IHL is that a state of armed conflict does not thereby permit any form of destruction or killing but rather the only permissible purpose is to disable the opposing military force.[51] In this context, military necessity is often referred to as being one of the main three (or four) principles of IHL.[52] When used in this context, it is not required to assess military necessity on a case-by-case basis. Rather, in this context military necessity is a principle that guides the development and interpretation of other rules.[53] Accordingly, once the rules on attack on combatants and the limitations thereon (eg, prohibiting attacks on combatants that are *hors de combat*) are considered, the effect of the principle of military necessity is spent. Accordingly, there is no need for an enemy combatant to be posing a direct threat or be taking part in hostilities at the time of an attack on that combatant.[54] Rather, it is always permissible due to

47 *Legal Issues Arising from the War in Afghanistan and Related Anti-Terrorism Efforts* (2002) Human Rights Watch <http://www.hrw.org/campaigns/september11/ihlqna.htm> at 2 March 2005. See also Dinstein, *The Conduct of Hostilities under the Law of International Armed Conflict*, above n 66 (chapter 2), 94.

48 Henckaerts and Doswald-Beck (eds), *Customary International Humanitarian Law*, vol II, above n 64 (chapter 1), 190–3.

49 See generally *Expert Meeting: "Targeting Military Objectives"*, above n 27 (chapter 1), 13.

50 HCP, above n 11 (chapter 2), art 4(2).

51 See the preamble of the *St Petersburg Declaration*, above n 64 (chapter 1); and API, above n 2 (chapter 1), art 35(1).

52 The three general principles of IHL are usually listed as military necessity, humanity and proportionality (see, for example, Air Power Development Centre, above n 81 (chapter 1), 49–50). Sometimes a fourth principle of *distinction* is also listed. It is my opinion that distinction is merely a subset of military necessity when viewed in a targeting context.

53 See Sassoli and Bouvier, above n 10 (chapter 1), 113.

54 See *Why They Died: Civilian Casualties in Lebanon during the 2006 War*, above n 3 (chapter 2), 126.

military necessity to attack the enemy's combatants. This is so because an individual soldier will always be adding to the military capability of the enemy until the point that they are *hors de combat*—be that through surrender, capture or wounding. Even though "evidence shows attrition levels of 20 to 50 percent usually render a military force combat ineffective",[55] the individual soldiers can still fight and may form up with other units to reconstitute or strengthen those units. Accordingly, the principle of military necessity does not impose a limitation on attacking combatants who are not *hors de combat*. Therefore, and for example, soldiers asleep in their barracks remain legitimate targets. It has also been suggested that the principle of humanity "enjoins that capture is to be preferred to wounding, and wounding to killing".[56] Once again, while as a moral principle this may well be correct, it is not a legal principle or rule of IHL.[57]

4.1.2 Inviting or offering an opportunity to surrender

Does IHL require an attacker to either invite an offer of surrender or at least present an opportunity for a combatant to surrender, particularly where the enemy is overwhelmed or unarmed? To take an example from the 1991 Gulf War:

> [A] controversial incident involving coalition forces occurred on the last day of the ground campaign, as an entire column of Iraqi troops was retreating from Kuwait. These troops had not surrendered, making them legitimate military targets. Yet, they put up only minimal resistance, while coalition aircraft dropped Rockeye fragmentation bombs and other antipersonnel arms, killing thousands. The ICRC concluded that the attacks "cause[d] unnecessary suffering and superfluous injury," and that they were tantamount to "a denial of quarter." Many other observers, however, counter that the concept of denial of quarter does not apply to forces that have not surrendered.[58]

The starting point in analysing this type of situation is that the standard requirement is not to attack a combatant who either is recognised, or in the circumstances should have been recognised, as clearly expressing an intention to surrender. Therefore, attack by snipers is lawful as is attacking a retreating enemy. As Barber points out, retreating soldiers are "neither in the power of the adverse Party nor clearly expressing an intention to surrender, so attacking them would appear legitimate on these two grounds."[59] Henckaerts and Doswald-Beck report that the legal view of the United States is that a retreating enemy may be attacked even if defence-

---

55 US Department of Defense, *Conduct of the Persian Gulf War: Final Report to Congress*, above n 29 (chapter 3), 146.

56 CE/4b, above n 77 (chapter 2), 5.

57 See CE 1972 Report, vol I, above n 25 (chapter 1), 131, where a draft rule that some experts considered might be interpreted as an obligation to capture was considered unacceptable. The adopted rule in API, art 41(3) differs significantly from the 1972 draft.

58 Smyth, above n 103 (chapter 1).

59 Barber, above n 74 (chapter 2), 690.

less, and there is no legal obligation to offer an opportunity to surrender.[60] Finally, whether there should be a legal obligation to offer an opportunity to surrender was expressly considered during the drafting of API but is not expressed as a requirement in any article of API.[61]

The other reason for arguing against the existence of a rule that prohibits the attack on a retreating enemy or a surrounded enemy is that it is contrary to military sense.[62] From a military perspective, it is obviously better to attack a retreating enemy than an enemy putting up a defence; and it is better to attack an enemy who is surrounded by your forces than one who has freedom of manoeuvre. However, this does not mean a defending combatant has no protection under IHL. As argued above, the defending combatant is protected from attack if he or she expresses an intention to surrender and IHL also imposes a positive obligation on an attacker to respect the right of an enemy to surrender.[63] A retreating enemy is not a surrendering enemy—not even if flying a white flag.[64] If not attacked, the retreating enemy will presumably come back and fight another day, or at the very least be in a position to do so.

The same reasoning applies where an enemy is clearly overwhelmed but has not retreated (perhaps because they are surrounded or have no avenue for retreat). The options available to the defending enemy are to surrender (and thereby become *hors de combat*) or not surrender and thereby remain combatants. The options available to the attacker depend upon the defending party's actions. If the defending party surrenders, the combatants become *hors de combat* and, therefore, are protected from attack. If they do not surrender, they remain combatants and are subject to attack. To argue otherwise would be to confuse the law relating to attacking combatants (ie, IHL) with domestic law concerning self-defence and murder. It is a fundamental rule of IHL that combatants are lawful targets, and the definition

---

60 Henckaerts and Doswald-Beck (eds), *Customary International Humanitarian Law*, vol I, above n 64 (chapter 1), 168.

61 See CE/4b, above n 77 (chapter 2), 7 and annex II, 10.

62 "The decisive test for any rule of humanitarian law is whether, to the soldier in an active combat situation, it would appear to be an instinctively apparent and reasonable rule." (Robbie Sabel, 'Chivalry in the Air? Article 42 of the 1977 Protocol I to the Geneva Conventions' in Michael Schmitt (ed), *International Law Across the Spectrum of Conflict: Essays in Honour of Professor L.C. Green on the Occasion of his Eightieth Birthday* (2000) 439, 439)

63 API, above n 2 (chapter 1), art 40. Note that the obligation is to *not attack* a surrendering person. There is no strict obligation under IHL to *capture* a surrendering person party and take that person as a prisoner of war.

64 See Paul Walker, *U.S. Bombing: The myth of Surgical Bombing in the Gulf War* (1992) <http://deoxy.org/wc/wc-myth.htm> at 11 August 2003, who appears to criticise the United States of America for an attack on retreating Iraqi forces during the 1991 Gulf War when many of the retreating Iraqi forces "had affixed white flags to their tanks which were clearly visibly to the U.S. pilots" (footnote omitted). However, this was a misuse of the white flag. The flying of a white flag is not a definite symbol of surrender, but merely a sign of truce carried by a parlementaire who has been authorized by one of the belligerents to enter into communication with the other side (see HIVR, above n 10 (chapter 2), art 32). A person retreating can hardy be retreating whilst also be trying to enter into a truce communication. Alternatively, even if being used as symbol of surrender, once again person retreating can hardy be retreating whilst also surrendering.

of a combatant does not include a requirement that for a person to be a combatant the person must also be currently posing a direct and immediate threat to the attacking party.

There would be significant practical difficulties if an attacker were to be prevented from attacking an overwhelmed force. How is it that an attacking party is to know that it has overwhelmed the defending party? At what point does a defending party go from being militarily disadvantaged to overwhelmed? What is an attacker supposed to do with enemy combatants who due to extremely unfavourable circumstances should be wise enough to surrender but do not do so? As they have not surrendered, presumably they are not willing to be taken as a prisoner of war. Military necessity and humanity are adequately addressed through an attacking party being under an obligation not to attack a person who clearly expresses an intention to surrender[65] and by the positive obligation on an attacker to respect the right of an enemy to surrender and thereby for the enemy to be protected from attack.[66]

Accordingly, the better view of the law is that an attacker is not prevented from attacking an overwhelmed force and—with the one exception being for certain parachutists —[67] there is no obligation to offer an opportunity to surrender. However, an attacker does have a minimum obligation to be prepared to accept surrender and call off the attack as quickly as possible if surrender is forthcoming.[68]

4.1.3 Parachutists

The one exception to the rule that there is no legal obligation to give an enemy combatant an opportunity to surrender arises in the limited case of occupants descending from disabled aircraft. Article 42(1) API provides that persons parachuting from an aircraft in distress shall not be made the object of attack during their descent.[69] This rule can be thought of as a qualified form of *hors de combat*.[70] The history of the rule can be traced back to when:

> [m]ilitary aviation really began to develop during the First World War. The novelty of this weapon, the spirit of adventure of its devotees, the prestige of its missions, and the sharing of risks created a sort of fraternity between the airmen of the two camps at that time, which was characterized by a spirit of camaraderie and by practices which are suggestive of chivalry. The adversary who had been brought down in flames was entitled, not to bullets, but to a salute as he went down, to wishes for his recovery if he were wounded, and flowers if he were dead.[71]

65 API, above n 2 (chapter 1), art 41.

66 Ibid, art 40.

67 See section 4.1.3.

68 US Department of Defense, *Conduct of the Persian Gulf War: Final Report to Congress*, above n 29 (chapter 3), 719.

69 The rule does not apply to airborne troops (API, above n 2 (chapter 1), art 42(3)).

70 Sabel, above n 62 (chapter 4), 443.

71 Sandoz, Swinarski and Zimmerman (eds), above n 68 (chapter 1), [1633].

In addition to not be made an object of attack during descent, providing an opportunity to surrender is addressed in article 42(2) API. That article provides that where a person has parachuted from an aircraft in distress, then in the limited case of where that person lands:

> in territory controlled by an adverse Party, [that person] shall be given an opportunity to surrender before being made the object of attack, unless it is apparent that he is engaging in a hostile act.[72]

A hostile act is not defined. Obviously firing upon the adverse party would amount to a hostile act. Consistent with what would amount to a hostile act for the purposes of *hors de combat* under article 41(2) API, attempting to destroy destroying installations or military equipment would be considered a hostile act.[73] A further example given of a hostile act includes commencing to destroy "important military documents."[74] It has been suggested that commencing an attempt to escape, although not mere movement in the direction of his or her own lines, would also amount to a hostile act.[75] I agree with this. As the prohibition on attack was for the purpose of allowing the person who has parachuted from the aircraft in distress an opportunity to surrender, once the person has manifested an intention not to surrender there can be no good reason to continue the immunity from attack. The mere fact that the parachutist is likely to or will land in friendly territory is not grounds for attack.[76] The *ICRC Commentary* then states:

> if an airman in distress refuses to lay down arms or to surrender, tries to escape or engages in any other way in an obviously hostile act when he reaches the ground, only such force as is necessary in the circumstances to capture him or render him *hors de combat* may be used.[77]

No support for this statement is referred to, and I have not come across any support for it. It is directly contrary to the statement on this point in the Canadian *LOAC*

72 API, above n 2 (chapter 1), art 42(2).

73 Sandoz, Swinarski and Zimmerman (eds), above n 68 (chapter 1), [1622] and [1650].

74 Rogers, *Law on the Battlefield*, above n 84 (chapter 1), 50.

75 CDDH/XV, above n 98 (chapter 3), 386 and 429.

76 See CE/4b, above n 77 (chapter 2), 8; Sandoz, Swinarski and Zimmerman (eds), above n 68 (chapter 1), [1648]; Henckaerts and Doswald-Beck (eds), *Customary International Humanitarian Law*, vol I, above n 64 (chapter 1), 171–2; Sabel, above n 62 (chapter 4), 446. See also the unsuccessful amendment put forward by a coalition of countries—CDDH/III, above n 28 (chapter 3), 173. See the discussion at CDDH/VI, above n 77 (chapter 2), 104–7; and at CDDH/XV, above n 98 (chapter 3), 88, 94–5, 97–8, 104–5, 386, 450 and 519. *Contra* Green, above n 83 (chapter 1), 150; although it is not clear whether Green's remarks apply to API, above n 2 (chapter 1), art 42 or just the relevant customary international law rule.

77 Sandoz, Swinarski and Zimmerman (eds), above n 68 (chapter 1), [1651].

Manual[78] and impliedly contrary to the quoted practice in *Customary International Humanitarian Law* where the quoted practice touches upon the issue.[79]

Assuming the person is a military member, then the person is a combatant. Article 42 API provides only temporary immunity from attack to allow time for the person to surrender. Rogers writes that the "normal rules on surrender apply once a person parachuting from an aircraft in distress reaches the ground."[80] I agree, with the exception that unlike an ordinary combatant a parachutist is to "be given an opportunity to surrender before being made the object of an attack, unless it is apparent that [the parachutist] is engaging in a hostile act."[81] Once the person evinces an intention not to surrender, the temporary immunity ceases; therefore, as a combatant they are liable to attack and not just capture or rendering *hors de combat*. As there is no general obligation to use only such force as is necessary in the circumstances to capture a combatant or render a combatant *hors de combat*, I can find no legal reason why this would be the case for an airman or airwomen who has left an aircraft in distress. Rather, such personnel may be attacked "if it becomes obvious by their commission of a hostile act that that they intend to continue combat."[82] As well as obviously hostile acts such as firing upon the opposing armed force, in this context hostile acts would also include "refuse[ing] to lay down arms or to surrender, [or trying] to escape".[83]

Having reviewed the lawfulness of attacks on combatants, the next issue is the lawfulness of attacks on civilians.

4.2 Civilians

Article 50 API divides the world into two neat categories for the purposes of targeting, which we can refer to as combatants and non-combatants. While the term non-combatant is not a defined term, it does have a popular meaning. While historically the term non-combatant was used to describe a *member of the armed forces* who was not a combatant,[84] the term is now usually used to mean *any person* who is not a combatant.[85] Therefore, in common parlance non-combatants are members of the armed forces who are exempt from attack[86] and civilians. It is important to

78 Quoted in Henckaerts and Doswald-Beck (eds), *Customary International Humanitarian Law*, vol II, above n 64 (chapter 1), 980.

79 Ibid, 978–86.

80 Rogers, *Law on the Battlefield*, above n 84 (chapter 1), 49.

81 API, above n 2 (chapter 1), art 42(2).

82 Oeter, above n 24 (chapter 2), 442.

83 Sandoz, Swinarski and Zimmerman (eds), above n 68 (chapter 1), [1651].

84 See generally Knut Ipsen, 'Combatants and Non-Combatants' in Dieter Fleck (ed), The *Handbook of Humanitarian Law in Armed Conflicts* (1995) 65, [313]. See also Sandoz, Swinarski and Zimmerman (eds), above n 68 (chapter 1), [1667]—"The armed forces of the belligerent parties may consist of combatants and noncombatants."

85 See Anthony Rogers, *Combatant Status*, Crimes of War Project <http://www.crimesofwar.org/thebook/combatant-status.html> at 27 April 2006.

86 Medical personnel, religious personnel, and, I would include in this category for targeting considerations, members of the armed forces exclusively and permanently assigned to civil defence organisations.

appreciate that the terms *civilian* and *non-combatant* are not synonyms, not the least of which because many of the IHL rules that apply to military personnel who are non-combatants are different from the IHL rules that apply to civilians. Therefore, in this section I use the term *civilian* in preference to the term *non-combatant*.

Article 50(1) API defines civilians as all personnel who do not belong to one of the groups that form the class of combatants (including non-combatant military personnel). This style of definition is a useful drafting tool to avoid any gaps through which (metaphorically) a person could fall. All persons who are not combatants are ipso facto civilians.[87] This is particularly important because article 51(2) then re-states one of, if not the most important principles of IHL: civilians, individually and collectively, enjoy general protection from attack.[88] The importance of this protection cannot be overstated. As Spaight wrote back in 1924:

> If a certain measure of immunity is to be granted to that portion of the population which does not engage actively in hostilities, it is obviously important that the line between that portion and the active, fighting portion should be sharply drawn and loyally maintained.[89]

Indeed, so important is the concept of protection for the civilian population, API provides that there is only one circumstance in which civilians lose their protection from direct attack and that is "*for such time* as they take a *direct part in hostilities*."[90] Unless a civilian is taking a direct part in hostilities, the civilian remains protected from attack. [91] There is not a third category of person, sometimes called a 'quasi-

---

87 Sandoz, Swinarski and Zimmerman (eds), above n 68 (chapter 1), [1913].

88 API, above n 2 (chapter 1), art 51(2).

89 Spaight, above n 1 (chapter 4), 59.

90 API, above n 2 (chapter 1), art 51(3) (emphasis added). It is perhaps worth noting that it is not a war crime or other offence for a civilian to take a direct part in hostilities. Rather, the consequences are that, first, a civilian so participating loses immunity from direct attack and, second, the civilian may be prosecuted under domestic law if the actions of the civilian amount to domestic crimes. See *Third Expert Meeting on the Notion of Direct Participation in Hostilities: Summary Report*, above n 53 (chapter 2), 9.

91 I note that in a 2007 report, Human Rights Watch made a mistake when it stated that:

> attacks may be carried out only against military objectives, defined as *persons*, objects or places whose nature, location, purpose or use make an effective contribution to military action, and whose destruction at that time offers a definite military advantage. (*Civilians under Assault: Hezbollah's Rocket Attacks on Israel in the 2006 War* (2007) Human Rights Watch, 7 <http://hrw.org/reports/2007/iopt0807/iopt0807webwcover.pdf> at 19 September 2007 (emphasis added))

That is the test for whether an object is a lawful target, not for whether a person is a lawful target. I do note that the correct test is stated in a 2003 Human Rights Watch report:

> Military objectives are members of the armed forces, other persons taking a direct part in hostilities for the duration of their participation, and "those objects which by their nature, location, purpose or use make an effective contribution to military action and whose total or partial destruction, capture or neutralization, in the circumstances ruling at the time, offers a definite military advantage." (*Off Target: The Conduct of the War and Civilian Casualties in Iraq* (2003) Human

combatant'[92] or 'unlawful combatant'.[93] As recently held by the Israeli Supreme Court (sitting as the High Court of Justice):

> We shall take no stance regarding the question whether it is desirable to recognize this third category [of unlawful combatants]. The question before us is not one of desirable law, rather one of existing law. In our opinion, as far as existing law goes, the data before us are not sufficient to recognize this third category. That is the case according to the current state of international law, both international treaty law and customary international law … It is difficult for us to see how a third category can be recognized in the framework of the *Hague* and *Geneva Conventions*.[94]

It is incorrect to suggest that a civilian who significantly contributes to the military operations but not to the extent of taking a direct part in hostilities becomes a quasi-combatant and by so being is subject to attack.[95] Equally, just because there is a "military rationale for an attack on civilians does not transform those targeted into valid military objectives".[96]

For such a significant provision, exactly what is meant by taking a *direct part of hostilities* is not settled.[97] It has been described as a "currently vague notion".[98] Indeed, in the context of a case involving, inter alia, alleged crimes against persons taking no direct part in hostilities, it was held by the trial chamber of the ICTY:

> It is unnecessary to define exactly the line dividing those taking an active part in hostilities and those who are not so involved. It is sufficient to examine the rel-

Rights Watch, 8 <http://www.hrw.org/reports/2003/usa1203/usa1203.pdf> at 4 November 2007)

92 This term is usually used when dealing with civilians who make a substantial contribution to the war effort but do not bear arms—eg, munition factory workers.

93 This term is usually used when dealing with civilians who do regularly bear arms but do not meet the criteria for combatant status.

94 *The Public Committee against Torture in Israel v The Government of Israel*, HCJ 769/02 (13 December 2006) [28] (Barak P (emeritus), Beinisch P concurring). Rivlin V-P generally concurred with Barak P (emeritus) but partly dissents from this point at para 2 of his honour's judgement. See also Mark Maxwell, 'The Law of War and Civilians on the Battlefield: Are We Undermining Civilian Protections?' (2004) September-October *Military Review* 17, 17 and 19 <http://usacac.leavenworth.army.mil/cac/milreview/download/English/SepOct04/maxm.pdf> at 8 March 2007; Sandoz, Swinarski and Zimmerman (eds), above n 68 (chapter 1), [1677].

95 See CE/3b, above n 27 (chapter 3), 21; Dinstein, *The Conduct of Hostilities under the Law of International Armed Conflict*, above n 66 (chapter 2), 124.

96 *Civilians under Assault: Hezbollah's Rocket Attacks on Israel in the 2006 War*, above n 91 (chapter 4), 7.

97 Schmitt, '"Direct participation in hostilities" and 21st century armed conflict' above n 58 (chapter 1), 507.

98 *Third Expert Meeting on the Notion of Direct Participation in Hostilities: Summary Report*, above n 53 (chapter 2), 6.

> evant facts of each victim and to ascertain whether, in each individual's circumstances, that person was actively involved in hostilities at the relevant time.[99]

This point was not overruled on appeal. While it is an understandable approach, a clear difficulty with this line of reasoning is the question of how is a civilian to know beforehand whether his or her conduct amounts to a direct participation in hostilities. Should not combatants have a test available to them so they can determine, with as much certainty as the fog of war allows, whether a civilian is a lawful target or not?

The main problem is where to draw the line between a civilian who undertakes an activity that contributes indirectly and remotely to military action and a civilian who by his or her actions presents an immediate and clear physical danger to an opposing combatant. The ICRC was well aware of this issue during the conferences that resulted in the adoption of API. A suggested draft clause presented to the 1971 *Conference of Government Experts on the Reaffirmation and Development of International Humanitarian Law Applicable in Armed Conflicts* explicitly drew a distinction between civilians who took part in military operations—and thereby lost protection from attack—and civilians whose activities contributed directly to the military effort—and who thereby did not lose protection from attack.[100] The ICRC also presented an alternative draft clause where civilians who took part in military operations were mentioned explicitly but civilians whose activities contributed directly to the military effort were not mentioned. The commentary on the two clauses states that the clauses contain the same idea, with the second clause requiring an "interpretation a contrario."[101] Romania also put forward an amendment at the 1974–77 *Diplomatic Conference on the Reaffirmation and Development of International Humanitarian Law Applicable in Armed Conflicts*, which would have put this matter beyond doubt.[102]

That the interpretation of article 51(3) API remains controversial is attested to by the fact that the ICRC, in cooperation with the TMC Asser Institute, has already held three expert meetings (in 2003, 2004 and 2005) to discuss the issue.[103] The next two sections contain discussion in some detail of article 51(3) API and in particular the meaning of the words *for such time* and *direct part in hostilities*. Before moving to the next section, there are two important points to note. The exemption from immunity from attack set out in article 51(3) API applies only to civilians per se. Where a person is in fact a combatant under the extended definition provided for in article 44(3) API, such a person is liable to attack at all times; not just when

99 *Prosecutor v Tadic*, (*Trial Chamber*) Case No IT-94-1 (7 May 1997) [616]. The judgment refers to *active* part in hostilities as the case dealt with common art 3 of the 1949 Geneva Conventions. However, the court's reasoning can also be applied to API, above n 2 (chapter 1), art 51(3).

100 CE/3b, above n 27 (chapter 3), 26.

101 Ibid (underlying in original).

102 "Persons whose activity may contribute directly to the military effort do not for that reason lose their civilian status." (CDDH/III, above n 28 (chapter 3), 199)

103 See *Direct Participation in Hostilities*, above n 66 (chapter 1). I understand a fourth and final meeting was held in 2006, but at the time of finalising this study a report of that meeting was still not available.

and for such time as they take a direct part in hostilities. In considering the correct interpretation of article 51(3) API, it is worth recalling that as article 51(3) API "is an exception to the duty to refrain from causing harm to innocent civilians, great caution must be employed when removing the law's protection of the lives of civilians in the appropriate circumstances."[104]

4.2.1 For such time

A civilian loses their protection from attack only *for such time* as they take a direct part in hostilities. This is a clear temporal limitation on the loss of immunity from attack and can be compared to the limitation of an object being a military objective only "in the circumstances ruling at the time".[105] Unlike combatants who lose protection from attack by the act of becoming a combatant,[106] a civilian does not lose protection from attack once and for all by a single act of taking a direct part in hostilities. If a civilian farmer were to take a direct part in hostilities by shooting at the enemy and then if that farmer is observed farming two days after shooting upon an armed force, the farmer cannot be attacked. Rather, if any action is to be taken, an attempt must be made to arrest the farmer. The farmer has regained immunity from attack; however, the farmer nonetheless would be subject to penal sanction for his or her activities in the hostilities.[107] Of course, reasonable force, including, if required by the circumstances, lethal force,[108] could be used in effecting the arrest.

Not only does one act of taking a direct part in hostilities not result in future loss of protection from attack, but strictly interpreted article 51(3) API seems to mean that a civilian can take direct part in hostilities, go back to farming, take part in hostilities again, go back to farming and so on and still be immune from attack while farming.[109] This is often called the 'revolving door' problem.[110] After referring to the *ICRC Commentary* on *unless and for such time*, Schmitt writes:

> This explanation provokes the notorious 'revolving door' debate. Can an individual be a guerrilla by night and a farmer by day? Do illegal combatants regain their immunity from direct attack whenever they successfully return from an operation, only to reenter the fray later?
>
> Again, in humanitarian law one must interpret gray area issues in light of the underlying purposes of the law. If civilians could repeatedly opt in and out of hostilities, combatants victimized by their activities will quickly lose respect for

---

104 *The Public Committee against Torture in Israel v The Government of Israel*, HCJ 769/02 (13 December 2006) (Beinisch P).

105 See API, above n 2 (chapter 1), art 52(2).

106 For example, by joining the armed forces or becoming part of a militia.

107 Unless the participation in hostilities was as part of a *levee en masse*—GCIII, above n 7 (chapter 2), art 4(A)(6).

108 Noting that in our example the alleged crime would probably be murder or attempted murder.

109 See Parks, 'Air War and the Law of War', above n 181 (chapter 3), 118.

110 Schmitt, '"Direct participation in hostilities" and 21st century armed conflict', above n 58 (chapter 1), 510.

> the law, thereby exposing the civilian population as a whole to greater danger. Moreover, the greater their susceptibility to attack, the greater their incentive to stay out of the conflict. The best approach is therefore the only one that is practical in actual combat operations. Once an individual has opted into the hostilities, he or she remains a valid military objective until unambiguously opting out. This may occur through extended non-participation or an affirmative act of withdrawal. Further, since the individual who directly participated did not enjoy any privilege to engage in hostilities, it is reasonable that he or she assume the risk that the other side is unaware of such withdrawal.[111]

The difficulty with Schmitt's article at this point is that it is hard to discern whether he is offering an interpretation of the law or a view as to what the law should be. Certainly his line of argument does not seem to be supported by the wording of article 51(3) API. Indeed, it has been suggested that it has "to be recognized that the phenomenon of the 'revolving door' was not only unavoidable but even intended by the drafters of the Protocols."[112] Accordingly, whereas Schmitt's point makes a lot of sense, I must disagree with Schmitt's view as a matter of current law. The only time a civilian loses complete protection from attack is where that person's direct participation in hostilities is so continuous as to amount to uninterrupted participation. This last point is supported by the judgment of the Israeli Supreme Court:

> a civilian who ... commits a chain of hostilities, with short periods of rest between them, loses his immunity from attack "for such time" as he is committing the chain of acts. Indeed, regarding such a civilian, the rest between hostilities is nothing other than preparation for the next hostility.[113]

Admittedly, this issue is further complicated where the civilian is not acting alone but as part of an organised armed group. The:

> IHL applicable in such situations remains unclear as to whether members of organized armed groups are "civilians"—and thus subject to direct attack only for such time as they directly participated in the hostilities—or whether they can be directly attacked according to the same principles as members of state armed forces, that is to say, irrespective of their individual direct participation in hostilities.[114]

In my view, the better approach is that, assuming that the organised armed group does not meet the criteria for combatant status, the members of the group remain civilians. As held by the Israeli Supreme Court, there are only two categories of

111 Ibid.

112 *Third Expert Meeting on the Notion of Direct Participation in Hostilities: Summary Report*, above n 53 (chapter 2), 50.

113 *The Public Committee against Torture in Israel v The Government of Israel*, HCJ 769/02 (13 December 2006) [39] (Barak P (emeritus), Rivlin V-P and Beinisch P concurring).

114 *Third Expert Meeting on the Notion of Direct Participation in Hostilities: Summary Report*, above n 53 (chapter 2), 41.

personnel under IHL—combatants and civilians.[115] However, to the extent that they are part of the armed faction of the group they can for the period of membership be considered as taking a direct part in hostilities.[116] The periods between actual acts of hostility are "nothing other than preparation for the next hostility."[117] By becoming a member of the armed faction of an organised armed group, a person's direct participation in hostilities is ipso facto so continuous as to amount to uninterrupted participation. I acknowledge that this approach has some limitations. In particular:

> Not only is there is no clear and generally accepted definition of 'organized armed group', but the practical identification of membership in such groups is also a serious problem.[118]

However, it is my view that this is where the jurisprudential work should focus. In addition, intelligence agencies are well practiced in endeavouring to identify both criteria and facts by which persons can be associated with various groups. If IHL and militaries can deal with the concept of a *levee en masse*, then I suggest the concept of an organised armed group should be able to be equally accommodated.

Schmitt identifies another issue, namely:

> A second issue lacking clarity is the temporal boundary of direct participation. Specifically, when does direct participation cease, such that the individual involved may no longer be directly targeted?[119]

While Schmitt introduces this issue just before his discussion of the revolving door problem, the point he raises has another context. Namely, is the time spent preparing for and returning from combat operations to be considered as part of direct participation in hostilities or are these periods outside of that period? This issue remained the subject of divergent views at the 1974–77 *Diplomatic Conference*[120] and the various views are discussed at some length in the *ICRC Commentary*.[121]

I agree with the view expressed by a number of the delegates to the Diplomatic Conference that the time period should also include the time spent directly prepar-

115 *The Public Committee against Torture in Israel v The Government of Israel*, HCJ 769/02 (13 December 2006) [28] (Barak P (emeritus), Beinisch P concurring). Rivlin V-P generally concurred with Barak P (emeritus) but partly dissents from this point at para 2 of his honour's judgement.

116 *Third Expert Meeting on the Notion of Direct Participation in Hostilities: Summary Report*, above n 53 (chapter 2), 44 and 48.

117 *The Public Committee against Torture in Israel v The Government of Israel*, HCJ 769/02 (13 December 2006) [39] (Barak P (emeritus), Rivlin V-P and Beinisch P concurring).

118 *Third Expert Meeting on the Notion of Direct Participation in Hostilities: Summary Report*, above n 53 (chapter 2), 53.

119 Schmitt, '"Direct participation in hostilities" and 21st century armed conflict', above n 58 (chapter 1), 509.

120 Sandoz, Swinarski and Zimmerman (eds), above n 68 (chapter 1), [1714]. See also below n 123 (chapter 4).

121 Ibid, [1706–1714].

ing for and returning from combat.[122] Just what this encompasses though is still not completely clear. For instance, does it mean just any movement towards the place of a military operation (eg, from the time of departure from the assembly area) or does it just mean the final movement towards a firing position?[123] There appears to be no reason why the period should not also include the deployment phase of military operations, as at this stage a civilian has clearly indicated an intention to take part in hostilities.[124] It would be illogical if the law provided that a civilian who, perhaps in company with other civilians, is travelling with explosives for the purpose of destroying military equipment is immune from attack until he or she is within manoeuvring distance of the desired objective.

4.2.2 Direct part in hostilities

When put forward in draft form in 1971, the intent behind the draft wording that became article 51(3) API was to deal with acts "such as to cause damage [to the adversary, on the military level] in the ordinary course of events and according to experience of armed conflicts."[125] Most commentary on the meaning of taking a direct part in hostilities is consistent with a view that the phrase "usually means

---

122 CDDH/XV, above n 98 (chapter 3), 274 and 330; Bothe, Partsch and Solf, above n 87 (chapter 1), 303; *Third Expert Meeting on the Notion of Direct Participation in Hostilities: Summary Report*, above n 53 (chapter 2), 61.

123 See Sandoz, Swinarski and Zimmerman (eds), above n 68 (chapter 1), [1709–14], where the meaning of "military deployment preceding the launching of an attack" in API, above n 2 (chapter 1), art 44 is discussed. The differing views of the delegates to the 1974–77 *Diplomatic Conference on the Reaffirmation and Development of International Humanitarian Law Applicable in Armed Conflicts* were clearly influenced by their position on non-State armed groups fighting wars against colonial domination, alien occupation or racist regimes. This divide also appeared to affect a State's understanding on the purpose behind, what is now, API, art 44(3). States who were in favour of a broader interpretation of the meaning of "deployment" generally emphasised that the purpose of API, art 44(3) was to ensure protection of the civilian population by maintaining a minimum acceptable level of distinction, while States who favoured a much narrower interpretation tended to emphasise that guerrilla fighters needed to operate successfully and this required them to be able to move about undetected as much as possible. States who were in favour of a broader interpretation included Israel, Australia, the United Kingdom, the Federal Republic of Germany, the Netherlands, the United States of America, and Japan (CDDH/VI, above n 77 (chapter 2), at pages 123, 128, 132, 135, 142, 150, 151 respectively), and the Republic of Korea, Australia, the Federal Republic of Germany, the Netherlands, Canada, the United States of America (CDDH/XV, above n 98 (chapter 3), at pages 162, 165, 167, 171, 176, 179 respectively). States who favoured a much narrower interpretation included Egypt, the United Arab Emirates, the Observer for the Palestine Liberation Organization, Qatar (CDDH/VI, above n 77 (chapter 2), at pages 145, 146, 148, and 149 respectively), and the Democratic Republic of Viet – nam, Egypt, the Syrian Arab Republic, the Palestine Liberation Organization (CDDH/XV, above n 98 (chapter 3), at pages 138, 160, 161, 184 respectively). For a summary of the positions and rationales, see CDDH/XV, above n 98 (chapter 3), 453–4. The meaning of 'military deployment' was left for later defining (CDDH/XV, above n 98 (chapter 3), 138), which did not occur. For a statement of the purposes behind API, art 44(3), see CDDH/XV, above n 98 (chapter 3), 402–3.

124 Rogers, *Law on the Battlefield*, above n 84 (chapter 1), 11.

125 CE/3b, above n 27 (chapter 3), 28.

attacking enemy combatants or military objectives"[126] or "engaging in acts of war directed toward enemy personnel or materiel."[127] The ICTY has held that to "take a 'direct' part in the hostilities means acts of war which by their nature or purpose are likely to cause actual harm to the personnel or materiel of the enemy armed forces".[128] The fact that such acts meet the test is uncontroversial. More challenging perhaps is the identification of acts that do not amount to taking a direct part in hostilities.

When looking to interpret API in general, and article 51 in particular, it is important to realise that the concept of wars being fought by nations with entire populations contributing to the war effort pre-dates API. As Solf[129] wrote in 1986:

> The Napoleonic war and the French Revolution put an end to the era of limited warfare. Thereafter, wars were fought by entire nations in arms. The entire population was mobilized for the war effort, blurring the distinction between combatants and civilians, putting great strain on the customary law of war.[130]

The negotiators and drafters of API were aware of the roles civilians can perform in wartime and the need to resolve the issue.[131] So, if desired, they could have chosen to make workers in a munitions factory the subject of attack or exempt for the proportionality equation. And similar to my earlier comment about economic targets, in both World War I and World War II "the bulk of the adult population was engaged in some activity concerned with the war effort."[132] Nonetheless, API did not make provision for targeting civilians engaged in the war effort in circumstances other than when they "take a direct part in hostilities."[133] I open with these comments to emphasise that the wording of articles 50 and 51 API were not produced either in a vacuum or in a time where armed conflicts were significantly simpler than they are in the early 21st century.

A useful starting point for interpreting what would amount to taking a direct part in hostilities is to look at what it is lawful for a combatant and only a combatant to do. This is often called the combatant's privilege. So, what is the combatant's privilege? Peter Rowe provides a standard but well expressed definition when he writes:

> Soldiers have rights, insofar as they are members of the armed forces, as defined in international humanitarian law (IHL). They are known as combatants and have the right to *participate directly in hostilities*. This means, in practical terms, that

126 Rogers, *Combatant Status*, above n 85 (chapter 4).

127 Air Force Pamphlet 14-210 Intelligence, above n 53 (chapter 1), [A4.2.1.1].

128 *Prosecutor v Galic, (Trial Chamber)* Case No IT-98-29-T (5 December 2003) [48].

129 Amongst other things, Solf was a member of the US Delegation to the Diplomatic Conference on International Humanitarian Law, 1974–77.

130 Solf, above n 90 (chapter 2), 120.

131 CE/3b, above n 27 (chapter 3), 27–8. See Gardam, *Non-combatant Immunity as a Norm of International Humanitarian Law*, above n 28 (chapter 4), 113.

132 Robertson Jr, above n 105 (chapter 1), 47.

133 API, above n 2 (chapter 1), art 50(3).

> combatants are entitled to attack enemy forces, kill or injure them, and destroy property as part of military operations—activities that if done not in wartime or not by combatants would all be criminal behavior.[134]

It is helpful to consider Rowe's statement in light of a similarly useful statement in the *ICRC Commentary*:

> Direct participation in hostilities implies a direct causal relationship between the activity engaged in and the harm done to the enemy at the time and the place where the activity takes place.[135]

Taken together, we can see that to amount to a 'direct participation in hostilities', it is not enough to look at the result of an act performed by a person (ie, death or injury to enemy forces or destruction of property), but also was there a sufficiently direct casual relationship between that act and the result.

It has been suggested that "the illegality or legality of an act of civilian violence under domestic or international law is irrelevant for its qualification as direct participation in hostilities."[136] While only a rule of thumb test and not a strict legal test, it is my view that considering whether the actions of a civilian amount to criminal behaviour goes a fair way towards determining whether those actions might amount to taking a direct part in hostilities. The reverse, however, is not true, and some lawful activities may still amount to taking a direct part in hostilities (eg, see the discussion on coast-watch activities below).

Solf writes that the protection afforded to a civilian from attack is lost "in the event of direct participation in hostilities with the *intent* to cause physical harm to enemy personnel and objects."[137] When read in context, it is my view that this sentence should not be understood to mean that *intent* in the criminal law sense is required. That would be practical only in a trial and not during the heat of battle. Rather, I understand that Solf was defining direct participation in hostilities as meaning actions *likely* to directly lead to causing 'physical harm to enemy personnel and objects', as opposed to actions that unexpectedly have that result. For example, one expert has suggested "that the stealing of military equipment, as opposed to the actual use of such equipment in hostilities, should not be regarded as sufficient to qualify as direct participation in hostilities."[138] I disagree. From a military operational perspective, having equipment stolen is just as detrimental to operational effectiveness as having that equipment damaged or destroyed.[139] Soldiers cannot

134 Peter Rowe, *Soldiers, Rights of*, Crimes of War Project <http://www.crimesofwar.org/thebook/soldiers-rights-of.html> at 26 May 2006 (emphasis added).

135 Sandoz, Swinarski and Zimmerman (eds), above n 68 (chapter 1), [1679].

136 *Third Expert Meeting on the Notion of Direct Participation in Hostilities: Summary Report*, above n 53 (chapter 2), 9.

137 Solf, above n 90 (chapter 2), 130 (footnote omitted) (emphasis added).

138 *Third Expert Meeting on the Notion of Direct Participation in Hostilities: Summary Report*, above n 53 (chapter 2), 27.

139 Arguably more so. Stolen equipment can be used against an armed force and also can be exploited for intelligence value.

be expected to have to arrest and interrogate a person to determine the motivation behind that person's action. Whether an act amounts to direct participation in hostilities must be assessed on objective criteria and not on the subjective intent of the participant.[140]

The *ICRC Commentary* states that taking a direct part in hostilities should be understood to be acts "which by their nature and purpose are likely to cause actual harm to the personnel and equipment" of the armed forces.[141] While I am in general agreement with this statement in the *ICRC Commentary*, it does warrant some further comment. In my view, it would seem as a matter of practicality that in some circumstances the word *likely* should be given a broad meaning to include possible and not just probable. So, for instance, a civilian firing a light weapon on a heavily defended location surely must be considered to be taking a direct part in hostilities, regardless of the likelihood of injury. It is the act of "opening fire at members of the enemy armed forces"[142] that constitutes taking a direct part in hostilities, regardless of the likelihood of successfully harming those armed forces.[143] As argued above, an armed force that is being fired upon cannot be expected to make fine judgments about the likelihood of actual harm being caused. Also, the forces being shot at cannot be expected to know exactly what types of weapons are available to the attacker at the given time. My interpretation is also consistent with the definition given just two paragraphs earlier in the *ICRC Commentary*, where it states:

> Hostile acts should be understood to be acts which by their nature and purpose are *intended* to cause actual harm to the personnel and equipment of the armed forces.[144]

While not necessarily excluded by the definition in the *ICRC Commentary*,[145] it is also my view of the law that civilians lose their protection from attack not just when they are personally firing a weapon but also when they are acting as part of a weapon system. If a civilian is acting as a forward observer for the purposes of guiding an artillery barrage, then clearly in those circumstances the civilian is taking a direct part in hostilities.[146]

As a way of determining how directly involved a civilian is in acts of hostilities, Schmitt suggests:

---

140 *Third Expert Meeting on the Notion of Direct Participation in Hostilities: Summary Report*, above n 53 (chapter 2), 34.

141 Sandoz, Swinarski and Zimmerman (eds), above n 68 (chapter 1), [1944].

142 Rogers, *Law on the Battlefield*, above n 84 (chapter 1), 11.

143 See *Third Expert Meeting on the Notion of Direct Participation in Hostilities: Summary Report*, above n 53 (chapter 2), 31.

144 Sandoz, Swinarski and Zimmerman (eds), above n 68 (chapter 1), [1942] (emphasis added).

145 The first one quoted at para 1944 of Sandoz, Swinarski and Zimmerman (eds), above n 68 (chapter 1)—see above n 141 (chapter 4).

146 Bothe, Partsch and Solf, above n 87 (chapter 1), 303; *Third Expert Meeting on the Notion of Direct Participation in Hostilities: Summary Report*, above n 53 (chapter 2), 31.

> Perhaps the best tack when analyzing a particular act is assessing the criticality of the act to the direct application of violence against the enemy. Consider intelligence. Rendering strategic-level geopolitical estimates is certainly central to the war effort, but will have little bearing on specific combat missions. By contrast, tactical intelligence designed to locate and identify fleeting targets is the sine qua non of time-sensitive targeting; it is an integral component of the application of force against particular targets. Civilians providing strategic analysis would not be directly participating in hostilities, whereas those involved in the creation, analysis, and dissemination of tactical intelligence to the "shooter" generally would.[147]

I agree with Schmitt's distinction between various levels of intelligence activity. In support, I note that the Israeli Supreme Court has held that a person providing "general strategic analysis" would not be taking a direct part in hostilities.[148] Similarly, Rogers lists "assessing aerial photography for likely targets" as one of his examples of acts that do not amount to taking a direct part in hostilities.[149] An analogy could be made with arms production or distribution in a rear area[150] compared with the delivery of munitions to soldiers in contact with the enemy.[151] Where a civilian merely contributes to "building up the capacity of a party to a conflict to harm its adversary",[152] this should not be viewed as taking a direct part in hostilities. I would join in with those experts who are of the view that "only intelligence gathering that had a direct connection to attack or defence should be regarded as part of the hostilities."[153] In military terms, there is a distinction between strategic intelligence gathering and tactical intelligence gathering; with only the latter amounting to the taking of a direct part in hostilities.[154] This is consistent with the *ICRC Commentary*, which states:

> Direct participation in hostilities implies a direct causal relationship between the activity engaged in and the harm done to the enemy at the time and the place where the activity takes place.[155]

---

147 Schmitt, 'Humanitarian Law and Direct Participation in Hostilities by Private Contractors or Civilian Employees', above n 21 (chapter 1), 534.

148 *The Public Committee against Torture in Israel v The Government of Israel*, HCJ 769/02 (13 December 2006) [35] (Barak P (emeritus), Rivlin V-P and Beinisch P concurring). Other actions the court considered as not amounting to taking a direct part in hostilities include providing monetary aid and distributing propaganda.

149 Rogers, *Law on the Battlefield*, above n 84 (chapter 1), 11.

150 Which would not amount to taking a direct part in hostilities (Schmitt, '"Direct participation in hostilities" and 21st century armed conflict', above n 58 (chapter 1), 508).

151 Which would amount to taking a direct part in hostilities (Ibid, 50; *Third Expert Meeting on the Notion of Direct Participation in Hostilities: Summary Report*, above n 53 (chapter 2), 33).

152 *Third Expert Meeting on the Notion of Direct Participation in Hostilities: Summary Report*, above n 53 (chapter 2), 21.

153 Ibid, 22.

154 Ibid, 39.

155 Sandoz, Swinarski and Zimmerman (eds), above n 68 (chapter 1), [1679].

Schmitt writes:

> Direct participation, therefore, seemingly requires "but for" causation (i.e., the consequences would not have occurred but for the act) and causal proximity to the foreseeable consequences of the act. Returning to the ammunition truck driver, one who transports ammunition from the factory to ammunition depots would clearly not be directly participating; an individual who delivered it to the front lines, however, arguably would.[156]

Applying his own tests, Schmitt discusses a variety of contemporary situations in which civilians are involved in logistics and maintenance during armed conflicts. He draws a distinction between two different scenarios. One scenario is "regularly scheduled maintenance on equipment, even near the front, [which] does not impact in any direct way on specific operations",[157] and therefore does not in his view amount to direct participation in hostilities. The other is "preparing equipment for battle[, which] has a direct impact on the course of battle",[158] and which does in his view amount to direct participation in hostilities. The latter category includes "activities such as fueling aircraft, loading weapons, conducting preflight checks, performing life-support functions, and locally repairing minor battle damage".[159] Other examples that would amount to taking a direct part in hostilities include repairing target acquisition or missile guidance equipment in the middle of a battle,[160] and "driving ... ammunition to the place from which it will be used for the purposes of hostilities".[161] I agree with both of Schmitt's points, whilst fearing that his distinctions are legally neat but practically difficult.[162]

As can be deduced from the above discussion, merely being employed in the Ministry of Defence (howsoever called) does not cause a civilian to lose protection from attack.[163] This was suggested as a discrete category at the 1972 *Conference of Government Experts on the Reaffirmation and Development of International Humanitarian Law Applicable in Armed Conflicts* but was not adopted.[164] *A fortiori*,

156 Schmitt, '"Direct participation in hostilities" and 21st century armed conflict', above n 58 (chapter 1), 508.

157 Schmitt, 'Humanitarian Law and Direct Participation in Hostilities by Private Contractors or Civilian Employees', above n 21 (chapter 1), 545.

158 Ibid.

159 Ibid.

160 Bothe, Partsch and Solf, above n 87 (chapter 1), 304.

161 *The Public Committee against Torture in Israel v The Government of Israel*, HCJ 769/02 (13 December 2006) [35] (Barak P (emeritus), Rivlin V-P and Beinisch P concurring).

162 In light of my opinion on what is the current state of law, but the practical difficulties that may arise, see my comments at the end of section 4.2.3. In summary, it is my policy view that to ensure the greatest respect for the principle of distinction, and thereby to avoid or in any event minimize the risk to civilians, civilians should to the maximum extent possible be kept away from front-lines, combat areas and military installations.

163 Rogers, *Law on the Battlefield*, above n 84 (chapter 1), 11; *Why They Died: Civilian Casualties in Lebanon during the 2006 War*, above n 3 (chapter 2), 29.

164 CE 1972 Report, vol I, above n 25 (chapter 1), 144.

mere political support of a belligerent does not amount to direct participation in hostilities.[165]

Schmitt makes the very good point that proximity to the battlefield, or put another way, proximity to the point at which the harm to the enemy is manifested, is not directly relevant.[166] There is little difference between a civilian pulling a trigger on a rifle and a civilian hundreds or thousands of kilometres away controlling an unmanned aerial vehicle armed with air-to-surface missiles. And, of course, as the ICTY has held:

> There is no necessary correlation between the area where the actual fighting is taking place and the geographical reach of the laws of war. The laws of war apply in the whole territory of the warring states ... whether or not actual combat takes place there... A violation of the laws or customs of war may therefore occur at a time when and in a place where no fighting is actually taking place.[167]

It is partly due to this point that I agree with Schmitt's distinctions between different types of maintenance activity. If the civilian who performs routine scheduled maintenance on an aircraft in a rear area well removed from the theatre of operations is not liable to attack, why should a similar civilian be merely because that State has opted to have maintenance conducted closer to or in the theatre of operations? Or to take the 1991 Gulf War, is the American civilian aircraft maintainer in the continental United States of America immune from attack when his or her Iraqi counterpart is liable to attack merely because the main bombing operations are occurring over Iraqi territory? Equally, therefore, the civilian who refuels the long-range bomber many thousands of kilometres from the intended target is as much liable to attack as the civilian who refuels a military aircraft while enemy aircraft are circling overhead.

The term *direct part in hostilities* is also used in article 77(2) API in relation to the participation of children who have not yet attained the age of 15 years. The *ICRC Commentary* on this article states:

> Can this lead to the conclusion that indirect acts of participation are not covered? Examples would include, in particular, gathering and transmission of military information, transportation of arms and munitions, provision of supplies etc.[168]

In my view, the examples listed are indirect only when considered in light of the discussion above. For example, transportation of munitions is indirect only when

---

165 *Why They Died: Civilian Casualties in Lebanon during the 2006 War*, above n 3 (chapter 2), 8.

166 Schmitt, '"Direct participation in hostilities" and 21st century armed conflict', above n 58 (chapter 1), 510–2.

167 *Prosecutor v Kunarac, Kovac and Vukovic, (Appeals Chamber)* Case No IT-96-23&23/1 (12 June 2002) [57] (footnote omitted).

168 Sandoz, Swinarski and Zimmerman (eds), above n 68 (chapter 1), [3187].

not related to immediate hostilities. When ammunition is being delivered to soldiers in the midst of battle, such actions are a direct participation in hostilities.[169]

With respect to article 13(3) APII,[170] the ICTR has held: "To take a 'direct' part in the hostilities means acts of war which by their nature or purpose are likely to cause actual harm to the personnel and equipment of the enemy armed forces."[171] The court delivered a similar ruling in *Prosecutor v Semanza*,[172] where the court held that to "take a direct part in hostilities means, for the purposes of these provisions, to engage in acts of war that strike at personnel or equipment of the enemy armed forces."[173] The provisions being referred to are common article 3 of the 1949 Geneva Conventions and article 4(1) APII. This is interesting, because while article 4(1) APII refers to persons "who do not take a direct part … in hostilities", common article 3 refers to persons "taking no active part in the hostilities". It would seem that the test propounded by the ICTR would certainly be applicable to the wording of article 51(3) API. However, it is not clear whether the test espoused should be considered as stating what *can* amount to taking a direct part in hostilities or whether the test was meant to be an exhaustive definition. Due to the facts of the cases, the ICTR does not appear to have considered examples such as a civilian of State B attempting to destroy a bridge on an important route of advance. In such circumstances, the civilian could not be considered immune from attack.[174] Therefore, in my view the better interpretation of the ICTR cases is that taking a direct part in hostilities includes, but is not limited to, causing harm to personnel or equipment of the other side.[175] In addition, taking a direct part in hostilities includes activities directly intended to impede the military operations of the opposing Party, including acts of sabotage.[176] Likewise, a civilian who was covertly engaging in espionage and is now about to transmit intelligence by radio that would limit the successfulness of a military operation would be taking a direct part in hostilities. Indeed, article 16 of HAW states that the "term 'hostilities' includes the transmission during flight of military intelligence for the *immediate* use of a belligerent."[177] Take, for example, the interesting case of civilians acting as coast watchers in their own territory and thereby providing advance warning of the approach of enemy forces.[178] While such activities are clearly completely lawful (both under local domestic law

169 Bothe, Partsch and Solf, above n 87 (chapter 1), 303.

170 APII, above n 61 (chapter 1), art 13(3) is similar to API, above n 2 (chapter 1), art 51(3) but for non-international armed conflicts.

171 *Prosecutor v Rutaganda, (Trial Chamber)* Case No ICTR-96-3-T (6 December 1999) [100].

172 *Prosecutor v Semanza, (Trial Chamber)* Case No ICTR-97-20-T (15 May 2003).

173 Ibid, [363–6]. This aspect of the ruling was not addressed in the separate dissenting opinions, nor was it challenged on the appeal.

174 See Rogers, *Law on the Battlefield*, above n 84 (chapter 1), 11.

175 See *Third Expert Meeting on the Notion of Direct Participation in Hostilities: Summary Report*, above n 53 (chapter 2), 14.

176 Bothe, Partsch and Solf, above n 87 (chapter 1), 303.

177 Emphasis added.

178 See, for example, the activities of civilians, including clergy, in the Pacific during World War II referred to in Parks, 'Air War and the Law of War', above n 181 (chapter 3), 132 (fn 396).

and clearly there is no aspect of 'spying'), such civilians are, nonetheless, taking a direct part in hostilities and are liable to attack.

The final point I wish to make in this section is that a civilian does not take a direct part in hostilities or become an actual combatant merely by engaging in activities that are politically or even legally unacceptable to the other Party. To take the situation in Kosovo in 1999 as an example, the police force of the Federal Republic of Yugoslavia were attacking a particular group of their own fellow citizens and were not attacking NATO forces.[179] The citizens being attacked were not acting, generally speaking, in concert with NATO forces. Accordingly, these actions alone did not make members of the Federal Republic of Yugoslavia police force combatants as defined in API,[180] other treaties or customary international law; nor could they legally have been classified as civilians taking a direct part in hostilities under article 51(3) API.[181] The result is that NATO could not rely on IHL rules concerning attack on combatants as a legal basis to target the Federal Republic of Yugoslavia police.[182] If the opposite was the case, an attacking Party could lawfully attack any person whose actions were contrary to the stated political or strategic aims of the attacker. This is completely antithetical to the preamble to the *St Petersburg Declaration of 1868*.[183] However, this does not mean that force could not be used to protect innocent civilians from attack, ethnic cleansing or genocide.[184] Rather, what I am arguing is that IHL is not the apposite legal paradigm to regulate the use of force in such a situation.

4.2.3 Direct contribution to the war effort: factory workers and scientists

A civilian loses immunity from direct attack if he or she takes a direct part in hostilities. A problem of interpretation arises because "conventional IHL made exten-

179 Peter Rowe, 'Kosovo 1999: The Air Campaign—Have the Provisions of Additional Protocol I Withstood the Test?' (2000) 837 *International Review of the Red Cross* <http://www.icrc.org/Web/eng/siteengo.nsf/iwpList177/B98F42CBD37BB2D3C1256B66005E3504> at 4 June 2006.

180 Unless API, above n 2 (chapter 1), art 43(3) had been complied with.

181 See Rowe, 'Kosovo 1999: The Air Campaign—Have the Provisions of Additional Protocol I Withstood the Test?', above n 179 (chapter 4). However, it is not completely clear whether my view on this point is contrary to that of Rowe. While Rowe discusses the issue, he does not clearly state his position on the point. Note that in *The Public Committee against Torture in Israel v The Government of Israel*, HCJ 769/02 (13 December 2006) [33] (Barak P (emeritus), Rivlin V-P and Beinisch P concurring), the court stated that "acts which by nature and objective are intended to cause damage to civilians should be added to [the definition of taking a direct part in hostilities]". I suggest that from the context of the decision the court was referring to acts against the civilians of State A by non-State A actors, and not acts by State A itself against its own civilians.

182 A view has also been expressed that "the mere fact of attacking civilians would not constitute [direct participation in hostilities] unless such attacks were used as a means of facilitating future military operations"—*Second Expert Meeting: Direct Participation in Hostilities under International Humanitarian Law: Summary Report* (2004) International Committee of the Red Cross, 4 <http://www.icrc.org/Web/Eng/siteengo.nsf/iwpList74/459B0FF70176F4E5C1256DDE00572DAA> at 10 April 2006.

183 See the discussion at section 3.1.

184 See *Expert Meeting: "Targeting Military Objectives"*, above n 27 (chapter 1), 11–12.

sive use of the notion of "hostilities" without, however, providing a definition [of that term]."[185] As a result, there is some uncertainty over whether a civilian working in a munitions factory, or a civilian scientist conducting weapons research, is taking a direct part in hostilities.

Workers in factories that are seen to be integral to an enemy's military capability have long been considered as lawful targets by some and as targets that should be lawful by others. For example:

> Lauterpacht, as editor of Oppenheim in 1952 ... conceded that the principle of immunity of non-combatants does not mean absolute immunity, and that sections of the civilian population 'closely identified with military objectives proper' may be legitimately exposed to air attack.[186]

And writing in 1954 on air warfare, Stone stated that there should be a distinction between what he called "true civilians" and civilians "in the hinterland who make, equip or service the aeroplanes, tanks, ships, and munitions, and the multitude of machine tools and precision instruments on which military success depends."[187] In Stones's view, the latter group should be lawful targets both at work and while at home.[188] Whether or not this was the position under customary international law in the 1950s,[189] this is not the case under API.

First, and as we have seen above, factory workers are not combatants. Therefore, the only basis on which they could lose protection from attack is by taking a direct part in hostilities. However, while the concept of *hostilities* is wider than the concept of *attack* as used in API, it is nonetheless not synonymous with the armed conflict as a whole.[190] The requirement of taking a direct part in hostilities is narrower than merely making a direct contribution to the war effort.[191] As Rowe argues, contributing to the war effort by way of arms production, military engineering works or military transportation does not amount to taking a direct part in hostilities.[192] Even Hays Parks, who could not be considered as a proponent of limiting targeting options, notes that the aircraft of the Swiss Air Force are maintained by civilian factory workers but under API those civilians remain protected from direct attack.[193] Accordingly, a factory worker is not considered to be taking a direct part

185 *Third Expert Meeting on the Notion of Direct Participation in Hostilities: Summary Report*, above n 53 (chapter 2), 17.

186 Louise Doswald-Beck, 'The Value of the 1977 Geneva Protocols for the Protection of Civilians' in Michael Meyer (ed), *Armed Conflict and the New Law: Aspects of the 1977 Geneva Protocols and the 1981 Weapons Convention* (1989) 137, 147 (footnote omitted).

187 Stone, above n 21 (chapter 4), 628.

188 Ibid, 629.

189 Due to his style of writing, it is difficult to determine on many points whether Stone is expressing a view of the law *lex lata* or *de lege ferenda*.

190 *Third Expert Meeting on the Notion of Direct Participation in Hostilities: Summary Report*, above n 53 (chapter 2), 17.

191 CE 1972 Report, vol I, above n 25 (chapter 1), 143.

192 Rogers, *Law on the Battlefield*, above n 84 (chapter 1), 8–9.

193 Parks, 'Air War and the Law of War', above n 181 (chapter 3), 132 (fn 397). See CE/3b, above n 27 (chapter 3), 39.

in hostilities even where the factory is involved in the production, distribution or storage of ammunition, tanks etc.[194]

In an example from World War II, Hays Parks refers to the role of a civilian scientific officer serving with the RAF's No. 604 Squadron. The scientific officer's role was the servicing of newly developed Mark VII air-intercept radar—a radar that was critical to the squadron's night air-intercept role. The scientific officer's expertise was essential to the servicing of the radar. Hays Parks concludes that the scientific officer would be immune from direct attack in accordance with article 51(3) API.[195] In my view, this is clearly the correct conclusion to draw if applying article 51(3) API. A civilian does not lose protection from attack just because of the value of his or her contribution to the war effort.[196]

A review of the reports of the 1971 and 1972 conferences of government experts, and the 1974–77 diplomatic conferences that negotiated API reveals that the delegates were aware of the roles many civilians played during WWII and other conflicts up to the early 1970s. If there was an intention to have included civilian scientists, technical maintenance workers or workers in munition factories, this could easily have been achieved. Instead, API clearly limits the loss of protection from attack to the much more limited circumstance of taking a direct part in hostilities and not just a direct part in the war effort.[197]

Solf comments on the same issue when discussing article 52(2) API:

> while a civilian may not lose his protection against individualized attack while working in a munitions plant, he assumes the risk of collateral injury when he is in the vicinity of the munitions plant, although he continues to retain full protection while at home.[198]

Solf's comment needs clarification. Under API, whereas a munitions worker may de facto assume the risk of an attack, de jure the munitions worker is still a civilian and accordingly must be counted as such when an attacker is estimating the expected collateral damage before determining the proportionality of the attack.[199] This is the same view taken by the United Kingdom's Ministry of Defence.[200]

While discussing the meaning of discrimination and article 48 API, Schmitt writes that "some have cited mission-essential civilians working at a base during

194 Bothe, Partsch and Solf, above n 87 (chapter 1), 294.

195 Parks, 'Air War and the Law of War', above n 181 (chapter 3), 127 (fn 386). Care must be taken when reading this article by Parks, as he is often contrasting the law under API with the law where API is not applicable. However, he is careful to distinguish between the two when making statements on the law, so a careful reader can distinguish the two as long as his words are read in context.

196 Rogers, *Law on the Battlefield*, above n 84 (chapter 1), 9.

197 CE/3b, above n 27 (chapter 3), 39.

198 Solf, above n 90 (chapter 2), 131.

199 See Sassoli, above n 47 (chapter 3), 9: "Military objectives, such as armament factories, may be attacked, and, subject to the principle of proportionality, the attack on a military objective does not become unlawful because of the risk that a civilian who works or is otherwise present in a military objective may be harmed by such an attack."

200 UK Ministry of Defence, above n 14 (chapter 1), [2.5.2] and [2.6.3].

hostilities, even though not directly engaging in acts of war, as legitimate targets."[201] However, the above argument concerning the civilian workforce in military objectives can be extrapolated to cover all forms of civilian activity that contribute to the war effort but do not amount to taking a direct part in hostilities. Indeed, this issue was specifically addressed in a draft clause presented to the 1971 *Conference of Government Experts on the Reaffirmation and Development of International Humanitarian Law Applicable in Armed Conflicts*. The clause provided that:

> civilians whose activities directly contribute to the military effort, assume, within the strict limits of these activities and when they are within a military objective, the risks resulting from an attack directed against that objective.[202]

This draft clause is not reflected in API. As will be further discussed in section 8.3.4, civilians inside a military objective remain both protected from direct attack and form part of the collateral damage equation when assessing the proportionality of an attack.[203]

In conclusion, it is my view that the rule that a civilian factory worker remains a non-combatant extends to other civilians engaged in contributions to a belligerent's war effort and that this is the case irrespective of that person's value, no matter how great, to that belligerent's war effort.

Schmitt raises a further interesting point:

> there is an increased proclivity ... to contract out many activities which previously were performed by military personnel, and which are integral to the effective conduct of military operations. The U.S. military, for example, has at times contracted out aircraft maintenance, security, transportation of troops and supplies, housing, and even training in basic combat functions. ...Clearly, if the trend towards militarizing civilian activities and civilianizing military ones continues, the consequences for the principle of discrimination are grave. There will be measurable pressure to interpret the universe of targetable objects and individuals more liberally than today simply because each side will seek to deny its opponent potential advantage.[204]

I agree with Schmitt's final point. Just because there are many activities that a civilian can perform without thereby losing protection from attack, this does not mean that it is good policy to adopt such a course of contracting out. Respect for IHL depends not only upon obeying the strict letter of the law but also a good-faith application. One wonders whether it truly is within the spirit of IHL to use civilians in quasi-military roles in combat areas or on military bases.[205]

The next class of civilian discussed is civilian leaders during wartime.

---

201 Michael Schmitt, 'The Principle of Discrimination in 21st Century Warfare' (1999) 2 *Yale Human Rights & Development Law Journal* 143, [13] (footnote omitted).

202 CE/3b, above n 27 (chapter 3), 38.

203 Rogers, *Law on the Battlefield*, above n 84 (chapter 1), 9.

204 Schmitt, 'The Principle of Discrimination in 21st Century Warfare', above n 201 (chapter 4), [42–3].

205 See generally Maxwell, above n 94 (chapter 4).

4.2.4 Heads of State and senior politicians

The status of Heads of State and other political leaders is an often-debated point in IHL discussions. There are three types of Heads of State and other political leaders relevant to this discussion. First, the military commander who is also the political leader. Second, the ceremonial commander-in-chief. Third, the civilian political leader with real authority. The lawfulness of targeting the first class is not really in doubt: such people are lawful targets.[206] However, as regards my second and third categories:

> Senior leaders who are not members of the armed forces, but lie in the chain of command, are more difficult to categorize. Their legitimacy as a target must be assessed contextually and holistically.[207]

In practice, there is little concern about the ceremonial commanders-in-chief, as it is realized that they do not exercise military authority. Accordingly, from a purely effectiveness point of view, an attack on such a person would have little military benefit. However, there might be some who would wish to pursue such an attack for its propaganda or moral value. In any event, in a work like this one it is a point that should be addressed.

The difficulty with some ceremonial positions is that they have the trappings of a military position. As Schmitt notes:

> wearing military uniforms, carrying weapons, or using military rank suggest combatant status, but are not dispositive. The Queen of England wears a uniform and carries a ceremonial dagger during the "trooping of the colours", but is hardly a combatant by virtue of doing so.[208]

Schmitt concludes:

> It would be incongruous to suggest that all such individuals are legitimate targets. Obviously, if a post is purely ceremonial, or otherwise solely de jure in nature, i.e., if it involves no military decision-making, then the incumbent is a civilian who enjoys protected status.[209]

---

206 A contemporary example comes from the 2003 Gulf War. "Australian forces could try to kill Saddam Hussein because he was a legitimate target under their rules of engagement, senior military figures have confirmed. A Defence spokesman said military leaders could legally be attacked. The Iraqi Government fell within this definition. 'The military leadership, including Saddam, is a legitimate target,' the spokesman said." (Forbes, above n 165 (chapter 3)) See *Off Target: The Conduct of the War and Civilian Casualties in Iraq*, above n 91 (chapter 4), 40.

207 Schmitt, 'Targeting and Humanitarian Law: Current Issues', above n 42 (chapter 1), 77.

208 Ibid.

209 Ibid, 78 (footnote omitted). See also Dinstein's reference to Buckingham Palace in London not being a legitimate military target as the Queen's role is not analogous to that of American President as Commander-in-Chief—Dinstein, *The Conduct of*

I agree that certain purely traditional or ritualistic positions should not attract combatant status. While IHL sets out the requirements for combatant status, there is also a need to look to domestic law to see how each State organises its military.[210] Where it is clear that a person has no real connection with the military except in a purely ceremonial sense, IHL must be interpreted in a practical way to exclude classifying such a person as a combatant.

Having briefly considered ceremonial positions, there is perhaps the practically more interesting group who are the opposite of what we have just discussed. These are the political leaders who are not members of the armed forces, who do not wear uniform etc, but who do have substantive roles in the conduct of an armed conflict.[211] Despite not being combatants, are those who are directly responsible for controlling and directing the war effort legitimate targets? For example, Human Rights Watch (who could be considered to be reasonably moderate in their views on IHL) state that "political leaders who are effectively commanders of a state's forces would be legitimate targets but absent some unusual circumstance, officials of, say, a ministry of education would not."[212]

The two main arguments that are used for contending that heads of State and senior politicians are lawful targets are as follows:

(a) First, these people are taking a direct part in hostilities through controlling and directing the use of the armed forces.
(b) Second, on purely practical grounds, it is argued that a successful attack on these people might save more lives (both civilian and military) than not attacking them.

In my view, there are no legal difficulties with the first argument, but only if the controlling and directing the use of the armed forces rises above the level of *political* control and direction and becomes one of *military* control and direction. It would appear that Schmitt does not make this distinction when he writes that "civilian leaders who engage in tactical level planning or approval are directly participating and thereby legitimate targets."[213] I argue that a distinction needs to be drawn between *planning* and *approving*. Having civilian leaders exercise ultimate approval or veto of an aspect of a military operation is quite different from having civilian leaders propose targets, suggest means and methods of attack or defence, etc. That said, Schmitt does emphasise the tactical aspect of the planning, and it would be quite unusual for civilian leaders to engage at that level. However, in the modern battlefield, it would not be unusual for Western militaries to have access to extensive communication facilities. And in a low-level conflict, civilian leaders may well be

---

Hostilities under the Law of International Armed Conflict, above n 66 (chapter 2), 98. I infer from this that he is of the view that the Queen herself is not a lawful target.

210 See Ipsen, above n 84 (chapter 4), 86.

211 Such as ministers of defence (howsoever described in domestic law or practice), prime ministers and presidents.

212 *Legal Issues Arising from the War in Afghanistan and Related Anti-Terrorism Efforts*, above n 47 (chapter 4).

213 Schmitt, 'Humanitarian Law and Direct Participation in Hostilities by Private Contractors or Civilian Employees', above n 21 (chapter 1), 543 (footnote omitted, emphasis added).

overseeing operations to an extent unprecedented in earlier conflicts. Accordingly, the emphasis should be on the type of decision being made and not whether that decision is classified as tactical, operational or strategic. Schmitt engages in classification to some extent when he writes:

> State practice would also suggest that decision-making at the strategic level of war does not render the participant a combatant (legal or illegal), because such decisions are in essence political. As an example, attempting to build an international coalition would not alone suffice. However, if an individual occupying a de jure position makes decisions affecting the operational or tactical level of war, he or she is sufficiently involved in military operations to become legitimately targetable.[214]

My concern with this statement is that it requires agreement on what is tactical, operational and strategic. For example, is it a tactical decision to decide to shoot an individual, or is it a strategic decision because that individual is the senior military leader of the enemy? Would a prime minister be taking a direct part in hostilities if the prime minister vetoed the attack (perhaps for the reason that it is hoped that the military commander proposed for targeting might have a significant role to play in normalising post war relations)? Accordingly, I believe Schmitt more correctly states the position when he writes that "[e]ssentially, leaders who decide how and where to use military force are directly participating in hostilities".[215] However, I would add the qualification that mere approval or vetoing of decisions proposed by military commanders does not amount to direct participation. The test for direct participation by political leaders should focus on the type of decision being made and not the level at which the decision is being made nor the long-term effect of the decision. With the death of Slobodan Milosevic prior to the completion of his trial in the ICTY, we will probably have to wait for the ICC to judicially deal with at least some of these issues in its future cases.

With respect to the second argument as to why attacking heads of State should be, or is, lawful,[216] there is a significant problem with this line of argument. Once the test for taking a direct part in hostilities moves away from including personal involvement in either the use of force, or the direct impeding of the military activities of the opposing Party, there would be legal support to include in the category of civilians taking a direct part in hostilities too many groups of civilians. For instance, should we now start to include factory workers in a munitions plant, or scientists in a research laboratory? To avoid this indeterminate expansion of the category of civilians taking a direct part in hostilities, the focus should be on the distinguishing characteristic of the exercise of control and direction over military operations. The advantages of focusing on this aspect are that it distinguishes a prime minister from the chief engineer in a munitions factory and avoids nomenclature issues becoming a determining factor. An example of the latter would arise

214 Schmitt, 'Targeting and Humanitarian Law: Current Issues', above n 42 (chapter 1), 78 (footnote omitted).

215 Ibid, 79.

216 The second argument being that a successful attack on political leaders might save more lives (both civilian and military) than not attacking them.

when trying to determine whether a king is a legitimate target where in one State the king might be the actual commander-in-chief of the armed forces, in another State purely the honorary commander-in-chief of the armed forces, and in a third State might have no role whatsoever with respect to the armed forces.

While the characteristic of the exercise of control and direction over military operations is helpful in determining the role of a certain politicians and heads of State, it is not determinative of the issue of whether a person is taking a direct part in hostilities. The criterion in article 51(3) API is whether the civilian is taking a direct part in *hostilities*. In many cases, when acting in the usual course of their duties, senior government officials will more correctly be classified as taking a direct part in the *armed conflict* and not a direct part in *hostilities*. For example, a minister of defence who decides on the composition of a task force to participate in a coalition operation would be making a decision concerning the armed conflict. If, however, a Minister suggested a target for attack, or proposed a route of advance, that would be taking part in hostilities. Again, a minister who vetoed a proposed route of advance (perhaps because of foreign relation sensitivities) would not be taking part in hostilities. It is important to give effect to the fact that API uses *hostilities* rather than *armed conflict*. As can be seen from the negotiating history of article 51 API, this was a deliberate choice of words.[217] In addition, *armed conflict* appears not only in the very title of API but also in the preamble and various articles. At the same time, the term *hostilities* appears not only in various articles of API but in some cases it is used in a context that clearly implies it is being used to mean the destructive effects of the armed conflict rather than the armed conflict itself.[218]

In this context, I disagree with a point used by Hays Parks to argue that certain classes of civilians should be subject to lawful attack. When discussing the very high value to the war effort during World War II made by, amongst others, certain scientists, Hays Parks writes:

> Consideration of the legality of attack on certain quasi-civilians (or quasi-military personnel) who are providing direct support to a nation's military effort should not be taken to the extreme of suggesting that every one of them would be pursued to their homes and attacked. It would take a person of extraordinary importance to a nation's military effort to generate such a mission by the enemy. Such persons generally would be at risk only while at their place of duty.[219]

The conclusion that can be drawn from the above quote is not that it would be illegal to attack such civilians, but rather that while legal it would not be militarily efficient. The premise for the quote overlooks the reality of modern technology that can facilitate significant individual and collaborative research and development being conducted from a person's home or other venue; and it could be argued that a special forces attack or bombing attack on a civilian property is easier to mount

217 CE/3b, above n 27 (chapter 3), 39.

218 See specifically API, above n 2 (chapter 1), arts 47(2)(a) and (b), where armed conflict is used in paragraph (a) and hostilities in paragraph (b).

219 Hays Parks, 'Air War and the Law of War', above n 181 (chapter 3), 135 (fn 402).

than an attack on a defended locality.[220] If Hays Parks were right, then a civilian would be legally liable to direct attack in circumstances were the civilian has not posed a direct threat to a third party.[221] As the use of force by a combatant against the civilian would be a lawful use of force under international law, it should also amount to a lawful use of force under any applicable domestic law.[222] As the civilian does not enjoy any form of combatant immunity, or have any other right under international law to use force, the usual consequence of this would be that any response by way of force by the civilian would not be lawful under domestic law.[223] As this makes no sense, then for this reason alone (as well as the other reasons argued above) Hays Parks's view cannot be adopted as a part of the correct interpretation of article 51(3) API.

There is a final point I wish to make in this section to address the argument that is sometimes advanced that more lives might be saved by conducing attacks on senior political leaders. In his work titled *Operations Against Enemy Leaders*, Hosmer notes:

> With the single exception of the shoot-down of Admiral Isoroku Yamamoto's aircraft in World War II, all U.S. operations to neutralize senior enemy leaders by direct attack have failed. The targets that have escaped elimination by aerial or other direct U.S. attack include Fidel Castro, Muammar al-Qaddafi, Saddam Hussein, Mohamed Farah Aideed, Osama bin Laden, and Slobodan Milosevic.[224]

Similar lack of success continued during the 2003 Gulf War, with Saddam Hussein and one of his senior military commanders[225] not being captured until after the end

220 For example, during the 2003 Gulf War, two coalition aircraft used laser-guided munitions to attack Ali Hassan al-Majid (aka 'Chemical Ali'—at the time a senior Iraqi military commander in charge of Iraqi forces in the south of Iraq) when he was believed to be in is house in Basra—Tini Tran, '"Chemical Ali" reported killed in Basra', *The Age* (Melbourne), 8 April 2003. Contrary to early reports, he was not killed in the attack. However, there is no reason to believe the attack itself did not occur. This is also an example of an attack outside of a place of duty.

221 See the discussion in section 4.2.2 on the meaning of taking a direct part in hostilities.

222 This last point assumes for the purposes of argument that the relevant domestic law is in conformity with international law.

223 By way of a domestic law analogy, a person cannot claim self-defence or any plead any other defence to a charge of assault if the person who was the victim of the assault was a police officer exercising a lawful right of arrest or, in those countries that still award the death penalty, an executioner putting the death penalty into effect. In other words, there are legal situations in which person A can use force against person B and in which person B has no lawful right to use force (either initially or by way of self-defence) against person A.

224 Stephen Hosmer, *Operations Against Enemy Leaders* (2001) RAND xii <http://www.rand.org/publications/MR/MR1385/> at 1 May 2005.

225 Hassan al-Majid (aka 'Chemical Ali')—see Tran, above n 220 (chapter 4).

of major combat operations.[226] Indeed, Human Rights Watch report that during the 2003 Gulf War "[a]ll of the fifty acknowledged attacks targeting Iraqi leadership failed."[227] Under the heading *Even Successful Attacks Often Have Not Produced Desired Results*, Hosmer writes:

> The demise or incapacitation of an enemy leader often does not result in a favorable change in enemy policy or behavior. Belligerent states and nonstate organizations are often governed by a collective leadership or possess competent second-echelon leaders who are as strongly motivated to continue a struggle as was the fallen leader. The frequent futility of leadership attacks is borne out by the experience of Israel in its attempts to suppress Palestinian terrorism and Russia in its attempts to pacify Chechnya. Indeed, analyses of the effects of political assassinations from antiquity through modern times document the infrequency with which the killing of a particular leader has produced the results hoped for by the assassin.[228]

I am not trying to suggest by these quotes from Hosmer that leadership targets that meet the previously discussed test for being lawful targets are, nonetheless, somehow immune from attack. However, Hosmer's points are very relevant to considering the value of such attacks. This is particularly important if there is any expected collateral damage arising from the planned attack. I suspect that leadership attacks are often considered to have a high "pay off",[229] and accordingly even significant expected collateral damage may be considered as not being excessive. Hosmer's analysis indicates that this may not be the case. As Human Rights Watch state:

> the continued resort to decapitation strikes despite their complete lack of success and the significant civilian losses they caused can be seen as a failure to take "all feasible precautions" in choice of means and methods of warfare in order to minimize civilian losses as required by international humanitarian law.[230]

To conclude, there is no concept of quasi-combatants. In particular, a civilian working in a munitions factory, a civilian scientist involved in weapons research,[231] and a civilian minister for defence or prime minister are all civilians and are entitled to protection as such. The corollary, of course, is that these civilians have no right to take up arms and could be punished for doing so.

---

226 Major combat operations are considered to have ceased on 1 May 2003 (*The War in Iraq: ADF Operations in the Middle East in 2003*, above n 170 (chapter 3), 35).

227 *Off Target: The Conduct of the War and Civilian Casualties in Iraq*, above n 91 (chapter 4), 6.

228 Hosmer, above n 224 (chapter 4), xiii.

229 In legal terms, a large 'concrete a direct military advantage' is anticipated from the attack.

230 *Off Target: The Conduct of the War and Civilian Casualties in Iraq*, above n 91 (chapter 4), 40.

231 Rogers, *Law on the Battlefield*, above n 84 (chapter 1), 11.

That concludes the general discussion on the direct targeting of civilians. What are now covered are some specific areas of contemporary controversy concerning attacks that affect the civilian population.

Article 51 API offers further protection for civilians beyond just protection from direct attack. As well as the general protection from attacks provided by article 51(3) API, the following are also specifically prohibited:

(a) acts or threats of violence the primary purpose of which is to spread terror among the civilian population,[232]
(b) indiscriminate attacks,[233] and
(c) attacks against the civilian population or civilians by way of reprisals.[234]

There is no need to discuss the API issues covering reprisals, as the statement in article 51(6) hardly needs to be elaborated upon. However articles 51(2) and 51(4) API warrant comment.

4.2.5 Terrorising civilians

"Numerous public Iraqi military communiqués issued during the war used very explicit language to indicate that the missile attacks were intended to terrorize the civilian populations of both Israel and Saudi Arabia."[235] For States bound by API, such attacks are explicitly prohibited by the second sentence of article 51(2) API, which states: "Acts or threats of violence the primary purpose of which is to spread terror among the civilian population are prohibited". Due to the inclusion of the word primary, it is clear that attacks, or threats of attacks, which have the incidental effect of spreading terror among the civilian populace are not prohibited by article 51(2) API.[236] However, it needs to be emphasised that the effect must be incidental. This view is supported by Human Rights Watch, who state:

> Iraq's statements accompanying its missile attacks must be examined in light of the customary law prohibition codified in Article 51(2) of Protocol I, which enjoins "[a]cts or threats of violence the primary purpose of which is to spread terror among the civilian population." While customary law does not immunize civilians against fear and anxiety as a consequence of legitimate attacks against military targets, the principle affirmed in Article 51(2) "is intended to prohibit acts of violence the primary purpose of which is to spread terror among the civilian population without offering substantial military advantage."[237]

232 API, above n 2 (chapter 1), art 51(2).

233 Ibid, art 51(4).

234 Ibid, art 51(6).

235 *Needless Deaths in the Gulf War: Civilian Casualties During the Air Campaign and Violations of the Laws of War*, above n 38 (chapter 3).

236 CDDH/XV, above n 98 (chapter 3), 274; Sandoz, Swinarski and Zimmerman (eds), above n 68 (chapter 1), [1940]; Bothe, Partsch and Solf, above n 87 (chapter 1), 301 (fn 6); Dinstein, *The Conduct of Hostilities under the Law of International Armed Conflict*, above n 66 (chapter 2), 116.

237 *Needless Deaths in the Gulf War: Civilian Casualties During the Air Campaign and Violations of the Laws of War*, above n 38 (chapter 3) (footnotes omitted).

I should add that while I draw support from the opening words of the second sentence, I do not completely agree with the last sentence in the above quote. The final words of the quote seem to indicate that if an attack offers a substantial military advantage, then it is lawful even if the primary purpose of the attack is to spread terror among the civilian population. I disagree. The prohibition in the second sentence of article 51(2) API is not subject to some sort of proportionality or balancing argument. If the primary purpose of the attack is to spread terror among the civilian population, then it is prohibited in all circumstances. A review of State practice in *Customary International Humanitarian Law* under the heading "Violence aimed at Spreading Terror among the Civilian Population" is consistent with my conclusion, in that none of the State practice listed permits acts the primary purpose of which is to spread terror just because there is a substantial military advantage to the attack.[238]

As already stated, while an attack is not lawful if the primary purpose is to spread terror among the civilian population, as long as an attack is on a legitimate military objective, an attack would be permissible if a desired *secondary* effect was to spread terror. As unpalatable as the proposition in the preceding sentence may be, it is nonetheless correct. However, strict limitations would apply as article 51(1) API states that the rules in article 51 API are in addition to other applicable rules of international law and that those additional rules must still be observed. These limitations would be as follows. First, the attack is restricted to a legitimate military objective, be that a combatant, a civilian who has lost protection from attack, or an object that satisfies the test set out in article 52(2) API. Second, if the attack is on an object, the spreading of terror is not counted as part of the definite military advantage to be gained by the attack when determining whether the object is a military objective.[239] Third, when choosing between the means and methods of attack, no extra civilian loss of life or injury, or damage to civilian objects, is caused to enable the secondary purpose of spreading terror.[240] Fourth, it cannot be decided to withhold effective advance warning of the attack in the hope that this will either cause or increase the spreading of terror when circumstances would otherwise have permitted the giving of a warning.[241] Fifth and finally, if there is a choice between two or more military objectives that offered the same military advantage, no extra civilian loss of life or injury, or damage to civilian objects, is caused by choosing to attack the military objective that enables the secondary purpose of spreading terror.[242]

Human Rights Watch has stated that article 51 API:

> also prohibits bombing to attack civilian morale. Although technically there may be a distinction between morale and terror bombing, they are, in practice, treated the same. It has often been observed that what is morale bombing to the attacking

238 Henckaerts and Doswald-Beck (eds), *Customary International Humanitarian Law*, vol II, above n 64 (chapter 1), 68–70.

239 See definition of military objectives in API, above n 2 (chapter 1), art 52(2).

240 Ibid, art 57(2)(a)(ii).

241 Ibid, art 57(2)(c).

242 Ibid, art 57(3).

> force is terror bombing to the civilians who are targeted. … Attacks intended primarily to induce the civilian population to rebellion or to overthrow its leadership would be examples of unlawful attacks.[243]

It would appear that Human Rights Watch might have been mixing up concepts, even though I partly agree with their conclusion. I agree that an attack could not be launched for the primary purpose of inciting the civilian population where the means of that incitement is by spreading terror amongst the population. For example, escalating attacks of barbarity that cause the civilian population to be put in fear with a message that the attacks will stop if they overthrow their leaders are not lawful. However, to the extent that an attack is on an otherwise legitimate military objective, and the means of inciting the population is to show that they could now conduct (for example) a popular rebellion, that form of attack does not come within the prohibition in article 51(2) API. Take the following illustration. Assume a civilian population is being governed against their will and that the oppression is being enforced by military units and military communication facilities. In such a case, as an attack on military communication facilities, re-supply routes etc would be lawful, the attack on such military objectives remains lawful even where the main purpose for the attack is to encourage a civilian revolt. The important point, though, is that this primary purpose cannot be taken into account when determining the *ab initio* lawfulness of the attack (eg, whether the target is a military objective or whether the attack is in compliance with the proportionality test). In addition, it cannot add to the assessed quantum of military advantage to be gained from the attack.

The above point is a specific case of a more general question: is it lawful to select targets for the purpose of affecting civilian support for the war as long as article 51(2) API is not breached? Certainly, this seems to be attractive to military planners. For example, Human Rights Watch quotes a military planner as saying that "military planners hoped that the unrelenting aerial bombardment would provoke a coup against Saddam Hussein."[244] There is a particular irony in this, as during the Iran-Iraq war in the 1980's:

> Iraq noted publicly that civilian morale was an objective of its missile attacks on Iranian urban areas. The commander of Iraq's Fourth Corps, Major-General Thabit Sultan, stated in April 1985 that Iraq wanted to bring the war home to the Iranian people: We want to bring the Iranian people into the front lines of the war. We hope this will encourage the Iranian people to rebel against their government and bring the war to an end.[245]

Nor is this a very recent phenomenon. Part of the Allied bombing campaign during World War II, especially the area bombing campaign, involved a determined

243 *Needless Deaths in the Gulf War: Civilian Casualties During the Air Campaign and Violations of the Laws of War*, above n 38 (chapter 3).

244 Ibid.

245 Ibid.

policy to undermine, inter alia, "the morale of the German people".[246] Interestingly, putting aside the legality for one moment, the effectiveness of this tactic is not beyond doubt. In support of the tactic, it has been suggested that in World War II there was in Japan a "'rapid weakening of morale' due to the strategic air offensive."[247] Also, Hays Parks quotes authority to support the view that worker output in factories decreased as a result of bombing campaigns on both sides during World War I.[248] However, on the contrary, Barber writes that "bombing civilians has proven counterproductive in previous campaigns … [as] it usually tends to consolidate opposition rather than undermine morale."[249] Given the divergent opinion on its effectiveness, I expect the issue is unlikely to go away. In particular, in limited campaigns where target sets are restricted and the enemy is a developed country where the civilian population are not used to living without modern conveniences, directly targeting the civilian population is likely to be seen as very attractive to campaign planners. For example:

> During the NATO action on Kosovo, at least one US Air Force leader advocated a relatively unrestricted air campaign against Serbia. "Just think if after the first day, the Serbian people had awakened and their refrigerators weren't running, there was no water in their kitchens or bathrooms, no lights, no transportation system to get to work".[250]

Brown comments that "this line of reasoning is morally defunct."[251] Morals aside, it is not legally permissible under API. Human Rights Watch directly states its view that attacks justified on the basis of affecting civilian morale or support for the war effort are not permitted:

> "Bringing the war home to the enemy," to demoralize civilians and lead them to pressure their leaders to surrender, is a tactic that has marked military history. But civilian morale is not a permissible military objective under the laws of war, as discussed in Chapter One. The balance of this report operates from the premise that attacks intended to weaken the morale of the civilian population in order to force capitulation, surrender, or a change of government, are prohibited under the rules set forth in Chapter One of this report.[252]

---

246 DeSaussure, 'Belligerent Air Operations and the 1977 Geneva Protocol I', above n 13 (chapter 2), 474.

247 Ibid, 475.

248 Parks, 'Air War and the Law of War', above n 181 (chapter 3), 21.

249 Barber, above n 74 (chapter 2), 688.

250 Gary Brown, *Proportionality for Military Leaders* (2000) Air Command and Staff College, Air University, 19 <http://www.au.af.mil/au/awc/awcgate/acsc/00-208.pdf> at 26 May 2006 (footnote omitted).

251 Ibid.

252 *Needless Deaths in the Gulf War: Civilian Casualties During the Air Campaign and Violations of the Laws of War*, above n 38 (chapter 3).

As Amnesty International state, if "weakening the enemy population's resolve to fight were considered a legitimate objective of armed forces, there would be no limit to war".[253] And as Dinstein states, even if such attacks could truly bend the will of the civilian populace—which he doubts—they are not lawful.[254]

Noting that some have argued that in the 1991 Gulf War one of Iraq's only options in the armed conflict was to try to split the coalition, it is worth noting that Human Rights Watch considered this very point:

> Although Iraq might claim that it sought a military advantage from its missile attacks —splitting the military coalition, either by prompting Israel to attack Iraq or by encouraging Saudi civilians under attack to rise against their leaders—those objectives do not justify targeted or indiscriminate attacks on civilians or efforts to terrorize civilians. Just as it would be illegal for allied forces intentionally to target Iraqi civilians with the aim of encouraging them to overthrow Saddam, so it was illegal for Iraq to target civilians in Israel and Saudi Arabia with the aim of furthering Iraq's military or political objectives. Acts violative of the laws and customs of war cannot be justified or made lawful by a military necessity argument.[255]

Human Rights Watch then correctly point out that:

> Deliberately creating hardships for civilians so that they might rise up against their dictatorial leader would violate that essential distinction [between civilians and civilian objects and combatants and military objectives].[256]

I have found no support for the argument that such attacks are permissible under API. Rather, the most that can be found is argument that such attacks *should be* allowed or at least allowed in part. So, we see Meyer arguing:

> It is only the recent, restrictive interpretations of Article 52(2) that attempt to limit state practice, customary international law, and conventional law—all of which have allowed for targeting objectives with at least the partial purpose of affecting enemy morale. Clearly, the targeting of civilians to affect morale through the intentional killing and injuring of civilians is not allowed, and has been rejected

253 *Israel/Lebanon: Deliberate destruction or "collateral damage"? Israeli attacks on civilian infrastructure* (2006) Amnesty International, 5 <http://web.amnesty.org/library/pdf/MDE180072006ENGLISH/$File/MDE1800706.pdf> at 19 September 2007.

254 Dinstein, *The Conduct of Hostilities under the Law of International Armed Conflict*, above n 66 (chapter 2), 116.

255 *Needless Deaths in the Gulf War: Civilian Casualties During the Air Campaign and Violations of the Laws of War*, above n 38 (chapter 3). See also *Civilians under Assault: Hezbollah's Rocket Attacks on Israel in the 2006 War*, above n 91 (chapter 4), 7; where Human Rights Watch correctly state that Hezbollah could not target Israeli civilians "to compel Israel to mount a ground offensive in Lebanon, thereby giving Hezbollah certain fighting advantages it lacked when facing a war from the air."

256 *Needless Deaths in the Gulf War: Civilian Casualties During the Air Campaign and Violations of the Laws of War*, above n 38 (chapter 3).

> by states both in practice and doctrinally. This Part will explore how affecting the morale and will of the enemy, including its civilians, through other means has not been rejected, and, how, until recently, it has been accepted as a lawful use of air power and how recent restrictive interpretations of Article 52(2) attempt to unilaterally change that status, regardless of state practice and customary international law.[257]

I disagree with her interpretation of article 52(2) API. Rather, it is not possible to base the attack on a legitimate military purpose and at the same time include in the calculation of the anticipated military advantage a component that allows for the affect of the attack on the morale of the enemy civilians.

The confusing aspect of Meyer's article is that she seems to be arguing that any interpretation of article 52(2) API that is not in accordance with customary international law is an incorrect interpretation of article 52(2) API. This is a line of reasoning I fail to understand—particularly as API did not purport merely to codify the law but also to develop IHL.[258] Meyer also fails to address the fact that IHL generally, and API in particular, has placed limits on the *means* by which the *ends* of an armed conflict can be achieved. For example, after correctly pointing out that war is not an end unto itself,[259] she does not deal with the issue that, nonetheless, IHL imposes limits on the conduct of the armed conflict. Indeed, explicitly contrary to the preamble in the *St Petersburg Declaration*, she states that "[d]efeat of the enemy forces is but one way to achieve this end".[260] It seems that for Meyer, IHL should generally not restrict the means and methods used to achieve the ultimate goals of an armed conflict (noting that she does admit a few exceptions to this broad statement). Meyer's argument is on the face of it superficially attractive, as she attempts to argue from an efficiency and humanity perspective. For example, she argues:

> The type of conflicts prevalent in the world today center more than ever on the application of force to bend the will of the enemy. Moreover, destruction of military-oriented targets is not always the most efficient or humane way in which to achieve that goal.[261]

In making her arguments, Meyer makes regular use of the Kosovo air campaign in which "the conflict pitted the military force of NATO against the will and resolve of Milosevic and the Serbian leadership."[262] The following is typical of her examples and argument.

---

257 Jeanne Meyer, above n 53 (chapter 3), 163 (footnote omitted).

258 For example, the following paragraph appears in the Preamble to API, above n 2 (chapter 1): "Believing it necessary nevertheless to reaffirm and *develop* the provisions protecting the victims of armed conflicts" (emphasis added).

259 "The goal of war is not simply to defeat the enemy's military forces. 'We don't go to war merely to have a nice fight; rather, we go to war to attain something of political value to our organization.'" (Jeanne Meyer, above n 53 (chapter 3), 167 (footnote omitted))

260 Ibid.

261 Ibid, 181.

262 Ibid, 175 (footnote omitted).

> NATO specifically targeted objects intended to affect the morale of the enemy forces and civilian population. While the affect on enemy troop morale arguably is allowed under Article 52(2), current restrictive interpretations of the Article do not allow for targeting enemy civilian morale.

Up to that point, I completely agree with Meyer. However, in relation to the prohibition on targeting enemy civilian morale, she then proceeds to write:

> If so, then it appears that a majority of the NATO air campaign against Kosovo, while a key component of the overall campaign, was illegitimate under some current interpretations of what constitutes a legitimate military objective. This unusual result is not only inconsistent with prior state practice, but clearly points out the difficulty with interpreting Article 52(2) in a restrictive manner. If the very real possibility exists, as was the case of Kosovo, that 'the Serbian population forced Milosevic to call the war off when the life of the Serbian population was made very uncomfortable,' then removal of that strategic option for overcoming the will of the enemy may ultimately lead to longer and more destructive wars.[263]

This, of course, is an ends justifies the means line of argument. There are, however, a number of problems with her argument. First, and perhaps foremost, it could well be that the Kosovo campaign itself was illegal. It is arguable that the Kosovo campaign did not comply with the *jus ad bellum*, in that it amounted to the use of force by a coalition of States to impose their political will on a third State in circumstances where neither article 51 or Chapter VII of the *Charter of the United Nations*, nor the inherent right of self defence—and perhaps not even the currently uncertain concept of humanitarian intervention—applied. Of course, the *jus in bello* is independent of the *jus ad bellum*; but it is slightly ironic to argue that a particular interpretation of IHL may not have allowed the successful prosecution of what may have been an unlawful goal.

The second problem is that she seems to be arguing that because a certain interpretation of article 52(2) API is inconsistent with NATO activities, that this is somehow 'unusual'. It is an unfortunate fact of armed conflict that prisoners of war are not always treated in accordance with GCIII. Yet, few seem to argue that this means GCIII needs revision or the standard interpretations of GCIII are wrong. Rather, what it means is that some States and some individuals act contrary to IHL.

Finally, she resorts to an old argument that certain aspects of IHL may prolong wars. Of course, this is not new. I refer in particular to the famous quote that is attributed to Admiral Sir John Fisher, the senior British naval representative to the First Hague Peace Conference:

> If you rub it in, both at home and abroad, that you are ready for instant war, with every unit of your strength in the first line and waiting to be first in, and hit your enemy in the belly and kick him when he is down, and boil your prisoners in oil

263 Ibid, 176–7 (footnotes omitted).

> (if you take any), and torture his women and children, then people will keep clear of you.[264]

Sassoli has summarised the position well:

> The rule that only military objectives may be attacked is based on the principle that, while the aim of a conflict is to prevail politically, acts of violence for that purpose may only aim at overcoming the military forces of the enemy ... Acts of violence against persons or objects of political, economic or psychological importance may sometimes be more efficient to overcome the enemy, but are never necessary, because every enemy can be overcome by weakening sufficiently its military forces. Once its military forces are neutralized, even the politically, psychologically or economically strongest enemy can no longer resist.[265]

Accordingly, I disagree with Meyer to the extent that she argues that the morale or will of the civilian population may be directly targeted.[266] I also disagree with her line of argument that where an interpretation of a rule of IHL places restrictions on a belligerent's means and methods and it is believed (or even proved) that adopting those means or methods may have resulted in a shorter armed conflict, then somehow that interpretation must be revisited. As succinctly put by the Israeli Supreme Court: "Not every efficient means is also legal."[267]

---

264 Hays Parks, 'Air War and the Law of War', above n 181 (chapter 3), 12 (fn 50).

265 Sassoli, above n 47 (chapter 3), 3.

266 I note here that while Dunlap argues that the will of the enemy civilian population should be directly targeted, he states to legally do so will require a change in IHL—Dunlap, 'The End of Innocence: Rethinking Noncombatancy in the Post-Kosovo Era', above n 79 (chapter 1), 14 and 17.

267 *The Public Committee against Torture in Israel v The Government of Israel*, HCJ 769/02 (13 December 2006) [63] (Barak P (emeritus), Rivlin V-P and Beinisch P concurring).

Chapter 5

Effects-based operations and controversial military objectives

In this chapter, I discuss two contemporary and related topics. The first topic is an approach to the operational and strategic planning of military operations known as EBO. Following that are sections that deal with some currently controversial classes of military objectives, noting that these classes of targets are frequently referred to in EBO targeting discussions.

Effects-based operations is a modern theory of targeting. Traditional targeting theory focused on attrition where targets are progressively attacked with a view to cumulatively weakening the enemy's military forces.[1] However, in EBO targets are attacked for systematic effect[2] and attention is paid to not only direct effects but also indirect effects.[3] In section 5.1, I consider whether EBO are consistent with IHL. As they are classic EBO target sets, I then discuss the lawfulness of targeting certain targets of contemporary interest (television and radio broadcasting stations, electrical power generation stations, economic targets, and a government's power base).

The rationale for attacking television and radio broadcasting stations extends from the uncontroversial (eg, when actually being used to transmit military orders) through to perhaps the most controversial (eg, the dissemination of propaganda). In this chapter, I consider in some detail some of the various rationales for attacking television and radio broadcasting stations in previous conflicts and the resulting learned articles and commentaries. Attacks on electrical power generation stations raise similar issues, in that at one end the rationale appears perfectly lawful (eg, where the generating station directly supports military operations, while at the other end it is quite debatable (eg, as a way of influencing civilian morale). A focus of my discussion is how legally to categorise an attack where both rationales are present concurrently.

The last two sections are not concerned with types of targets per se (eg, oil export facilities) but rather the rationale behind attacking targets (eg, an object that provides economic support to a belligerent's war effort). For economic targets, I note that there may be a need to distinguish between obligations under API and under customary international law. When considering targeting a government's power base, I draw a distinction similar to that raised in chapter 3 between the political or national-strategic goals of a conflict and the military goals.

---

1 Michael Schmitt, 'Targeting and Humanitarian Law: Current Issues' (2004) 34 *Israel Yearbook on Human Rights* 59, 60.

2 Ibid.

3 Ibid, 62.

5.1 Effects-based operations

First, there is a need to define what is meant by EBO.[4] Unfortunately, this is not as easy as it might seem. As Das writes:[5]

> Effects-Based Operations (EBO) is a phrase used to represent a host of concepts permeating current military thinking regarding planning and operations. These concepts are still evolving, and much literature exists espousing different points of view. These differences exist because of the different aspects that have been emphasised by different proponents. Nonetheless there is a universal agreement that, for meaningful EBO analysis, the adversary should be treated as an integrated complex system.[6]

Accordingly, the discussion will focus on those aspects of EBO relevant to this study. In the targeting context, Schmitt sets out some aspects of EBO that are useful. First, he writes:

> Effects-based operations (EBO) have replaced attrition targeting in US doctrine. In attrition warfare, extensive pre-planned target lists are developed and targets are then destroyed serially, while engaging targets of opportunity as located. Reduced to basics, the enemy is defeated by progressively weakening its military forces. In contrast, effects-based operations represent "the maturation of ... technologies merged with the theory of targeting for systematic effect rather absolute destruction".[7]

While this is of some assistance in determining that EBO are different from classical attrition warfare, it is not the complete picture. Another important point is that one of the defining aspects of EBO is the attention to direct and indirect effects.

> Direct effects are "immediate, first order consequences", *i.e.*, the damage directly caused by the weapon. Classic attrition warfare emphasizes direct effects. However, effects-based planning also factors in indirect effects—"the delayed and/or displaced second-and third-order consequences of military action". A typical example is loss of support for a regime that appears inept or impotent in the face of repeated enemy attacks.[8]

---

4 For an interesting critique of EBO generally (although not dealing with the IHL aspects of EBO), see Brigadier Justin Kelly and Lieutenant Colonel David Kilcullen, 'Chaos Versus Predictability: A critique of Effects-Based Operations' (2004) vol II(1) *Australian Army Journal* 87.

5 An article that has 'Simulations with Cellular Automata' in the title was never going to be light reading.

6 Balaram Das, *Effects-Based Operations: Simulations with Cellular Automata* (2004) DSTO, iii <http://www.dsto.defence.gov.au/publications/2677/DSTO-RR-0275.pdf> at 24 December 2005.

7 Schmitt, 'Targeting and Humanitarian Law: Current Issues', above n 42 (chapter 1), 60 (footnote omitted).

8 Ibid, 62 (footnotes omitted).

There is nothing inherently contrary to IHL in EBO. Rather, it is in the detail of how EBO may be applied that IHL issues arise. For example, while indirect effects can be planned for, and even desired, with one exception these effects cannot be counted when assessing whether an object is a military objective or determining military advantage as part of the proportionality equation under API. The reason why they cannot be counted is because by definition they are indirect and therefore contrary to the requirements of articles 52 and 57 API. The exception when indirect effects can be counted is when assessing whether an individual attack as part of an overall attack offers a military advantage.

Another IHL problem with the methodology of EBO is that API consistently uses the term *anticipated* military advantage—be that when defining military objectives,[9] when assessing whether expected collateral damage will be proportional to the military advantage to be gained from the attack,[10] or in prohibiting indiscriminate attacks.[11] Additional Protocol I does not refer to the *desired* military advantage to be gained from the attack. In this respect, it is notable that EBO remains more of a theory than a concrete tool. For example, Kelly and Kilcullen state:

> On present trends, it seems probable that EBO will remain at best a worthy aspiration. The pluralistic nature of Western democracies, including that of Australia, limits the coherence and unity of an effects-based approach to strategy. Moreover, Clausewitz's trinity of chance, uncertainty and friction continues to characterise war and will make anticipation of *even the first-order consequences of military action highly conjectural.* Interaction between personalities and events means that any given military action may have totally unpredictable effects on different actors. In addition, a systems approach to warfare does not guarantee that second- and third-order consequences of actions can be predicted, let alone managed.[12]

In this respect, EBO could be likened to a 'smart' weapon that was designed to seek out only enemy combatants; however, due to technological limitations the weapon had unpredictable results. In such a case, the concept behind the weapon is not contrary to IHL; but rather the concept does not match reality. This can be contrasted with the next point, which is a fundamental objection to how EBO is sometimes discussed.

A significant legal problem with EBO is that it is often associated with an approach to armed conflict in:

> an era in which technological advances and dramatic asymmetry in military capabilities make possible coercive strategies that seek to compel (a compellance strategy) an opponent to engage in, or desist from, a particular course of conduct.[13]

---

9 See API, above n 2 (chapter 1), art 52(2).

10 See ibid, arts 57(2)(a)(iii) and (b).

11 See ibid, art 51(5)(b).

12 Kelly and Kilcullen, above n 4 (chapter 5), 97 (emphasis added).

13 Schmitt, 'Targeting and Humanitarian Law: Current Issues', above n 42 (chapter 1), 64 (footnote omitted).

Two problems arise here. First, the courses of conduct under discussion are often unrelated to the military actions of the adversary. To take a recent example, one of the stated military goals of the NATO bombing campaign in the FRY was to:

> attack Yugoslav military and security forces and associated facilities with sufficient effect to degrade its capacity to continue repression of the civilian population and to deter further military actions against its own people.[14]

As discussed earlier, as this is a national or strategic goal, targets cannot be selected solely on the basis of seeking to attain this goal (or effect). Second, the concept of EBO is often considered to be a means by which a broader range of targets than those traditionally permissible under IHL can be selected; thereby allowing the attacker to avoid the use of significant military assets (in particular, the committing of significant numbers of ground troops). For example, in the context of discussing what is a lawful military objective, Schmitt writes:

> For instance, one respected academic [Marco Sassoli] has opined that:
>
> > Acts of violence against persons or objects of political, economic or psychological importance may sometimes be more efficient to overcome the enemy, but are never necessary, because every enemy can be overcome by weakening sufficiently its military forces. Once its military forces are neutralized, even the politically, psychologically or economically strongest enemy can no longer resist.
>
> Such assertions are overly simplistic. First, they assume that both sides of a conflict are willing to commit the resources necessary to conquer the enemy. Operation Allied Force demonstrates that this is not always the case. It may well be that one side is seeking limited objectives and therefore only prepared to employ (or risk) forces necessary to achieve those specific objectives.[15]

The problem with Schmitt's response is that it is based on a premise that IHL should permit the use of force to achieve political or diplomatic ends. This is not the case, and in this respect I agree with Sassoli's statement that lawful targets are limited to those that contribute to overcoming the enemy's military forces. This last point leads to the conclusion for this section. While EBO is not per se contrary to IHL, EBO cannot be used to overcome or avoid IHL. In particular, EBO cannot be used to avoid the fundamental legal limitations on what are military objectives.

The following discussion deals with some particular objects that generate significant debate in both the popular media and the legal literature concerning whether the objects are lawful targets.

---

14 Clark, above n 123 (chapter 3), 203.

15 Schmitt, 'Targeting and Humanitarian Law: Current Issues', above n 42 (chapter 1), 67 (footnote omitted).

5.2 Television and radio broadcasting stations

It is in no way an overstatement to say:

> There is considerable debate as to when traditionally civilian objects, such as TV and radio stations, make an effective contribution to military action and therefore become legitimate military targets.[16]

Whole articles can be found on this topic alone. In this discussion, it would be useful to start with a synopsis of the military reasoning behind attacking television and radio broadcasting stations. A convenient summary is provided in the April 1992 *Final Report to Congress* on the conduct of the 1991 Persian Gulf War:

> More than half of Iraq's military landline communications passed through major switching facilities in Baghdad. Civil TV and radio facilities *could* be used easily for C3 backup for military purposes. The Saddam Hussein regime also controlled TV and radio and used them as *the principal media for Iraqi propaganda*. Thus, these installations also were struck.[17]

In a summary of the effects and results of the first week (17–23 January 1991) of the campaign, the *Final Report to Congress* states:

> Saddam Hussein's internal telecommunications capability was so badly damaged that, while he could broadcast televised propaganda to the world by portable satellite uplinks, he was limited in the use of telecommunications to influence the Iraqi populace.[18]

Other examples of recent attacks include:

(a) "On 23 April 1999, at 0220, NATO intentionally bombed the central studio of the RTS (state-owned) broadcasting corporation at 1 Aberdareva Street in the centre of Belgrade. … While there is some doubt over exact casualty figures, between 10 and 17 people are estimated to have been killed."[19]

(b) "On March 26 [2003], the United States used Cruise missiles and bombs in an attack on Iraq's main television station and other broadcasting facilities."[20]

So, what is the law in this area? Interestingly, this issue has a long history. As Rado states:

---

16 Kellenberger, above n 23 (chapter 1).

17 US Department of Defense, *Conduct of the Persian Gulf War: Final Report to Congress*, above n 29 (chapter 3), 149 (emphasis added).

18 Ibid, 179.

19 *OTP Report*, above n 90 (chapter 1), [72]. 'RTS' stands for Radio Televizije Srbije (Radio Television Serbia).

20 Anthony Dworkin, *Iraqi Television: A Legitimate Target?* (2003) Crimes of War Project <http://www.crimesofwar.org/print/onnews/Brief-tv-print.html> at 2 April 2006 (emphasis added).

> Unbeknownst to most television reporters, customary law long ago deemed radio and television stations to be military objectives as are other military-industrial, military research, infrastructure, communications, and energy targets. The logic is that they can usually be put to military use and are essential for the functioning of any modern military in time of conflict.[21]

This statement is presumably based on the 1956 ICRC *Draft Rules for the Limitation of Dangers incurred by the Civilian Population in Time of War.*[22] However, the Draft Rules never became law. And while of interest in determining what is customary international law, the Draft Rules cannot be considered declarative of customary international law. And, of course, we are now interested in what article 52(2) API provides rather than the Draft Rules. As a result, notwithstanding the Draft Rules, the controversy over attacks on television broadcasting stations continues. This is nicely highlighted by the grammar of the heading to Anthony Dworkin's article in the Crimes of War Project. His article is titled "Iraqi Television: A Legitimate Target?"[23] Indeed, despite being a very lengthy report, Andreas Laursen notes that the *OTP Report* fails to draw a firm and clear conclusion on whether the media is a "legitimate target group".[24] Part of the problem seems to be that some commentators seem to do little more than re-state the question. For example, Ronzitti writes:

> The view that media are a legitimate military objective, or may become one, is supported by the compilation of military objectives made by the ICRC in the context of its 1956 Draft Rules for the Limitation of the Dangers incurred by the Civilian Population in Time of War. According to that list of military objectives (which should have become an annex to Article 7, paragraph 2 of the Draft Rules), "installations of broadcasting and television stations" are military objectives. It must be added that radio and TV stations are used (or can easily be used) for military purposes, i.e. for C3 ...[25]

Looked at carefully, what Ronzitti seems to have said is that in some cases the media are legitimate targets and in other cases the media may become a legitimate target. However, Ronzitti does not make it clear whether the media are legitimate targets because they can easily be used for military purposes or whether they become targets only when used for military purposes. Since the introduction of article 52(2) API, we know that any object, in the right circumstances, can be a military objective. Accordingly, the discussion needs to be tightly focused if we are

21 Gaby Rado, *Legitimate Military Targets,* Crimes of War Project <http://www.crimesofwar.org/thebook/legit-military-target.html> at 26 May 2006.

22 See above n 16 (chapter 3).

23 Dworkin, *'Iraqi Television: A Legitimate Target?'*, above n 20 (chapter 5).

24 Laursen, above n 19 (chapter 3), 777.

25 Natalino Ronzitti, 'Is the non liquet of the Final Report by the Committee Established to Review the NATO Bombing Campaign Against the Federal Republic of Yugoslavia Acceptable?' (2000) 840 *International Review of the Red Cross* <http://www.icrc.org/Web/eng/siteengo.nsf/iwpList180/73C2B0D8BBFE408CC1256B66005F37FE> at 4 June 2006 (footnote omitted).

to go beyond a mere general statement that TV and radio stations may or may not be lawful targets.

Dworkin sets out the issue accurately when he writes:

> It has been generally recognized in international law that TV and radio stations *can* make a contribution to military action as part of the network of command, control and communication, and therefore that they are legitimate targets *under certain conditions*. The problem comes in deciding whether they are being attacked for this reason, or instead because of their propaganda value—which has not generally been regarded as a contribution to military action.[26]

Considered this way, the problem can be reduced to two questions. First, under what conditions may TV and radio stations be attacked? Second, do those conditions include the spreading of propaganda?

On the first question, it is readily apparent that if a TV or radio station meets the test set out in article 52(2) API then it is a military objective. While this point seems basic, it is worth making—particularly because of what it means in practice. And what it means is that TV and radio stations as a class are neither military objectives nor not military objectives. Rather, and like all other objects,[27] each particular TV or radio station must be looked at and assessed. For example, it is not enough that, as a class, radio stations may be used as part of the military communication system. Instead, each individual radio station must be assessed to determine whether that station is contributing to the military communication system (eg, by current use or by intended future use (ie, the *purpose* aspect of the article 52(2) API test)).

Having determined that a TV or radio station may be lawfully attacked if it comes within the article 52(2) API definition of a military objective, the second issue is, is the mere spreading of propaganda sufficient to meet the article 52(2) API test? This is particularly important, as in some cases this has been the sole justification for the basis on which a station has been attacked. For example, Amnesty International has stated that it asked NATO for an explanation regarding the NATO attack on the RTS headquarters, with the reply being that "the attack was carried out because the RTS was a propaganda organ"[28] and that NATO "argued that propaganda is direct support for military action."[29] In other cases, one can imagine that a TV or radio station that is being used to support military communications and is also being used to spread propaganda. In that case, if an attack can be justified based on the spreading of propaganda then there would be an increased military advantage

26 Dworkin, *'Iraqi Television: A Legitimate Target?'*, above n 20 (chapter 5) (emphasis added).

27 Recalling that *all* objects must be assessed as to whether they are military objectives, not just so called dual-use objects—see the discussion at section 3.2.

28 *Amnesty International's initial comments on the review by the International Criminal Tribunal for the Former Yugoslavia of NATO's Operation Allied Force*, above n 89 (chapter 1). See also *"Collateral damage" or Unlawful Killings?: Violations of the Laws of War by NATO during Operation Allied Force* (2000) Amnesty International <http://web.amnesty.org/library/index/ENGEUR700182000> at 26 May 2006.

29 Ibid.

to the attack compared with counting just the military communications aspect. The consequence would be that more collateral damage would be proportional, as the military advantage anticipated from the attack would be higher.

Laursen correctly summarises the issues when he asks: "Does propaganda provide an 'effective contribution to military action' and would its destruction offer a 'definite military advantage?'"[30] The authors of the *OTP Report* seem to be of the view that propaganda does not contribute to military action,[31] as do Human Rights Watch[32] and Amnesty International.[33] Similarly, Ronzitti concludes that:

> The lawfulness of the attack on the Serbian radio and TV station in Belgrade is even more controversial. Radio and TV are dual-use objects, which can be employed for civilian use as well as for military purposes. If they are used for military communication, it is clear that they can be targeted. If they are used only for propaganda, their destruction does not give a "definite military advantage" within the meaning of Article 52, paragraph 2 of Protocol I.[34]

Dunlap disagrees and states that because popular support of a government can be a centre of gravity, then attacking an object that affects that popular support (such as radio and television) does offer a direct and concrete military advantage.[35] He goes on to state that:

> To military professionals it is absurd – and even duplicitous – to contend, as the ICTY report seems to do, that it is somehow preferable to slaughter masses of enemy troops to achieve victory – in lieu of merely destroying a propaganda organ propping up a perverse regime (at the price of small, albeit regrettable, numbers of civilian casualties).[36]

Unfortunately, Dunlap is arguing from what he sees as preferable as opposed to what the law allows. As is so often the case, determining what is a military advantage as that term is understood under IHL cannot be considered in isolation but must be understood in the totality of IHL.[37] And under IHL, a touchstone is always that an action must conform with military necessity; and in the context of targeting, this principle is expressed in the preamble to the *St Petersburg Declaration*: "The only legitimate object which States should endeavour to accomplish during war is to

---

30 Laursen, above n 19 (chapter 3), 782.

31 *OTP Report*, above n 90 (chapter 1), [76].

32 *Why They Died: Civilian Casualties in Lebanon during the 2006 War*, above n 3 (chapter 2), 75.

33 *Israel/Lebanon: Deliberate destruction or "collateral damage"? Israeli attacks on civilian infrastructure*, above n 253 (chapter 4), 16.

34 Ronzitti, above n 25 (chapter 5).

35 Dunlap, *Law and Military Interventions: Preserving Humanitarian Values in 21st Conflicts*, above n 168 (chapter 3), 15.

36 Ibid, 15–6.

37 See Ian Sinclair, *The Vienna Convention on the Law of Treaties* (2nd ed, 1984) 139.

weaken the military forces of the enemy".[38] I also suggest that he has perhaps misunderstood a United State of America, Department of Defense, General Counsel advice. In a footnote, Dunlap quotes the General Counsel advice as:

> [w]hen it is determined that civilian media broadcasts are directly interfering with the accomplishment of the military force's mission, there is no law of war objection to using minimum force to shut it down.[39]

However, the next sentence in the General Counsel advice is:

> The extent to which force can be used for purely psychological operations purposes, such as shutting down a civilian radio station for the sole purpose of undermining the morale of the civilian population, is an issue that has yet to be addressed authoritatively by the international community.[40]

I respectfully suggest that Dunlap has paid insufficient attention to that part of the advice that says that the "civilian media broadcasts must be *directly* interfering with the accomplishment of the military force's mission";[41] not to mention that the advice says that minimum force is permitted.[42]

Returning to statement by Ronzitti that radio and television stations that broadcast military communications are lawful targets but those that broadcast pure propaganda are not, the difficulty remains that:

> Part of the problem is that there is no consensus about where to draw the line between military communication and propaganda. For instance, when Saddam Hussein is shown on television in military uniform, exhorting his supporters to rise up and "slit the throats" of U.S. troops, is that a contribution to military action or not?[43]

In this simple statement, Dworkin has in fact pointed us towards the solution. The mistake that is often made is to try to determine whether propaganda as a class contributes to military action and consequently whether stopping the dissemination of propaganda offers a military advantage. The difficulty is that propaganda is a very broad class, and what some would class as propaganda others would class as something else. The correct approach is not to try to determine whether the use of a TV or radio station to spread propaganda makes the TV or radio station a military objective. Rather, it is whether the use of the TV or radio station to disseminate

38 *St Petersburg Declaration*, above n 64 (chapter 1).

39 Dunlap, *Law and Military Interventions: Preserving Humanitarian Values in 21st Conflicts*, above n 168 (chapter 3), fn 80.

40 Department of Defense, Office of General Counsel, *An Assessment of International Legal Issues in Information Operations* (1999) Maxwell-Gunter AFB, 9 <http://www.au.af.mil/au/awc/awcgate/dod-io-legal/dod-io-legal.pdf> at 27 November 2007.

41 Ibid (emphasis added).

42 Ibid.

43 Dworkin, *'Iraqi Television: A Legitimate Target?'*, above n 20 (chapter 5), 2.

a particular message or type of message makes the TV or radio station a military objective. As has been previously discussed, under API we need to move away from deeming classes of objects to be military objectives to applying the article 52(2) API test in each case.

To use an analogy, we can liken a radio station to a bridge, a truck to one particular style of propaganda broadcast, and the contents of the truck to the contents of the broadcast. Looked at this way, in the same way that a bridge may or may not be a military objective depending upon what the cargo is inside a truck passing over or about to pass over the bridge, a radio station may or may not be a military objective depending not on classing the broadcast as propaganda but rather by assessing the actual contents of the message. Of course, in practice the test may be difficult, as it may remain the case that it will be "very difficult to quantify the impact of propaganda from a certain outlet on the military action."[44] Nonetheless, at least the correct test will be being applied.

So, how might this work in practice? In an article discussing IHL and the NATO action in Kosovo, Burger writes that "communication facilities were used to send orders to military forces and receive their reports, spread Serbian propaganda, and generally prolong the war." He concludes that their "destruction or damage was consistent with the definition of 'military objective'".[45] If we break this into three sub-points, the argument for communication facilities being legitimate military objectives is that they were used to: send orders to military forces and receive their reports, spread Serbian propaganda, and generally prolong the war.

It is not clear whether Burger is using the API or customary international law test for military objectives. When assessed against article 52(2) API, I agree that point (a) can lead to assessing a communication facility as a military objective. I, for reasons stated above, disagree that merely stating that communication facilities were used to spread propaganda can support an assessment of an object as a military objective. Rather, the content of the messages must be assessed. I am also of the view that use to 'generally prolong the war' is not a definitive enough assessment for determining whether an object is a military objective. Many things might assist in prolonging the war,[46] but the test in article 52(1) API is stricter.

There are two further aspects of propaganda that need specific consideration. First, the truthfulness of the message is irrelevant. A justification for an attack during the NATO bombing campaign was that "a propaganda machine that creates false propaganda constantly is a legitimate target and that's why it was hit."[47] To paraphrase Laursen, why logically limit to false propaganda?[48] When considering

44 Laursen, above n 19 (chapter 3), 783.

45 James Burger, 'International humanitarian law and the Kosovo crisis: Lessons learned or to be learned' (2000) 837 *International Review of the Red Cross* <http://www.icrc.org/Web/eng/siteeng0.nsf/iwpList177/1A257FE6E1DC3A57C1256B66005E3484> at 4 June 2006.

46 For example, statements concerning the moral or religious rightness of the conflict or, in a prolonged conflict, mothers having babies.

47 *Briefing by the International Development Secretary, Ms Clare Short, and the Chief of Joint Operations, Admiral Sir Ian Garnett on 23 April 1999* (1999) <www.kosovo.mod.uk/brief230499.htm> at 26 December 2005.

48 Laursen, above n 19 (chapter 3), 783.

whether a radio or TV station can be targeted, there is no legal distinction between a radio or TV station that broadcasts true propaganda and one that broadcasts false propaganda. Rather, the issue is the content of the message.

Second, the issue of propaganda aimed at civilian morale was considered in the *OTP Report*. After noting that "whether the media constitutes a legitimate target group is a debatable issue",[49] the *OTP Report* states that if the media is "merely disseminating propaganda to generate support for the war effort, it is not a legitimate target."[50] The *OTP Report* goes on to state:

> The media does have an effect on civilian morale. If that effect is merely to foster support for the war effort, the media is not a legitimate military objective. If the media is the nerve system that keeps a war-monger in power and thus perpetuates the war effort, it may fall within the definition of a legitimate military objective.[51]

I agree with the statement that where propaganda does no more than rally general civilian support for the war effort (eg, exhortations to work harder, buy government bonds or enlist), then that is not sufficient to meet the test required by article 52(2) API. Attacks on "radio stations, newspaper agencies, and the like ... [are not lawful if] only attacked to affect civilian morale."[52] While not offering direct legal support for my argument, I see this result as being similar in principle to the prohibition on attacks designed to spread terror among the civilian population. In a similar vein, British Defence Doctrine states:

> The civilian population and civilian objects must not be deliberately targeted; the morale of an enemy's civilian population is not a legitimate target and attacks designed to spread terror among the civilian population are expressly prohibited.[53]

The first statement after the semi-colon is that "the morale of an enemy's civilian population is not a legitimate target". The reference to the prohibition on "attacks designed to spread terror among the civilian population" is not a qualifier but an additional point or elaboration. My view is supported by Human Rights Watch. In relation to an attack by NATO on RTS (ostensibly, because it was transmitting propaganda supportive of the Yugoslav war effort), Human Rights Watch stated:

> While stopping such propaganda may serve to demoralize the Yugoslav population and undermine the government's political support, neither purpose offers

49 *OTP Report*, above n 90 (chapter 1), [47].

50 Ibid.

51 Ibid, [55].

52 *Expert Meeting: "Targeting Military Objectives"*, above n 27 (chapter 1), 10.

53 *British Defence Doctrine* (JWP 0-01) issued by the British Minister of Defence in 1996, in Rogers, 'Zero-casualty warfare', above n 94 (chapter 3).

> the 'concrete and direct' military advantage necessary to make them a legitimate military target.[54]

While I agreed with the first statement in the quote from the *OTP Report*,[55] I disagree with the last statement.[56] First, as matter of principle and law, IHL needs to be applied equally. Accordingly, there should be no difference between how IHL is applied when in a conflict with totalitarian State or a fully functioning democracy.[57] If attacks were lawful on media outlets that supported a war-monger, then consider the following example. State A is involved in a coalition operation against State B. State A is a democracy, with two main parties (Parties C & L) and two main media conglomerates (Media M and Media P). An election is due in four weeks. Party C is in currently power. Party C committed State A's armed forces to the conflict and supports their continued involvement. Party L opposed the initial involvement and supports a withdrawal. Both Parties are campaigning consistent with the above, and Media M is widely considered to support both continued involvement in the armed conflict and re-election of Party C. Based on the conclusions of the *OTP Report*, it could be argued that Media M is a lawful target and the party headquarters and branches of Party C are legitimate targets. This is clearly wrong in principle and wrong in law, and demonstrates the inaccuracy of the conclusion reached in the *OTP Report*.

However, there is also a second point that shows the conclusion in the *OTP Report* is wrong. To allow an attack on a media organisation merely because of general support for the war effort is surely no different from permitting attacks on any object that can be shown to support the war effort. But, mere contribution to the war effort is no longer considered as coming within the test laid down by article 52(2) API.

There is a further aspect of the role of the media that I wish to discuss, and that is where media outlets are used to incite war crimes—be that by the military or by

54 *Civilian Deaths in the NATO Air Campaign*, above n 88 (chapter 1). Similar comments are made in *Off Target: The Conduct of the War and Civilian Casualties in Iraq*, above n 91 (chapter 4), 49.

55 That if the effect of the media "is merely to foster support for the war effort, the media is not a legitimate military objective." (*OTP Report*, above n 90 (chapter 1), [55])

56 "If the media is the nerve system that keeps a war-monger in power and thus perpetuates the war effort, it may fall within the definition of a legitimate military objective." (Ibid)

57 I note that Dunlap argues that IHL should be applied differently in some circumstances, particularly against "societies psychologically disposed to champion ethnic cleansing and similarly maniacal behaviour by their militaries." However, it seems clear from his argument that while that is what he argues should occur, he recognises that is not the current law; and, therefore, he also argues for a change in the law to accommodate his argument. (Dunlap, 'The End of Innocence: Rethinking Noncombatancy in the Post-Kosovo Era', above n 79 (chapter 1), in particular at pages 10 and 14–7) Interestingly, in subsequent article, Dunlap sates that the US traditionally focuses on attacking an opposing State's military strength while current opponents of the United States "focus on the people element and seek to diminish the strength of their support for the military effort." (Dunlap, *Law and Military Interventions: Preserving Humanitarian Values in 21st Conflicts*, above n 168 (chapter 3), 4)

the civilian population. If the media are not a legitimate target due to spreading propaganda in general support of the war effort, can the media become a legitimate target if used to incite war crimes? For example, some argue that RTS broadcasts were calculated to incite genocide and racial hatred during the Kosovo conflict.[58] Also, there is strong evidence of such actions during the Rwanda conflict.[59] In any event, as Laursen states, whether or not this occurred during the Kosovo conflict, the issue is nonetheless difficult and challenging.[60]

Returning to the discussion in the *OTP Report* about the media as targets, it is stated that "[i]f the media is used to incite crimes, as in Rwanda, then it is a legitimate target."[61] Unfortunately, no argument or support for this assertion is provided. When commenting on the *OTP Report*, Ronzitti appears to agree with this aspect of the *OTP Report* as he writes:

> Moreover, there are instances in which the media are used to incite the population to commit war crimes and crimes against humanity, as happened in Rwanda. As the Report states: "If the media is the nerve system that keeps a warmonger in power and thus perpetuates the war effort, it may fall within the definition of a legitimate military objective." In such a case, the media may be targeted as a military objective, particularly also by those States which are not bound by Protocol I, such as the United States, whose broad definition of military objective is not in keeping with the narrow delimitation given by Protocol I.[62]

The above quote joins two slightly different topics, and therefore it is not possible to be definite about Ronzitti's position. As argued above, there is a distinction between perpetuating the war generally and inciting the commission of war crimes inside that war. Therefore, while the arguably broader interpretation adopted by the United States of America of what amounts to a military objective may extend to support for the war effort, that is different from whether the United States of America approach or the stricter API definition covers the incitement of war crimes.

Laursen does a very good job of asking the interesting question that arises from this issue when he writes that "[e]ven if the definition of a military target found in API is accepted as authoritative, it is very difficult to place institutions that incite genocide within this definition."[63] What is important about Laursen's statement is that it refocuses our attention on the correct issue, which is the definition of a military objective. It is not enough that we abhor war crimes and consequently believe that armed force can be used to prevent not only the commission of war crimes but also the incitement thereof. What Laursen causes us to do is to look for the legal justification, not just the conclusion. As Fenrick states, while "the Protocol I defi-

---

58 See generally *Hate Radio: Europe* (2002) Radio Netherlands <http://www2.rnw.nl/rnw/en/features/media/dossiers/hateradioeur.html> at 26 December 2005.

59 See generally *Prosecutor v Nahimana, Barayagwiza and Ngeze, (Trial Chamber)* Case No ICTR-99-52-T (3 December 2003).

60 Laursen, above n 19 (chapter 3), 785.

61 *OTP Report*, above n 90 (chapter 1), [47].

62 Ronzitti, above n 25 (chapter 5) (footnotes omitted).

63 Laursen, above n 19 (chapter 3), 785.

nition of military objective is not beyond criticism, it provides the contemporary standard which must be used when attempting to determine the lawfulness of particular attacks."[64]

Laursen goes on to write:

> On the surface at least, a broadcasting station that incites genocide does not make an effective contribution to military activities and its destruction would, therefore, not constitute a clear military advantage. On the contrary, to the extent the armed forces participate in the genocide, this would appear, from a cynical point of view, to detract from their contribution to legal military efforts.[65]

Importantly, this remains the case even where the reason for the armed conflict is some form of intervention to prevent genocide. Laursen writes:

> One could argue, however, that the genocide was an integral part of the military campaign, in which case military "success" had to be measured according to the number of civilian casualties from a specific ethnic group. From such a perspective, the criteria of "effective contribution" would have been fulfilled. Even such a distorted deliberation, however, would not account for "definite military advantage" if the enemy regarded genocide as being without military significance.[66]

It is important to distinguish what a military does from what, under IHL, amounts to a contribution to military action or a military advantage. Those terms must be considered as relating only to the conflict between opposing armed forces. If this were not the case, then the whole concept of military necessity, as first expounded in the preamble to the *St Petersburg Declaration*, would be distorted. The previous point is essentially a manifestation of the distinction between the *jus in bello* and the *jus ad bellum*. The reasons for going to war do not affect the application of IHL. As Laursen identifies:

> Consider a revolutionary government that announces over its radio stations that it intends to destroy all private property in territory it has occupied. If such policy is assumed to violate Article 53 of the Fourth /Geneva Convention, does the said statement make radio stations legitimate military targets? Clearly, it does not.[67]

Laursen also correctly points out that while there is arguably a huge difference between the destruction of private property and genocide, it is difficult—if not impossible—to distinguish formally between the two examples.[68]

While this study is concerned with targeting under IHL, it needs to be remembered that this is not the only legal justification for the use of force. Accordingly,

---

64 Fenrick, 'Attacking the Enemy Civilian as a Punishable Offense', above n 20 (chapter 3), 544.

65 Laursen, above n 19 (chapter 3), 786.

66 Ibid.

67 Ibid.

68 Ibid.

I am not stating that force, including maybe even lethal force, cannot be used to prevent the commission or incitement of war crimes. What I am arguing is that the legal basis is not based on an attack on a lawful military objective as defined by article 52(2) API. As for another legal basis, Fenrick has suggested:

> a facility which is being used to incite the commission of a serious violation of international humanitarian law or to provide the location for the commission of such an offence may be lawfully attacked even if it did not meet the criteria for a military objective. For example, attacks on the gas chambers at Auschwitz or on the facilities of Radio Mille Collines in Rwanda which were used to incite genocide would, it is suggested, be lawful because of some generalized right to prevent the continuing commission of crimes.[69]

While Laursen is understandably sceptical, he does say that this may be the best, even if not ideal, option at present.[70] Similarly, at a meeting of experts to discuss the meaning of direct participation in hostilities:

> no objection was raised to the argument that, in exceptional circumstances, lethal force could be used outside the framework of the conduct of hostilities, namely within a law enforcement framework or in case of international interventions for the suppression of massive inter-civilian atrocities, such a genocide and ethnic cleansing, in so far as these interventions were not governed by IHL on the conduct of hostilities.[71]

Regrettably, as this issue is outside the scope of this book, further discussion will have to wait for another occasion.

5.3 Electrical power generation stations

Electrical power generation stations appear as regular targets in armed conflicts, dating as far back as World War I.[72] A good example of the military reasoning behind attacking the electricity grid is provided in the April 1992 *Final Report to Congress* on the conduct of the 1991 Persian Gulf War.

> Electricity is vital to the functioning of a modern military and industrial power such as Iraq, and disrupting the electrical supply can make destruction of other facilities unnecessary. Disrupting the electricity supply to key Iraqi facilities

69 William Fenrick, 'Targeting and Proportionality during the NATO Bombing Campaign against Yugoslavia' (2001) 12:3 *European Journal of International Law* 489, 496.

70 Laursen, above n 19 (chapter 3), 787.

71 *Third Expert Meeting on the Notion of Direct Participation in Hostilities: Summary Report*, above n 53 (chapter 2), 11.

72 J.W. Crawford, III, *The Law of Noncombatant Immunity and the Targeting of National Electric Power Systems* (1996) Defense Technical Information Centre, 1 <http://stinet.dtic.mil/cgi-bin/GetTRDoc?AD=ADA312110&Location=U2&doc=GetTRDoc.pdf> at 26 November 2007.

> degraded a wide variety of crucial capabilities, from the radar sites that warned of Coalition air strikes, to the refrigeration used to preserve biological weapons (BW), to nuclear weapons production facilities.
> To do this effectively required the disruption of virtually the entire Iraqi electric grid, to prevent the rerouting of power around damaged nodes. Although backup generators sometimes were available, they usually are slow to come on line, provide less power than main sources, and are not as reliable.
> During switch over from main power to a backup generator, computers drop off line, temporary confusion ensues, and other residual problems can occur. Because of the fast pace of a modern, massed air attack, even milliseconds of enemy power disruption can mean the difference between life and death for aircrews.[73]

Waxman then shows us why, despite what will often be a clear military value, this target set remains problematic when he writes:

> Distinguishing between military and civilian infrastructure is sometimes difficult and, especially with respect to support systems that provide basic needs such as electricity, it may be impossible to destroy or disrupt only those portions servicing the military. This last point is especially true when the military, generally the priority user during crises, can be expected to utilize any residual capacity.[74]

So, what can usefully be said about the IHL issues concerning attacks on electrical power stations? First, it is generally accepted that in the right circumstances, and that these circumstances would not be unusual, power stations can be military objectives. Power stations are listed in the 1956 ICRC *Draft Rules for the Limitation of Dangers incurred by the Civilian Population in Time of War*,[75] and see also article 56(1) API.[76]

Second, it is important not to make assumptions or generalisations about power stations. For example, Hays Parks notes that in an integrated system power will be transferred from different power plants and how in the United States power can be transferred from opposite sides of the US.[77] However, as late as March 2005 not only does Australia not have a national integrated grid, not even all the eastern States are part of an integrated grid.[78] Therefore, it would be very difficult to argue as to why a power station in Western Australia needed to be targeted if the desired effect was to reduce power to a military installation in Victoria.

---

73 US Department of Defense, *Conduct of the Persian Gulf War: Final Report to Congress*, above n 29 (chapter 3), 148–9.

74 Waxman, above n 56 (chapter 1), 20.

75 See above n 16 (chapter 3).

76 While API, above n 2 (chapter 1), art 56(1) provides protection from attack for, inter alia, nuclear electrical generating stations, the very existence of the article indicates that it was believed that such power stations were likely to be the subject of lawful attack if special protection was not provided.

77 Hays Parks, 'Air War and the Law of War', above n 181 (chapter 3), 141 (fn 415).

78 'What's up with our power supply?' (March 2005) *Choice* 26, 29.

Third, the reason for attack on a power station must be in accordance with article 52(2) API. The following justification for an attack would not be lawful under API:

> For example, one Air Force planner stated in an interview with *The Washington Post* that the attacks on the country's electrical system were intended to send a message to the Iraqi people: "We're not going to tolerate Saddam Hussein or his regime. Fix that, and we'll fix your electricity."[79]

As Human Rights Watch state, "[d]irect attacks of this sort on civilian morale and well-being are clearly impermissible under the rules of law."[80] As argued in section 5.4, justifying an attack based on affecting civilian morale is not permissible. But what about the following case that Waxman has identified?

> Planners sometimes view the dual-use nature of infrastructure systems opportunistically, because military usage arguably legitimizes these systems as targets, even though it may in fact be the incidental effects on the civilian population that planners hope to manipulate.[81]

In that case, if an attack is otherwise lawful (ie, the justification for the attack meets the requirements of article 52(2) API), then consistent with what I stated back in section 4.2.5, the attack does not become unlawful just because there is a concurrent, even primary, purpose to affect civilian morale.[82] The attack would be unlawful if the primary purpose was not just to affect civilian morale but was to spread terror among the civilian population contrary to the second sentence of article 51(2) API.

The final aspect that requires consideration is the secondary effects of attacks on power generation stations (or distribution networks).

> Allied forces destroyed many electrical power stations in Iraq. The attacks adversely affected Iraq's civilian population, as they rendered sewage plants in many civilian areas inoperable and left many hospitals without power.[83]

As this issue concerns not the initial assessment of the target as a military objective, but rather whether the attack on an otherwise legitimate military objective is lawful in particular circumstances, this point is pursued in section 8.3.2. The next topic I wish to discuss is not a *type* of target per se, but the *justification* for attacking a particular target.

---

79 *Needless Deaths in the Gulf War: Civilian Casualties During the Air Campaign and Violations of the Laws of War*, above n 38 (chapter 3).

80 Ibid.

81 Waxman, above n 56 (chapter 1), 21.

82 *Expert Meeting: "Targeting Military Objectives"*, above n 27 (chapter 1), 10. I note, however, that Crawford doubts the actual likelihood of achieving the desired effect—Crawford, above n 72 (chapter 5) 5–6 and 12.

83 Smyth, above n 103 (chapter 1). See also Crawford, above n 72 (chapter 5) 13.

5.4 Economic targets

The arguments for and against attacking economic targets are, in essence, an argument about whether the test for the definition of a military objective, be that under customary international law or article 52(2) API, should be interpreted broadly or narrowly. In particular, how remote from the immediacy of the battlefield can an object's effect be on military action, and, therefore, how remotely can an attacker consider what amounts to a military advantage from a particular attack and that object still be considered a legitimate military objective? The problem is a manifestation of the fact that IHL by its very nature imposes limits on means and methods of warfare, and reasonable people can differ as to where those limits should be placed. For example:

> The Protocol I definition of military objective has been criticized by W. Hays Parks, the Special Assistant for Law of War Matters to the U.S. Army Judge Advocate General as being focused too narrowly on definite military advantage and paying too little heed to war sustaining capability, including economic targets such as export industries.[84]

The interesting thing about that quote is that it indicates that Hays Parks is critical of API definition, as opposed to interpretations of that definition. In other words, if the quote is accurate, one can conclude that Hays Parks is of the view that an object cannot be assessed as being a military objective because of its war sustaining capability. Robertson devotes a number of paragraphs to this issue in his article on military objectives.[85] He refers to the definition of military objective in *The Commander's Handbook on the Law of Naval Operations* (the '*Commander's Handbook*'), which is:

> Military objectives are combatants and those objects which, by their nature, location, purpose, or use, effectively contribute to the enemy's *war-fighting or war-sustaining capability* and whose total or partial destruction, capture, or neutralization would constitute a definite military advantage to the attacker under the circumstances at the time of the attack.[86]

The *Commander's Handbook* then states that "[e]conomic targets of the enemy that indirectly but effectively support and sustain the enemy's war-fighting capability may also be attacked."[87] Robertson is of the view that the main point of difference between the *San Remo Manual* and the *Commander's Handbook* is exports. The *Commander's Handbook* includes exports as military objectives (at least where they are the sole or principal source of financial resources), whereas the San Remo Round Table "firmly rejected the broadening of military objectives to include such targets

84 Fenrick, 'Attacking the Enemy Civilian as a Punishable Offense', above n 20 (chapter 3), 544 (footnote omitted).

85 Robertson Jr, above n 105 (chapter 1), 50–1.

86 US Department of the Navy, *Annotated Supplement to the Commander's Handbook on the Law of Naval Operations* (1997) [8.1.1] (my emphasis).

87 Ibid.

because the connection between exports and military action would be too remote."[88] Of course, as the *Commander's Handbook* is a United States of America manual, one assumes this expresses the United States Navy's opinion on the customary international law definition of military objective.[89] However, why it is important to this work is that Robertson then notes that the San Remo Round Table specifically addressed the issue of whether to adopt the definition in the *Commander's Handbook* or in API. The *San Remo Manual* adopted the API definition. Why this is interesting is that it lends some support to the view that the API definition is narrower than the United States Navy definition, and that arguably the API definition of military objective does not include economic targets.

It is notable that in both World War I and World War II "the economies of all the major parties involved were completely mobilized in support of the war effort."[90] Nonetheless, the definition of military objective in article 52(2) API did not clearly adopt economic targets. Robertson also refers to Kalshoven being against the view that contribution to the war effort makes a target a legitimate military objective.[91]

In a one-page article on "Total War" in the Crimes of War Project, Rowe sets out various (non-legal) definitions of Total War, including:

> It has also been used to mean war conducted against an enemy's military and economic infrastructure, across all of its territory, in order to cripple the enemy's ability to wage war; Great Britain used the term in this sense in both World Wars.[92]

In the next paragraph, he then writes:

> It is even possible, although more difficult, to fight a war attacking military-economic infrastructure legally, provided that the attacking forces respect IHL rules regarding indiscriminate attack.[93]

While it would appear from this that he is of the view that at least some economic targets can be legitimate military objectives, his article deals with IHL generally and the above comments are not necessarily dealing with API—it may well have been the case that he was discussing military objectives under customary international law. Alternatively, whereas he may have meant his comments to apply to article 52(2) API, as he was non-specific about how military-economic infrastructure might become a legitimate military objective, and as he uses words like *more difficult*, his comments cannot be adopted to either support or deny the legitimacy of

88 Robertson Jr, above n 105 (chapter 1), 51.

89 The United States of America does not have one authorative document that can be considered to express that State's position on many IHL points, nor even a single military manual. So, and for example, at a 2005 expert meeting, "[t]here was continued disagreement on whether the notion of 'war-sustaining capability' reflected the official US position or not." (*Expert Meeting: "Targeting Military Objectives"*, above n 27 (chapter 1), 5)

90 Ibid, 47.

91 Ibid, 55.

92 Peter Rowe, *Total War*, Crimes of War Project <http://www.crimesofwar.org/thebook/total-war.html> at 26 May 2006.

93 Ibid.

attacking economic targets under API obligations.[94] Some further, limited support for the view that economic targets are not lawful military objectives can be drawn from an unattributed assertion by an expert at a meeting to discuss the meaning of direct participation in hostilities. That expert is attributed as stating that "the question of whether significant oil sales revenues could transform the oil industry into a military objective had generally been answered in the negative."[95]

The section of the report of the expert meeting on targeting military objectives that deals with "Economic Targets and their 'Effective Contribution to Military Action' or 'War-Sustaining Capability'" is not as helpful as it might be.[96] Unfortunately, the report does not consistently make it clear whether any particular expert's comment is dealing with customary international law or article 52(2) API. However, I suggest the general tenor was that 'war-sustaining' targets do not come within the test to be applied under article 52(2) API. But, as I note, it is a difficult section upon which to reach a firm and conclusive view as to what was the majority opinion.

Finally, Dinstein specifically discusses this issue and rejects 'war-sustaining' objects as coming within the definition of military objective in article 52(2) API.[97]

So, when one notes that, generally speaking, the main commentators who include objects contributing to the war effort as military objectives are discussing customary international law, and that the majority of the military manuals United States armed forces always add some extra words to the article 52(2) API definition of military objectives, then the better conclusion is that objects that contribute to a belligerent's war sustaining capability, including economic targets, are not military objectives as defined in article 52(2) API.

The following section deals with perhaps one of the most controversial of all current target sets, which is the opposing government itself.

5.5 Government power base

Perhaps because a number of recent conflicts have involved being in direct conflict with the opposing government (as opposed to the people of that State), the direct targeting of the government, or the ability of that government to stay in power, has been very topical. By way of example, in previous wars it was normal to consider the whole population of the other belligerent as the enemy. One would talk of being at war with 'Germany' or with 'Japan'. However, a number of recent conflicts have used language like liberating the people of Iraq from the Iraqi leaders,[98] and removing the Taliban and allowing the people of Afghanistan to elect their own

---

94 My comments are not meant to be a criticism of the article, as it was a one-page article that no doubt was aimed at a different audience with a different purpose than a lengthy article published in an international law legal journal.

95 *Third Expert Meeting on the Notion of Direct Participation in Hostilities: Summary Report*, above n 53 (chapter 2), 15.

96 *Expert Meeting: "Targeting Military Objectives"*, above n 27 (chapter 1), 6–7.

97 Dinstein, *The Conduct of Hostilities under the Law of International Armed Conflict*, above n 66 (chapter 2), 87.

98 It would seem, though, that *Operation Iraqi Liberation* had a rather unfortunate abbreviation compared with *Operation Iraqi Freedom*.

leaders.[99] I have discussed previously attacks on the actual leadership.[100] However, there remains a 'grey area concern[ing] political sites (like government ministries) that aren't a direct part of the military chain of command, or the personal assets of the leadership.'[101]

While an attack directly on a government or its power base may seem attractive, that does not mean it is lawful. As is rightly pointed out in a *Crimes of War* article on targeting during the 2003 Gulf War, the test for what is a military objective, '[a]s with the rest of the laws of war, … represents a hard-fought trade-off between military requirements and humanitarian concerns'.[102] In an article discussing targeting decisions made in light of the stated objective of regime change in the 2003 Gulf War, Dworkin writes:

> In practice this meant that the military campaign of the United States and its allies was targeted not so much against the Iraqi army as against the security apparatus that Saddam Hussein and his regime used to maintain their hold on power. … a central focus of coalition efforts throughout the war remained on such targets as Saddam Hussein's palaces, Iraqi government ministries, and the local headquarters of the Ba'ath Party.
>
> The law does not appear to allow scope for attacks designed to weaken the domestic power base of an oppressive regime, at least where this apparatus of control is clearly distinct from the country's military infrastructure.[103]

---

99 "American and coalition forces are steadily advancing against the regime of Saddam Hussein. With each new village they liberate, our forces are learning more about the atrocities of that regime, and the deep fear the dictator has instilled in the Iraqi people. Yet no crime of this dying regime will divert us from our mission. We will not stop until Iraq is free." (President George W. Bush, *Operation Iraqi Freedom* (2003) The White House <http://www.whitehouse.gov/news/releases/2003/04/20030405.html> at 27 December 2005) "We express our continued support for the people of Afghanistan in their effort to establish a government that can bring peace and stability to Afghanistan, close down terrorist camps, and end Afghanistan's use as a platform for international terrorists. … The United States and Russia do not intend to, and cannot, create the future government of Afghanistan. It is up to the Afghans themselves to determine their future. … We agree that the Taliban as a movement should have no place in future bodies of state power in Afghanistan." (President George W. Bush and President Vladimir Putin, *Joint Statement on Afghanistan* (2001) The White House <http://www.whitehouse.gov/news/releases/2001/11/20011113-9.html> at 27 December 2005) "Our overall objective is to eliminate terrorism as a force in international affairs. … The immediate objectives are: … (d) assuming that Mullah Omar will not comply with the US ultimatum we require sufficient change in the leadership to ensure that Afghanistan's links to international terrorism are broken." (UK Government, *Defeating International Terrorism: Campaign Objectives* (2001) Global Security <http://www.globalsecurity.org/military/library/news/2001/10/uk-011016-terror-objectives.htm> at 27 December 2005)

100 See section 4.2.4.

101 *In America's Sights: Targeting Decisions in a War with Iraq* (2003) Crimes of War Project <http://www.crimesofwar.org/print/onnews/iraq-print.html> at 4 March 2005.

102 Ibid.

103 Anthony Dworkin, *The Iraq War in Retrospect* (2003) Crimes of War Project <http://www.crimesofwar.org/print/onnews/iraq33-print.html> at 4 March 2005. As I noted in my introduction, this book is about general principles of law and not particular cases.

I would go further and delete the words *appear to* in the last sentence above. The reason for my view is the stated rule in article 52(2) API. A target must meet the test for being a military objective, and military objectives are viewed independently of the ultimate goal of the armed conflict. As argued back in section 3.5.1, there is a need to distinguish between the national-strategic goals being pursued in an armed conflict and the attainment of a definite military advantage.[104] I agree with Oeter when he writes that prohibited attacks include attacks 'of a purely political purpose, whether to demonstrate military strength, or to intimidate the political leadership of the adversary.'[105] The achievement of national-strategic goals is not a military advantage.

However, care needs to be taken not to exclude valid targets. A target supporting the government can also support the military. For example, during Operation FALCONER, '75 Squadron conducted four ... planned strikes against a variety of military targets including Iraqi Intelligence Service facilities.'[106] In the case of the dictatorship then in power in Iraq, an intelligence service could be used to support both the regime remaining in power (by discovering and dealing with internal attacks and rebellions) as well as providing intelligence about opposing military forces. For example:

> The Directorate of General Security (DGS), the Iraqi security organization responsible for monitoring political dissent, was a fixture throughout Iraq. During the war, DGS was responsible for coordinating local militias.[107]

Of course, the roles and functions of any given intelligence service must be assessed and not merely presumed. The point is that an agency like an intelligence service can be as much a dual-use target as a bridge or power station.

In conclusion, the government as a whole, the organisations that assist to keep a government in power, and the personal assets of the government's elite are not lawful military objectives per se. Rather, they can become military objectives only when assessed to be of a military value. The assessment cannot be influenced by the fact that the goal or objective of the attacker in the conflict may be regime change or regime policy change.

However, so as not to be seen to be quoting out of context, while the point I quoted remains valid, I do note the following sentence in Dworkin's article: "In fact, in the case of the war with Iraq, the distinction may be less significant than it first appears, since all the resources of Saddam's regime were deployed against the invading coalition forces."

104 See Solf, above n 90 (chapter 2), 128.

105 Oeter, above n 24 (chapter 2), 158 (footnote omitted).

106 *The War in Iraq: ADF Operations in the Middle East in 2003*, above n 170 (chapter 3), 28.

107 *Off Target: The Conduct of the War and Civilian Casualties in Iraq*, above n 91 (chapter 4), 53.

Chapter 6

United Nations operations: does the law of targeting differ?

The generally accepted view is that the legality of the resort to force does not affect the IHL obligations of the parties to the conflict.[1] While I agree with this as a general proposition, it is my view that this is a simplified view and is not a completely accurate statement of the law. In 1971, the ICRC drew a distinction between the humanitarian rules of IHL—which the ICRC considered it be essential that these rules apply equally between parties to a conflict—and some other rules that apply in an armed conflict[2] (on which issue the ICRC did not wish to take a stand but noted that some others had expressed a view that such rules may not apply equally).[3] For example, under customary international law a captured enemy military aircraft is considered war booty and title to the aircraft passes to the capturing State.[4] This makes sense under a traditional view of armed conflict being fought between two or more States. However, when a State's sole legal authority for engaging in armed conflict is to enforce a UNSCR, does it still make sense that a State can appropriate certain public property for retention after the conclusion of the conflict?

In this chapter, I discuss whether the interpretation of the applicable targeting law is affected by the fact that one party's legal justification for the armed conflict includes UN authorisation or approval for its actions. I argue that where a State is acting pursuant to a UNSCR, the IHL applicable to target selection, and even more particular still, the lawfulness of particular targets, may vary depending upon the terms of the UNSCR authorising the military action. As UN authorisation for participation in an armed conflict is an aspect of the *jus ad bellum*, the starting point for this chapter is to discuss the relationship between the *jus ad bellum* and the *jus in bello*.

1 Greenwood, 'Historical Development and Legal Basis', above n 45 (chapter 1), 7–8.

2 For example, the "rules concerning economic war, the law applicable after the end of hostilities, especially in relation to enemy property, as well as the law of neutrality." (CE/1b, above n 13 (chapter 1), 35)

3 Ibid.

4 Wolff Heintschel von Heinegg, 'The Law of Armed Conflict at Sea' in Dieter Fleck (ed), *The Handbook of Humanitarian Law in Armed Conflict* (1995) 405, 424.

6.1 The *jus in bello* is independent of the *jus ad bellum*

The contemporary legal view is that the *jus in bello* is independent of the *jus ad bellum*.[5] This is shown by such statements as:

(a) 'The unique aspect of international humanitarian law is that it applies without judgment of the merits of the causes being fought over.'[6]

(b) 'After much soul-searching in the 1970s, the Institut de Droit International came to the conclusion that the rules of armed conflict—whether within the scope of international humanitarian law or otherwise—must be equally respected by both sides, even in hostilities in which UN forces are engaged.

This is still good law today.'[7]

(c) 'Whatever be the merits or otherwise of resorting to the use of force (the province of the ius ad bellum), when once the domain of force is entered, the governing law in that domain is the ius in bello. The humanitarian laws of war take over and govern all who participate, assailant and victim alike. ... The reality is, of course, that while the ius ad bellum only opens the door to the use of force (in self-defence or by the Security Council), whoever enters that door must function subject to the ius in bello.'[8]

(d) 'Accordingly, this report does not address who was responsible for the armed conflict between Hezbollah and Israel or which party was justified in waging war—the justness of the cause does not affect the international humanitarian law analysis.'[9]

As an aside, perhaps the one clear exception is that '[a]rticle 47 [API] effectively excludes mercenaries from the protection of the Geneva Conventions as either 'combatants' or 'prisoners of war'.'[10] Essentially, this is a variation of the *jus in bello* based on the individual *jus ad bellum*. As McCoubrey notes, "[t]his is an overtly moral judgment inserted in Protocol I".[11]

It would appear that a contrary view on the independence of *jus in bello* from the *jus ad bellum* was recently expressed by James Burger, who writes:

---

5 See generally Dinstein, *War, Aggression and Self-Defence*, above n 112 (chapter 3) 156–62.

6 Duncan Kerr, 'Opening Remarks' in William Maley (ed), *Shelters from the Storm: Developments in International Humanitarian Law* (1995) 2, 3.

7 Yoram Dinstein, 'Remarks' in ASIL Proceedings, *Implementing Limitations on the Use of Force: The Doctrine of Proportionality and Necessity* (1992) 54. See also Dinstein, *The Conduct of Hostilities under the Law of International Armed Conflict*, above n 66 (chapter 2), 4.

8 *Nuclear Weapons Case* [1996] ICJ Rep 226, 57 (Separate Opinion of Judge Weeramantry). See generally Gardam, *Non-combatant Immunity as a Norm of International Humanitarian Law*, above n 28 (chapter 4), 38–41.

9 *Civilians under Assault: Hezbollah's Rocket Attacks on Israel in the 2006 War*, above n 91 (chapter 4), 8.

10 McCoubrey, above n 91 (chapter 1), 35.

11 Ibid.

> The questions to be addressed in this article are: what was the application of the law of armed conflict to this crisis, how was it applied, and what can be learned from it? However, the application of appropriate rules, such as those that apply to targeting, the treatment of participants who fall into hostile hands and other victims of the conflict, cannot be adequately judged without consideration of the underlying causes and reasons for the action. Were the military actions appropriate and proportionate to the stated political objectives and results?[12]

However, on my reading, his article does not make specific reference back to assessing the *jus in bello* in light of the stated political objectives and results. Rather, the focus is on whether an armed conflict existed in certain situations and, therefore, whether IHL did or did not apply. The better view is that a belligerent's stated political objectives and results can be used only to assess compliance with the *jus ad bellum* and the (non-legal issue) of the moral correctness of the actions of one of the belligerents to the conflict. It has no bearing on the lawfulness of the actions when assessed against the *jus in bello*. Nonetheless, parties that believe they are in the right will still try to link the two issues. So, we see:

> Nato's [sic] often repeated contention that anything it did wrong in Kosovo should be judged in the light of the humanitarian cause it was pursuing can be seen as a plea for more lenient standards to be applied to NATO than to FRY.[13]

Regardless of whether NATO was pursuing a humanitarian objective or not, compliance with the *jus ad bellum* does not obviate the need for compliance with the *jus in bello*.[14] As the ICJ has clearly held in the *Nuclear Weapons Case*: "A weapon that is already unlawful *per se*, whether by treaty or custom, does not become lawful by reason of its being used for a legitimate purpose under the Charter."[15] Is there, however, a difference when the 'just' side is more clearly identified by being associated with a UN sanctioned operation?

6.2 Application of IHL to UN forces

For the purposes of this section, it will be helpful to make a preliminary remark about operations conducted under UN auspices. There is a distinction between UN conducted operations and UN authorised operations. A UN conducted operation is where the UN organises, controls and conducts the operations itself using forces committed to it by member States. A UN authorised operation is where the

---

12 Burger, above n 45 (chapter 5).

13 Claudio Cordone and Avner Gidron, *The Kosovo conflict: NATO on trial* (2000) Le Monde diplomatique <http://mondediplo.com/2000/07/02kosovo> at 26 May 2006.

14 Christopher Greenwood, 'The Advisory Opinion on nuclear weapons and the contribution of the International Court to international humanitarian law' (1997) 316 *International Review of the Red Cross* <http://www.icrc.org/Web/eng/siteengo.nsf/iwpList159/C724E78E1FDDD9F5C1256B66005A623C> at 4 June 2006. See also Faite and Grenier, above n 68 (chapter 2), 9–10.

15 *Nuclear Weapons Case* [1996] ICJ Rep 226, [39].

UN authorises member States to take action directly to enforce a UNSCR.[16] To allow both types of operations to be covered under one term, the term 'UN sanctioned operations' is used to encompass both operations conducted under UN command and control as well as operations authorised by the UN but conducted under national command and control.[17]

There was a brief challenge to the proposition that the *jus in bello* was independent of the *jus ad bellum* if the armed conflict involved UN forces. It was argued that a UN force acting under Chapter VII of the *Charter of the United Nations* was not legally bound by IHL. This argument did not gain majority support and has "no support in subsequent United Nations practice, regulations and agreements."[18] Nonetheless, the issue was controversial enough to result in a resolution by the prestigious Institute of International Law, affirming that the humanitarian rules of IHL apply to UN forces as of right (ie, not just as a matter of discretion by the UN).[19] And also:

> Subject to the exceptions provided for in the following Articles, the rules of armed conflict shall apply to hostilities in which United Nations Forces are engaged, even if those rules are not specifically humanitarian in character.[20]

While such resolutions are not legally binding in the sense of being a treaty, they are highly persuasive, and perhaps even likely to amount to "the teachings of the most highly qualified publicists" for the purposes of article 38(1)(d) of the *Statute of the International Court of Justice*. In this respect, the Institute adopts both resolutions and declarations and with the resolutions purporting to state the *lex lata* and the declarations to be *de lege ferenda*.[21] The other notable point for UN authorised operations is that "[t]he national contingents of UN forces participating in an

---

16 Major Jim Waddell, 'UN Peacekeeping' in Hugh Smith (ed), *The Force of Law: International Law and the Land Commander* (1994) 47, 48.

17 For a general and detailed discussion of the types of operations see Joseph Bialke, 'United Nations Peace Operations: Applicable Norms and the Application of the Law of Armed Conflict' (2000) 50 *Air Force Law Review* 1.

18 Sir Kenneth Keith, 'The Protection of United Nations and Associated Personnel' in William Maley (ed), *Shelters from the Storm: Developments in International Humanitarian Law* (1995) 87, 88–9. See generally Christopher Greenwood, 'International Humanitarian Law and United Nations Military Operations' (1998) 1 *Yearbook of International Humanitarian Law* 3; Umesh Palwankar, 'Applicability of International Humanitarian Law to United Nations Peace-Keeping Forces' (1993) 294 *International Review of the Red Cross* 227.

19 *Conditions of Application of Humanitarian Rules of Armed Conflict to Hostilities in which United Nations Forces May be Engaged* (1971) Institute of International Law, art 2 <http://www.idi-iil.org/idiE/resolutionsE/1971_zag_03_en.pdf> at 1 March 2005.

20 Ibid. See also Dinstein, *The Conduct of Hostilities under the Law of International Armed Conflict*, above n 66 (chapter 2), 5.

21 See *History*, Institute of International Law <http://www.idi-iil.org/idiE/navig_history.html> at 2 March 2005.

armed conflict would, however, be bound by the conventions to which their States are parties."[22]

Notwithstanding the above, there is still the reality of operations and the assessment of the operations to be considered. As Gardam writes:

> Most commentators take the position that the rules must be applied equally, as exemplified in the Preamble to Protocol I. Events in the recent gulf conflict demonstrate that this analysis is too simplistic. The practice of states in that conflict reveals that the legality of a state's resort to force has a subtle impact on the perception by that state of the means that can legitimately be used to achieve its goal. Thus, in reality, the *jus ad bellum* to some extent may determine the *jus in bello*. The coalition forces interpretation of the requirements of proportionality in attacks on military targets that involved heavy civilian casualties is a case in point.[23]

While Gardam does not make it immediately clear what she means by her last sentence, it appears as though she is arguing that the coalition forces look a more liberal view of what would be proportionate collateral damage and that the role of the Security Council in determining the aggressor was a significant factor. Accordingly, it appears as though her conclusion is that the coalition forces applied a lower standard due to Iraq being determined to be the aggressor by the Security Council. This interpretation is supported by the following sentence from the second last page of her article:

> In the assessment of proportionality, civilians, and to a lesser extent combatants, of the aggressor state were accorded less weight in the balancing process than combatants of the "just side".[24]

She then writes, probably correctly, that:

> It seems unlikely that the international community would have tolerated the scale of civilian casualties in the conflict if it were not for the consensus that Iraq's action had no legal or moral basis.[25]

So, while IHL applies to UN sanctioned operations, there is also the reality that the application of that law may be judged unevenly. Gardam sees that it might be judged in favour of UN sanctioned forces. However, I wonder if the opposite may not also apply. Might not UN forces be held to a higher standard by politicians, the media and the public?

Shraga notes:

---

22 Shearer, above n 12 (chapter 1). See also Roberts and Guelff, above n 14 (chapter 1), 723.

23 Judith Gardam, 'Proportionality and Force in International Law' (1993) 87 *American Journal of International Law* 391, 393.

24 Ibid, 412.

25 Ibid.

> while the principle of its applicability to UN forces and operations is now well established, it is the scope of application of international humanitarian law in any given context which is still debatable.[26]

Following on from Shraga's point, what I am interested in exploring is whether the goals of the campaign specified in a UNSCR mandate might affect the overall military advantage sought and thereby affect the lawful target set?

6.3 UN sanctioned operations and military objectives

Greenwood writes:

> In cases where the United Nations force is a party to an international armed conflict, IHL applicable to international conflicts applies in its entirety. The only question is whether the involvement of the United Nations leads to any difference in the application of those rules.[27]

Greenwood went on to conclude that the differences in application of IHL are probably limited to rules concerning neutrality and belligerent occupation.[28] He also stated that, in any event, any potential differences in the application of IHL by UN forces does not include the principles of distinction and proportionality.[29] I do not disagree with Greenwood. However, what I believe needs to be explored is not *whether* the rules of IHL apply to UN sanctioned operations, but *how* those rules are to be applied. It is my argument that while the principle of distinction applies to a belligerent operating in accordance with UN sanction, there may be limits on what can be considered a military objective in such a situation.

My argument is as follows. For an objective to be a military objective, the object must not only contribute to the military action of the defending party but attacking the object must also offer a definite military advantage to the attacker. Where a conflict has a limited outcome (eg, the desired outcome is not the complete submission of the defending Party but some lesser goal), an attack that does not contribute towards this ultimate outcome does not amount to a definite military advantage in the actual circumstances of the conflict.

Contrary to my argument, Normand and af Jochnick write:

> The widespread approval for coalition conduct in the Gulf War lends credence to the notion that under United Nations mandate a belligerent may legitimately

26 Daphna Shraga, 'The United Nations as an Actor Bound by International Humanitarian Law' (1998) 5:2 *International Peacekeeping* 64, 64.

27 Greenwood, 'International Humanitarian Law and United Nations Military Operations', above n 18 (chapter 6), 27.

28 Ibid, 33.

29 Greenwood also argues that these principles apply to UN forces in situations of less than armed conflict, and how this should be uncontroversial as "it is difficult to see how it could be argued that a United Nations force not participating in an armed conflict should be entitled to … attack targets which would be forbidden to that same force if it were to become a party to an armed conflict"—ibid, 29.

> employ military force to secure its war objectives, unrelated to the weakening or surrender of the enemy's military.[30]

For the reasons that follow, it is my view that as a *legal* statement it is incorrect. As argued in section 3.5.1, an object cannot be targeted purely on the basis that an attack on that target will contribute to the political goals of the conflict.

Bothe poses the interesting counter-view to the quote from af Jochnick and Normand.

> Do traditional considerations of military necessity and military advantage have a legitimate place in a conflict the declared purpose of which is a humanitarian one, namely, to promote the cause of human rights? The thought would deserve further consideration that in such a conflict, more severe restraints would be imposed on the choice of military targets and of the balancing test applied for the purposes of the proportionality principle than in a 'normal' armed conflict.[31]

In my view, that is the current state of the law. In direct support of my argument, I note that the United States Army *Law of War* handbook states that "[i]n a limited war, the act must be indispensable to attain the *limited* objective."[32] And any action being taken pursuant to a UNSCR is ipso facto a limited war, in that the resolution will set out the basis for the action and the goals associated with the use of force.

In 1992 Hampson suggested that the test for a military objective should include a "proposed additional requirement ... that the destruction, etc., of the objective is necessary to the achievement of the war aim."[33] She then writes:

> At present, there is no legal requirement to define the war aim, but political leaders come under considerable internal pressure to define what they are trying to achieve by the use of force. That is even more likely to be a condition in operations undertaken in the name of the United Nations.[34]

She emphasises that this would be an additional requirement for defining a military objective, not an alternative requirement. It is my view that her proposed test is in fact already part of the law, as this requirement is implicit in the test of whether the attack will offer a definite military advantage.

There is a recent example of targeting outside the strict scope of the lawful basis for the operation. During the United States of America and United Kingdom's enforcement of no-fly zones over Iraq in March 2003, and prior to the commencement of the 2003 Gulf War in late March 2003, senior United States of America Defense officials are referred to as the source of a report that new targets in Iraq

---

30 af Jochnick and Normand, above n 76 (chapter 2), 410. It should be noted that they do not condone this conclusion.

31 Bothe, above n 25 (chapter 3), 535.

32 US Army, *Operational Law Handbook* (2000) chapter 5, 4 (emphasis added).

33 Hampson, 'Proportionality and Necessity in the Gulf Conflict', above n 23 (chapter 3), 51.

34 Ibid.

were being attacked by coalition patrols. The new targets included surface-to-surface missile systems and multiple-launch rockets. These objects were targeted on the basis that these objects could be used against ground troops in an invasion or against neighbouring nations.[35] The news article then quotes defence analyst Loren Thompson of the Lexington Institute: "The U.S. military is taking advantage of the no-fly zones to prepare the battle space for war".[36] Presuming for the purposes of argument that the enforcement of the no-fly zones was pursuant to UNSCRs,[37] then the attacks would have been unlawful. This is because in the context of the operation pursuant to the extant UNSCRs, there was no military advantage to the attack.

To summarise, IHL applies fully to UN sanctioned operations. However, the scope of the mandate will affect what is a military advantage that may lawfully be sought from any particular attack. Before concluding this chapter, I point out that the reverse of the above argument is not true. So, for example, if humanitarian intervention is authorised, this does not expand the scope of legitimate targets.

35 'Target scope extended in no-fly zones', *Gulf News Online Edition* (Dubai) 3 March 2003 <http://www.gulf-news.com/Articles/news.asp?ArticleID=79241> at 9 September 2003.

36 Ibid.

37 The United States of America and United Kingdom, and to some extent France, argued that the enforcement of the no-fly zones was pursuant to UNSCRs, but this line of argument has been criticized. See, for example, Chris Mooney, *Did the United Nations Authorize 'No-Fly' Zones Over Iraq?* (2002) Slate <http://slate.msn.com/id/2074302> at 2 March 2005.

Part II

The Law Concerning Attacking a Target Lawfully

Chapter 7

Precautions in attack

> Determining the proper relation between means and ends in situations of great complexity and uncertainty is never easy. Decision makers are faced with their own inadequacies and lack of knowledge, together with the pressures inherent in conflict. They cannot forget the risks and costs of restraint, yet they must also be mindful of the legal imperative to avoid unnecessary and disproportionate force.[1]

Part I dealt with the law concerning lawful target selection. But, this is not the end of the matter. As well as a general obligation to target only military objectives, articles 57(2) and 57(3) API provide for certain precautions that must be taken when planning or executing the attack itself. In other words, not only must the target of an attack be lawful but lawful targets must be attacked lawfully. In this chapter, article 57 API in discussed in some detail; however, due to size of the topic, the law relating to the rule of proportionality (which is just one aspect of the precautions to be taken when conducting an attack) is dealt with in its own chapter (chapter 8).

Before turning to the actual requirements of article 57 API, a significant preliminary issue that is covered in this chapter, and which is not clearly addressed in API, is the level at which the precautions set out in article 57 API must be applied? For instance, Switzerland made a reservation stating that the "provisions of Article 57, paragraph 2, create obligations only for commanding officers at the battalion or group level and above."[2] I argue that this is an overly restrictive view and a misunderstanding of what is required by article 57 API. I argue that the obligations in article 57 API apply to all personnel who have the authority and practical possibility to affect the course of an attack. To support my conclusion, I set out a method for compliance in chapter 9 along with references to how article 57 API has been complied with at the individual pilot level by Australian military aircrew.

One of the precautions to be taken when conducting an attack is to do everything feasible to verify that the target is a military objective subject to lawful attack.[3] I review the law and arrive at a conclusion as to what amounts to *everything feasible* and what level of certainty is implied by *verify*. When planning an attack,

---

1 Oscar Schachter, 'Remarks' in ASIL Proceedings, *Implementing Limitations on the Use of Force: The Doctrine of Proportionality and Necessity* (1992) 39, 39.

2 Reservation 1 by Switzerland, Roberts and Guelff, above n 14 (chapter 1), 509. Switzerland, as well as Austria, made similar statements during the 1974–77 *Diplomatic Conference on the Reaffirmation and Development of International Humanitarian Law Applicable in Armed Conflicts*—CDDH/VI, above n 77 (chapter 2), 212.

3 API, above n 2 (chapter 1), art 57(2)(a)(i).

when "a choice is possible between several military objectives for obtaining a similar military advantage, the objective to be selected shall be that the attack on which may be expected to cause the least danger to civilian lives and to civilian objects."[4] This requires an assessment of the relative quantum of collateral damage that might be caused by different attacks. Therefore, in this chapter I consider how to asses the value of different objects when conducting a proportionality assessment.

Before turning to considering the law, it is worth noting that while the difficulties faced by planners and commanders needs to be remembered when endeavouring to provide further meaning to the obligations imposed by article 57 API, the importance of taking precautions cannot be overstated. The estimates of civilian casualties in armed conflict are truly concerning. For instance:

(a) "The 1994 United Nations Human Development Report shows that in conflicts at the start of the 20th century 90 per cent of war casualties were military, whilst now at the end of the century, 90 per cent are civilian."[5]
(b) According to the Swiss Federal Office for Civilian Protection, the ratio of persons killed during in the First World War was 200 military: 1 civilian; in the Second World War nearly 1:1, in the Korean War 1:5, and in the Vietnam War 1:20.[6]
(c) "In 1988 it was estimated that there were approximately three million casualties from the twenty-five wars going on in the world at the time. Four-fifths of these casualties were civilians."[7]

As it can, regrettably, be assumed that in some cases civilians are not injured or killed only incidentally but are directly targeted, it is not possible to conclude that all civilian injuries and deaths are attributable to attacks on lawful targets.[8] Nonetheless, the taking of appropriate—and legally required—precautions when attacking lawful targets will have a direct impact on the extent and number of civilian injuries and deaths.

The Battle for Manila in February 1945 provides a chilling reminder of how civilian casualties can be terrible. During the battle, General MacArthur refused to allow the air and ground commanders to use aerial bombardment out of concern for civilian casualties; however, the:

> American commanders made frequent use of artillery bombardment to assist in clearing the city and to save the lives of their own troops. … An estimated 16,000 Japanese soldiers died in the battle and American forces lost 1,000 killed and

---

4 Ibid, art 57(3).

5 Kerr, above n 6 (chapter 6), 3.

6 Sassoli and Bouvier, above n 10 (chapter 1), 145 (fn 98).

7 Gardam, *Non-combatant Immunity as a Norm of International Humanitarian Law*, above n 28 (chapter 4), 1.

8 "In the new warfare that has emerged, the impact of armed conflict on civilians goes far beyond the notion of collateral damage. Targeted attacks, forced displacement, sexual violence, forced conscription, indiscriminate killings, mutilation, hunger, disease and loss of livelihoods collectively paint an extremely grim picture of the human costs of armed conflict." (*Report of the Secretary-General on the Protection of civilians in armed conflict*, [3], UN Doc S/2005/740 (2005))

5,000 wounded. Manila was devastated and the bodies of 100,000 Filipino civilians were found in the rubble, most of them killed in the exchange of fire between American and Japanese forces.[9]

7.1 The obligation to take precautionary measures applies to all levels of armed conflict

On a simple reading of articles 57(2) and 57(3) API, the obligation to take precautions in attack applies to all forms of attack. Article 49(1) API defines attack extremely broadly, including that an attack covers actions in both offence and defence. Indeed, the definition provided is so broad that Fenrick states that the "act of a single soldier shooting a rifle [is] an attack"[10] for the purposes of article 49(1) API. However, notwithstanding this broad definition of attack, Fenrick is of the view that the acts of single soldiers would not constitute an attack for the purposes of articles 51(5)(b) and 57(2) API. He submits it would be "inappropriate and impractical to classify an operation below divisional or equivalent level as an "attack" for the purposes of these articles."[11] His reasoning for this is that the articles of API require the gathering and assessing of information as part of a planning process, and article 57(2)(a)(i) API "clearly envisages 'attack' as an action directed against several military objectives."[12] Presumably, this last point is based on the use of the plural 'objectives' in article 57(2)(a)(i) API. I find neither argument persuasive. Rather, there is no logical or practical reason why the requirements should not apply to all forms of attack (as that word is defined in article 49(1) API). In Boivin's words, "the obligations apply at whatever level the regulated functions are being performed."[13] Despite the number of declarations and reservations concerning article 57 API made by parties to the protocol, only two address the issue currently under discussion. Switzerland made a reservation stating that the "provisions of Article 57, paragraph 2, create obligations only for commanding officers at the battalion or group level and above."[14] The declaration of understanding by the United Kingdom is particularly interesting. The United Kingdom declared that with respect to article 57(2) API, the "UK understands that the obligation to comply with paragraph 2(b) only extends to those who have the authority and practical possibility to cancel or suspend the attack."[15] The

9 William Fenrick, 'The Rule of Proportionality and Protocol I in Conventional Warfare' (1982) 98 *Military Law Review* 91, 91 (footnote omitted). Interestingly, later in his article, Fenrick writes: "A review of the facts clearly indicates that American forces and their commanders did not commit an indiscriminate attack causing excessive civilian casualties within the meaning of Protocol I" (at 121).

10 Ibid, 102.

11 Ibid.

12 Ibid; see also page 108.

13 Boivin, above n 19 (chapter 1), 35.

14 Reservation 1 by Switzerland, Roberts and Guelff, above n 14 (chapter 1), 509. Switzerland, as well as Austria, made similar statements during the 1974–77 *Diplomatic Conference on the Reaffirmation and Development of International Humanitarian Law Applicable in Armed Conflicts*—CDDH/VI, above n 77 (chapter 2), 212.

15 See the United Kingdom's declaration of understanding (n), Roberts and Guelff, above n 14 (chapter 1), 511.

United Kingdom's declaration is also interesting in that it did not purport to limit the application of the rest of article 57 per either Switzerland's position or the more conservative position again of Fenrick.[16]

Arguably, New Zealand adopts a middle position. New Zealand's military manual states that the:

> Obligation presupposes that the measures are to be taken by a level which possesses a formalised planning process and a substantial degree of discretion concerning methods by which medium-term objectives are to be attained. It is unlikely that the proper level would normally be below a divisional or equivalent level of headquarters.[17]

I am of the view that the United Kingdom's declaration accurately states the general position, and that the United Kingdom's view can be accommodated with that expressed by New Zealand. There is no obvious reason to interpret the text of API in the way that Switzerland and Austria have. Rather, looking back at the statement made at the *Diplomatic Conference*, Switzerland's position seems to be based on the view that the precautions would impose too great a burden on junior military personnel[18] and Austria's position seems to be based on an assumption that only higher echelons of command would be apply to comply with the required precautions.[19] Also, New Zealand is arguably taking too conservative a view in its manual. Rather, what article 57(2) API does presuppose is that the obligations imposed apply where they can be met. This is what the United Kingdom have said. Consistently in my view, the Netherlands have stated that the "higher the level [of command] the stricter the required compliance is."[20] Therefore, as a simple matter of treaty interpretation, I agree with Boivin and favour the United Kingdom's position but understood in light of the statement made by the Netherlands.

I also see no reason why the United Kingdom's position cannot be adopted as a general statement across article 57 API. So, the general principle would be that the obligations in article 57 API apply to all personnel who have the authority and practical possibility to affect the course of an attack.

Whether the actions of a single soldier will constitute an attack or not will depend upon the context in which the acts of that soldier are conducted. An attack should be understood to be:

16 I say more conservative, as a division is higher up the command chain than a battalion.

17 New Zealand, *Military Manual* (1992), [518(2)] in Henckaerts and Doswald-Beck (eds), *Customary International Humanitarian Law*, vol II, above n 64 (chapter 1), 359.

18 CDDH/VI, above n 77 (chapter 2), 212.

19 Ibid.

20 Henckaerts and Doswald-Beck (eds), *Customary International Humanitarian Law*, vol II, above n 64 (chapter 1), 359 (insertion in square brackets in original).

> co-ordinated acts of violence against the adversary by a specific military formation engaged in a specific military operation, rather than ... each act of violence of the individual combatants who are members of that formation.[21]

Understood in this way, whether an act of violence by a sniper or single bomber aircraft amounted to an *attack* or not would depend upon the context in which the act was conducted. A single strike aircraft (or, more likely, a pair of strike aircraft) tasked in isolation against a particular target is clearly conducting an attack. As Rogers points out, where a pilot has been tasked to fly over an area of operations and attack targets of opportunity, then the pilot will have to comply with the obligations imposed by article 57 API.[22] However, where a squadron of strike aircraft are tasked against a military installation, each aircraft is contributing to the attack but the actions of a single aircraft against its assigned target(s) are not considered in isolation as an attack for the purposes of article 57 API.

Where the acts of violence did amount to an attack for the purposes of article 57 API, the standard expected of the planners and deciders of the attack will be different in different contexts. For example, what would be feasible precautions for a divisional commander planning an assault are likely to be more onerous than what would be feasible for a single soldier armed with a sniper rifle. The exact obligations will depend upon a person's "individual responsibilities in relation to planning, deciding upon or executing attacks."[23]

Finally, the author has seen the requirements successfully applied at the single pilot level during Operation FALCONER. For more detail on this, and a method showing how the requirements can be applied at all levels, see the discussion in chapter 9 of a 6-step targeting process.

7.2 Verifying the objectives to be attacked

Article 57(2)(a)(i) API requires that those who plan or decide upon an attack shall do everything feasible to verify that the objectives to be attacked are military objectives and also are not subject to some other form of protection. The words of most interest in article 57(2)(a)(i) API are 'everything feasible'.

As to the meaning of *feasible*, the "it was preferred by most representatives [to the 1974–77 *Diplomatic Conference*] to the word 'reasonable', and it was intended to mean 'that which is practicable or practically possible'."[24] A number of States made declarations to the same effect. The United Kingdom's declaration is illustrative, which states that feasible means "that which is practicable or practically possible, taking into account all the circumstances ruling at the time, including humanitar-

21 Bothe, Partsch and Solf, above n 87 (chapter 1), 288.

22 Rogers, *Law on the Battlefield*, above n 84 (chapter 1), 112.

23 Ibid, 362.

24 CDDH/XV, above n 98 (chapter 3), 285. Referred to with apparent approval in Blix, above n 78 (chapter 2), 148. See also CDDH/XV, above n 98 (chapter 3), 353; Fenrick, 'The Rule of Proportionality and Protocol I in Conventional Warfare', above n 9 (chapter 7), 108–9.

ian and military considerations."[25] It is interesting that the definition provided for 'feasible precautions' in article 1(5) of Protocol III to the *Convention on Prohibitions or Restrictions on the Use of Certain Conventional Weapons which may be deemed to be Excessively Injurious or to have Indiscriminate Effects*[26] is "those precautions which are practicable or practically possible taking into account all circumstances ruling at the time, including humanitarian and military considerations." What is feasible will also depend upon the resources and technology available to an attacker.[27] Of course, within reason and perhaps more as a moral exhortation:

> it is the duty of Parties to the conflict to have the means available to respect the rules of the Protocol. In any case, it is reprehensible for a Party possessing such means not to use them, and thus consciously prevent itself from making the required distinction.[28]

When determining what is practical, another common declaration is that commanders have to reach their decisions based on the information available to them at the time.[29] While the proceeding points all represent settled law, they do not provide the complete answer. The obligation in article 57(2)(a)(i) API is to do *everything* feasible. In this respect, the declaration made by Spain is worth mentioning. Spain declared that for articles 51–58, the decisions to be made by commanders "which may have repercussions on civilians, or civilian or similar objects, cannot necessarily be based on more than relevant information available at the time and

25 Declaration (b), Roberts and Guelff, above n 14 (chapter 1), 510. Similar statements were made by many States at the 1974–77 *Diplomatic Conference on the Reaffirmation and Development of International Humanitarian Law Applicable in Armed Conflicts*, although 'humanitarian' considerations were not mentioned and 'military considerations' was expressed as "relevant to the success of military operations"—see the statements of Turkey, the United Kingdom, Canada, the Federal Republic of Germany, and the United States of America (CDDH/VI, above n 77 (chapter 2), at pages 211, 214, 224, 226, and 241 respectively). Italy made what I believe is a similar statement, but in the following terms: that the obligations imposed by the word *feasible* "are conditional on the actual circumstances really allowing the proposed precautions to be taken, on the basis of the available information and the imperative needs of national defence"—CDDH/VI, above n 77 (chapter 2), 231. See generally the consistent State practice on this point referred to in Henckaerts and Doswald-Beck (eds), *Customary International Humanitarian Law*, vol II, above n 64 (chapter 1), 359–60.

26 Opened for signature 10 April 1981, 1342 UNTS 137 (entered into force 2 December 1983).

27 Sandoz, Swinarski and Zimmerman (eds), above n 68 (chapter 1), [2199]; Schmitt, *Precision Attack and International Humanitarian Law*, above n 30 (chapter 3), 460. See the statement to this effect made by the Indian delegation to the 1974–77 *Diplomatic Conference on the Reaffirmation and Development of International Humanitarian Law Applicable in Armed Conflicts*—CDDH/VI, above n 77 (chapter 2), 228. See also the Indian statement at CDDH/VI, above n 77 (chapter 2), 188.

28 Sandoz, Swinarski and Zimmerman (eds), above n 68 (chapter 1), [1871].

29 See, for example, United Kingdom declaration (c), reprinted in Roberts and Guelff, above n 14 (chapter 1), 510.

which *it has been possible to obtain* to that effect."[30] It is my view that the Spanish declaration states the general law. Accordingly, while article 57(2) API does not require a commander to know "everything when [the commander] makes a decision",[31] a commander must not only reach his or her decision based on the information available to them at the time, but "must make a reasonable effort to discover pertinent information"[32] before making that decision. In other words, did "the commander, planner or staff officer do what a reasonable person would have done in the circumstances?"[33] Where information was reasonably available but not collected or assessed, the reasonableness of the decision of the commander, planner or staff officer can be judged based on not only what information the person did have but also what information was reasonably available to that person;[34] while noting that was is reasonably available is judged in light of the "urgent and difficult circumstances under which judgements are usually made."[35]

The *ICRC Commentary* states that a commander planning an attack must "in case of doubt, even if there is only a slight doubt ... call for additional information and if need be give orders for further reconnaissance".[36] With respect, this is setting the standard too high. For example, the intelligence available might indicate that a building was used as a munitions factory two weeks ago. The intelligence might be intercepted communications that are supported by human intelligence reports obtained before the commencement of the armed conflict. Such a factory would clearly be a military objective. Should the commander have a doubt in these circumstances as the intelligence is two weeks old? What if aerial reconnaissance will reveal no more than a building and the coming and going of civilian trucks? This example is different from intelligence indicating that military communications equipment was stored in a certain building. The reason for the difference is that the tooling of a factory to make munitions is quite extensive, whereas the mere storage of communications equipment could occur just about anywhere and it could be easily re-located. As Bothe, Partsch and Solf write: "command decisions have to be made in the fog of battle under circumstances when clinical certainty is impossible and *when the adversary is striving to conceal the true facts, to deceive and confuse.*"[37]

The original draft put forward at the 1971 *Conference of Government Experts on the Reaffirmation and Development of International Humanitarian Law Applicable in Armed Conflicts* used the words "*ensure* that the objective or objectives concerned ... are identified as military objectives."[38] However, 'ensure' has been replaced with 'do

30 Spanish declaration E., ibid, 509 (translation, and lettering of declarations added by Roberts and Guelff) (emphasis added).

31 Barber, above n 74 (chapter 2), 689.

32 Ibid.

33 Quote from the Canadian *LOAC Manual* (1999) in Henckaerts and Doswald-Beck (eds), *Customary International Humanitarian Law*, vol II, above n 64 (chapter 1), 359.

34 See the practice of States on this point referred to in Henckaerts and Doswald-Beck (eds), *Customary International Humanitarian Law*, vol II, above n 64 (chapter 1), 363–5.

35 Canada's *LOAC Manual*, quoted in ibid, 364.

36 Sandoz, Swinarski and Zimmerman (eds), above n 68 (chapter 1), [2195].

37 Bothe, Partsch and Solf, above n 87 (chapter 1), 279 (emphasis added).

38 CE/3b, above n 27 (chapter 3), 136 (emphasis added).

everything feasible to verify'. Whereas there will be occasions when the intelligence available to a commander leaves the commander with no doubt, by the very nature of armed conflict intelligence will often be less than 100 per cent.

There is also a difference, for example, between not being sure whether the enemy is using a particular bridge or not compared with not being sure whether a building is a command and control bunker or a bomb shelter. The reason for the difference is that the consequences of a mistake are more serious in the latter case. Where collateral damage is more likely, there should be an increase in the level of caution employed when endeavouring to identify the target.[39] In other cases, "occasions may arise which require instantaneous decisions on available evidence and some doubt is certain to exist."[40] It cannot be expected that armed conflict will be reduced to the point where a commander can act only when he or she is 100 per cent certain in all cases. Rather, the level of certainty should vary based on the consequences for the civilian population. In this respect, see article 52(3) API, which imposes a presumption of civilian character in cases of doubt only with respect to objects which are "normally dedicated to civilian purposes, such as a place of worship, a house or other dwelling or a school".[41]

Of course, this is not just a legal question. A military commander has no interest in wasting valuable, and often scarce, resources on striking non-military objectives. So, there is a beneficial congruence of interests. Therefore, it is not surprising to read:

> "Recent operational experience has sown that the ability of the US armed forces to engage and prosecute targets of interest is severely hampered by uncertainty in target identify and location," says the AFRL [Air Force Research Laboratory]. "The problem of detecting, identifying and maintaining target identification in realistic battlefield conditions is among the most difficult issues facing the US military today."[42]

General Schwarzkopf is reported to have observed that "commanders must have the courage to make decisions based on insufficient information. In war, information is always imperfect and often late."[43] International humanitarian law permits commanders to make the decisions but the decisions must be informed and reasonable in the circumstances.

Having started this section by stating that requiring a commander to call for additional information even in cases of only slight doubt was setting the standard too high, I should add that at the other end, the test under API is not one of *substan-*

39 See *The Public Committee against Torture in Israel v The Government of Israel*, HCJ 769/02 (13 December 2006) [5] (Rivlin V-P).

40 DeSaussure, 'Belligerent Air Operations and the 1977 Geneva Protocol I', above n 13 (chapter 2), 470.

41 API, above n 2 (chapter 1), art 52(3).

42 *US Air Force grapples with continuous target identification* (2002) International Defense Review <http://idr.janes.com/public/idr/index.shtml> at 15 May 2005 (subscription to website required to access article).

43 Fred Green, 'Remarks' in ASIL Proceedings, *Implementing Limitations on the Use of Force: The Doctrine of Proportionality and Necessity* (1992) 62, 66.

tial doubt[44] or *significant doubt*.[45] Rather, based on the above discussion of the meaning of feasible, I conclude that a commander is required to take all practicable steps to obtain information to enable the making of a good-faith assessment. What steps are considered practical will depend upon the difficulty in obtaining the necessary information. A "high priority [should be assigned] to the collection, collation, evaluation and dissemination of timely target intelligence."[46] Then, when making the decision, the level of verification required to reduce doubt, and the degree of acceptable doubt, will vary depending upon the likely adverse consequences of a wrong decision. Taking all of the above into consideration, a commander is then required to come to a *reasonable belief* about whether the object meets the criteria for being a military objective.[47]

Applying this test, take the example during the NATO bombing campaign in Kosovo of a B-52 strike that "was mistargeted against the Chinese embassy in Belgrade—and killed three Chinese diplomats and wounded 27".[48] In these circumstances, the number of civilians killed or injured is indirectly relevant to whether API was breached. I say indirectly, as what is relevant is what a commander knew, or should have known, at the time of the attack and not in hindsight. However, the actual casualty figures can be a guide as to what should have been known. Whether a breach occurs or not when a mistake is made is partly dependent upon the likely adverse consequences if a mistake does occur. If the building being targeted had not been an office building in the middle of a major city but rather say an unmanned radio relay station (and the radio relay station turned out to be a non-military objective), its unmanned status would be relevant to determining whether the attacker had complied with its obligations under API to verify the target prior to undertaking the attack.

Assuming what I have just discussed is good law and the process I have outlined is followed by a commander, what are the consequences where the decision is wrong and a civilian target is hit? Rowe writes:

44 See New Zealand State practice referred to in Henckaerts and Doswald-Beck (eds), *Customary International Humanitarian Law*, vol II, above n 64 (chapter 1), 243.

45 See Israeli State practice referred to in ibid, 244. While Israel is not a party to API, it does accept the definition of military objective set out in API, art 52(2) as reflecting customary international law—*Preserving Humanitarian Principles While Combating Terrorism: Israel's Struggle with Hizbullah in the Lebanon War*, above n 101 (chapter 3), 9–10. The qualification of *doubt* with *significant* had disappeared in Israel's 2007 communiqué—*Preserving Humanitarian Principles While Combating Terrorism: Israel's Struggle with Hizbullah in the Lebanon War*, above n 101 (chapter 3), 13.

46 Bothe, Partsch and Solf, above n 87 (chapter 1), 363.

47 *Prosecutor v Galic, (Trial Chamber)* Case No IT-98-29-T (5 December 2003) [51]. See also Boivin, above n 19 (chapter 1), 20. I note that in the 2003 Gulf War, the United States of America appears to have adopted a test of 'reasonable certainty' but if there was not reasonable certainty that a target was a legitimate target, then higher command was to be contacted for a decision—*Off Target: The Conduct of the War and Civilian Casualties in Iraq*, above n 91 (chapter 4), 99. This seems to imply that the higher command could apply a lesser test than that of 'reasonable certainty'.

48 Cordesman, above n 97 (chapter 1), 95.

> During the air campaign there were a number of mistakes made when an unintended civilian object was attacked. ... The Protocol is silent as to the effect of a mistake in these circumstances.[49]

I disagree. Rather, as Benvenuti states:

> [I]f the precautionary measures have worked adequately in a very high percentage of cases, this does not mean that they are generally adequate, so as to excuse violations occurring in a small number of cases. In practice, it is only when each attack is considered in its specific circumstances that it is possible to say whether or not all practicable precautions have been taken and whether or not the attack constitutes a breach of IHL.[50]

I agree with Benvenuti. The better view is that IHL imposes standards of care and it is only if these standards are met and a mistake still occurs that no breach occurs. However, one further point needs to be made. Where the targeting system[51] is working and is not leading to breaches of IHL, then, unless there were some obvious and easy steps which where not being taken, a commander may quite reasonably be of the view that he or she is taking all practicable precautions. I agree with the following extract from the *OTP Report*:

> Further, a determination that inadequate efforts have been made to distinguish between military objectives and civilians or civilian objects should not necessarily focus exclusively on a specific incident. If precautionary measures have worked adequately in a very high percentage of cases then the fact they have not worked well in a small number of cases does not necessarily mean they are generally inadequate.[52]

Barber is clearly of a similar view when, in his discussion of the coalition bombing of the Iraqi 'Amiriya Bomb Shelter',[53] he writes:

> It is not possible to determine exactly what "everything feasible" incorporates, but if normal intelligence gathering methods that had proven reliable in the past had been used on this occasion, it is probable that this would meet the required standard.[54]

---

49 Rowe, 'Kosovo 1999: The Air Campaign—Have the Provisions of Additional Protocol I Withstood the Test?', above n 179 (chapter 4).

50 Benvenuti, above n 78 (chapter 3), 514–5.

51 By this I mean everything from gathering of information, the assessment of that information, the immediate staff process for making targeting decisions, the communication to the operator of the weapon system, and the mechanical operation of that weapon system itself.

52 *OTP Report*, above n 90 (chapter 1), [29].

53 I have put these words in quotes to indicate the fact that this is just one possible description of the target.

54 Barber, above n 74 (chapter 2), 689.

To be clear, I interpret him to be saying that if the normal intelligence methods had been used and a mistake still occurred, there would be no violation of the law. Accordingly, the first mistake should normally not be judged too harshly. Of course, that mistake should be reviewed to see if any of the procedures require modification or new procedures adopted. Equally, where a method of attack is resulting in a high number of civilian casualties, it would be appropriate to review the methodology being employed.[55] Where a mistake is repeated, that is a better indication that the required steps are not being taken. However, the standard is never one of infallibility:

> There may be no way of ever knowing whether the attack on the Chinese Embassy was deliberate. ... However, even assuming that the attack was a mistake, the fact that such a mistake could be made at all suggests serious problems with the NATO campaign.[56]

This is an overstatement. To suggest 'serious problems' with a targeting process on the basis of the misidentification of one fixed target is to misinterpret the requirements of customary international law[57] and, where applicable, API. As Fenrick states in the abstract to his article on the NATO bombing campaign: "There are no such things as error-free wars".[58] It would appear that during "the bombing campaign, NATO aircraft flew ... 10,484 strike sorties."[59] I have not been able to determine how many of the strike sorties were against fixed targets (like buildings) as opposed to mobile targets (like tanks and artillery pieces). However, I have not come across any reports of misidentification of fixed targets other than the Chinese Embassy incident. Aerial bombing in particular will often occur in territory under the control of the opposing party. In few cases will Party A be bombing territory once held by Party A but now occupied by Party B. As Cordesman notes:

> Kosovo raised a number of issues regarding maps and mapping. *The most politically sensitive was the need for up-to-date and accurate maps of al* [sic] *of all key politically important facilities where collateral damage was a problem.* This is much easier to ask force than provide. Ironically, China found it very difficult to understand how NATO and the US could have used data maps that contributed to the strike on the Chinese embassy in Belgrade, but have virtually no fully up-to-date maps of their own cities, or of state and state-owned facilities.[60]

55 See *Why They Died: Civilian Casualties in Lebanon during the 2006 War*, above n 3 (chapter 2), 7.

56 Tania Voon, 'Pointing the Finger: Civilian Casualties of NATO Bombing in the Kosovo Conflict' (2001) 16:4 *American University International Law Review* 1083, 1110.

57 Noting that in this example customary international law was the particular standard that applied to the attacker (which was the United States of America).

58 Fenrick, 'Targeting and Proportionality during the NATO Bombing Campaign against Yugoslavia', above n 69 (chapter 5), 489.

59 Ibid.

60 Cordesman, above n 97 (chapter 1), 206 (footnote omitted).

7.3 Minimising collateral damage

After doing everything feasible to determine that a target is subject to lawful attack, the next legal obligation is to take "all feasible precautions in the choice of means and methods of attack with a view to avoiding, and in any event to minimizing" collateral damage.[61] Perhaps the most important point about this sub-paragraph is that it comes before the obligation not to cause excessive collateral damage (the proportionality principle). In other words, there is a requirement to minimise collateral damage and not merely to cause no more than proportional collateral damage.[62] Pursuant to the requirements of article 57(2)(a)(ii) API, it is not sufficient when planning an attack to conclude that the expected collateral damage is not excessive (ie, is proportionate) to the anticipated military advantage. There is also a positive obligation to reduce the expected collateral damage by taking all feasible precautions. Therefore, the relevant law can be stated as: an attack must not cause more than the minimum collateral damage feasible, and the attack may proceed only where that minimum collateral damage is not excessive. As a result, an attack that causes proportionate collateral damage may still be legally reviewed to see if the collateral damage was higher than what it could have been if feasible precautions were taken.

As a brief aside, the following statement in the report from a workshop on *Understanding Collateral Damage* is interesting:

> A major point stressed by military participants was the importance of considering strategy rather than simply tactics when evaluating the morality, legality, or effectiveness of a military effort. Strategic choices, such as the decision to use air power exclusively or to rely upon proxy forces or to disperse rather than destroy an enemy, may have far greater implications for civilians on the ground than tactical decisions to use Cluster Bomb Units (CBUs) or bomb an office building.[63]

In other words, the methods for minimising collateral damage arise not just during an individual attack but also as part of the operational and campaign planning as a whole. While I certainly agree with the sentiment and the conclusion of the working paper as matter of fact, there is no specific IHL obligation to conduct *campaign* planning to minimise collateral damage.[64]

As to the meaning of 'all feasible precautions' in article 57(2)(a)(ii) API, this is the equivalent of 'everything feasible' as just discussed above in section 7.2. Accordingly, 'all feasible precautions' means doing everything that is practicable. In this respect, there is no difference between this interpretation and that of Human Rights Watch who when commenting on the 1991 Gulf War stated that certain actions by the coalition "appear to have involved deliberate decisions by

---

61 API, above n 2 (chapter 1), art 57(2)(a)(iii).

62 *Expert Meeting: "Targeting Military Objectives"*, above n 27 (chapter 1), 13.

63 *Understanding collateral damage workshop*, above n 150 (chapter 3), 5.

64 *Expert Meeting: "Targeting Military Objectives"*, above n 27 (chapter 1), 12. There is, of course, an obligation to conduct campaign planning in accordance with the *jus ad bellum*—in particular, the action must be necessary and proportional.

allied commanders to take less than the *maximum* feasible precautions necessary to avoid harm to civilians."[65] While it is best to use the words of API (ie 'all' or 'everything'), as long as 'feasible' appears after 'maximum' then the statement by Human Rights Watch is correct. However, it should be remembered that while all feasible precaution have to be taken for each attack:

> The availability of alternative means and methods depends on the context and has to be made in the light of the conflict as a whole. For instance, an attacker who has precision guided munitions available is not necessarily under an obligation to use them in a particular attack, even if they would cause less damage than another weapon. The attacker may prefer to withhold these munitions for a later stage of the conflict, which is expected to involve urban warfare.[66]

The following is a list of some typical examples of what have been considered feasible precautions in certain circumstances:

(a) Only precision-guided munitions ('PGM') were used to destroy key targets in downtown Baghdad in order to avoid damaging adjacent civilian buildings.[67]

(b) As part of developing the master attack list, a six-mile area around each target was scanned for schools, hospitals, and mosques to identify those targets where extreme care was required. Further, using imagery, tourist maps, and human-resource intelligence reports, these same types of areas were identified for the entire city of Baghdad.[68]

(c) During World War II, the Allies would bomb factories in territories occupied by German forces when the workers were not expected to be at work.[69]

(d) During bombing attacks conducted by the United States of America in the 1991 Gulf War, the weapon system, munition, time of attack, direction of attack, desired impact point, and level of effort were carefully planned. For example, attacks on known dual-use facilities normally were scheduled at night, because fewer people would be inside or on the streets outside.[70]

(e) "NATO made a detailed effort to review the range of possible collateral damage for each target, and to plan its strikes so that the weapon used, the angle of approach, and the aim point would minimize collateral damage."[71]

(f) During the 2003 Gulf War, coalition forces "employed other methods to help minimize civilian casualties, such as bombing at night when civilians were less likely to be on the streets, using penetrator munitions and delayed fuzes to

---

65 *Needless Deaths in the Gulf War: Civilian Casualties During the Air Campaign and Violations of the Laws of War*, above n 38 (chapter 3) (emphasis added).

66 *Expert Meeting: "Targeting Military Objectives"*, above n 27 (chapter 1), 16.

67 US Department of Defense, *Conduct of the Persian Gulf War: Final Report to Congress*, above n 29 (chapter 3), 153. Clearly though, this would be feasible only for a belligerent who had access to PGMs.

68 Ibid.

69 Sandoz, Swinarski and Zimmerman (eds), above n 68 (chapter 1), [2200].

70 US Department of Defense, *Conduct of the Persian Gulf War: Final Report to Congress*, above n 29 (chapter 3), 153.

71 Cordesman, above n 97 (chapter 1), 94.

ensure that most blast and fragmentation damage was kept within the impact area, and using attack angles that took into account the locations of civilian facilities such as schools and hospitals."[72]

The importance of these examples is that if they were considered feasible in one situation, they might equally be feasible in another. Or, put differently, if these precautions are not taken, a Party might be called upon to explain why the precautions were not taken. Of course, what is feasible depends upon the capability of a belligerent. To take an example from the NATO bombing campaign:

> each target required legal review and review for collateral damage. As a result, it often took nine or more people in different locations, working together over a secure communications system, to compete the review of a single target, and the procedures involved additional review in any case where 20 or more civilians might be killed.[73]

Clearly, not every military would have this capability. Nonetheless, when using PGMs the types of issues that might be considered are quite numerous. For example:

> Coalition planners followed stringent procedures to select and attack targets. Attack routes were planned to minimize the results of errant ordnance; the norm was to use PGMs, rather than less-accurate gravity weapons, in built-up or populated areas. Attack procedures specified that if the pilot could not positively identify his target or was not confident the weapon would guide properly (because of clouds, for example), he could not deliver that weapon.[74]

It would appear as though procedures allowed for both errant weapons and weapons that may not guide correctly. What this indicates is that allowance was made for what might occur and not just the best-case scenario. This is the correct position under API. For example, certain types of guided munitions will tend, on average, to fall short rather than go long.[75] Therefore, this should be factored into the planning process and where possible attack routes should be chosen that will minimise the likely collateral damage if a weapon does fall short.

While looking at previous State practice is a useful guide, it would be helpful to be able to identify more generally the types of feasible precautions that should be taken by planners and commanders. This can be achieved by looking at the problem in reverse. The purpose of taking the precautions is to minimise collateral damage.

---

72 *Off Target: The Conduct of the War and Civilian Casualties in Iraq*, above n 91 (chapter 4), 17 (footnote omitted).

73 Cordesman, above n 97 (chapter 1), 117.

74 US Department of Defense, *Conduct of the Persian Gulf War: Final Report to Congress*, above n 29 (chapter 3), 228.

75 See, for example, the explanation of the Paveway II guidance system at Carlo Popp, *Desert Storm: Precision Guided Munitions* (2005) Air Power Australia <http://www.ausairpower.net/TE-PGM-ODS-92.html> at 29 December 2005.

If we look at what causes collateral damage, we can then consider what precautions could be taken to address those causes. Waxman states that collateral damage:

> is largely a product of three factors: (1) information about exactly where a military target is, (2) the ability to aim at and hit a desired point, and (3) the ability to regulate the quantum of destruction a hit inflicts.[76]

Looked at this way, we can now see the issues that need to be addressed when considering what would be feasible precautions. First, precautions should be taken to identify accurately where the target is. This is different from determining whether the target is a military objective, as required by article 57(2)(a)(i) API.[77] The issue here is that by having a greater knowledge of the location of the target, an attacker can be more discriminate with the targeting and thereby reduce the likelihood of damage to other objects.

The second general precaution concerns both weapon choice and how the weapon is employed. For example, a shot fired from rifle will usually be more accurate than a shot fired from pistol. Further, a rifle shot fired from a stable position will be more accurate than the same shot rifle fired from an unstable position. Also, a rifle fired by a person with more training will be more accurate than a shot fired by a person with less training.[78] By 'hit a desired point', Waxman's analysis addresses the consequence of errors. Therefore, further precautions under this point include the reliability and accuracy of the weapon system[79] and allowing for the consequences of a miss.

Third, the choice of weapon may affect the possible collateral damage. In simple terms, a larger bomb is more likely to cause collateral damage than a smaller bomb with similar characteristics due to the increased blast and fragmentation range. Equally, a bomb that has fuse set to detonate some milliseconds after impact is

---

76 Waxman, above n 56 (chapter 1), xiv. See also Schmitt, 'The Principle of Discrimination in 21st Century Warfare', above n 201 (chapter 4), [53]. See also Sandoz, Swinarski and Zimmerman (eds), above n 68 (chapter 1), [2212], where it is stated that:

> The danger incurred by the civilian population and civilian objects depends on various factors: their location (possibly within or in the vicinity of a military objective), the terrain (landslides, floods etc.), accuracy of the weapons used (greater or lesser dispersion, depending on the trajectory, the range, the ammunition used etc.), weather conditions (visibility, wind etc.), the specific nature of the military objectives concerned (ammunition depots, fuel reservoirs, main roads of military importance at or in the vicinity of inhabited areas etc.), technical skill of the combatants (random dropping of bombs when unable to hit the intended target).

77 I am using *target* in the sense of the desired object for attack, as opposed to the desired point of impact of a weapon. To take an example from the NATO bombing campaign, it could be said the desired object for attack was the Federal Directorate for Supply and Procurement, while the desired point of impact was the building now known to have been occupied by the Chinese Embassy.

78 See Sandoz, Swinarski and Zimmerman (eds), above n 68 (chapter 1), [2212]; quoted with approval in *Why They Died: Civilian Casualties in Lebanon during the 2006 War*, above n 3 (chapter 2), 34.

79 Both the human and non-human aspects.

likely to produce less fragmentation problems than the same bomb designed to explode on or just prior to impact.

None of the above points is determinative, and each must be assessed in light of the particular attack. For example, if there is a military advantage to using a point detonating weapon, and use of a delay fuse would not achieve the desired effect, then use of a delay fuse would not be a feasible precaution.[80]

There is one more factor I would add to Waxman's list, and that is knowledge of the presence of civilians or civilian objects. A bridge could be accurately assessed as a military objective, it could be precisely hit, and the minimum force might have been used, but if it was unknown that civilians were present, collateral damage might still occur. This is a particularly important point in the context of taking precautions, as article 57(2)(a)(iii) API requires an attacker to refrain from launching an attack if the expected collateral damage will be disproportionate. As Human Rights Watch state, "[c]ollateral damage assessments are a key way for the military to fulfil its obligations under international humanitarian law."[81] It is, therefore, important to have an obligation on an attacker to take steps to determine what might be the expected collateral damage. The Kosovo bombing campaign provides yet another useful example.

> In Brussels, NATO officials told Amnesty International that an aircrew flying at 15,000 feet would be able only to identify whether the objective was the intended one according to the planning preparations, but would be unable to tell whether, for example, civilians had moved within its vicinity. The 15,000-feet rule thus effectively made it impossible for NATO aircrew to respect the obligation to suspend an attack once circumstances had changed on the ground rendering the objective no longer legitimate. They told Amnesty International that following the bombing of civilians in a convoy at Djakovica, the Rules of Engagement were amended to require visual confirmation that there were no civilians in the target area.[82]

The obligation in this case is to observe the target in such a way as to be able to determine whether collateral damage will be an issue. I should add that, despite how it has been expressed by Amnesty International, observing the potential target area is often an issue under article 57(2)(a)(i) and (ii) API and is not an issue under article 57(2)(b) API. Article 57(2)(b) API applies only where the full planning for an attack has already been carried out. In a number of cases, the final assessment cannot be made until the target is observed immediately prior to the attack. This would certainly have been the case with the convoy at Djakovica, as the type of

---

80 Recalling that at this point I am discussing minimising collateral damage and not whether any expected collateral damage is proportional. It may well be that in a particular case the use of a point detonating weapon is permitted under API, above n 2 (chapter 1), art 57(2)(a)(ii) but is not permitted under art 57(2)(a)(iii).

81 *Off Target: The Conduct of the War and Civilian Casualties in Iraq*, above n 91 (chapter 4), 18.

82 *"Collateral damage" or Unlawful Killings?: Violations of the Laws of War by NATO during Operation Allied Force*, above n 28 (chapter 5).

convoy is question would not have been a pre-planned target.[83] Accordingly, in the above example, the aircrew would have been required to comply with, inter alia, article 57(2)(a)(ii) API.

Having considered what an attacker can do by way of precautions, it is worth re-iterating that it is only those precautions that are feasible that are required to be done. What is feasible will vary for military to military, and even attack to attack.

At the moment, the issue being discussed is what precautions are feasible to minimise collateral damage and not whether the expected collateral damage is proportional. To take an example, imagine a scenario where an attack by bombing is expected to result in 10 civilian deaths. Alternatively, an attack by inserting special forces reduces the expected civilian death toll to zero. But, for the purposes of the example, say the likelihood of the special forces team surviving the mission is less than one percent. Arguably, the precaution of using special forces instead of aerial bombing is not feasible due to the high risk to own forces.[84] Accordingly, that particular precaution need not be taken. But, this does not mean that 10 civilian deaths is proportional. That is another question entirely. If, however, it were concluded that 10 civilian deaths was proportional, then article 57(2)(a)(ii) API would not have been breached just because a possible but not feasible precaution to reduce the civilian death toll had not been taken.

An interesting example of what may be considered feasible precautions, and the requirement not to cause excessive collateral damage, is provided by weapons that either fire automatically, or whilst requiring manual firing, automatically track and locate a target. The following is an example of the use of such a weapon.

> As part of Operation Grapes of Wrath in April 1996, Israel's attacks culminated "in the shelling of a makeshift refugee compound at a UN post south of Tyre in which more than one hundred displaced civilians were killed." Israel said Hizbollah had fired mortars and Katyusha rockets from a position three hundred meters from the UN post. ... The International Committee of the Red Cross (ICRC) one day later issued a statement in which it 'firrmly condemned' the Israeli shelling at Qana and reiterated there was an 'absolute ban' on indiscriminate attacks. However, a senior ICRC official said after an investigation that the real problem here was the fact that the Israeli system was designed to automatically fire back on the source of the original attack. Therefore Israel did not take sufficient precautions in their attack to ensure that it would not result in disproportionate civilian deaths.[85]

Arguably, there are in fact two issues here. The first is the taking of feasible precautions. This can be considered by stepping through Waxman's three points. First, how accurate was the counter-barrage in the sense of was the aim-point the same as where the mortars were fired from? Second, how accurate was the counter-bar-

83 See a description of the attack sequence in *OTP Report*, above n 90 (chapter 1), [65].

84 See section 8.2 for further discussion concerning risk to own forces and proportionality of attacks.

85 Roy Gutman and Daoud Kuttab, *Indiscriminate Attack*, Crimes of War Project <http://www.crimesofwar.org/thebook/indiscriminate-attack.html> at 26 May 2006.

rage in the sense of what was the circular error probable ('CEP')[86] for the shells with respect to the aim point? Finally, what were the shells' blast and fragmentation properties and was this commensurate with the desired military result?

There is also a further issue. Even if all of the above was acceptable, was there any assessment of the anticipated collateral damage? In other words, is it the case that inadequate precautions were taken to minimise collateral damage (and possibly thereby avoid disproportionate collateral damage), or is it the case that feasible precautions were taken but nonetheless the collateral damage was disproportionate? It appears as though the ICRC may have mixed up the two concepts.

Before concluding this section, an observation by Hays Parks merits comment. Hays Parks is critical of the way that API has placed the onus for reducing collateral damage on an attacker without recognising that it is a shared obligation between attacker, defender and the civilian population.[87] His point has some merit. First, while article 51(7) API prohibits what are often term human shields, article 51(8) API expressly states that a violation of, inter alia, article 51(7) API does not relieve an attacker of its obligations to the civilian population, and in particular the obligations to take precautionary measures under article 57 API still apply in full.[88] Second, while article 58 API does explicitly place obligations on the defending party, API is silent on whether non-compliance with those obligations lessens an attacker's obligations. As API is silent on the point, and article 57 API is not expressed in conditional language, then the obligations of article 57 API apply in full despite non-compliance with article 58 API by the defending party.[89] That said, non-compliance with article 58 API by a defender may reduce what it is feasible for an attacker to do in compliance with articles 57(2)(a)(i) and (ii) API. But, this is of little effect, because article 57(2)(a)(iii) API requires an attacker to refrain from launching an attack where the expected collateral damage will be disproportionate. And importantly, this obligation exists independently of what precautions it was feasible to take. Hays Parks is also correct in relation to collateral damage in that API does not place any obligations on civilians directly. However, as Hays Parks recognises, API now reflects the law for State parties and the above criticisms do not change the interpretation of API obligations.

The following paragraphs deal with one particular precaution, and that is the height of attacking aircraft. In some recent conventional conflicts, the restrictions on the minimum height flown by strike aircraft have attracted attention. The reasons for, and the consequences of, minimum height restrictions provides a good example for many of the points just discussed. A good starting point is the often-quoted example of NATO aircraft during the 1999 bombing campaign. During the early part of that campaign, NATO aircraft were restricted by orders from

86 The CEP "is the radius of a circle within which one-half of the weapons will fall"—Schmitt, *Precision Attack and International Humanitarian Law*, above n 30 (chapter 3), 446. For example, the Joint Direct Attack Munition has an unclassified CEP of 20 feet, whereas bombs dropped from a B-17 during World War II had a CEP of approximately 3,300 feet—Schmitt, *Precision Attack and International Humanitarian Law*, above n 30 (chapter 3), 449 and 456.

87 Hays Parks, 'Air War and the Law of War', above n 181 (chapter 3), 28–9.

88 The issue of human shields is further discussed at section 8.3.3.

89 See *Prosecutor v Galic, (Trial Chamber)* Case No IT-98-29-T (5 December 2003) [61].

flying below 15,000 feet to minimise risk to the aircrew from anti-aircraft weapons.[90] While presumably not solely a function of the operating height restriction, the risk to the aircrew was clearly well managed.

> The air campaign began on 24 March 1999. It ended with the conclusion of the Military Technical Agreement between the International Security Force and the Governments of the Federal Republic of Yugoslavia and the Republic of Serbia of 9 June 1999. Between these two dates 10,484 strike sorties were flown by NATO aircraft and 23,614 munitions were released. No NATO casualties were reported arising out of these strike sorties.[91]

Why 15,000 feet? There are two reasons. The one usually discussed, and as the following quote illustrates, is that there can be a significant anti-air threat at lower altitudes.

> The Coalition's aggressive SEAD defeated most Iraqi radar systems. This enabled Coalition aircraft to conduct operations in the middle altitudes (about 15,000 feet) in relative safety because they were less vulnerable to IR-guided SAMs or unguided AAA. One of the greater dangers Coalition pilots faced was from IR- or EO-guided SAMs while they were flying at relatively low altitudes, supporting Coalition ground forces. Although sortie rates were relatively constant, approximately half of its fixed-wing combat losses occurred during either the first week of Operation Desert Storm (17 aircraft), before enemy defenses had been suppressed, or during the last week (eight aircraft), when aircraft were operating at lower altitudes in the IR SAM threat region.[92]

However, there is also a second and less discussed reason. For a number of PGM, medium altitude release provides the greatest accuracy (in the sense of hitting as close as possible to the aim point):

> Dropping a PGM in the midaltitude range—from 15,000 to 23,000 feet—achieves maximum accuracy, allowing enough time for the weapon to correct itself in flight and hit its designated target as close to a bull's-eye as possible. Dropping it from a lower altitude gives the weapon's steering fins less opportunity to correct the aim, decreasing its accuracy. From the pilot's perspective, this altitude range is also the most desirable for attacks on a fixed or preplanned target. The middle altitudes allow time to identify the target at sufficient distance, "designate it" (if the weapon is laser guided), and release. In short, for PGMs used against a fixed target in an

90 Waxman, above n 56 (chapter 1), xii.

91 Rowe, 'Kosovo 1999: The Air Campaign—Have the Provisions of Additional Protocol I Withstood the Test?', above n 179 (chapter 4) (footnotes omitted).

92 US Department of Defense, *Conduct of the Persian Gulf War: Final Report to Congress*, above n 29 (chapter 3), 229. SEAD is Suppression of Enemy Air Defences, IR is Infra-Red, SAM is Surface-to-Air Missiles, AAA is Anti-Aircraft Artillery, and EO is Electro-Optical.

> established position—true of most of the targets struck in Serbia—the optimum altitude to ensure accuracy lies at or above 15,000 feet.[93]

For the purposes of this discussion, what exact height aircraft fly at is not the issue as such. Rather, what is important is whether flying at a higher altitude significantly and adversely affects likely collateral damage.[94] In this respect, aircraft height could affect collateral damage in either or both of the first two ways that Waxman has identified.[95] First, flying at a higher altitude could make target identification less accurate. Second, flying at a higher altitude may make hitting the aim point harder. It is convenient to deal with the second point first, as this point has already been partly addressed.

Assuming that a target has been correctly identified, the issue then is how accurately can that target be struck. As we saw just above, for correctly identified targets, if an aircraft is dropping a PGM, a higher altitude may in fact be the preferred altitude for weapon accuracy. Concerning the Kosovo campaign in particular, NATO's Supreme Allied Commander Europe from 1997–2000 states that the "airmen assured me that we were flying at the right altitudes to optimize their weapons without slipping down into the range of most of the antiaircraft weapons."[96] So, flying at 15,000 feet when using PGMs might actually make weapon delivery more accurate.

But, what about UGMs?

> Because nonguided munitions or "dumb bombs" are inherently less precise than their more intelligent brothers, their optimum drop altitude is lower than that of a PGM. Even so, acquisition remains a limiting factor—coming in too low makes acquiring the target, lining up, and putting the bomb on target nearly impossible. One can imagine the difficulty of such target acquisition for a pilot roaring in at low altitude and 500 knots. At that speed and altitude, pilots generally have their hands full just trying to avoid hitting the ground. As a result, the compromise altitude for the delivery of unguided bombs is around 5,000 feet, putting the delivery aircraft right in the thick of fire from ground defenses. Allied Force air commanders resolved this dilemma by keeping aircraft at medium altitudes but restricting the use of non-PGMs to areas where there was little or no chance of civilian casualties or collateral damage.[97]

So, prima facie flying at a lower altitude, but not too low, will lead to more accurate delivery of UGM. However, as Meilinger alludes to, this is relevant only if less accuracy is likely to affect anticipated collateral damage. To take the Kosovo campaign as an example, I am not aware of any allegations of collateral damage arising

93 Phillip Meilinger, *Precision Aerospace Power: Discrimination, and the Future of War* (2001) Air & Space Power Chronicles <http://www.airpower.maxwell.af.mil/airchronicles/apj/apj01/fal01/meilinger.html> at 30 December 2005. The relationship between aircraft operating height, accuracy and threat is discussed in some detail in Rebecca Grant, *Altitude* (2001) Air Force Magazine Online <http://www.afa.org/magazine/oct2001/1001altitude.asp> at 23 May 2006.

94 Meilinger, above n 93 (chapter 7) (footnote omitted).

95 See above n 76 (chapter 1).

96 Clark, above n 123 (chapter 3), 225.

97 Meilinger, above n 93 (chapter 7).

from the use of UGM; or in particular, the use of UGM in circumstances where the UGM fell too far from a military objective and thereby caused collateral damage. If any collateral damage concerns are sufficiently outside of the CEP of the intended UGM, then the use of a UGM compared to a PGM is not a relevant legal issue. Indeed, a PGM might cause more risk of harm, as if a PGM suffers guidance failure it may go outside of the likely target area of a UGM.

Of course, the above are generalisations and different weapons have different characteristics. For example, when discussing the employment of cluster munitions by aircraft flying above 15,000 feet by NATO aircraft during the bombing campaign in Kosovo, Benvenuti writes:

> This is an altitude which makes it difficult to select accurately military objectives in the targeted area, and to control properly the trajectory of the projectiles, in conformity with the principle of distinction.[98]

The issue of identification is considered below. However, with respect to control over the weapon, Benvenuti is quite right in saying that the height (or range) from which certain weapons are employed will affect their accuracy. Importantly, this will vary from weapon to weapon. Some weapons are inaccurate if fired from too far away, while conversely some weapons can be inaccurate if fired from too close.

There is another point that I believe Meilinger would have been aware of but has not clearly spelt out. The compromise altitude of 5,000 feet is based on the aircrew having an unimpeded run at the target. However, by flying at a height where anti-air defences are high, the aircrew are not only put at risk but are also distracted by the threat. An interesting but seemingly overlooked aspect to this debate is that, as one would logically suppose, bombing accuracy decreases when an aircraft comes under attack.[99] As Spaight noted as far back as 1924 in regard to World War I operations (when aircraft and anti-aircraft defences were in their infancy): "The bombing airmen were very far from being able to drop their bombs serenely and at their leisure. They were for the most part fighting for their own lives."[100]

Along with other factors, a bombing attack is a compromise between attacking in such a way to hit accurately the target, hitting the target with sufficient weapons effect to achieve the desired damage to the target, the minimisation of collateral damage, and the safety of the aircrew.[101] By operating at an altitude that lessens the aircrew's exposure to ground-based threat, the aircrew can increase their focus on targeting rather than their own survival.[102] While in the abstract flying lower will usually improve the ability to distinguish between civilian objects and military objectives, and also improve the accuracy of the weapon,[103] targeting does not occur

98 Benvenuti, above n 78 (chapter 3), 513.

99 Bothe, Partsch and Solf, above n 87 (chapter 1), 364.

100 Spaight, above n 1 (chapter 4), 220.

101 Email from Michael Kitcher (Commanding Officer, Number 3 Squadron, Royal Australian Air Force) to Ian Henderson, 4 December 2003.

102 Ibid.

103 Subject to the discussion above on optimum heights for weapon release across different weapon types.

in the abstract. The lower the aircraft flies, often the greater the risk to the aircraft. And as risk increases, pilots will usually take other measures like flying faster, regular changes in altitude and direction, etc to reduce risk. This will result in decreased discrimination and accuracy.[104] Hays Parks quotes a figure of a 200% increase in the CEP when an aircraft comes under fire.[105]

The other affect altitude may have is on the ability to identify the target in the first place. I say may, because as Voon notes:

> In some cases, lower level flying may not have increased the pilot's ability to distinguish between civilian objects and military objectives, so flying at 15,000 feet would not of itself affect the legality of the conduct of the campaign.[106]

Additionally, not all identification is done with the naked eye. In the Kosovo bombing campaign, a system was set up to enable NATO aircraft:

> to descend well below 15,000 feet, if necessary, to identify targets on the ground, but the pilots reported that they were usually more effective using high-powered binoculars and orbiting well above antiaircraft machine gun altitudes.[107]

The issue of identification will not normally arise with pre-planned fixed targets, as these are generally not only large, but even where the targets are small, by the use of the global positioning system, visual cues and other ways of identifying the correct aim point, the right target can be struck. Rather, the problem will usually arise:

> during attacks on mobile or transitory targets. In such cases, the key factor becomes target identification. Is the column below comprised of military or civilian vehicles? If both, which is which? Aircraft at medium altitudes have difficulty making such a determination.[108]

Three things can occur in these circumstances. First, the aircrew may try to identify the object themselves. Second, the aircrew may seek assistance from other sources, such as:

---

104 See Schmitt, *Precision Attack and International Humanitarian Law*, above n 86 (chapter 3), 449. Bothe, Partsch and Solf refer to an unsuccessful attempt by the ICRC during the negotiations of API to extend the protection from attack for aircrew parachuting from disabled aircraft (now codified in API, above n 2 (chapter 1), art 42) to occupants of aircraft in distress whether or not the aircraft is abandoned. The rationale was to increase the aircrew's probability of survival in heavily defended attacks, and therefore reduce the aircrew's hesitation with a resultant improvement in the accuracy of the attack and thereby reduce collateral damage—Bothe, Partsch and Solf, above n 87 (chapter 1), 226–7.

105 Hays Parks, 'Air War and the Law of War', above n 181 (chapter 3), 53 (fn 197).

106 Voon, above n 56 (chapter 7), 1098.

107 Clark, above n 123 (chapter 3), 276.

108 Meilinger, above n 93 (chapter 7).

> a forward air controller (FAC), who pilots an aircraft that generally operates at lower altitudes, or an un[inhabited] aerial vehicle (UAV). The latter also flies at low altitude and can relay video it takes of the suspected target to an analyst, who rapidly determines its identity and sends that information either to the airborne aircraft or spotters on the ground. After one of these sources makes the determination, strike aircraft can attack from the optimum altitude.[109]

Finally, if the aircrew cannot identify the object themselves, and have no FAC, UAV, or ground spotters to consult, they can elect not to drop their bombs.[110] This occurred, for example, during Operation FALCONER. During that Operation, "Australian pilots could, and on occasion did, abort missions to avoid the risk of unintended casualties if their target could not be clearly identified from the air."[111]

Finally, the 15,000 limitation may not be absolute. Rather, it may be a general restriction from which derogations are permitted. In a discussion post the Kosovo bombing campaign, Britain's Defence Secretary during the Kosovo crisis writes:

> Some have criticised the fact that the majority of offensive missions were flown at medium level. It is true that offensive aircraft were initially restricted to operating above 15,000 feet (and some continued to do so throughout the campaign). Given the multitude of small arms, anti-aircraft artillery and shoulder launched missile systems, the decision not to fly at low level was entirely correct. However, as the Serbian air defence systems were degraded, operating height restrictions were eased and, for the latter half of the campaign, some aircraft operated down to 6,000 feet when target identification or weapons delivery profile required it.[112]

What can be seen from the above is that it is not as simple as the lower an aircraft flies the more accurate the targeting and the higher it flies the increased likelihood of misidentification and collateral damage. Rather, where potential collateral damage is an issue, some of the things that need to be considered are as follows:

(a) What types of weapons are being employed and what is the optimal height for weapons release?
(b) What type of mission is being flown and has the target been pre-identified?
(c) If the target has not been pre-identified, are other assets available to assist with target identification?
(d) What types of anti-aircraft defences are present and is the attack aircraft vulnerable to these defences?
(e) To what extent will targeting accuracy be degraded by the aircrew diverting some attention to survivability?

Of course, these types of considerations apply not just to aircraft height. Similar factors, suitably adjusted, would also apply to the positioning of artillery, mortars

109 Ibid.

110 Ibid.

111 *The War in Iraq: ADF Operations in the Middle East in 2003*, above n 170 (chapter 3), 13.

112 Lord George Robertson, 'Kosovo—An account of the crisis: NATO Air strikes' <http://www.kosovo.mod.uk/account/nato.htm> at 30 December 2005.

etc. Indeed, even an urban action by an infantry squad could be analysed in these terms. Rogers provides a good conclusion to this point. As he notes, it is not the height restriction that is important. What is important is how that height restriction operates in practice. Rogers suggests the following:

> If the target is sufficiently important, higher commanders may be prepared to accept a greater degree of risk to the aircraft crew to ensure that the target is properly identified and accurately attacked. …
> However, if the target is assessed as not being worth that risk and a minimum operational altitude is set for their protection, the aircrew involved in the operation will have to make their own assessment of the risks involved in verifying and attacking the assigned target. If their assessment is that (a) the risk to them of getting close enough to the target to identify it properly is too high, (b) that there is a real danger of incidental death, injury or damage to civilians or civilian objects because of lack of verification of the target, and (c) they or friendly forces are not in immediate danger if the attack is not carried out, there is no need for them to put themselves at risk to verify the target. Quite simply, the attack should not be carried out.
> Rules of engagement could make this clear with a test like: "Are you sure that the target is a military objective? If you are in any doubt, would you or friendly forces be placed in danger if the attack were not carried out? If not, the attack is NOT to be carried out."[113]

Rogers raises the interesting issue of danger to friendly forces if the attack is not carried out. It is not clear whether he is of the view that where there is such danger does this mean that the attack can be carried out without descending in altitude; or does it mean that the aircrew should accept greater risk to themselves and descend? Both situations could apply. Preventing danger to friendly forces is clearly a military advantage. Accordingly, where such a risk exists, the anticipated military advantage from the attack is higher; and, therefore, the level of collateral damage that would be proportional is also higher. However, this is only acceptable as an argument where there is sufficient certainty about the target and expected collateral damage. In such a case, the issue in not descending is not identification but the accuracy of weapon delivery. Where, conversely, the issue is not accurate weapon delivery but identification of the target and potential collateral damage, then the second option of descending is the more appropriate one.

Notwithstanding that all appropriate precautions are taken, article 57(2)(a)(iii) API imposes a further obligation to nonetheless not launch an attack if excessive collateral damage is expected. That is the issue discussed in the next section.

7.4 Proportionality

Article 57(2)(a)(iii) API expresses in rule form one version of the proportionality principle that is applicable to armed conflict. However, the principle of proportionality has three distinct areas of application in armed conflict as three different rules of proportionality are to be found in the *jus ad bellum* and the *jus in bello*.

113 Rogers, 'Zero-casualty warfare', above n 94 (chapter 3).

With respect to the *jus ad bellum*, the ICJ has held that the entitlement to resort to self-defence under Article 51 of the *Charter of the United Nations* is subject to the customary international law conditions of necessity and proportionality.[114] As to one of the rules under the *jus in bello*, belligerent reprisals[115] are governed, inter alia, by a rule of proportionality.[116] Finally, there is the *jus in bello* rule that expected collateral damage must not be excessive to the anticipated military advantage. While the terms used in API are 'excessive damage' or 'excessive injury',[117] these terms are generally understood as reflecting a *jus in bello* principle of proportionality and the term proportionality is regularly used in that way.[118] When used in this sense:

> The principle of proportionality acknowledges the unfortunate inevitability of collateral civilian casualties and collateral damage to civilian objects when non-combatants and civilian objects are mingled with combatants and targets, even with reasonable efforts by the parties to a conflict to minimize collateral injury and damage.[119]

As this study considers only the *jus in bello* applicable to targeting, the following discussion is limited to the IHL targeting aspect of the principle and not the *jus ad bellum* or belligerent reprisal issues.

The proportionality rule requires commanders to refrain from deciding to launch an attack against a military objective which may be expected to cause the "incidental loss of civilian life, injury to civilians, damage to civilian objects, or a combination thereof, which would be excessive in relation to the concrete and direct military advantage anticipated."[120] In other words, "attacks on lawful targets only remain lawful if the incidental civilian casualties or damages are not excessive."[121] Despite the long history of IHL treaties, API was the first time that the customary international law principle of proportionality was codified in a multilateral treaty.[122] While some may find that surprising, perhaps the most interesting

---

114 *Nuclear Weapons Case* [1996] ICJ Rep 226, [40]-[41]. See also *Military and Paramilitary Activities in and against Nicaragua (Nicaragua v United States of America) (Merits)* [1986] ICJ Rep 14 [176].

115 Belligerent reprisals are "measures taken in the context of an existing armed conflict by one of the parties in response to unlawful conduct by an adversary"—Christopher Greenwood, 'Reprisals and Reciprocity in the New Law of Armed Conflict' in Michael Meyer (ed), *Armed Conflict and the New Law: Aspects of the 1977 Geneva Protocols and the 1981 Weapons Convention* (1989) 227, 227.

116 For a discussion on proportionality and belligerent reprisals, see ibid 230–3.

117 See API, above n 2 (chapter 1), arts 51(5)(b), 57(2)(b), and 85(3).

118 Fenrick, 'Attacking the Enemy Civilian as a Punishable Offense', above n 20 (chapter 3), 545 (footnotes omitted).

119 US Department of Defense, *Conduct of the Persian Gulf War: Final Report to Congress*, above n 29 (chapter 3), 698.

120 API, above n 2 (chapter 1), art 57(2)(a)(iii).

121 Kellenberger, above n 23 (chapter 1).

122 Ibid. Fenrick provides a concise review of the history of the proportionality rule in Fenrick, 'The Rule of Proportionality and Protocol I in Conventional Warfare', above n 9 (chapter 7).

aspect of the principle is not in the detail of the rule but the fact that it exists at all. As explained by Major Pfaff:

> In the criminal model, police are not permitted to engage in courses of action in which innocent civilians will knowingly be harmed, but soldiers are permitted to do this in war. In the former, the protection police owe civilians is nearly absolute, but in the latter, soldiers have greater permissions to put civilians at risk.[123]

Indeed, this is one of the very reasons why when lecturing on this topic I try to get the audience to view IHL as permissive rather than as imposing restrictions. One could rightly argue that what restrictions there are in IHL are in fact merely limits of the permissions.

Having introduced the topic now due to its place in article 57(2)(a)(iii) API, there are so many interesting issues in this one rule that the topic deserves its own chapter. Accordingly, I leave discussing the proportionality rule in detail until chapter 8 and will now move on to the next part of article 57 API.

7.5 Cancelling or suspending an attack

An attack must be cancelled or suspended:

> if it becomes apparent that the objective is not a military one or is subject to special protection or that the attack may be expected to cause collateral damage which would be excessive in relation to the concrete and direct military advantage anticipated.[124]

The interesting aspect of article 57(2)(b) API is that, unlike article 57(2)(a) API, it is not addressed solely to those who plan or decide upon attacks, but it is also aimed at those who execute attacks. Indeed, arguably the article is primarily aimed at those who execute attacks.[125] The obligation in article 57(2)(b) API is conditional upon it becoming *apparent* that something might be amiss. Rogers quotes an interesting example of this from the NATO air campaign in Kosovo:

> At the NATO press briefing on 18 April 1999, an account was given of how a pilot launched an attack against a radar and, noting that the site was close to a church, pulled his weapon off the target so that it exploded harmlessly in a wood.[126]

However, as Blix has noted, those "who actually perform the attack will often, with modern methods and means of combat, be unable to see in advance what they

123 Tony Pfaff, *Non-combatant Immunity and the War on Terrorism* (2003) United States Air Force Academy <http://www.usafa.af.mil/jscope/JSCOPE03/Pfaff03.html> at 26 May 2006.

124 API, above n 2 (chapter 1), art 57(2)(b).

125 Sandoz, Swinarski and Zimmerman (eds), above n 68 (chapter 1), [2220].

126 Rogers, 'Zero-casualty warfare', above n 94 (chapter 3). A copy of the weapons-system video showing this incident is held by the author of this book.

attack."[127] In such a case, it is unlikely that anything will become apparent to an attacker, and article 57(2)(b) API will be likely to have little to no operation vis-à-vis the person executing the attack. However, where the attacker does observe the target and, to take but one example, discovers "that the target has been wrongly identified, they must refrain from attack."[128] So, the first notable thing about article 57(2)(b) API is that this article does not impose an additional obligation beyond the obligations imposed by article 57(2)(a) API to positively gather information about the target and target location. It is interesting, therefore, that in relation to the Kosovo bombing campaign Voon has observed:

> However, in most cases, pilots and weapons system officers were not in a position to verify that the targets remained legitimate. For example, the pilots were generally unable to obtain visual confirmation that civilians had not moved into the target area before the planes approached. Amnesty International criticized NATO for focusing on the planning phase without giving enough attention to subsequent verification, by the attacking force, to ensure the intelligence relied on was accurate and up to date.[129]

Amnesty International's criticism would be valid only if the subsequent verification could be considered a feasible action or precaution under article 57(2)(a) API. This would partly depend upon just how old the planning intelligence was and also the availability of assets to conduct verification. Another factor would be whether there was any evidence of increased collateral damage because of not conducting pre-attack verification.

The next interesting issue about the article is how to apply it in practice. To use the air force as an example, the crew of a strike aircraft might receive their tasking through an Air Task Order ('ATO'). The only information in the ATO relevant to the target might be the type of weapon to be used, the aim point (ie, the desired point of impact of the weapon) and the time on target. Based on this information, how are the crew to decide whether the target is or is not a military objective, if, for instance, the target is an otherwise nondescript building? Or, assuming it is obviously a military objective, as the crew do not know the anticipated military advantage that the commander is hoping to gain, how can the crew apply the proportionality rule and decide whether the collateral damage will be excessive? Bothe, Partsch and Solf note that in a coordinated operation, the military advantage anticipated from the attack "is not a matter which can be determined by individual tank leaders, the commanders of lower echelon combat units or individual attacking bomber aircraft."[130] Fenrick is of the view that the personnel who are required to take action to cancel or suspend an attack under article 57(2)(b) API are those who are "higher in the chain of command and, possibly, those subordinates with a sufficient knowledge of all aspects of the attack to determine that excessive incidental

127 Blix, above n 78 (chapter 2), 147.
128 Ibid.
129 Voon, above n 56 (chapter 7), 1097–8.
130 Bothe, Partsch and Solf, above n 87 (chapter 1), 367.

losses will probably be incurred."[131] He rightly points out that the authority to cancel or suspend an attack may not be exercisable by every military member, as for example, a private soldier may not have sufficient information available to assess properly whether an attack should be cancelled or suspended.[132] Fenrick makes a good point. But, the best way to address the issue is for States to put in place procedures to give effect to article 57(2)(b) API.[133] The conclusion that I draw is that in practice, article 57(2)(b) API is confined in operation to either clear cases of mistaken targeting or where the target or target areas is different from what was briefed. What article 57(2)(b) API does not do is to impose a burden on those who execute attacks to second-guess their commanders. To take a very simple example, a pilot might be tasked to strike a certain aim point with a particular weapon within a particular period of time. The tasking might come with a target folder, which might include, amongst other things, imagery of the target and the surrounding area. If, in accordance with procedure, the headquarters that tasked the pilot is responsible for assessing whether the target is a military objective and that the expected collateral damage will be proportional, the pilot is entitled to rely on this information.[134] The pilot is required to cancel or suspend the attack only if it becomes apparent to the pilot that something might be amiss. So, if the pilot sees a church right next to the aim point but that church was clearly visible and marked as a church in the target folder imagery, then the pilot would be entitled to rely upon the assessment made at the higher headquarters. Conversely:

> aircrew may be ordered to bomb what the mission planner believes to be a command and control centre. If, in the course of the mission, the command and control centre is displaying an unbriefed symbol of protection, eg Red Cross symbol, then aircrew must refrain from completing their attack.[135]

Having refrained from completing the attack, the aircrew either could abort or could seek further orders. A recent Australian example of this issue is provided by "Australia's squadron of 14 F/A-18 Hornet jets …, [which] on occasion, pulled out of bombing raids at the last minute when it was realised civilians were in the

131 Fenrick, 'The Rule of Proportionality and Protocol I in Conventional Warfare', above n 9 (chapter 7), 109.

132 Ibid.

133 See the discussion of the IHL 6-step targeting process at chapter 9.

134 *OTP Report*, above n 90 (chapter 1), [85].

135 Houston, above n 4 (chapter 1). The symbol may be on a flag that has been flown subsequent to the date of imagery or perhaps was always there but was not visible in the briefing pack photographs due to the angle of the imagery and the position of the flag (footnote added). It is important that the symbol is unbriefed. For example, Human Rights Watch refer to an example from the 2003 Gulf War of the misuse of the ICRC emblem—*Off Target: The Conduct of the War and Civilian Casualties in Iraq*, above n 91 (chapter 4), 70. If this was known during the planning phase of the attack, then subject to verification and perhaps a warning to the enemy to desist, the aircrew might have been briefed to attack the building displaying the ICRC emblem.

vicinity."[136] Presumably, the presence of civilians was not part of the target brief. Alternatively, the brief might be to expect up to say 15 civilians. If more civilians were present, the proportionality of the attack would have to be re-assessed.

7.6 Effective advance warning of attacks

"[E]ffective advance warning shall be given of attacks which may affect the civilian population, unless circumstances do not permit."[137] The obligation under article 57(2)(c) API needs to be considered separately from similar but different obligations to warn a defending party before attacking an object with special protection where it is alleged that the object with special protection has ceased to be protected from attack due to it being used to commit, outside its proper use, acts harmful to the attacker.[138] This added obligation does not apply, as a matter of law, to all civilian objects.

There have been many examples of such warnings in the past. During the Second World War, particularly in the case of objectives situated in occupied territory, warnings were made by radio or by means of pamphlets; there were also cases in which aircraft flew very low over the objective, giving civilians, workers or just townspeople, time to leave.[139] Further examples from World War II and the Korean war are provided by Hays Parks.[140] And in the 2006 armed conflict between Israel and Hezbollah forces in Lebanon:

> Israel repeatedly sent warnings to the population in southern Lebanon to evacuate the area south of the Litani River. It issued such warnings by Arabic-language flyers dropped from airplanes, Arabic radio messages broadcast into southern Lebanon, recorded voice messages sent to some Lebanese cellphones, and loudspeakers along the Israel Lebanese border.[141]

Accordingly, a claim that this rule does not reflect the practice in armed conflict would be misleading.[142]

Consistent with the words 'unless circumstances do not permit' in article 52(2)(c) API, the *ICRC Commentary* states that giving a warning may be inconven-

136 Tom Allard, 'Hill Credits ADF for Lower Civilian Toll', *The Age* (Melbourne), 24 April 2003.

137 API, above n 2 (chapter 1), art 57(2)(c).

138 See GCI, above n 5 (chapter 2), art 21 for medical units and establishments; GCIV, above n 8 (chapter 2), art 19 and API, above n 2 (chapter 1), art 13(1) for civilian medical facilities; and API, art 65(1), for civil defence facilities.

139 Sandoz, Swinarski and Zimmerman (eds), above n 68 (chapter 1), [2224].

140 W Parks, 'Air War and the Law of War', above n 181 (chapter 3), 157 (fn 466).

141 *Why They Died: Civilian Casualties in Lebanon during the 2006 War*, above n 3 (chapter 2), 6–7.

142 An interesting website with propaganda leaflets (some of which could be classified as warnings) dating back as far as World War I is *psywar.org* <http://www.psywar.org/leaflets.php> at 26 May 2006.

ient when the element of surprise in the attack is a condition of its success.[143] An example where surprise is very likely to be an element would be a mobile target. If the enemy is given advance warning of the attack, the target can be relocated. While the *ICRC Commentary* uses the word inconvenient, I suggest a better word would be *disadvantageous*. It is not necessarily any more *inconvenient* to give a warning when surprise is an aspect of the attack compared with when surprise is not an element of the attack. However, giving a warning in such circumstances is likely to be *disadvantageous* to the success of the attack. Accordingly, notwithstanding the use of the word inconvenient, the *ICRC Commentary* should be understood as stating that where surprise is a condition for the success of an attack, a warning need not be given. This is supported by Oeter, who states that a warning need not be given where "the specific circumstances of the planned operation do not make it possible to inform the defender because the purpose of the operation could not then be achieved".[144]

The *ICRC Commentary* notes that:

> During the Second World War, particularly in the case of objectives situated in occupied territory, warnings were made by radio or by means of pamphlets; there were also cases in which aircraft flew very low over the objective, giving civilians, workers or just townspeople, time to leave.[145]

The *ICRC Commentary* then proceeds to state that, "the possibility of giving such warning depends to a large extent on who has air control and on what air defences there are."[146] Once again, while *possibility* is the word in the *ICRC Commentary*, the better word would be *risk*—where risk is used in the sense of physical risk to the attacking force. Following on from the point raised in the *ICRC Commentary*, as Rowe points out:

> The often-quoted phrase "surprise in attack is the key to victory" does not have a great deal of significance if the attacking State has complete supremacy of the air, [and] *is virtually immune from the defensive measures of the attacked State*[.][147]

---

143 Sandoz, Swinarski and Zimmerman (eds), above n 68 (chapter 1), [2223]. By way of background, a proposal by the experts from Romania at the 1972 *Conference of Government Experts on the Reaffirmation and Development of International Humanitarian Law Applicable in Armed Conflicts* would have resulted in the obligation to give a warning being mandatory in all circumstances where an attack threatened civilians—CE 1972 Report, vol II, above n 53 (chapter 2), 74. See also the proposal by the experts from Spain—CE 1972 Report, vol II, above n 53 (chapter 2), 80.

144 Oeter, above n 24 (chapter 2), 172. See also Rogers, *Law on the Battlefield*, above n 84 (chapter 1), 115.

145 Sandoz, Swinarski and Zimmerman (eds), above n 68 (chapter 1), [2224].

146 Ibid, 686–7.

147 Rowe, 'Kosovo 1999: The Air Campaign—Have the Provisions of Additional Protocol I Withstood the Test?', above n 179 (chapter 4). Note that in this quote Rowe is focusing on surprise and risk to the attacking force. There is the other element of surprise already discussed which relates to the success of the attack itself.

As indicated by the *ICRC Commentary* and spelt out by Rowe, where the defending force poses virtually no risk to the attacking force, then giving an advance warning of the attack is not precluded. Importantly though, risk to the attacker is not minimal merely because the enemy does not have a significant air force. For anything more than just general advance warnings to be given, there must also be a lack of surface-to-air threat. Examples of a negligible air-to-air threat but of a significant surface-to-air threat include the 1990–91 Gulf War, the NATO campaign in Kosovo, the 2001–3 coalition action against the Taliban in Afghanistan and the 2003 Gulf War.

In a commentary on the NATO bombing campaign, Amnesty International state:

> NATO officials told Amnesty International in Brussels that as a general policy they chose not to issue warnings, for fear that this might endanger the crew of attacking aircraft. Given all the other measures taken in order to avoid NATO casualties (including high-altitude bombing), one might question whether sparing civilians was given sufficient weight in the decision not to give warnings. Nor does the consideration of pilot safety explain why there was no warning to civilians when Cruise missiles were used in attacks.[148]

To take their last point first, Amnesty International are quite right in referring to attacks by cruise missiles as coming within the scope of giving warnings.[149] While NATO might argue surprise or some other factor, clearly aircrew safety cannot be relied upon. This leads into my second point. A general policy cannot be adopted. Rather, the requirements of article 57(2)(c) API must be considered for each attack. As per the quote from Oeter above, an effective advance warning may be dispensed with only where "the *specific circumstances of the planned operation* do not make it possible to inform the defender because the purpose of the operation could not then be achieved".[150]

Warnings may have a general character. A belligerent could, for example, give notice by radio that attacks will be conducted on certain types of installations or factories. A warning could also contain a list of the objectives that will be attacked.[151] For example, during Operation Southern Watch, the coalition enforcing a No Fly Zone over southern Iraq warned repair workers that the coalition would be re-attacking communications links if they were being repaired.[152]

The *ICRC Commentary* states that even though ruses of war are not prohibited in this field, they would be unacceptable if they were to deceive the population and nullify the proper function of warnings, which is to give civilians the chance

148 *"Collateral damage" or Unlawful Killings?: Violations of the Laws of War by NATO during Operation Allied Force*, above n 28 (chapter 5).

149 See API, above n 2 (chapter 1), art 49(3); Oeter, above n 24 (chapter 2), 166.

150 Oeter, above n 24 (chapter 2), 172 (emphasis added).

151 Sandoz, Swinarski and Zimmerman (eds), above n 68 (chapter 1), [2225].

152 See Herbert Friedman, *Psychological Operations in Iraq: No-Fly Zone Warning Leaflets to Iraq, 2002–2003* (2003) *psywar.org* <http://www.psywar.org/noflyzone.php> at 26 May 2006.

to protect themselves.[153] I agree with this statement, noting its careful wording. I am assuming that *unacceptable* was carefully chosen rather than *unlawful* or *illegal*. A distinction can be drawn between a ruse that causes an unnecessary evacuation, and thereby limits the effectiveness of future warnings,[154] and a ruse that actually contributes to collateral damage. For example, if an attacker gave a warning that a certain TV station was to be attacked but then attacked a military HQ with no civilians present, while that would be unacceptable, it would be lawful. However, if an attacker gave a warning that a certain TV station was to be attacked, but then attacked a different communication facility where civilians where present and perhaps included civilians who had relocated from the first installation, that would not be just unacceptable but would also be likely to be unlawful.

A point not addressed in the *ICRC Commentary* is that as a warning is to be given where the attack might *affect* the civilian population, what is meant by affect? In my view, affect has to be narrowly construed consistent with the purpose of article 57 API as a whole. For instance, mere loss of a job could not warrant advance warning. Affect should be interpreted narrowly to mean directly affected in the sense of injured or killed, as well as property damage.

Article 57(2)(c) API is silent on how and to whom the warning is to be given. What is required is an *effective* warning. Compare this to article 26 HIVR *Warning of bombardment,* which requires the officer commanding an attacking force to "do all in his power" to warn the authorities before commencing a bombardment (except in the case of an assault).[155] Whether a warning to the authorities of the area under attack would amount to an *effective* warning will depend upon the circumstances. For instance, during Operation Desert Storm, one of the stated, and achieved, goals of the coalition was to disrupt the ability of the Iraqi authorities to communicate orders and instructions.[156] In such circumstances, clearly a warning to the central authority would not amount to an effective warning to civilians, especially those civilians in remoter regions. Like the decision to give a warning at all, the nature of the warning must be considered in the particular circumstances of the given attack.

Finally, it is important to note that the issuing of a warning does not relieve an attacker of the obligation take other precautions to protect civilians from harm.[157] In particular, it does not entitle an attacker to presume that any person remaining in an area that civilians had been warned to leave is ipso facto a combatant or is otherwise subject to lawful attack. The principles of distinction and proportionality

153 Sandoz, Swinarski and Zimmerman (eds), above n 68 (chapter 1), [2225].

154 ie, a 'cry wolf' scenario.

155 HIVR, above n 10 (chapter 2), art 26. Query whether authorities means the authorities of the town, village etc that is about to be bombarded or whether notification to the enemy's military authorities or higher government levels is sufficient or required.

156 US Department of Defense, *Conduct of the Persian Gulf War: Final Report to Congress*, above n 29 (chapter 3), 149.

157 Henckaerts and Doswald-Beck (eds), *Customary International Humanitarian Law*, vol I, above n 64 (chapter 1), 65; quoted with approval in *Why They Died: Civilian Casualties in Lebanon during the 2006 War*, above n 3 (chapter 2), 65.

must still be complied with,[158] albeit I suggest that the giving of the warning is one aspect of compliance.

The next, and last, point considered in this chapter concerns choosing between military objectives to minimise collateral damage.

7.7 Choosing between several military objectives

> When a choice is possible between several military objectives for obtaining a similar military advantage, the objective to be selected shall be that the attack on which may be expected to cause the least danger to civilian lives and to civilian objects.[159]

This article raises some very complicated issues, and one of those issues is, in my view, ultimately unresolvable.

The first issue is that calculating military advantage is not exact. As Cordesman notes:

> It also seems clear that NATO encountered a classic problem in strategic bombing. It could speculate on the importance of given targets to Serbia, but had no reliable way of knowing their importance. As a result, it tended to bomb by category and judge its success largely by perceived damage to physical facilities, rather than any clear insights into enemy perceptions and behavior.
>
> … *This does not mean that strategic and interdiction bombing were not effective in many ways, but it is almost impossible to know how effective they were, whether a different mix of targets would have been more effective, and how much of the damage inflicted was actually justified by the results.*[160]

The conclusion to be drawn is that it is next to impossible to assign a particular value to the military advantage anticipated from attacking a particular target. As a result, article 57(3) API will only occasionally be applicable in practice. The occasions where it might be applicable are where the goal of the attack is distinct and more than one target is readily available to achieve that distinct goal. For example, if the goal of the attack is to disrupt electricity distribution, then an attack on either the power generation station or the distribution network might be equally as effective in achieving that goal. However, even in these circumstances an attacker might be justified in conducting a concurrent attack on the entire system to ensure success.

The second issue, and one that is possibly unresolvable, concerns the second half of the requirement in article 57(3) API: causing the least danger to civilian

158 *Why They Died: Civilian Casualties in Lebanon during the 2006 War*, above n 3 (chapter 2), 65. This point was also made at the 1972 *Conference of Government Experts on the Reaffirmation and Development of International Humanitarian Law Applicable in Armed Conflicts*, although for unknown reasons the proposed amendment did not make it into API—CE 1972 Report, vol I, above n 25 (chapter 1), 152.

159 API, above n 2 (chapter 1), art 57(3).

160 Cordesman, above n 97 (chapter 1), 157–8 (emphasis in original).

lives and civilian objects. While I generally refer to just collateral damage in this work, it is important to remember that collateral damage is made up of three components: loss of civilian life, injury to civilians, and damage to civilian objects; with collateral damage being the total of the combination thereof. Often it is sufficient to use the collective term collateral damage, as it is usually the case that it is the expected amount of the combination of the three components that is being compared to the anticipated military advantage. However, article 57(3) API is one of the times when this is not the case. The next chapter deals in some detail on how one of the problems with the proportionality rule is that it requires the comparison of unalike objects; namely *military* advantage against *civilian* death, injury and destruction. In article 57(3) API, we meet the same problem in a different context. Suppose that there are three military objectives available for attack, and that the attack on any one of those objectives will offer the same military advantage. Now suppose the expected collateral damage from attack on Military Objective 1 (MO1) is 10 civilian deaths and no property damage. The expected collateral damage from attack on MO2 is five civilian deaths and five houses destroyed. And finally, the expected collateral damage from attack on MO3 is no civilian deaths and 10 houses destroyed. The problem is, attack on which one of these military objectives causes the least danger to civilian lives and to civilian objects? Put in the bluntest terms, how many destroyed houses equals one civilian death?

In reviewing the literature, investigations, reports and cases in this area, one might conclude that property has very low value. For example, the *OTP Report* investigated only "the more well known incidents"[161] and "... all other incidents in which it appears three or more civilians were killed."[162] Not one case of alleged property damage was reviewed. In her article on the NATO bombing campaign in Kosovo, Voon's discussion similarly "focuses on civilian deaths and injuries caused by the bombing, largely ignoring issues concerning civilian property and infrastructure".[163] In a paragraph discussing attacks on military objectives located adjacent to civilian property (eg, a tank next to a house) during the Kosovo bombing campaign, General Clark writes: "We weren't going to disregard risks to civilians but the alternative to taking risks with property damage was that we might ultimately have to put our troops in on the ground."[164] In other words, General Clark was saying that he was prepared to accept a higher risk of damage to property than to risk human life. Most directly, Rowe states: "Although Part IV of the Protocol refers to the protection of the civilian population and civilian objects, protection of the former is clearly more important than of the latter."[165] Bothe, Partsch and Solf write that "[h]umanitarian inclinations would tend to suggest that the avoidance of danger to civilian lives should be preferred over that of property."[166] See also the many cases referred to by Hays Parks stating the even one life is of more value than say the Louvre or histori-

161 *OTP Report*, above n 90 (chapter 1), [13].

162 Ibid.

163 Voon, above n 56 (chapter 7), 1086.

164 Clark, above n 123 (chapter 3), 277.

165 Rowe, 'Kosovo 1999: The Air Campaign—Have the Provisions of Additional Protocol I Withstood the Test?', above n 179 (chapter 4) (footnote omitted).

166 Bothe, Partsch and Solf, above n 87 (chapter 1), 368–9.

cal monuments in Italy.[167] It is interesting that in the cases cited and Hays Parks own examples, he is referring to soldiers of the United States of America on foreign soil. One wonders what would be the view of French soldiers to fighting to protect the Louvre, or an Italian soldier to defend the Sistine Chapel. Would American soldiers put themselves in harms way, or more pointedly, would an American commander order the commander's soldiers into harm's way, to defend an evacuated White House or perhaps Mount Rushmore—particularly where no tactical or operational military advantage was to be gained from protecting those places?

At a very practical level, the *Criminal Code Act 1995* (Cth) creates the war crimes of, *inter alia*, launching attacks that cause excessive incidental death, injury or damage. However, the maximum penalty varies depending upon whether the attack caused excessive incidental death or injury, or excessive incidental property damage. Pursuant to s 268.38(1) of the *Criminal Code Act 1995* (Cth), it is a war crime to launch an attack where the perpetrator knows that the attack will cause incidental death or injury to civilians and the perpetrator knows that the death or injury will be of such an extent as to be excessive in relation to the concrete and direct military advantage anticipated. The maximum penalty is imprisonment for life. However, pursuant to s 268.38(2) of the *Criminal Code Act 1995* (Cth), while it is still a war crime to launch an attack where the perpetrator knows that the attack will cause damage to civilian objects[168] and the perpetrator knows that the damage will be of such an extent as to be excessive in relation to the concrete and direct military advantage anticipated, the maximum penalty is not life imprisonment but rather imprisonment for 20 years. It can only be concluded that the Australian Commonwealth Parliament was of the view that death or injury to civilians is more serious than damage to civilian objects.[169]

Benvenuti makes the interesting point that "very deleterious consequences may result for civilians from material damage caused by an attack"[170] and that "it is unsatisfactory to assess the lawfulness of an attack with regard to the rule of proportionality if damage to civilian property is not evaluated."[171] Of course, Benvenuti's comments can be seen to still be looking at the physical effect on people—albeit now indirectly. We are still left with the problem of how to assess cultural property and the like against personal injury and death.

To go back to the question posed above, the only answer can be that there is no exact answer. Most people would probably agree that attacking MO3 is better than attacking MO1. But is attacking MO2 better than attacking MO1? If a confident answer of yes is given to the last question, then all that needs to be done is to change the examples. We can introduce MO4 and MO5. An attack on MO4 will cause only one death and no property damage. On the other hand, an attack on MO5 will cause no deaths but will destroy a historical church, a national museum of antiquities and a renaissance art gallery. Once again, an attack on either MO4 or

167 Parks, 'Air War and the Law of War', above n 181 (chapter 3), 148.

168 Or, alternatively, widespread, long-term and severe damage to the natural environment.

169 Or widespread, long-term and severe damage to the natural environment.

170 Benvenuti, above n 78 (chapter 3), 508.

171 Ibid.

MO5 will offer exactly the same military advantage. How is a commander to decide which one to attack? The only answer can be that the commander is to make the decision based on his or her subjective assessment of what is more important, and we should be slow to second guess where a commander, faced with "the lesser of two evils",[172] has made that assessment bona fides.

While the examples are a little bit fanciful, I hope the point is clear: article 57(3) API will be able to be applied only in the most straight forward of cases.[173] This discussion should not be taken as too harsh a criticism of the rule. The rule is a good reminder to planners to think through their targeting decisions. The goal of attacking a power station is not to destroy the power station per se but usually rather to disrupt the electricity flow to the military. If this goal can be achieved by attacking a sub-station or other target further away from the civilian population (and perhaps without preventing the flow of electricity to the civilian population), then that obviously should be considered. Rather, what I am trying to show is that we should be careful not to think of collateral damage and military advantage estimates as a precise science that is subject to clear-cut answers.

7.7.1 Are all civilian objects equal?

It is argued in the next chapter that when assessing proportionality, all civilians are counted equally, be they old or young, innocent or complicit.[174] Does the same reasoning apply to material things? I argue that the answer is no and that different material objects are weighed differently in the proportionality equation.

The reason for my view is not black letter law but logic. Unless we are to make distinctions based on age, sex, race etc, a person is a person. Except for in some extreme form of utilitarianism, we do not 'value' a farmer over an insurance salesperson, a healthy person over a sickly person, or indeed, a medical doctor over a lawyer. We, perhaps, even like to think that most people would find making such a decision repugnant. We would not want the law to impose an obligation on a person to make these kinds of value judgements. However, there is no law prohibiting this kind of discrimination amongst material objects. Indeed, I suspect most people would be surprised if the law prohibited this kind of value judgement. Interestingly, it has even been suggested that "non-military objects do not deserve protection in themselves, but only regards the importance which they have for the civilian population."[175] While personally I disagree with this statement *de lege ferenda*, it is a correct statement of the *lex lata*.[176] By definition, IHL takes as its basis *humanitarian* values. So, considered in this way, as different objects would have different amounts of importance, the values of objects will vary.[177]

172 Sandoz, Swinarski and Zimmerman (eds), above n 68 (chapter 1), [2226].

173 See, for examples, ibid, 687.

174 See sections 8.3.3 and 8.3.4.

175 CE/3b, above n 27 (chapter 3), 66.

176 As the court held in the *Hostages Trial*, "it is not our province to write International Law as we would have it—we must apply it as we find it." (*Hostages Trial*, Lauterpacht (ed), above n 45 (chapter 2), 642)

177 CE/3b, above n 27 (chapter 3), 66.

If there was a choice between causing collateral damage to a disused small factory and a house in which a family resides (albeit the family would not be home at the time of the attack), the choice seems relatively simple. Of course, not every choice would be so simple. How would a commander choose between causing collateral damage to ten homes compared with a small school? However, such examples do not refute the point that not only is it lawful but it is actually required for a commander to make such decisions and to assess the relative value of civilian objects that are likely to be damaged in an attack. International humanitarian law does not specify particular criteria upon which this assessment is to be made. However, relevant factors might include the 'utility' of the object, the objects 'replace-ability', and the cost of replacement. By utility, I mean what will be the objective effects of damaging or destroying the object. For instance, it is arguable that the consequences of incidentally destroying a pharmacy will have a more severe short to medium term impact on the civilian population than incidentally destroying a cinema. By replace-ability, what I am referring to is the time and effort involved in replacing an object. All other things being equal, if Object A can be rebuilt or otherwise replaced quicker and easier than Object B then presumably the consequential collateral effects of destroying Object A will be less severe than destroying Object B.[178] Another example is provided by Human Rights Watch, who state that:

> civilian electrical generation (production) facilities should not be attacked because replacement is costly and time consuming, thereby causing prolonged human suffering. As seen in Yugoslavia, attacks on electrical distribution facilities can have a lesser impact.[179]

Equally, if Object A is irreplaceable then that might make it 'worth' more than an object that can be replaced.

Further to what I have just argued, IHL also provides for special categories of civilian objects. How are these specially protected objects dealt with from a collateral damage point of view?

7.7.2 Specially protected objects

The issue that is addressed in this section is whether specially protected objects have some sort of extra weighting in the proportionality assessment compared with ordinary non-military objectives.

---

178 An example might be a bridge and a tunnel on the same rail line. While I confess to having no idea about the cost and time involved in rebuilding these objects, presumably a civil engineer or other expert would. In this respect, I note this is the kind of advice a commander would want in any event, as it will assist the commander in knowing either (a) how much effort it will take the enemy to rebuild or (b) what the commander might have to do if the area is occupied by friendly forces.

179 *Off Target: The Conduct of the War and Civilian Casualties in Iraq*, above n 91 (chapter 4), 45.

While there are a number of objects that receive special mention in IHL as protected objects, these objects belong to only two different classes.[180] The first class comprises objects that would, but for being given special protection, normally be capable of being classed as a military objective due to their making an effective contribution to military action. This class of objects is principally composed of the following objects: military medical units, equipment, vehicles, vessels and aircraft.[181] The second class comprises objects that prima facie do not contribute to military action. The second class of objects is composed of civilian medical units,[182] vehicles,[183] vessels[184] and aircraft;[185]dams, dykes and nuclear electrical generating stations;[186] cultural property;[187] objects indispensable to the survival of the civilian population;[188] and civil defence.[189]

It is interesting at this point to observe how there is some confusion between specially protected objects and certain civilian objects that do not have special protection but nonetheless attract special attention. A good example is that of schools.

> Adversaries sometimes take advantage of the special protected status granted certain types of structures, ... During the Gulf War, a cache of Iraqi Silkworm surface-to surface missiles was discovered inside a school in a densely populated Kuwait City area, ... During Operation Allied Force, the Yugoslav armed forces

180 I am not considering the natural environment in this context as, first, my study did not consider that issue; and second, the natural environment it is not so much an 'object' protected from attack but rather more a interconnection of objects that make up a whole.

181 Hereafter, referred to collectively as 'military medical units and transportation'.

182 API, above n 2 (chapter 1), art 12.

183 Ibid, art 21.

184 Ibid, art 23.

185 Ibid, art 24.

186 API, above n 2 (chapter 1), art 56 API. While API, art 56 is titled *Protection of works and installations containing dangerous forces*, due to the use of the word *namely* to introduce the list of protected objects, the article is specifically limited to just dams, dykes and nuclear electrical generating stations. The draft article presented to both the 1971 *Conference of Government Experts on the Reaffirmation and Development of International Humanitarian Law Applicable in Armed Conflicts* and the 1972 *Conference of Government Experts on the Reaffirmation and Development of International Humanitarian Law Applicable in Armed Conflicts* used the words 'such as' to introduce the list of protected objects. If this wording had have been adopted, the list of protected objects would have been indicative, not exclusive—CE/3b, above n 27 (chapter 3), 134; CE 1972 Report, vol I, above n 25 (chapter 1), 156. See also CDDH/XV, above n 98 (chapter 3), 282. For a suggestion that the article should be extended, *de lege ferenda*, to installations like petrochemical plants, see Sergey Egrov, 'The Kosovo crisis and the law of armed conflicts' (2000) 837 *International Review of the Red Cross* 183.

187 Ibid, art 53. See also HCP, above n 11 (chapter 2).

188 API, above n 2 (chapter 1), art 54.

189 Ibid, art 62. Also, it is my view that military materiel and buildings permanently assigned to civil defence tasks also come within my second category (see API, art 67). Unlike military medical units etc, military units assigned to civil defence tasks are no longer providing a military advantage.

reportedly used churches, schools, and hospitals to shield troops and equipment against NATO air strikes[.][190]

Schools do not have any special protection under IHL and there is no prohibition on a belligerent using a school for a military purpose.[191] Of course, the school should not have civilians, and in particular children, present as this would be contrary to, inter alia, articles 57(1) and 58 API.

Assuming that one of the specially mentioned objects itself is not being attacked, but rather a military objective nearby by is being considered for attack, the issue is: do any of the above types of objects deserve special consideration as collateral damage compared to ordinary civilian objects? However, there is a more fundamental question that I wish to address first and that is why I divided the specially protected objects into two classes in the first place. That question is: are military medical units entitled to consideration in the proportionality question at all?

7.7.3 Military medical units and proportionality

Military medical units occupy an interesting position in IHL, as they are otherwise legitimate military objects[192] that are protected from attack. In other words, where a military medical unit is being used legitimately and appropriately by the enemy, the medical unit prima facie meets the test for a military objective under article 52(2) API. Indeed, arguably it is because military medical units meet the test for being a military objective (be that under customary international law or API) that military medical units are granted special protection by article 19 GCI and article 12(1) API. However, while being protected from attack, there is a consequence to a military medical unit meeting the test for being a military objective. And that consequence is that because a military medical unit meets the test for being a military objective (albeit one that is protected from attack), the military medical unit is not a civilian object as defined by article 52(1) API. This is because article 52(1) API defines civilian objects negatively as being "all objects which are not military objectives". And the consequence of this is that because collateral damage with respect to objects is limited to "civilian objects",[193] military medical units are not collateral damage for the purposes of the proportionality test. Some might find this result incongruous and doubt that it is the intent of API. However, as well as the logic of the interpretation, this conclusion is supported by the wording of article 56 API (which deals with the protection of certain works and installations containing dangerous forces). Article 56(1) API defines works or installations containing dangerous forces as "dams, dykes and nuclear electrical generating stations". Of course, these objects are not inherently military in nature. So, while they could become military objectives (as is recognised in article 56(1) API), they are certainly not normally military objects. Accordingly, what is particularly interesting about article 56(1) API in the

190 Waxman, above n 56 (chapter 1), 50.

191 *Prosecutor v Kordic & Cerkez, (Appeals Chamber)* Case No IT-95-14/2-A (17 December 2004) [92] (overruling a decision by the trial chamber on this point).

192 Note the use of the word *objects* and not *objectives.*

193 API, above n 2 (chapter 1), art 57(2)(a)(iii).

current context is not that it provides for special protection from attack for works or installations containing dangerous forces, but that article 56(1) API also specifically makes mention of causing collateral damage to these objects.[194] Accordingly, there are no grounds for presuming that the drafters of API intended protection from attack necessarily to always include protection from collateral damage.[195] Rather, each class of object must be assessed separately.

Finally, while military medical units are to be "respected and protected",[196] there is nothing in the drafting history of article 19 GCI[197] or in the authorative *Pictet Commentary*[198] that indicates that 'respected and protected' extends so far as to mean that collateral damage to military medical units must be considered when determining the proportionality of an attack on a nearby military objective.

7.7.4 Civilian medical units and other specially protected objects

Returning to civilian objects with special protection, they are not entitled to more consideration due, ipso facto, to their special mention in IHL. Put another way, there is no article or other provision in the treaties or conventions that clearly requires civilian objects with special protection to be given *additional* consideration as possible collateral damage compared to other civilian objects.

However, some classes of specially protected objects should be accorded a high value in a proportionality assessment for the same *reason* that they are specially mentioned in IHL; namely, their humanitarian character. As argued in section 7.7.1, not all civilian objects should be treated equally. Rather, different types of civilian objects are to be afforded more or less weight in the proportionality assessment depending upon their, inter alia, utility and replace-ability. Using these criteria, most, if not all, specially protected objects should be considered highly valuable when considering whether an attack would be proportional.

194 The last sentence of ibid, art 56(1) states: "Other military objectives located at or in the vicinity of these works or installations shall not be made the object of attack if such attack may cause the release of dangerous forces from the works or installations and consequent severe losses among the civilian population."

195 A similar conclusion applies to members of the armed forces who are *hors de combat*—CDDH/XV, above n 98 (chapter 3), 384.

196 GCI, above n 5 (chapter 2), art 19.

197 See International Committee of the Red Cross, *Report of the Work of the Conference of Government Experts for the Study of the Conventions for the Protection of War Victims* (1947), 23–24.

198 Jean Pictet, *The Geneva Conventions of 12 August 1949: Commentary* (1952) vol I, 134–5 and 196–7.

Chapter 8

Proportionality

As stated back in chapter 7, there are many meanings and uses for the term proportionality when considering the laws applicable to an armed conflict. However, this chapter deals only with the IHL targeting aspect of the principle and not the *jus ad bellum* or belligerent reprisal issues.

The first time the customary international law principle of proportionality was codified was in API.[1] An attack is prohibited where the attack:

> may be expected to cause incidental loss of civilian life, injury to civilians, damage to civilian objects, or a combination thereof, which would be excessive in relation to the concrete and direct military advantage anticipated [from the attack].[2]

Notwithstanding this late codification, the "main problem with the principle of proportionality is not whether or not it exists but what it means and how it is to be applied."[3] Put another way, "the application of the principle of proportionality is more easily stated than applied in practice."[4] This chapter provides an in-depth analysis of the codified principle of proportionality. I review what can be considered as a military advantage when assessing the proportionality of an attack and what must be assessed as collateral damage. For example, can the security of the attacking force be considered as one aspect of the military advantage anticipated from the attack? Must an attack be considered in isolation or can an attack be viewed as a whole? My answers are partly based on a practical assessment of how a military commander would assess what is the military advantage to be gained from the attack. On the other side of the proportionality equation, how is a civilian who works in a munitions factory treated? Is such a civilian counted as collateral damage when considering an attack on that factory? What about voluntary or involuntary human shields? In this case, my argument for how to treat these categories is based on whether a person can be assessed as taking a direct part in hostilities.

---

1 Kellenberger, above n 23 (chapter 1).

2 API, above n 2 (chapter 1), art 57(2)(a)(iii). See also the combination of ibid, arts 51(4) and 51(5)(b).

3 Fenrick, 'Attacking the Enemy Civilian as a Punishable Offense', above n 20 (chapter 3), 545.

4 *OTP Report*, above n 90 (chapter 1), [19].

8.1 How the rule of proportionality affects targeting decisions

The proportionality rule affects the decision whether to attack a military objective, not whether an object is a military objective. This point is fundamental to the declaration made by Australia concerning article 52(2) API:

> It is the understanding of Australia that the first sentence of paragraph 2 of Article 52 is not intended to, nor does it, deal with the question of incidental or collateral damage resulting from an attack directed against a military objective.[5]

While this declaration would appear to state the obvious, it would appear as though it is nonetheless a useful declaration due to the following:

> The *New Rules* notes that the rule of proportionality imposes "an additional limitation on the discretion of combatants in deciding *whether an object is a military objective* under paragraph. 2 of article 52." If an attack is expected to cause incidental casualties or damage, the requirement of an anticipated "definite" military advantage under Article 52 (one of the minimum requirements for an object to be a proper military target) is heightened to the more restrictive standard of a "concrete and direct" military advantage set forth in Article 5l(5)(b).[6]

This statement is not correct. Whether or not an object is a military objective is assessed against the test in article 52(2) API.[7] Whether an attack on that object in a certain way (eg, by a 2000 lb bomb) will cause disproportionate collateral damage does not affect the object's status as a military objective. Rather, and in accordance with the wording of article 57(2)(a)(iii) API, a party must refrain from deciding to launch the attack if the expected collateral damage would be excessive. For example, the status of a military air traffic control tower in close proximity to civilian housing does not change from not being a military objective if attacked using a 2000 lb unguided bomb to being a military objective if attacked using a 500 lb laser-guided bomb. Rather, the tower's status as a military objective is solely dependant upon the article 52(2) API test. What does change is whether in any given scenario it is lawful to launch a potential attack against the tower.

While the rule of proportionality allows for the causing of collateral damage, the intentional causing of proportionate but avoidable collateral damage when attacking military targets is not permissible.[8] For example, after referring to the NATO targeting of the RTS building and the discussion of this attack in the *OTP Report*, Benvenuti writes:

5 Roberts and Guelff, above n 14 (chapter 1), 500.

6 *Needless Deaths in the Gulf War: Civilian Casualties During the Air Campaign and Violations of the Laws of War*, above n 38 (chapter 3) (footnotes omitted, emphasis added in the latter part of the first sentence).

7 Leaving aside human targets for the moment for ease of example.

8 Benvenuti, above n 78 (chapter 3), 509.

> In fact, according to the Committee, the attack had two intentional goals; a primary military goal, and a secondary non-military goal. In other words, the civilian casualties as 'collateral damage' appear to be caused wilfully.[9]

There are two aspects to Benvenuti's comment. First, it is very clear that an attacker must "take all feasible precautions in the choice of means and methods of attack with a view to avoiding, and in any event to minimizing, [collateral damage]".[10] Only after this has been done is any remaining expected collateral damage assessed to see if it is proportional. Accordingly, the intentional causing of collateral damage that whilst proportional, is nonetheless greater than the minimum that would be caused by taking all feasible precautions is unlawful. However, there is a very important second point. As long as all feasible precautions are taken to minimise collateral damage, the collateral damage is proportional, and article 57(3) API is complied with,[11] then, whilst morally dubious, there is nothing actually unlawful in that particular collateral damage being considered desirable or beneficial by the attacker. Of course, the 'benefit' obtained from causing the collateral damage cannot be factored into the military advantage side of the proportionality equation, nor can it be considered as part of the military advantage when choosing between several military objectives pursuant to article 57(3) API.

8.2 What can be considered as the military advantage for the purpose of assessing proportionality?

There is detailed discussion in chapter 3 about what is meant by military advantage when determining whether an object is a military objective. However, what amounts to a military advantage for the purposes of assessing whether an object can be attacked is not necessarily identical to what amounts to a military advantage when executing an attack. For example, as stated back in chapter 3, a number of countries have made declarations with respect to the meaning of military advantage for the purposes of articles 51 and 57 API but not for article 52 API. The simplest example on point is the common declaration that for the purposes of articles 51 and 57 API, military advantage includes the security of the attacking force.[12] This makes

9 Ibid, 523.

10 API, above n 2 (chapter 1), art 57(2)(a)(ii).

11 Ibid, art 57(3) provides that: "When a choice is possible between several military objectives for obtaining a similar military advantage, the objective to be selected shall be that the attack on which may be expected to cause the least danger to civilian lives and to civilian objects."

12 Roberts and Guelff, above n 14 (chapter 1), 500. See also the State practice of Australia and Canada referred to in Henckaerts and Doswald-Beck (eds), *Customary International Humanitarian Law*, vol II, above n 64 (chapter 1), 328. To the extent that some States have stated that the security of the attacking force is a factor in determining whether there is a military advantage in attacking an object (the second part of the test for whether an object is a military objective), they are either mistaken or 'attacking force' has to be interpreted to mean the security of the armed forces generally of the attacker (ie, the attacking force or the friendly force) and not the security of the actual attackers of the target (for such statements, see Henckaerts and Doswald-Beck (eds), *Customary International Humanitarian Law*, vol II, above n 64 (chapter 1), 183–4). My view is sup-

sense, as when assessing merely whether an object is a military objective, the type of attack that may occur is not relevant. Accordingly, it is necessary to revisit the meaning of military advantage in the specific context of assessing proportionality.

When weighing up the military advantage anticipated against the expected collateral damage, a commander is limited to the concrete and direct military advantage anticipated. The words *concrete and direct* are clearly meant to limit the scope of military advantage that it is lawful to weigh against collateral damage to advantages that are readily apparent and tangible. Terms like *reasonably foreseeable* and *probable* come to mind. It is not enough that a military advantage might just conceivably occur. Rogers joins Solf in favouring *concrete* to mean *specific* or *perceptible*, and *direct* as meaning "without intervening condition of agency".[13] These are valid interpretations of the words used in articles 51 and 57 API.

When discussing the meaning of 'effective contribution' and 'definite military advantage' in article 52(2) API, Sassoli and Bouvier state that this means that indirect and possible advantages cannot be taken into account when deciding whether something is a military objective.[14] This commentary can also be applied to assessing whether the advantage to be gained from attacking that objective is concrete and direct. Importantly though, a word like *immediate* was not used in API to qualify what could amount to a military advantage. Accordingly, while the assessment of the anticipated military advantage cannot include indirect or only possible advantages, the assessment can include a military advantage that will not crystallise until sometime in the future.

It is generally agreed that when assessing the military advantage to be gained from an attack, the attack is an attack viewed as a whole and not each single target as part of an attack. For example, Laursen rejects the simplistic case-by-case (ie, target-by-target) approach to assessing military advantage as too narrow and simplistic. Laursen refers to various declarations by States to API to the effect that "the evaluation of military advantage … must be considered on the basis of the attack as a whole and not in relation to each action regarded separately."[15] This concept is without prejudice to the fact that in accordance with article 51(5)(a) API, distinct military objectives in an urban area cannot be treated as one objective.[16] In other words, each target must still be struck separately and the current point under discussion is not a license to area or carpet bomb.

While an attack may be viewed as a whole when assessing military advantage, there are, of course, limits as to what constitutes the whole of the attack. Laursen is critical of how the issue of military advantage is addressed in the *OTP Report.*

---

ported by Australia's practice referred to in ibid, 183. Whether or not an object is a military objective is determined independent of the means and methods of attack; and, therefore, is determined in isolation of the security of the potential attackers. This point is different from the argument below that after an object has been assessed as being a military objective, the security of the attacking force can be considered as part of the military advantage to be gained from the attack when assessing the proportionality of the attack.

13 Rogers, *Law on the Battlefield*, above n 84 (chapter 1), 99.

14 Sassoli and Bouvier, above n 10 (chapter 1), 161 (fn 142).

15 Laursen, above n 19 (chapter 3), 795.

16 Sandoz, Swinarski and Zimmerman (eds), above n 68 (chapter 1), [2218].

He describes the treatment of this issue in the *OTP Report* as "confusing".[17] He first quotes the report as stating that proportionality questions must be "addressed on 'a case by case basis.'"[18] He then quotes from the *OTP Report* that "the legal evaluation of 'the proportionality of the attack should not be premised on a specific incident'"[19] and that the attack "must be viewed as one phase of 'an integrated attack' against multiple objects."[20] Laursen's conclusion is that "[i]f consistently applied, the logic presented by the *OTP Report* will end by weighing the total number of casualties … against the entire Operation Allied Force."[21] And finally that "it is questionable whether such a comparison is useful for anything."[22] While his final statement is correct, this statement relates to his own conclusion of where the logic of the *OTP Report* might lead, a conclusion with which I disagree. I do not believe that the *OTP Report* was suggesting the conclusion that Laursen has drawn. Nonetheless, it is worth re-iterating that Laursen is correct in stating that proportionality is not assessed by looking at the total amount of collateral damage at the end of an armed conflict and then determining wether that collateral damage is excessive when compared against the goals of the armed conflict.[23]

If military advantage were not assessed by looking at an attack as a whole, there would be a serious gap between military practice and IHL. Rowe provides the following example to illustrate the point.

> It is, however, still possible to argue that only the destruction of all forms of certain types of dual purpose object would make an effective contribution to military action and offer a definite military advantage. If there are, for instance, two bridges across a strategically significant river, the destruction of one only may give no military advantage; only the destruction of both would achieve this objective.[24]

Another example would be modern communication nodes. An attack on a single node in a redundant system could be considered as having no effect. Does that mean no military advantage accrues, so the proportionate collateral damage can be no greater than zero? Hopefully, the question need only be put in this form to realise that the answer is no. The concept of assessing military advantage across the whole of the attack is not just a legal concept—this approach is supported by military practice. For example, the United States Air Force doctrine on targeting states:

---

17 Laursen, above n 19 (chapter 3), 791.

18 Ibid, 792.

19 Ibid.

20 Ibid.

21 Ibid.

22 Ibid.

23 Sassoli, above n 47 (chapter 3), 3. See also Dinstein, *The Conduct of Hostilities under the Law of International Armed Conflict*, above n 66 (chapter 2), 123.

24 Rowe, 'Kosovo 1999: The Air Campaign—Have the Provisions of Additional Protocol I Withstood the Test?', above n 179 (chapter 4).

> The target system concept is important because almost all targeting is based on targeting systems. A target is composed of components, and components are composed of elements. A single target may be significant because of its own characteristics, but often its importance lies in its relationship to other targets. Usually the effect of a strike or attack mission upon an enemy can be determined only by analyzing the target in the overall enemy's target system.[25]

The *ICRC Commentary* states that article 57(2)(a)(iii) API "is not concerned with strategic objectives but with the means to be used in a specific tactical operation."[26] It is hard to know whether I agree or disagree with this statement. If it means that an attacker cannot argue "this war is about national survival, therefore the allowable collateral damage is great", I agree. However, I would disagree if it means that attacks on strategic objectives cannot be assessed in context. For instance, say State A was aware that State B was about to succeed in developing the technology to intercept State A's encrypted communications. Surely, an attack on State B's military research and development laboratory has to be assessed in its strategic context.

The requirement to determine whether an attack on an object will offer a military advantage *in the circumstances ruling at the time* is well known and often stated.[27] What is less mentioned is that along with the mere existence of military advantage, the quantum of an object's military advantage is not fixed: it also varies with time. This fact is recognised in British Defence Doctrine, which states:

> The law stipulates that the military worth of the target needs to be considered in relation to the circumstances at the time. Therefore, a commander needs to have an up-to-date assessment of the significance of a target and the value of attacking it.[28]

It is for this reason that a target folder cannot assign a certain value to the military advantage of a target once and for all.[29]

An interesting final point is that as the military advantage of an attack must be assessed at the time of the attack, great care must be taken not to judge the attack on certain targets with hindsight. For instance, the attack on a factory producing tanks is arguably only of benefit if the enemy's current inventory of tanks will prove insufficient for its war effort. But, who knows how long a war might last. To take a simple example, the 1967 Six-Day Arab/Israeli war was not called that until after the war had ended! It would be a mistake to use hindsight and conclude that an attack by any of the belligerents during the Six-Day war on long-term military objectives like weapons research and development offered no military advantage as

25 Air Force Pamphlet 14-210 Intelligence, above n 53 (chapter 1), 18.

26 Sandoz, Swinarski and Zimmerman (eds), above n 68 (chapter 1), [2207].

27 See API, above n 2 (chapter 1), art 52(2).

28 *British Defence Doctrine* (JWP 0-01) issued by the British Minister of Defence in 1996, in Rogers, 'Zero-casualty warfare', above n 94 (chapter 3).

29 See generally Schmitt, 'The Principle of Discrimination in 21st Century Warfare', above n 201 (chapter 4), [17].

the war was over before any new weapons could have been developed. As recognised in the *Hostages Trial*:

> The course of a military operation by the enemy is loaded with uncertainties, such as the numerical strength of the enemy, the quality of his equipment, his fighting spirit, the efficiency and daring of his commanders, and the uncertainty of his intentions.[30]

It is against this background of uncertainty that a commander is called upon to estimate the military advantage from an attack.

Whether an attacker can consider the risk to the attacking force when assessing the proportionality of an attack is a debated issue. While not limited to the following case, the issue of risk to own forces is often discussed in the context of the operating height of attacking aircraft. As mentioned back in section 7.3, the national restrictions placed on the operating height of attack aircraft in some recent conflicts have proved controversial. In that section, I looked at how the operating height of the aircraft might affect discrimination. In summary, I concluded that operating height and discrimination are not directly linked and certainly not to the point that flying lower necessarily meant increased discrimination. In this section, the same issue is used to explore whether risk to own forces can be considered when assessing the proportionality of an attack.

For the sake of argument in this section, it is assumed that in a particular scenario flying lower will increase the accuracy of an attack and will reduce the likelihood of collateral damage but will also increase risk to the aircrew. In such circumstances, can an attacker choose to fly at a higher altitude to reduce the risk to the attacking force?

The report of a meeting of experts states:

> The experts agreed that the limitation of own side casualties was sensible military practice and not objectionable in itself. They also agreed that the protection of one's own forces must never be conducted at the cost of the civilian population.[31]

In my view, this overstates the requirements of IHL. While I disagree with his conclusion (for reasons that I shall explain), Fenrick does clearly set out the issue in the following quote:

> Determining the extent to which a military commander is obligated to expose his own forces to danger in order to limit civilian casualties or damage to civilian objects is almost impossible. Strictly speaking, resolution of the proportionality equation requires a determination of the relative worth of military advantage gained by one side and the civilian casualties or damage to civilian objectives

30 *Hostages Trial*, Lauterpacht (ed), above n 45 (chapter 2), 649.

31 *Expert Meeting: "Targeting Military Objectives"*, above n 27 (chapter 1), 17.

> incurred in areas in the hands of the other side. Military casualties incurred by the attacking side are not a part of the equation.[32]

What Fenrick has succinctly set out is that when assessing the proportionality of an attack, the only two issues are military advantage on one side and collateral damage on the other. Security of the attacking force is not a third issue. Either it comes within one of the two sides of the equation or it is not relevant. But, this is where I disagree with Fenrick. As I will show, the security of the attacking force can be assessed when determining the military advantage anticipated from the attack.

Regarding the meaning of military advantage in article 57(2)(a)(iii) API, Australia made a declaration of understanding that "the term 'military advantage' involves a variety of considerations, including the security of the attacking forces."[33] This declaration is not peculiar to Australia, and considering the security of the attacking force is often stated as forming part of the assessment when determining the proportionality of the attack.[34] While I am yet to find support for the following point as a principle of treaty interpretation, I submit that where a term (such as 'military advantage') appears more than once in a treaty, it is clearly preferable that it bears a similar meaning unless there are good grounds for giving the term different interpretations in different parts of the treaty.

While some might argue that when determining the military advantage to be gained from an attack that the only consideration should be by how much the other belligerent is weakened, such a line of argument is not in accordance with the law and is not logical. As the permitted goal of armed conflict is to weaken the enemy forces, then as I argued back in section 3.5, it follows that the protection of one's own forces is equally permissible; and this clearly would extend to the security of the attacking force itself. An example should illustrate why.

Suppose ground troops of State A are under enemy attack from combatants of State B. It would, of course, be lawful for other combatants from State A to attack the enemy attackers. In doing so, the anticipated military advantage to State A is not just the weakening of the military forces of State B but also the preservation of the forces of State A that were under attack. If the preservation of the forces under attack were a military advantage, why would not the preservation of the force conducting the defensive attack also be a military advantage? As Schmitt writes, "an attack in which the personnel or equipment are lost is self-evidently not as advantageous as one in which they survive to fight again".[35]

I am not suggesting that security of the attacking force takes primacy over collateral damage. So to argue would be the equivalent of arguing that achieving a military advantage outweighs causing collateral damage, and that clearly is not the law. I suggest this is where the report of an expert meeting goes wrong. The meet-

---

32 Fenrick, 'Attacking the Enemy Civilian as a Punishable Offense', above n 20 (chapter 3), 548–9 (footnote omitted).

33 Roberts and Guelff, above n 14 (chapter 1), 500.

34 See, Bothe, Partsch and Solf, above n 87 (chapter 1), 324; quoted with approval in Robertson Jr, above n 105 (chapter 1), 52.

35 Schmitt, *Precision Attack and International Humanitarian Law*, above n 30 (chapter 3), 462.

ing seems to have assumed that by factoring in the security of the attacking force, a large number of civilians could be killed even if the military objective under attack was of little importance.[36] That is not the case. Rather, what I am arguing is that security of the attacking force is a component when determining the quantum of military advantage anticipated from an attack. As Rogers states:

> In taking care to protect civilians, soldiers must accept some element of risk to themselves. The rule [of proportionality] is unclear as to what degree of care is required of a soldier and what degree of risk he must take. Everything depends on the target, the urgency of the moment, the available technology and so on.[37]

In a different work, Rogers quotes British Defence Doctrine by way of further explanation:

> If there is a choice of weapons or methods of attack available, a commander should select those which are most likely to avoid, or at least minimize, incidental civilian casualties or damage. However, he is entitled to take into account factors such as his stocks of different weapons and likely future demands, the timeliness of attack and risks to his own forces. Nevertheless, there may be occasions when a commander will have to accept a higher level of risk to his own forces in order to avoid or reduce collateral damage to the enemy's civil population.[38]

Accordingly, the correct statement of the law is that security of the attacking force is a factor when determining what would be proportional collateral damage.[39] In an effort to improve security of the attacking force, increased collateral damage is permissible. The amount of the increase will depend upon such factors as the size of the attacking force, the importance of that attacking force,[40] and the actual amount of risk. And, most importantly, there may come a point when, by taking measures

---

36 *Expert Meeting: "Targeting Military Objectives"*, above n 27 (chapter 1), 19, fn 45.

37 Rogers, 'Zero-casualty warfare', above n 94 (chapter 3).

38 *British Defence Doctrine* (JWP 0-01) issued by the British Minister of Defence, in Rogers, 'Zero-casualty warfare', above n 94 (chapter 3).

39 Bothe, Partsch and Solf, above n 87 (chapter 1), 311. See also Rogers, *Law on the Battlefield*, above n 84 (chapter 1), 20.

40 To put it crudely, certain elements of a military are more valuable to it in terms of their military capabilities and replaceability than other parts. An interesting example comes from the case law on belligerent reprisals. In brief, an Italian court had to decide whether the killing of 335 prisoners, many of whom were captured Italian soldiers, could be a lawful reprisal for a bomb attack that killed 33 German military policemen. "The court found that the reprisal was disproportionate because, inter alia, the Italian soldiers who were executed included five generals and eleven colonels, whereas the German military policemen killed in the bomb attack were men of much lower rank." (Greenwood 'The twilight of the law of belligerent reprisals', above n 74 (chapter 1), 45) However, note that Fenrick writes: "as no written judgments were rendered and as five more Italians were killed than the order required, it is not possible to determine whether findings of guilty were rendered because the ten to one ratio was considered excessive or because five extra persons were killed." (Fenrick, 'The Rule of Proportionality and Protocol I in Conventional Warfare', above n 9 (chapter 7), 117)

to improve the security of the attacking force, the increase in the expected collateral damage outweighs the anticipated military advantage. In such circumstances, article 57(2)(a)(iii) API provides that the attack cannot proceed.

That the security of the attacking force is a military advantage is important because it affects how to calculate the anticipated military advantage. Noting this, Waxman makes an interesting point when he writes that "[p]ublic and coalition sensitivity to friendly casualties and collateral damage or civilian injury may reduce operational flexibility more severely than does adherence to international law."[41] The important point here is that when a commander is considering public and coalition sensitivity, that is not a legal factor; and in particular, is not a part of the proportionality assessment.

Having looked at one side of the proportionality equation (military advantage), the next issue to consider is the other side of the equation.

8.3 What is counted as collateral damage?

While the term collateral damage is often used, there has been only limited discussion in case law and legal literature of exactly what is and what is not legally considered collateral damage. It is essential to determine this if a proper assessment of the proportionality of an attack is to be undertaken, either prior to the attack or as part of an analysis after the event.

8.3.1 Only civilians and civilian objects are counted

Starting with the basics, collateral damage is loss of civilian life, injury to civilians and damage to civilian objects.[42] What is immediately apparent is that any injury or loss of life caused to a combatant or to a military objective, even if unintended, is not collateral damage. As argued back in section 7.7.2, military medical units are not counted as collateral damage because they are not civilian objects. In addition, due to the definition of civilian in article 50 API, injury or loss of life to military medical personnel and military chaplains is equally not collateral damage. Such injury or death must not be intended, and steps should be taken to protect such persons from the affects of an attack;[43] but, nonetheless, such injury or death is not collateral damage and does not form part of the proportionality assessment. Equally, incidental injury or death to a combatant who is *hors de combat* does not form part of the collateral damage calculation. The statement to the contrary in Bothe, Partsch and Solf should be understood as an appeal to principles of humanity and not a statement of the law.[44]

It is worth pointing out that, conversely, there are also two small groups of civilians that while taking a more active role in an armed conflict than the traditional civilian are still counted as collateral damage. They are those civilians that

41 Waxman, above n 56 (chapter 1), xi.

42 See API, above n 2 (chapter 1), art 57(2)(a)(iii).

43 GCI, above n 5 (chapter 2).

44 Bothe, Partsch and Solf, above n 87 (chapter 1), 220–1.

fall within the categories set out in articles 4A(4) and (5) GCIII.[45] Once again, this is because of the definition of civilian in article 50(1) API.

There can be confusion about how to consider a civilian object that by its purpose has been assessed as a military objective. When determining whether an object is a civilian object for the purposes of collateral damage, the law is that if the object has become a military objective then it is no longer considered a civilian object per article 52(1) API. This is particularly important when considering dual-use objects. As Hampson notes: "There is no special category of dual-use targets. An objective is either a military objective, in which case it may be the object of attack, or it is not."[46] Accordingly, when a civilian object meets the test for being a military objective then the civilian object itself does not form part of the collateral damage assessment. Once it is subject to attack, the object itself is not collateral damage.

8.3.2 Indirect harm

A significant issue of contemporary debate is whether to count injury or death to civilians only where the injury or death is a direct result of the attack, or also to count the harm that arises as an indirect result of the attack.[47] As evidenced in the following quote, Schmitt appears to be of the view that long-term effects are part of the current law:

> If first-tier collateral damage and incidental injury (i.e., damage and injury directly caused by the kinetic force of the attack) become rarer, it is probable that humanitarian attention will increasingly dwell on subsequent-tier, or reverberating, effects. ... Of course, reverberating effects were theoretically always calculated when assessing proportionality. However, it is only now that the means exist to limit dramatically direct collateral damage and incidental injury that we are being sensitized to reverberation. Improved capabilities inevitably lead to heightened humanitarian expectations.[48]

When Canestaro writes "[a]s yet, no consensus has been reached on how far removed from the initial attack harm should be before being included",[49] he also appears to be of the view that indirect harm is to be counted, with the issue merely

45 These groups can be informally categorised as persons who accompany the armed forces without being members thereof, the merchant marine and civil aircrew—GCIII, above n 7 (chapter 2).

46 Hampson, 'Proportionality and Necessity in the Gulf Conflict', above n 23 (chapter 3), 50.

47 Technically, the legal issue would also apply to damage to civilian objects; but the debate seems to be limited to civilians. This is probably because indirect and long-term harm is more likely to arise, whereas usually an object is either damaged in an attack or it is not. Nonetheless, as indirect damage certainly could arise, it is worth noting that the discussion in this section is equally applicable.

48 Schmitt, 'The Principle of Discrimination in 21st Century Warfare', above n 201 (chapter 4), [55] (footnotes omitted).

49 Nathan Canestaro, 'Legal and Policy Constraints on the conduct of Aerial Precision Warfare' (2004) 37 *Vanderbilt Journal of Transnational Law* 431, 464.

being how indirect. Rowe writes that "[i]ncidental injury to civilians or to civilian objects may be direct or indirect." From the context in which this sentence occurs, Rowe appears to be stating that indirect injury and damage forms part of the assessment of proportionality to be conducted under article 57(2)(a)(iii) API, although no authority or reasoning for this proposition is provided. Human Rights Watch also seems to consider indirect harm as being legally part of the collateral damage assessment. For example, in an open letter to NATO Defense Ministers concerning the 2001–3 conflict in Afghanistan, the executive director of Human Rights Watch wrote:

> certain roads, bridges and airports may ordinarily be legitimate military targets; in the case of Afghanistan they may also be essential to the delivery of humanitarian relief throughout the winter. In such circumstances, the harm incurred to the civilian population by attacking them would be disproportionate to the military advantage gained, and so would be prohibited under international humanitarian law.[50]

Amnesty International make a similar point about destroying a road and the effect that might have "on civilians, especially the most vulnerable, such as those requiring urgent medical attention."[51] Back in 1996, Crawford discussed the issue in the context of attacks on electric power systems and concluded that the consequential effect on the civilian population must be considered.[52]

However, other commentators believe only direct affects need be counted. So, when Kalshoven asks whether military planners are legally required to consider the long-term potential after effects of attacks "to the point of modifying their plans so as to avoid them?",[53] he answers: "It would be wonderful if the law provided an affirmative answer to this question, but I am not convinced that it does so."[54] Further on, he refers to article 57(3) API and says that strategic planners would be "well advised to heed this rule of common sense, which especially on the

50 Kenneth Roth, *International Humanitarian Law Issues and the Afghan Conflict: Open Letter to North Atlantic Treaty Organization (NATO) Defense Ministers* (2001) Human Rights Watch <http://www.hrw.org/press/2001/10/nato1017-ltr.htm> at 28 February 2005. As an aside, it is interesting to note that in the same letter a mistake on the interpretation of proportionality is made. When discussing attacks on so called dual-use objects, the letter states "attacks should not be undertaken if the civilian harm outweighs the definite military advantage" (emphasis added). This is not the test. Definite military advantage is used when determining whether an object is a military objective, while the test when assessing proportionality is the concrete and direct military advantage anticipated from the attack. The suggested test in the letter actually lessens the protection afforded to civilians, as while a concrete and direct military advantage will have to be definite to be concrete and direct, a definite military advantage need not be concrete and direct.

51 *Israel/Lebanon: Deliberate destruction or "collateral damage"? Israeli attacks on civilian infrastructure*, above n 253 (chapter 4), 5.

52 Crawford, above n 72 (chapter 5) 15. See also Dunlap, *Law and Military Interventions: Preserving Humanitarian Values in 21st Conflicts*, above n 168 (chapter 3), 8.

53 Kalshoven, 'Remarks', above n 126 (chapter 3), 45.

54 Ibid.

strategic level and in the overall planning of military operations may contribute to the mitigation of foreseeable, long-term damage."[55] However, from the context, it would appear that this is an exhortation, rather than advice that compliance in such circumstances is legally required. Hampson also appears to be of the view that long-term effects do not form part of the proportionality equation. She states that when assessing proportionality, the collateral damage must be "caused by the *attack*, not by the choice of target."[56] I find this particular argument unconvincing, as the choice of target is one aspect of the attack.

With respect to the commentators who have a different view (and who find more clarity in the law on this point than I can), the text of article 57(2)(a)(iii) API is less than clear on whether indirect deaths as the result of an attack are counted as part of the proportionality equation, and if they are counted at all, to what extent are they counted. Certainly the section on "Proportionality and Reverberating Effects" in the report on the meeting of a group of experts comes to no conclude view on this point.[57] Perhaps the most telling commentary comes from Waxman, who writes:

> Some disagreement exists with respect to how to calculate adverse civilian effects of attacks on military targets. One view holds that planners must consider the long term, indirect effects of attacks on a civilian population, whereas the U.S. military adheres to a narrower interpretation emphasizing direct civilian injuries or deaths.[58]

Interestingly, on the other side of the scale it is clear that the only military advantage that can be counted is the concrete and direct military advantage anticipated.[59] These words are specifically meant to exclude from the calculation an assessment of the military advantage that would only appear in the long term.[60] Should we not, therefore, conclude that the same applies to assessing incidental deaths?

The answer to this can be determined by looking at the problem in two parts. In basic terms, there is a need to distinguish between deaths that are inevitable as the result of the attack and deaths that result not only from the attack but also from a lack of possible remedial action. Put another way, there is a need to distinguish between collateral damage that—in the ordinary course of events—can be expected[61] (and, therefore, must be counted as part of the proportionality equation) and collateral damage that one would expect might be avoided (and, accordingly, is not counted as part of the proportionality equation). Why I prefer to stay with the

55 Ibid.

56 Hampson, 'Proportionality and Necessity in the Gulf Conflict', above n 23 (chapter 3), 51 (original emphasis).

57 *Expert Meeting: "Targeting Military Objectives"*, above n 27 (chapter 1), 14–15.

58 Waxman, above n 56 (chapter 1), 21 (fn 44).

59 See the wording of API, above n 2 (chapter 1), art 57(2)(a)(iii).

60 Sandoz, Swinarski and Zimmerman (eds), above n 68 (chapter 1), [2209].

61 Recalling that the opening words of API, above n 2 (chapter 1), art 57(2)(a)(iii) are "refrain from deciding to launch any attack which may be *expected* to cause incidental loss of civilian life" (emphasis added).

word *expected*, I do not disagree with proposed tests of whether "there was a *reasonable expectation of casualty*"[62] of the future harm or if the future harm was "a *likely* or *foreseeable* consequence of the attack".[63] Such an interpretation is consistent with other reprovisions of API that ban certain attacks based on the consequential and indirect effects of the attacks.[64]

It can be expected that some attacks will almost inevitably lead to civilian deaths in the long term. For instance, imagine an attack on a nuclear electrical generating station.[65] It is expected that the result of the attack will be the release of radioactive material into the surrounding city such that radioactive poisoning of 2,000 people will occur to a level such that those people can be expected to die within 5–10 years. I can see no reason why these deaths should not be considered for the purposes of assessing proportionality. Contrast that example with an attack on a conventionally power electrical generating station, where, in a simplified example, the generating station produces half of the country's power needs. For the purposes of the example, assume that the military uses half of the country's power production. The other half is used for civilian purposes, including hospitals and sewerage pumps. Say it is forecast that if the military was to appropriate the entire power output, then up to 10,000 civilians might die over the next year from inadequate hospital services and disease caused by an unsanitary environment. Should such possible, but not necessarily inevitable, deaths be counted? In my view, the answer is no. These deaths are not caused by the attack as such and cannot reasonably be termed as being expected as a result of the attack. Human Rights Watch appear to apply similar reasoning when discussing the use of cluster munitions when it states that "parties to a conflict must weigh the military advantages of cluster munitions against their documented harm to civilians both during and after strikes."[66] And similarly:

> The high dud rate of cluster munitions and the impact of duds on the civilian population also should be taken into account when determining whether a specific attack caused disproportionate harm to civilians.[67]

That cluster munitions have a dud rate and that these munitions often harm civilians well after an attack is well known. Accordingly, such harm can be expected when cluster munitions are used in areas where civilians live, work or gather.

---

62 *Expert Meeting: "Targeting Military Objectives"*, above n 27 (chapter 1), 15 (emphasis in original).

63 Ibid (emphasis in original).

64 See API, above n 2 (chapter 1), arts 54 and 56. Crawford discusses the issue of how not considering the 'reverberating effects' of attacks on electric power systems may in some cases be inconsistent with the intent behind API, art 56—Crawford, above n 72 (chapter 5) 14–5.

65 So as not to confuse issues, assume for the purpose of argument that the attack is not prohibited by API, above n 2 (chapter 1), art 56.

66 *Civilians under Assault: Hezbollah's Rocket Attacks on Israel in the 2006 War*, above n 91 (chapter 4), 45.

67 Ibid, 47.

By applying my reasoning, full affect is given to the word *expected* while at the same time the test is not transformed into one of mere possibility. In summary, I argue that the law requires indirect or consequential harm to be counted as part of the collateral damage assessment but only where that harm will arise as an expected consequence of the attack.

8.3.3 Human shields

This section discusses whether human shields, be they involuntary or voluntary human shields, are counted as collateral damage The status of human shields has attracted recent debate, even though the practice of using human shields is not new. For example, there are reports of the use of human shields in the American Civil War, the Boer War, the Franco Prussian war and both World Wars.[68] A more recent example comes from November 2006 in the Middle East:

> Palestinian armed groups must not endanger Palestinian civilians by encouraging them to gather in and around suspected militants' homes targeted by the Israel Defense Forces (IDF), Human Rights Watch said today. … According to media reports, on Saturday the IDF warned Mohammedweil Baroud, a commander in the Popular Resistance Committees, to leave his home in the Jabaliya refugee camp as they planned to destroy it. Baroud reportedly summoned neighbors and friends to protect his house, and a crowd of hundreds of Palestinians gathered in, around, and on the roof of the house. The IDF said that they called off the attack after they saw the large number of civilians around the house. On Monday, the BBC also reported that the IDF had warned Wael Rajab, an alleged Hamas member in Beit Lahiya, that that they were preparing to attack his home, and that a call was later broadcasted from local mosques for volunteers to protect the home.[69]

Similarly:

> On November 3 the BBC also reported that Hamas radio broadcasted an appeal to local women to go to a mosque to protect 15 alleged militants holed up inside from Israeli forces surrounding the building. Many women went to the mosque and reportedly two were killed and 10 more injured when Israeli forces opened fire.[70]

Assuming the women were unarmed and were 'merely' acting as human shields, were the Israeli forces under an obligation to consider the women as civilians to be assessed under the rule of proportionality, or could the women be considered as

68 Paolo Fusco, *Legal status of human shields* (2003) Centro Studi per la Pace <http://www.studiperlapace.it/view_news_html?news_id=20050125105209> at 12 June 2005.

69 *Civilians Must Not Be Used to Shield Homes Against Military Attacks*, above n 59 (chapter 1).

70 Ibid.

taking a direct part in hostilities and, therefore, exempt from the proportionality equation?[71]

As we have previously seen, API makes reference to the concept, if not the term, human shields in article 51(7) API. Article 51(7) API imposes an obligation on the defending party by stating:

> The presence or movements of the civilian population or individual civilians shall not be used to render certain points or areas immune from military operations, in particular in attempts to shield military objectives from attacks or to shield, favour or impede military operations. The Parties to the conflict shall not direct the movement of the civilian population or individual civilians in order to attempt to shield military objectives from attacks or to shield military operations.[72]

The word *movements* also covers the situation where a civilian population moves of its own accord and not at the direction of a competent authority.[73] The use of human shields is not limited to placing civilians around objects but also extends to the mixing of combatants with non-combatants. To take an example from 1997:

> Zairean rebels fighting to overthrow the government of dictator Mobutu Sese Seko often complained that when they approached groups of Rwandan refugees who were then fleeing Zaire's civil war, they were often fired upon by armed elements hiding among the civilians.[74]

Similarly, but from as recent as July 2006:

> Israeli and Palestinian human rights groups have documented the IDF's forcible use of Palestinians as human shields in a well publicized incident during military operations in Beit Hanoun. According to the groups, the IDF blindfolded six civilians, including two minors, and forced them to stand in front of soldiers who took over civilian homes during a raid in northern Gaza.[75]

Like all rules of IHL that do not explicitly mention derogation in the event of military necessity, an appeal to military necessity, even the extreme case where "defenders seemingly might have no means to defend themselves except by hiding and

71 Of course, if voluntary human shields are considered to be taking a direct part in hostilities, not only are they not counted as collateral damage, they are also liable to direct attack.

72 API, above n 2 (chapter 1), art 51(7). See also ibid, art 58 for a more general statement on the obligations of both parties to take precautions in favour of the civilian population from the effects of attacks.

73 Sandoz, Swinarski and Zimmerman (eds), above n 68 (chapter 1), [1988].

74 Robert Block, *Shields*, Crimes of War Project <http://www.crimesofwar.org/thebook/shields.html> at 26 May 2006.

75 *Civilians Must Not Be Used to Shield Homes Against Military Attacks*, above n 59 (chapter 1).

dispersing themselves among non-combatants",[76] does not allow any breach of the rule in article 51(7) API. But, what are the consequences for an attacker if a defender does, nonetheless, breach article 51(7) API? Article 51(8) API goes on to state that "any violation of these prohibitions shall not release the Parties to the conflict from their legal obligations with respect to the civilian population and civilians, including the obligation to take the precautionary measures provided for in Article 57." While Hays Parks is critical of this sub-article, and submits that this is a change in the law, Gardam in direct response to Hays Parks writes:

> However, it has never been a principle of the law or armed conflict that an attacker can absolve itself from responsibility for compliance with the rule of non-combatant immunity on the basis that the defender has failed to meet their obligations.[77]

Regardless of who is right, what is important in the current context is that article 51(8) API is extant law for parties to API. Therefore, in accordance with article 51(8) API, even if the defending party places human shields around a military objective (involuntary human shields), the attacking party must still take the usual precautions in attack.[78] There also appears to be no reason why the 'value' assigned to the collateral damage can be reduced (eg, more civilians killed) merely because of their forced presence around the military objective. This conclusion is supported by DeSaussure, who writes that the "fact that civilians are used as a shield does not cause them to lose their normal protection."[79] Human Rights Watch also appear to be of this view when they state that where a party uses civilians the presence of civilians to attempt to render targets immune from attack or tries to direct the movement of civilians to shield a target from attack, nonetheless an attacker:

> remain[s] obliged under international humanitarian law to take precautionary measures and not to target civilians or cause excessive civilian injury or damage in relation to the anticipated concrete and direct military advantage.[80]

---

76 Kenneth Anderson et al, *A Public Call For International Attention to Legal Obligations of Defending Forces As Well As Attacking Forces to Protect Civilians in Armed Conflict* (2003) Crimes of War Project <http://www.crimesofwar.org/print/onnews/iraq3-print.html> at 4 March 2005.

77 Gardam, *Non-combatant Immunity as a Norm of International Humanitarian Law*, above n 28 (chapter 4), 122 (fn 63).

78 *Legal Issues Arising from the War in Afghanistan and Related Anti-Terrorism Efforts*, above n 47 (chapter 4). See also *Expert Meeting: "Targeting Military Objectives"*, above n 27 (chapter 1), 19–20; *Preserving Humanitarian Principles While Combating Terrorism: Israel's Struggle with Hizbullah in the Lebanon War*, above n 101 (chapter 3), 11.

79 Hamilton DeSaussure, *Military Objectives*, Crimes of War Project <http://www.crimesofwar.org/thebook/military-objective.html> at 26 May 2006. Although not explicitly stated, from the context it appears as though DeSaussure is referring to involuntary human shields.

80 *Civilians Must Not Be Used to Shield Homes Against Military Attacks*, above n 59 (chapter 1).

Rogers appears to suggest a slightly different view of the law when, after mentioning that:

> there is evidence to suggest that some States … deliberately put military assets close to protected objects or place civilians in military locations with the intention of protecting military objectives from attack[,][81]

Rogers then writes:

> Those carrying out attacks in such circumstances are not relieved of their obligation to attack military objectives only and reduce incidental damage as much as possible, but in considering the rule of proportionality, any tribunal dealing with the matter would be obliged to weigh in the balance in favour of the attackers any such illegal activity by the defenders.[82]

The United Kingdom's Ministry of Defence position on this point is hard to determine. While stating that the proportionality rule still applies when human shields are present, the United Kingdom's manual then states that where the defender has deliberately collocated military objectives with civilians or civilian objects,[83] "this is a factor to be taken into account in favour of the attackers in considering the legality of attacks on those objectives."[84] A subsequent paragraph makes it clear that the consideration in question is whether any collateral damage is proportional.[85] Presumably, it is being suggested that in such circumstances the collateral damage has a lower 'value' than in a non-shield case.

To the extent that Rogers is discussing the law under API and if I have correctly summarised the United Kingdom's manual, I must respectfully disagree. Article 51(8) API is clear that a breach of article 51(7) API does not release other parties from their obligations, and I can find no legal support for the argument that the obligations are reduced. Interestingly, claimed practice by the United States of America supports an argument that there is no lessening of obligation:

> Central Command (CENTCOM) forces adhered to these fundamental law of war proscriptions in conducting military operations during Operation Desert Storm through discriminating target selection and careful matching of available forces and weapons systems to selected targets and Iraqi defenses, without regard to Iraqi violations of its law of war obligations toward the civilian population and civilian objects.[86]

---

81 Rogers, 'Zero-casualty warfare', above n 94 (chapter 3).

82 Ibid.

83 By placing military objectives alongside civilians and civilian objects, or vice versa.

84 UK Ministry of Defence, above n 14 (chapter 1), [2.7.2].

85 Ibid, [5.22.1].

86 US Department of Defense, *Conduct of the Persian Gulf War: Final Report to Congress*, above n 29 (chapter 3), 697.

It is my conclusion that the law is that involuntary human shields are counted as collateral damage. In addition, IHL makes no distinction between classes of civilians. There are civilians, combatants and military non-combatants. Amongst civilians, there are no further graduations.[87] Accordingly, each civilian is 'worth' the same as every other civilian, and an involuntary human shield is given the normal weighting of any other civilian in the proportionality equation.[88]

Schmitt places an interesting twist on this issue in a recent article, where he writes:

> When one side intentionally places military objectives near civilian objects or places civilian objects close to military objectives in order to shield them ... , those objects may take on a status analogous to "military objective". Their use contributes directly to defense of the target and if their role as shields could be neutralized, a military advantage would accrue to the attacker. That said ... because their sole use is as a military shield, there is no need to attack them directly unless they physically impede attack on the intended target. Of course, they are vulnerable to damage during attack on the target, but, having taken on the character of a military objective through use, such damage should not be included within the proportionality calculation.[89]

As Schmitt clearly recognises, the principle of distinction in IHL has two prime consequences. First, only military objectives can be attacked. Second, everything that is not a military objective is immune from attack. A result of these two points is that anything that is not a military objective that is damaged or destroyed in an attack is collateral damage. However, there appears to be a flaw in Schmitt's argument. Schmitt does not appear to distinguish between the mere co-location of a civilian object with a military objective and the placing of an object in such a way as for the object to be taking an active role in shielding. Where a civilian object is deliberately placed in such a way as to impede military operations,[90] then I agree that such an object takes on the status of a military objective.[91] However, civilian objects do not become military objectives where a civilian object is merely co-located with a military objective or where a civilian object is placed in such a way

87 While not ruling on the point, see generally the discussion in *Prosecutor v Erdemovic, (Appeals Chamber)* Case No IT-96-22 (7 October 1997) [81] (Joint Separate Opinion of Judge McDonald and Judge Vohrah); [42] (Separate Opinion of Judge Cassese).

88 But see Dinstein, *The Conduct of Hostilities under the Law of International Armed Conflict*, above n 66 (chapter 2), 131.

89 Schmitt, 'Targeting and Humanitarian Law: Current Issues', above n 42 (chapter 1), 97.

90 For example, a civilian car placed across a narrow road to hinder movement of ground troops.

91 The same would apply when the object is positively used to facilitate military operations. For example, the use of a tall building as on observation post by an artillery spotter.

that the object does not impede military operations in the physical sense but merely causes reservations about causing collateral damage.[92]

The above discussion has dealt with involuntary human shields. But, what about the situation where civilians voluntary gather not as refugees or for other innocent reasons but rather to try to protect a military objective? For instance, the following quote comes from an article dealing with the NATO bombing campaign in the former Yugoslavia:

> Our bridges are still protected by the people who walk them during the day, and shield them during the night ... the students, professors, housewives and secretaries on those bridges are there on their own, not as NATO's perverted idea of military using civilians to protect the potential targets. Are they really so corrupt not to think that *anyone* would step up and protect their own country, their own homes, places of work, children's playgrounds? Wouldn't their own people do so, if the situation was reversed?[93]

An article by the Crimes of War project appears to draw a distinction between involuntary and voluntary human shields. In discussing the practice of human shields during the 2002 Gulf War, the article states:

> death or injury to human shields, whether Iraqi or non-Iraqi, who voluntarily take up positions at the site of legitimate military objectives does not constitute "civilian" collateral damage, because those voluntary human shields have assumed the risk of combat and, to that extent, have compromised their non-combatant immunity.[94]

Schmitt arrives at a similar conclusion. With respect to article 51(3) API, he takes the view that when determining whether a civilian has lost immunity from direct attack due to taking a direct part in hostilities, "the standard is participation in hostilities, not engagement therein."[95] On this basis, he concludes that a voluntary human shield is taking a direct part in hostilities and that while in:

> most cases, it will serve no valid military purpose to directly target the voluntary human shields themselves ... the fact that they are directly participating means that their injury or death would not factor into the required proportionality calculation.[96]

---

92 For example, the parking of military vehicles next to civilian houses in an effort to dissuade an air attack. Further on in this section, while discussing voluntary human shields, I refer to this as actions designed to provide a 'moral pause' to an attacker.

93 Biljana Marjanovic, *Collateral Damage: A View Into the Daily Lives of Yugoslavs Under the Bombs* <http://www.thing.net/~oliveworks/marjanovic.html> at 26 May 2006.

94 Anderson et al, above n 76 (chapter 8).

95 Schmitt, '"Direct participation in hostilities" and 21st century armed conflict', above n 58 (chapter 1), 521.

96 Ibid, 522. See also Schmitt, 'Humanitarian Law and Direct Participation in Hostilities by Private Contractors or Civilian Employees', above n 21 (chapter 1), 541, where he writes: "Voluntary shielding is unquestionably direct participation."

The Israeli Supreme Court cite Schmitt's articles in (sole) support of their opinion that voluntary human shields "should be seen as persons taking a direct part in the hostilities".[97] In 2004, a minority of experts at a meeting also took the view that voluntary human shields are taking a direct part in hostilities.[98]

Fusco directly discusses the issue of voluntary human shields and concludes that voluntary human shields must be counted in the collateral damage equation just like any other civilian. The reasoning for this conclusion is that voluntary human shields are not combatants as defined in IHL and nor in Fusco's view are they taking a direct part in hostilities within the meaning of article 51(3) API.[99] Human Rights Watch appears to be of a similar view. In discussing the situations quoted above from November 2006, Human Rights Watch writes:

> while civilians placing themselves in the way of military actions take on heightened risks, they cannot be considered legitimate targets by the opposing force, and parties to the conflict should cancel or suspend attacks where excessive civilian damage is anticipated.[100]

And at the 2004 meeting of experts:

> The majority view was that voluntary human shields, like weapons factory workers, were not taking a direct part in hostilities because they do not direct violence against the enemy. ... Therefore such voluntary human shields had to be factored into the proportionality evaluation like other civilians.[101]

In my view, the actions of the human shields needs to be looked at more closely before a conclusion can be reached as to whether it is Schmitt, the Israeli Supreme Court and the minority of experts at the 2004 meeting; or Fusco, Human Rights Watch and the majority of experts at the 2004 meeting, who are correct. What needs to be determined is whether the actions of the human shields are actually impeding military operations or merely providing a 'moral pause' to the attacker. By actually impede the progress of an attack, I mean (for example) to physically block a route of advance.[102] By 'moral pause', I mean a situation where the physical presence of the human shield will not practically impede the conduct of an attack. For

97 *The Public Committee against Torture in Israel v The Government of Israel*, HCJ 769/02 (13 December 2006) [36] (Barak P (emeritus), Rivlin V-P and Beinisch P concurring).

98 *Expert Meeting: "Targeting Military Objectives"*, above n 27 (chapter 1), 20. See also Dinstein, *The Conduct of Hostilities under the Law of International Armed Conflict*, above n 66 (chapter 2), 130; Dunlap, *Law and Military Interventions: Preserving Humanitarian Values in 21st Conflicts*, above n 168 (chapter 3), 9.

99 Fusco, above n 68 (chapter 8).

100 *Civilians Must Not Be Used to Shield Homes Against Military Attacks*, above n 59 (chapter 1).

101 *Expert Meeting: "Targeting Military Objectives"*, above n 27 (chapter 1), 20.

102 It is possible that this is what was understood by the term "shield, by their presence" at the 1972 *Conference of Government Experts on the Reaffirmation and Development of International Humanitarian Law Applicable in Armed Conflicts*—CE 1972 Report, vol I, above n 25 (chapter 1), 149–50.

example, I refer to the well-known footage of the Chinese man standing in front of a tank in Tiananmen Square.[103] From a practical point of view, the man's presence would not have actually impeded the physical progress of the tank if the tank driver had simply continued straight forward. However, the man's presence clearly caused the tank driver to pause from proceeding in what we can assume was the intended direction. This distinction between causing actual impediment and mere moral pause is not dissimilar to what I wrote about Schmitt's argument just above on co-location of objects. Human shields might not just be standing on a bridge in the hope of preventing an aerial attack but they may in fact be endeavouring to assist an attacker. The example we saw earlier was:

> US forces encountered "[a] Somali with a gun lying prone on the street between two kneeling women. The shooter had the barrel of his weapon between the women's legs, and there were four children actually *sitting* on him."[104]

If the purpose was to try and prevent the opposing force from being able to determine the source of the gun shots, this action by the women and children amounts to direct participation in hostilities and, therefore, the civilians have lost protection from attack. Accordingly, those civilians would not be counted as collateral damage. However, the mere presence of civilians on a bridge for the purpose of 'shielding' the bridge does not amount to direct participation in hostilities where the attacker is planning to bombard the bridge as the bridge is still in clear view. In such a case, the civilians are still counted as collateral damage. Further, as discussed above, as there is no graduation amongst civilians, each civilian is 'worth' the same as every other civilian, and where they are counted as collateral damage voluntary human shields are given the normal weighting of any other civilian in the proportionality equation.

8.3.4 Are workers inside a military objective counted in the collateral damage equation?

Some military objectives will have civilians located inside the objective itself. For example, a munitions factory is likely to have civilians working at that factory.[105] An attack on the factory might be expected to result in some of those civilians being wounded or killed. Are those factory workers assessed any differently in the proportionality equation from civilians outside the factory who are also wounded or killed by the attack?

---

103 An account is available at Pico Iyer, *The Unknown Rebel* (1998) Time <http://www.time.com/time/time100/leaders/profile/rebel.html> at 16 January 2007. A copy of the video footage is available at *Tiananmen revisited* (2001) CNN.COM <http://edition.cnn.com/SPECIALS/2001/tiananmen/> at 16 January 2007.

104 Waxman, above n 56 (chapter 1), 48 (fn 8) (original emphasis) (citation omitted).

105 Notwithstanding Winston Churchill's view during World War II that the "proper course for German Civilians and non-combatants is to quit the centres of munition production and take refuge in the countryside." (Charles Eade, *The Dawn of Liberation: War Speeches by the Right Honourable Winston S. Churchill 1944* (1945) 6)

The drafting history of API is illuminating in answering this question. The second part of article 6 of the *Draft Rules for the Limitation of the Dangers incurred by the Civilian Population in Time of War*, and which was presented to the 1971 *Conference of Government Experts on the Reaffirmation and Development of International Humanitarian Law Applicable in Armed Conflicts*,[106] had a clause that stated:

> Nevertheless, should members of the civilian population, Article 11 not withstanding, be within or in close proximity to a military objective they must accept the risks resulting from an attack directed against that objective.[107]

This clause is not reflected in what is now API. This is perhaps not surprising, as the Draft Rules had a clause on not causing disproportionate collateral damage[108] and it is hard to reconcile the two clauses.

The draft clause just referred to dealt with civilians both *in* and *in the vicinity of* military objectives. By the time of the 1972 *Conference of Government Experts on the Reaffirmation and Development of International Humanitarian Law Applicable in Armed Conflicts*, the focus had turned to consider only those civilians *inside* a military objective. The draft article (article 45) at the 1972 conference stated: "Nevertheless, civilians who are within a military objective run the risks consequent upon any attack launched against this objective."[109] This draft clause did not survive into what is now API, as its deletion was the prominent view at the 1972 conference.[110] However, it is arguably the case that at least some of the experts thought it should be deleted as it stated the law in any event. The comprise seemed to be that civilians did run a risk, but only if they ignored a prior warning.[111] This compromise position is not stated in any article of API.

Turing to the terms of API itself, API recognises that civilians can be involved in the war effort without thereby becoming combatants. As we have repeatedly seen, civilians lose their protection from attack only when they take a direct part in hostilities.[112] Mere participation in the general war effort does not lead to a civilian being a quasi-combatant and thereby a military objective in their own right.[113] With respect to article 51(3) API, the *ICRC Commentary* states:

> There should be a clear distinction between direct participation in hostilities and participation in the war effort. The latter is often required from the population as

106 CE/3b, above n 27 (chapter 3), 32.

107 *Draft Rules for the Limitation of the Dangers incurred by the Civilian Population in Time of War*, above n 16 (chapter 3). Article 11 deals with 'passive precautions', and is now broadly reflected in API, art 58.

108 Ibid, article 8. See now API, above n 2 (chapter 1), arts 51(5) and 57(2).

109 CE 1972 Report, vol I, above n 25 (chapter 1), 148.

110 Ibid.

111 Ibid, 149.

112 API, above n 2 (chapter 1), art 51(3).

113 Oeter, above n 24 (chapter 2), 163; Dinstein, *The Conduct of Hostilities under the Law of International Armed Conflict*, above n 66 (chapter 2), 124.

> a whole to various degrees. Without such a distinction the efforts made to reaffirm and develop international humanitarian law could become meaningless.[114]

If we accept that they are not subject to attack as combatants, then, like human shields, they must be civilians. And, like human shields, then civilians working in a military objective (eg, a munitions factory) must be counted as collateral damage when an attack is launched on that military objective.[115] Oeter believes there is still a further question:

> It must be asked whether the deliberate taking of the risk by any civilian who stays in a military installation should influence the balance which must be struck between the intended military advantage and the collateral damage to be taken into account. … Whether collateral damage to civilians working in military objectives (and thus contributing to the military endeavours of its state) is of lesser weight in striking a balance with the military advantage than potential damage to 'innocent' civilians is a question not yet answered, but which needs careful study. Although an affirmative answer might create serious ethical difficulties, reasons of military practicability (and of soldiers' common sense) might point in that direction.[116]

Bothe, Partsch and Solf write that it is doubtful whether collateral damage caused to civilians working alongside the armed forces in a military objective would weigh as heavily in the proportionality equation as collateral damage caused to civilians not so closely linked to military operations.[117] While some might consider this an accurate statement of reality, as I just argued in the section on human shields, IHL makes no distinction between classes of civilians. Accordingly, each civilian is 'worth' the same as every other civilian. Under IHL, there is no category of *innocent* civilians. There are only civilians who have lost protection from attack and those that have not. So, unlike Oeter, I am of the view that the question has been answered. And the answer is: the injury or death to any particular civilian is of no lesser weight than the injury or death to any other civilian.

That concludes the discussion on what is counted on each side of the equation. The next section deals with the law on how to determine what is proportional.

---

114 Sandoz, Swinarski and Zimmerman (eds), above n 68 (chapter 1), [1945].

115 Hans-Peter Gasser, 'Protection of the Civilian Population' in Dieter Fleck (ed), The *Handbook of Humanitarian Law in Armed Conflicts* (1995) 209, 233; *The Public Committee against Torture in Israel v The Government of Israel*, HCJ 769/02 (13 December 2006) [42] (Barak P (emeritus), Rivlin V-P and Beinisch P concurring). While Dinstein expresses the view that such workers enjoy no immunity while at work, it is hard to determine whether his conclusion is based on the fact that they are not counted as collateral damage or because of his robust view as to what would amount to proportionate collateral damage—see Dinstein, *The Conduct of Hostilities under the Law of International Armed Conflict*, above n 66 (chapter 2), 124. I suspect, though, that it is the latter, as he refers to such workers as "acceptable collateral damage".

116 Oeter, above n 24 (chapter 2), 163–4.

117 Bothe, Partsch and Solf, above n 87 (chapter 1), 295. Note, the authors are referring to civilians who in the circumstances are still not taking a direct part in hostilities per API, above n 2 (chapter 1), art 51(3).

8.4 What is meant by 'excessive'?

During Operation Allied Force, a NATO attack incidentally killed 16 civilians. The result of the attack was to disrupt "Serbian television broadcasts in the middle of the night for approximately three hours."[118] Amnesty International concludes that it "is hard to see how this can be consistent with the rule of proportionality."[119] On the other hand, the *OTP Report* concludes that "[a]ssuming the station was a legitimate objective, the civilian casualties were unfortunately high but do not appear to be clearly disproportionate."[120] It would seem that the test for what is excessive is not black and white.

Article 57(2)(a)(iii) API requires a balancing between the military necessity of attacking a target and the expected collateral damage that may result from that attack. More strictly speaking, a commander must refrain from deciding to launch any attack that may be expected to cause collateral damage that would be excessive in relation to the concrete and direct military advantage anticipated. Unfortunately, and perhaps unavoidably, article 57 API provides no guidance on what is proportional (ie, not excessive) in this balancing test. Indeed, the extensive list of State practice on this test referred to in the section on "Proportionality in Attack" in *Customary International Humanitarian Law* generally does little more than restate the rule that expected collateral damage must not be excessive to the anticipated military advantage.[121] But, having determined the anticipated military advantage and the expected collateral damage, how is a commander then to decide the worth or ratio of the combination of death, injury and damage to the military advantage anticipated (ie., what is meant by 'excessive')? As Kellenberger has noted, the:

> proportionality test is quite complex to apply in practice: ideally, balancing involves comparison of like values. In the case of proportionality the values are heterogeneous.[122]

How does one "objectively [calculate] the relative weight of a military aircraft, tank, or vantage point in terms of human casualties"?[123] To put it in very simple terms,

---

118 *"Collateral damage" or Unlawful Killings?: Violations of the Laws of War by NATO during Operation Allied Force*, above n 28 (chapter 5).

119 Ibid. It is implicit in Amnesty International's conclusion that it is assumed that the concrete and direct military advantage expected from the attack was limited to the 3-hour disruption.

120 *OTP Report*, above n 90 (chapter 1), [77]. The casualty estimate on which this sentence was based was 10–17 deaths (see paragraph 71 of the *OTP Report*). Once again, it is implicit in the *OTP Report's* conclusion that it is assumed that the concrete and direct military advantage expected from the attack was the 3-hour disruption.

121 Henckaerts and Doswald-Beck (eds), *Customary International Humanitarian Law*, vol II, above n 64 (chapter 1), 299–305.

122 Kellenberger, above n 23 (chapter 1). See also, Schmitt, 'The Principle of Discrimination in 21st Century Warfare', above n 201 (chapter 4), [16]; Fenrick, 'The Rule of Proportionality and Protocol I in Conventional Warfare', above n 9 (chapter 7), 95.

123 Kellenberger, above n 23 (chapter 1).

how many civilian deaths would be excessive in attacking a munitions factory? As recognised by the Israeli Supreme Court sitting as the High Court of Justice:

> [This] balancing is difficult when it regards human life. It raises moral and ethical problems. ... Despite the difficulty of that balancing, there's no choice but to perform it.[124]

This section deals with what guidance can be given to a commander to assist him or her in assessing whether an attack will be lawful when assessed against article 57(2)(a)(iii) API.

At least two commentators have concluded that that the determination of whether the expected collateral damage is excessive is a subjective assessment;[125] however, by this I take the commentators to mean that the assessment is not capable of precise analysis or determination by a mathematical equation. In other words, IHL does not currently allow us to say definitely know whether the incidental death of two civilians is proportional to the destruction of one tank. Importantly, I do not believe that they are using *subjective* in the sense that the correct legal answer will be only the one arrived at by the actual person who made the decision. Rather, as the ICTY has held:

> In determining whether an attack was proportionate it is necessary to examine whether a reasonably well-informed person in the circumstances of the actual perpetrator, making reasonable use of the information available to him or her, could have expected excessive civilian casualties to result from the attack.[126]

It can be seen, therefore, that there are both subjective and objective aspects to the proportionality test. An assessment of the proportionality of an attack is based on the circumstances of the commander and the information available to him or her. However, the *conclusions* to be reached on whether collateral damage is *expected* and whether it is *proportional* is then based on what a reasonable person would have concluded from that information. This is consistent with the *OTP Report*, which stated that:

> It is suggested that the determination of relative values must be that of the "reasonable military commander". Although there will be room for argument in close cases, there will be many cases where reasonable military commanders will agree

124 *The Public Committee against Torture in Israel v The Government of Israel*, HCJ 769/02 (13 December 2006) [46] (Barak P (emeritus), Rivlin V-P and Beinisch P concurring).

125 See Fenrick, 'The Rule of Proportionality and Protocol I in Conventional Warfare', above n 9 (chapter 7), 111; Blix, above n 78 (chapter 2), 148.

126 *Prosecutor v Galic, (Trial Chamber)* Case No IT-98-29-T (5 December 2003) [58]. See also the State practice of Ecuador (an "objective and reasonable estimate") and the USA (an "honest and reasonable estimate")—Henckaerts and Doswald-Beck (eds), *Customary International Humanitarian Law*, vol II, above n 64 (chapter 1), 334.

> that the injury to noncombatants or the damage to civilian objects was clearly disproportionate to the military advantage gained.[127]

So, the test for whether expected collateral damage will be *excessive* is an objective one based on what would a reasonable person (commander) would conclude in the circumstances. The problem this immediately raises is that that the subjective value placed on the lives of others may vary and, therefore, how do we determine what a reasonable person (commander) would conclude? Schmitt argues this well when he writes:

> On an immediate individual basis, of course, there is no distinction in the value placed on life by different societies. It would be absurd, for instance, to suggest that a Belgian valued the life of a loved one any more or less than a Somali. Yet, in some societies, death, poverty, and deprivation tragically are so widespread that their population can become desensitized to death in the more general sense. In much the same way that a doctor becomes less personally affected by death over time, or a criminal defense attorney learns to react somewhat impersonally to the crimes of her client, those who have the misfortune to live amongst death-filled circumstances may become inured to death when it is not personally relevant. This notion flies in the face of the objective valuation of life sought by humanitarian law, but represents an unfortunate reality that shades proportionality calculations. Among makers of proportionality calculations, therefore, the value attributed to the human suffering caused by a military operation may very widely with social or cultural background.[128]

Even once the subjective aspect is accounted for, there remains the fact that unalike values (military advantage and collateral damage) are being compared; and this is so even where it appears as though like things are being compared, as the alikeness is illusory. Even when the comparison is between the number of military casualties and civilian casualties, the comparison is still not between human lives and human lives. For example, suppose intelligence reveals that the senior intelligence officer of the enemy will be in a certain building at a certain time. Assume that the building is an apartment building and that the expected collateral damage from an attack designed to kill the senior intelligence officer is 10 civilian deaths. Even in this case, it is not as simple as saying one death versus 10 deaths. From the attacker's perspective, the military advantage to be gained is not the death of the senior intelligence officer as such but the significant disruption to the enemy's intelligence capability.

Human Rights Watch refer to an attack in the 2006 armed conflict between Israel and Hezbollah where an Israeli attack killed two armed members of the Lebanese Communist Party and incidentally killed four unarmed bystanders.

127 *OTP Report*, above n 90 (chapter 1), [50]. The first sentence of this quoted is quoted with approval in *Preserving Humanitarian Principles While Combating Terrorism: Israel's Struggle with Hizbullah in the Lebanon War*, above n 101 (chapter 3), 12.

128 Schmitt, 'The Principle of Discrimination in 21st Century Warfare', above n 201 (chapter 4), [18].

Human Rights Watch merely state, without referring to the proportionality of the attack, that:

> The four unarmed bystanders killed in the attack put themselves at risk by mixing with combatants during an Israeli military operation, and must be considered collateral casualties to a legitimate Israeli military strike.[129]

It would have been interesting to see what Human Rights Watch's view was on the question of proportionality, presuming, of course, that the attacker was aware of the presence of the unarmed civilians and that the attack might have been expected to kill or seriously injure those civilians.

The other point in this section concerns what is not meant be excessive. When discussing article 51(5)(a) API, the substantive wording of which is identical to article 57(2)(a)(iii) API, the *ICRC Commentary* states:

> The idea has also been put forward that even if they are very high, civilian losses and damages may be justified if the military advantage at stake is of great importance. This idea is contrary to the fundamental rules of the Protocol—in particular it conflicts with Article 48 '(Basic rule)' and with paragraphs 1 and 2 of the present Article 51. The Protocol does not provide any justification for attacks which cause extensive civilian losses and damages. Incidental losses and damages should never be extensive.[130]

These sentences were also quoted with approval in the Human Rights Watch report on the 1991 Gulf War.[131] Nonetheless, I disagree with the last three sentences of the quoted paragraph. First, article 48 API prohibits attacks directed at anything other than military objectives. Accordingly, as long as civilian losses and damages are incidental, such losses and damages are not contrary to article 48 API. Indeed, article 48 API does not even make mention of the proportionality principle. Second, article 51(2) API prohibits attacks on the civilian population as such, as well as individual civilians, and acts or threats of violence the primary purpose of which is to spread terror among the civilian population are prohibited. Therefore, like I argued for article 48 API, as long as the civilian losses and damages are incidental, such losses and damages are not contrary to article 51(2) API. Finally, *extensive* is not a synonym for, or a related word to, *excessive*. If the anticipated military advantage is high enough, then it is certainly arguable that extensive collateral damage would not be excessive collateral damage when *compared* to the military advantage anticipated.[132] The lawfulness of collateral damage cannot be assessed in isolation but only

129 *Why They Died: Civilian Casualties in Lebanon during the 2006 War*, above n 3 (chapter 2), 126.

130 Sandoz, Swinarski and Zimmerman (eds), above n 68 (chapter 1), [1980].

131 *Needless Deaths in the Gulf War: Civilian Casualties During the Air Campaign and Violations of the Laws of War*, above n 38 (chapter 3).

132 Dinstein, *The Conduct of Hostilities under the Law of International Armed Conflict*, above n 66 (chapter 2), 120–1; Dunlap, *Law and Military Interventions: Preserving Humanitarian Values in 21st Conflicts*, above n 168 (chapter 3), 9.

in comparison to the anticipated military advantage.[133] Some support for this point can be drawn from the decision in the *Nuclear Weapons* case. In that case the court advised, by seven votes to seven with the President casting the deciding vote, that:

> However, in view of the current state of international law, and of the elements of fact at its disposal, the Court cannot conclude definitively whether the threat or use of nuclear weapons would be lawful or unlawful in an extreme circumstance of self-defence, in which the very survival of a State would be at stake.[134]

As discussed in section 2.6, it is unfortunately not clear whether the court was saying that in such an extreme case military necessity would allow for disregarding IHL or whether in such an extreme case the military advantage to be gained would be so large as to make the use of a nuclear weapon probably lawful. However, as for current purposes the issue is whether collateral damage can be lawful even if extensive, the dissenting opinion of Higgins J is perhaps the most useful:

> For some States making submissions to the Court, the large number of civilian victims was said *itself to show* that the collateral damage is excessive. But the law of armed conflict has been articulated in terms of a broad prohibition—that civilians may not be the object of armed attack—and the question of numbers or suffering (provided always that this primary obligation is met) falls to be considered as part of the "balancing" or "equation" between the necessities of war and the requirements of humanity. ... It must be that, in order to meet the legal requirement that a military target may not be attacked if collateral civilian casualties would be excessive in relation to the military advantage, the "military advantage" must indeed be one related to the very survival of a State or the avoidance of infliction (whether by nuclear or other weapons of mass destruction) of vast and severe suffering on its own population; and that no other method of eliminating this military target be available.[135]

Similarly, Kalshoven asks whether there is an:

> upper limit beyond which collateral damage that is not excessive in view of the absolutely imperative military necessity of the attack, will by its terrible scale become unacceptable nonetheless?[136]

133 See Schmitt, *Precision Attack and International Humanitarian Law*, above n 30 (chapter 3), 457 where he writes: "The standard is 'excessive (a comparative concept), not 'extensive' (an absolute concept)." See also Rogers, *Law on the Battlefield*, above n 84 (chapter 1), 21.

134 *Nuclear Weapons Case* [1996] ICJ Rep 226.

135 *Nuclear Weapons Case* [1996] ICJ Rep 226, [20]-[21] (Separate Opinion of Judge Higgins).

136 Kalshoven, 'Remarks', above n 126 (chapter 3), 44.

His own answer is: "As far as I can see, there is no such further limit in the written or customary law of armed conflict."[137] The conclusion to be drawn is that where the military advantage is very high, a large number of civilian victims might not be excessive to that military advantage. Accordingly, it is quite correct to argue that as long as the direct and concrete military advantage anticipated is extremely significant then the permissible collateral damage can be extensive—it just cannot be excessive.[138] Extensive and excessive are two different words with very different meanings.

8.4.1 Expected not actual

When assessing whether a particular attack was proportional, it must always be remembered that the collateral damage to be considered is the collateral damage that was expected and not the actual collateral damage that was caused.[139] However, it is not uncommon to see commentators refer to the actual collateral damage caused. For example, when commenting on the NATO attack on the RTS television broadcasting station, Voon writes: "It is difficult to see how such a short interruption could achieve a degree of military advantage justifying the sacrifice of seventeen civilian lives."[140] The seventeen lives she is referring to are the actual civilian dead from the attack, which is not necessarily the same number as what was expected. Similarly, Fischer writes:

> As formulated in Additional Protocol I of 1977, attacks are prohibited if they cause incidental loss of civilian life, injury to civilians, or damage to civilian objects that is excessive in relation to the anticipated concrete and direct military advantage of the attack. This creates a permanent obligation for military commanders to consider the results of the attack compared to the advantage anticipated.[141]

Perhaps this should not be surprising, as it would be rare (and indeed, so rare that I have never seen it) for commentators to have access to an attacker's planning documents setting out the expected collateral damage from any particular attack.[142] But, this does not mean that we should not always take care in our use of language and

---

137 Ibid. Kalshoven does hope, nonetheless, that ethical considerations might come into play.

138 See Rogers, *Law on the Battlefield*, above n 84 (chapter 1), 21–2.

139 *Prosecutor v Galic, (Trial Chamber)* Case No IT-98-29-T (5 December 2003) fn 109.

140 Voon, above n 56 (chapter 7), 1098.

141 Horst Fischer, *Proportionality, Principle of*, Crimes of War Project <http://www.crimesofwar.org/thebook/proportion-principle.html> at 26 May 2006.

142 Although it is interesting to note that in a newspaper article discussing a computer program being used by the United States Air Force to assess potential collateral damage, Brigadier General Dunlap, a senior United States Air Force lawyer, was quoted as saying that such computer tools will create a record of the options that commanders faced in drawing up a war plan, thereby making them more accountable. They would also have to be able to explain themselves if they deviated from the options presented by the decision support tools. ('"Bugsplat" computer program aims to limit civilian deaths at targets', *The Seattle Times* (Seattle), 26 February 2003)

be very particular in setting out the correct test. There is, also, an interesting result from the point I have just made. If, unusually, documents became known showing that the expected collateral damage from an attack was disproportionate, the fact that the actual resulting collateral damage was not disproportionate is not relevant to whether article 57(2)(a)(iii) API was complied with.

In case I am misinterpreting Fischer, I do agree that commanders need to undertake after action reviews. However, the purpose of the reviews is not to see whether the attack was proportional; but rather to assess whether the planning methods being used are reliable. Cordesman makes the good point that:

> military history is filled with over-ambitious claims by air planners, and no wartime USAF estimate of the effect of bombing on supply and movement has yet proved to have been remotely correct in after-action studies.[143]

If planning staff regularly over-estimate the anticipated military advantage, and/or regularly underestimate the expected collateral damage, then the commander would not be able to rely upon those estimates when undertaking the proportionality assessment. Hampson has argued that if the planner of an attack "fails to consult an obvious source of information, he may be held responsible if that would have revealed the likelihood of high incidental civilian losses."[144] Not only do I agree with this point, I would go further and state that commanders also have an obligation to regularly check that the sources and methods they are using are reliable and approximate the actual consequences.[145]

8.4.2 Nationality of the civilians

When considering the immunity of the civilian population from indiscriminate attacks and, in particular, whether an attack is anticipated to cause excessive collateral damage, a very important point is that the nationality of the civilians is an irrel-

---

143 Cordesman, above n 97 (chapter 1), 171.

144 Hampson, 'Proportionality and Necessity in the Gulf Conflict', above n 23 (chapter 3), 48.

145 Rogers refers to Kalshoven's material on the sinking of the Japanese ship Awa Maru by the USS Queenfish in 1945. The IJN Awa Maru had been granted safe passage by authorities of the United States of America, and while this information had been received on board the USS Queenfish, the commander of the USS Queenfish (Commander Charles E. Loughlin) was unaware of it. At his court martial, Commander Loughlin was found guilty "because he was responsible for the inefficient internal procedures, which resulted in his not being informed." (Rogers, *Law on the Battlefield*, above n 84 (chapter 1), 110) However, as the trial was a court martial and the charge was one of negligence in obeying orders rather than a war crimes trial, I suggest the case has only limited relevance. Of interest, the court "sentenced [Commander Loughlin] to receive a career-crushing 'Letter of Admonition' from the Secretary of the Navy. He never held another command at sea; however, despite these set backs, Loughlin continued to be promoted, finally achieving Rear Admiral." (Bob Hackett, Sander Kingsepp and Peter Cundall, *IJN AWA MARU: Tabular Record of Movement* (1985–2005) Imperial Japanese Navy Page <http://www.combinedfleet.com/Awa_t.htm> at 12 February 2006)

evant consideration.[146] A State's own civilians are immune from the consequences of an attack just as much as are the enemy's civilians.[147] The issue may arise in occupied territory or disputed territory. It will also arise in coalition operations, where the civilians are nationals of an ally. For example, Fenrick quotes correspondence between Churchill and Roosevelt concerning civilian casualties in France from the pre D-Day allied bombing offensive. Churchill is quoted as having written "this slaughter of *friendly* civilian life"[148] and "this slaughter is among *friendly* people who have committed no crime against us, and not among the German foe, with all their record of cruelty and ruthlessness."[149] From a legal point of view, Churchill was mistaken in emphasising the friendly nature of the civilians. Roosevelt, on the other hand, was not prepared to balance military advantage and the security of allied forces against (even friendly) civilian casualties, as can be shown from this quote:

> No possibility of alleviating adverse French opinion should be overlooked, always provided that there is no reduction of our effectiveness against the enemy at this crucial time.
> However regrettable the attendant loss of civilian lives is, I am not prepared to impose from this distance any restriction on military action by the responsible commanders that in their opinion might militate against the success of 'Overlord' or cause additional loss of life to our Allied forces of Invasion.[150]

Gardam also falls into the trap of looking only at enemy civilians when she writes:

> The key to the dilemma is the subjective nature of assessing proportionality. It requires balancing between two *opposing* goals: the swift achievement of the military goal with the minimum losses of one's own combatants and the protection of the *other party's* civilian population. The military are extremely unwilling to see the balance shift from the emphasis on the former.[151]

Perhaps it is because Gardam has portrayed it in this way that the goals become, in her words, opposing. We have previously seen how assessing the expected collateral damage against the anticipated military advantage is like comparing apples

---

146 Sandoz, Swinarski and Zimmerman (eds), above n 68 (chapter 1), [1909].

147 But see ibid, [1925]. And, of course, it is totally unacceptable to make a distinction between certain ethnic groups as Hezbollah appeared to do in the 2006 armed conflict with Israel—see *Civilians under Assault: Hezbollah's Rocket Attacks on Israel in the 2006 War*, above n 91 (chapter 4), 13.

148 Winston Churchill, 'Closing the Ring (Vol 5, The Second World War)' (1951) 529–30, quoted in Fenrick, 'The Rule of Proportionality and Protocol I in Conventional Warfare', above n 9 (chapter 7), 119 (emphasis added). From the context, I understand 'German foe' to mean Germans generally, not just German combatants.

149 Ibid.

150 Ibid, 119–120. Of course, Roosevelt's decision not to impose restrictions does not, ipso facto, mean that the allied commanders did not themselves comply with the then applicable IHL.

151 Gardam, 'Proportionality and Force in International Law', above n 23 (chapter 6), 409 (emphasis added).

and oranges, and also how it is a subjective assessment by the commander. Not unsurprisingly, when engaged in an armed conflict against 'the enemy' there can be a tendency to distance oneself from the enemy's civilian population. This can lead to an acceptance of high collateral damage. Waxman identified the same point when he wrote:

> U.S. and Republic of Korea (ROK) forces attempting to dislodge invading North Korean forces from Seoul would likely be far less willing to demolish civilian property than if they were attempting to capture Pyongyang.[152]

Kendall provides a good example in his critique on the justifications for killing non-combatants in war. While discussing a book by Walzer on *Just and Unjust Wars*, Kendall writes:

> Walzer addresses the temptation to see the civilians in the enemy country as lesser in value or worth than the civilians in one's own or allied countries. This assimilation of ordinary men, women and children to their governments is a manifestation of what he calls "totalitarian" thinking. At worst, it adopts the likely premise of the enemy that some people are unworthy or, at least, that some are less worthy than others as people.[153]

However, there is a simple way to help commanders and other decision makers assess proportionality and that is by helping them to put the collateral damage issue into terms that are more easily grasped:

> The rule could perhaps be seen in more practical terms if it stated that an aerial attack expected to cause civilian casualties would be acceptable should it have the same degree of approval as a similar action taking place over a part of the country's own territory under enemy occupation, in which case the civilian casualties would be compatriots.[154]

By merely mentally thinking of the expected number of injured and dead civilians as being your own country-men and women, a commander is more likely to be able to appreciate the 'weight' of the expected collateral damage and more easily assess it against the anticipated military advantage. I have used this simple concept in lectures, exercises and operations and can attest to its usefulness in helping military members 'grasp' the concept of applying proportionality rather than merely thinking about it in abstract terms.

---

152 Waxman, above n 56 (chapter 1), 51.

153 Kendall III, above n 8 (chapter 1), 113. It would appear from the context in which this quote appears that the reference to the enemy was a reference to Germany and Japan during Word War II.

154 Javier Gomez, 'The Law of Air Warfare' (1998) 323 *International Review of the Red Cross* <http://www.icrc.org/Web/eng/siteengo.nsf/iwpList167/42F64C9A4212EA07C1256B66005C0BF1> at 4 June 2006.

8.5 Minimum force or proportionality

One particular IHL issue is often misstated. It is common to see statements such as "combatants can only use such force as is reasonably necessary to achieve a military objective",[155] or "the force used must not exceed the minimum required to achieve the military objective."[156] The correct statement of the rule is that the prohibition is on the *effects* from the force used and not the amount of force itself. For example, United States Air Force doctrine states "that the force used is no greater *in effect* on the enemy's personnel and property than needed to achieve his prompt submission (economy of force)".[157] The problem with using the word *force* is that it can lead commanders to think that not only do they have to be concerned with not causing superfluous injury and unnecessary suffering, and limiting collateral damage, but they also have to judge finely which weapon to choose when none of the aforementioned factors is relevant. To put it simply, if the enemy has constructed an unmanned radio relay tower in the wilderness, there is no prohibition on using overwhelming/excessive force to destroy that tower.[158] International humanitarian law places prohibitions on the consequences of the use of force, not on the amount of force used per se. The law requires a commander to choose a means of attack that will achieve the desired military advantage with the least collateral damage. Achieving the desired level of military advantage also includes factoring in the probability of success. It is permissible to use more force where greater certainty of success is desired. As Judge Schwebel stated:

> Nor is it as certain that the use of a conventional depth-charge would discharge the mission successfully; the far greater force of a nuclear weapon *could ensure* destruction of the submarine whereas a conventional depth-charge *might not*.[159]

Equally, proportionality does not mean meeting the enemy with proportional force. For example, in an action between the HMS *Shannon* and USS *Chesapeake* in 1813, the "Captain of the *Shannon* ordered the detachment of a companion frigate, HMS

---

155 Air Power Development Centre, above n 81 (chapter 1), [6.6].

156 Ibid, [6.9].

157 Air Force Pamphlet No. 110-31, *International Law—The Conduct of Armed Conflict and Air Operations*, (1976) [1–6] (emphasis added); quoted with apparent approval in *Needless Deaths in the Gulf War: Civilian Casualties During the Air Campaign and Violations of the Laws of War*, above n 38 (chapter 3). Almost exactly the same wording is used in Fenrick, 'The Rule of Proportionality and Protocol I in Conventional Warfare', above n 9 (chapter 7), 93.

158 Subject not to causing widespread, long-term and severe damage to the natural environment—API, above n 2 (chapter 1), art 35(3).

159 *Nuclear Weapons Case* [1996] ICJ Rep 226, 7 (Separate opinion of Vice-President Schwebel) (emphasis added). While noting that the use of nuclear weapons remains controversial, the point of this quote is to argue that using greater force to ensure success is permissible. So, the issue would also apply to choosing between a 500 lb bomb or a 2000 lb bomb; or dropping two bombs rather than one bomb.

Tenedos, in order not to have an 'unfair' advantage in a ship to ship 'duel'."[160] While chivalrous, the law neither then nor now requires this.

160 McCoubrey, above n 91 (chapter 1), 44. In case the reader is interested, the HMS *Shannon* won.

Chapter 9

Who owns the bomb?

The discussion in the previous chapters has dealt with what law applies to targeting and some of the finer points of that law. This final substantive chapter deals with a rarely discussed issue, namely: how is legal responsibility shared across the personnel involved for individual targeting decisions and execution of those decisions. In other words, who is it that has, or can have, the responsibility for making each of the decisions required by article 57 API when planning and executing an attack. Put colloquially—who owns the bomb?

Targeting decisions and the execution of the use of force in a modern conflict can range from factually very simple to extremely complex. At one end of the spectrum, a soldier may observe a person, conclude that the person is an enemy combatant, and shoot at that person. At the other end of the spectrum, a vast amount of information from various sources may be analysed to determine that an enemy combatant will be in a certain building at a certain time. Further work is then undertaken to determine where that building is geographically located. A pilot, who never sees the information that supported the analysis, is tasked to bomb the building. The attack may be conducted using a laser-guided weapon where the laser designation is provided by yet another person. Particularly in the more complicated cases, a question that may be asked by the 'trigger puller' (ie, the person who conducts the ultimate step in firing or releasing the weapon) is: am I responsible for the targeting decision as I am the one releasing the weapon? In other words, a pilot wants to know whether he or she is legally responsible for the assessment of the target as a military objective, the proportionality of the attack, and all the other associated IHL rules that apply to targeting decisions. Rogers raises this question in the following quote in his discussion of the 1999 NATO air campaign in Kosovo.

> Despite problems caused by cloud cover, care was taken to ensure that only military objectives were hit. There were, inevitably, some instances of collateral damage. But, by and large, things seemed to go well until an attack on a vehicle column by NATO aircraft operating at 15,000 feet raised an important question about the law of armed conflict: what is the precise legal obligation on an attacker to identify the target as a military objective before he launches his attack?[1]

That exact question is dealt with in this chapter. An IHL 6-step targeting process is set out, where the first four steps constitute the planning phase of an attack, and

1 Rogers, 'Zero-casualty warfare', above n 94 (chapter 3) (footnotes omitted).

the last two steps comprise the attack phase. The intent behind this IHL 6-step targeting process is not to set out additional obligations to those already found in IHL, but rather the process is meant as a way of conveniently expressing some of those obligations. This chapter concludes with applying the IHL 6-step targeting process to some case studies and an explanation of how the process can be reduced to a useful aide-memoire for use in combat.

9.1 Planning and executing an attack

To determine individual responsibility in a complex targeting situation, it is useful to break down the obligations imposed by API and to set those obligations out in a chronological sequence.

First, article 57(2)(a)(i) API requires that those who plan or decide an attack are to do everything feasible to verify that an objective is a military objective and that the objective is not subject to special protection. There are two issues to consider. The first involves locating and observing the potential target and the surrounding area.[2] This is, in effect, the information gathering phase of a targeting decision. This step is critical to enable the making of decisions that are required by article 57(2)(a) API.[3] The second issue is to take the information gathered and then apply the legal tests set out in API. For example, having observed a bridge and the movements of enemy personnel, it is then a legal step[4] to determine from the information available whether the bridge is a military objective. If the bridge is assessed as being a military objective, consideration is then given as to whether it is an object protected from attack (eg, is the bridge a historic monument within the meaning of that term in article 53 API?).[5] So, there are two steps. The first being information gathering and the second being information assessment. In reality, the steps might

2 "The precision revolution has made it possible for air power to put a bomb within feet of any point on earth. Of course, having the right intelligence to select that point remains a challenge"—Charles Dunlap, Jr, 'America's asymmetric advantage' (2006) September *Armed Forces Journal* 20, 24.

3 It would seem that the fact that this step is not always followed (for example, in the dropping of submunitions to clear a safe-path for helicopters or in counter-battery fire) is what leads to criticism by Human Rights Watch—*Off Target: The Conduct of the War and Civilian Casualties in Iraq*, above n 91 (chapter 4), 83 and 94. Human Rights Watch note that the United Kingdom "required forward observation even in the case of counter-battery fire." (ibid, 95) I note that as long ago as 1982, Bothe, Partsch and Solf recognised that interdiction fires would be lawful under API if "intelligence information shows that these critical points are heavily used *in the circumstances ruling at the time*" (Bothe, Partsch and Solf, above n 87 (chapter 1), 308); subject, of course, to not causing excessive collateral damage. See also Sandoz, Swinarski and Zimmerman (eds), above n 68 (chapter 1), [1955].

4 By 'legal step', I mean that the facts must be assessed in light of the applicable law to determine whether an object is a *lawful* military objective. I do not mean that it is necessarily a step for lawyers to make.

5 It is implicit in this step that the entirety of the rules concerning objects protected from attack are considered. For example, an object may be indispensable to the survival of the civilian population (API, above n 2 (chapter 1), art 54(2)) but the object is being used in direct support of military action by the defending party and an attack on the object is not expected to leave the civilian population with inadequate food or water as to cause

be cyclic in that information might be gathered and after assessment further information gathered to enable further assessment. I note here that those who make the decisions need not be the same persons who collected the information.[6] In other words, a commander can rely on information from third parties when determining whether an object is a military objective.

Second, article 57(2)(a)(ii) API requires that those who plan or decide an attack are to take all feasible precautions in the choice of means and methods of attack to avoid, and in any event minimise, collateral damage. The important point about this step is that it might be performed well before the attack itself. For example, the decision to use a precision-guided or unguided bomb will often be made before an aircraft takes off. Even more so, the type of force to be used (eg aircraft, ground assault, special forces or naval bombardment) is a decision about the means and methods of an attack. At the other end of the spectrum, an infantry soldier may choose, subject to his or her orders, between a grenade, a rifle or hand-to-hand combat.[7]

Third, article 57(2)(a)(i) API requires that those who plan or decide an attack are to determine whether, after article 57(2)(a)(ii) API has been complied with, the expected collateral damage is proportional. The most important issue with this step is that it comes after taking feasible precautions to avoid, and in any event minimise, collateral damage. An attack is not lawful where the attack is expected to cause proportional collateral damage if it was nonetheless feasible to take steps that would result in an expectation of causing even less collateral damage.

These four steps can be thought of as the *planning* phase of a targeting decision. From there, one moves into what can be termed the *execute* phase of an attack. During this phase, article 57(2)(b) API requires that the attack be cancelled or suspended if, contrary to expectations and the assessments made during the planning phase, it becomes apparent that the object is not a military objective, the object is subject to special protection from attack, or the expected collateral damage will be excessive (ie, disproportional). This obligation is imposed upon anyone who has effective control over the attack. This might be the person conducting the attack or it might be a commander who can issue orders to the person conducting the attack.

There is, though, another aspect to the execute phase, which is the actual execution of the attack. During the execution of an attack, there is an obligation to conduct the attack itself with care.[8] This step gives practical effect to the obligations set out in API. For example, this step reflects the fact that appropriate skill must be used in firing a weapon such that the attack is not indiscriminate. Appropriate skill means both the skills possessed by the actual combatant (not a hypothetical combatant), along with what is appropriate in the circumstances. This step can be considered as one aspect of choosing a 'means and methods' of combat that improve

---

starvation or forced movement of the civilian population (ibid, art 54(3)(b)). In such a case, the object is not an object protected from attack.

6 See Sandoz, Swinarski and Zimmerman (eds), above n 68 (chapter 1), [1952].

7 See section 7.1 for discussion on whether the activities of a single soldier can amount to an attack for the purposes of, inter alia, ibid, art 57.

8 Ibid, art 57(1).

the chances of actually hitting the desired target;[9] noting that we are considering the means and methods available to the particular combatant executing the attack, and not all the means and methods that were available to the commander who planned the attack.

The wording that is used to express the execution of the attack step is important. A person executing an attack is not under an obligation to take all possible steps to maximise the accuracy of an attack. Rather, the person is obligated to take such steps as are feasible in the tactical situation so as to take care in executing the attack to minimise collateral damage. For example, an infantry soldier who is under fire from enemy combatants cannot be expected to take the same steps to improve the accuracy of his or her shot as would be expected of a sniper in a camouflaged position whose presence is unknown to the enemy. In an air force context, the differences in permissible attack methods might be based on whether the defending party has ground-based air defences or fighter aircraft. Equally, some combatants will just be naturally better, or will have been better trained, than others. However, the choice of methods of attack to minimise collateral damage is part of the planning phase. During the execute phase, the obligation rests on the combatant conducting the attack, and by that stage, the law takes the combatant as the law finds him or her. If the target is in an isolated place well away from civilians and civilian objects, then the level of care required in conducting the attack is less. The issue when conducting the attack is not hitting the target as such, but rather not missing the target in such a way as to cause more collateral damage than what would be caused by accurately hitting the target. Finally, because presumably increased military advantage is gained from accurately hitting the target compared with missing, taking care to hit accurately the target is an aspect of complying with proportionality where collateral damage is anticipated from the conduct of a successful attack.

The other important point about the wording of the execution of the attack step is that in conducting the attack, the emphasis is on accurately attacking the desired target to the extent that not doing so may cause collateral damage. This has a number of consequences. First, the target itself may not be the desired point for the impact of a weapon.[10] For example, it may be preferable to aim a bomb between two small buildings with the desire of damaging both rather than aiming at one of the buildings. With an airburst weapon, the goal is for the weapon to detonate above (and not necessarily directly above) the target. If using a laser-guided weapon, the target itself may be a poor reflector and accordingly a point near the target must be illuminated.[11] Second, there may be occasions when to maximise

9 See generally ibid, art 51(4).

10 The desired point of aim is sometimes termed the 'desired mean point of impact' ('DMPI') or simply the 'aim point'.

11 For example, "[a]iming the [laser] designator into tunnels and other targets causes laser energy to be absorbed. Instead, the operator must aim the designator slightly above a tunnel opening which will allow a munition to impact at a critical point." (*Tactics, Techniques, and Procedures for the Strike/Recon Platoon (Striker)*, US Army Field Artillery School <http://sill-www.army.mil/fdic/doctrine/task%20force%202000/striker/chap7.htm#c7_2> at 23 March 2006) Interestingly, "[f]or munitions like laser-guided bombs that tend to impact short of the point being designated, this type of designation could guide the bomb into the tunnel opening." (ibid)

the probability of hitting the desired aim point, the weapon needs to be released in unusual circumstances. For example, certain laser-guided weapons need a certain amount of flight time to improve the accuracy of the glide path. If the target is lasered too early, the weapon loses energy in the glide path and will fall short.[12] In such circumstances, where there has already been a pass of the target to confirm identification, it might be more accurate to release the weapon on a subsequent pass prior to the target being completely visible. The target can then be lasered with the bomb already in flight as the target becomes visible.[13]

9.2 IHL 6-step targeting process[14]

As shown in the previous section, there are four steps that comprise the planning phase of an attack and two steps that comprise the execute phase of an attack. These steps can be expressed as a simple IHL 6-step targeting process as follows:

1. Locate and observe the potential target and its surrounding area.
2. Assess whether the target is a valid military objective and that it is otherwise unprotected from attack by IHL.
3. Take all feasible precautions to minimise collateral damage.
4. Assess whether any expected collateral damage is proportional (ie, not excessive) to the anticipated military advantage to be gained from the attack.
5. Take such care as is appropriate in the tactical situation to release or fire the weapon to achieve the best possible chance of hitting the selected aim point.[15]
6. Cancel or suspend the attack should it become apparent that any one of the assessments made under steps 2 or 4 is no longer valid.[16]

---

12 See generally *Laser Guided Bombs* (2000) Federation of American Scientists <http://www.fas.org/man/dod-101/sys/smart/lgb.htm> at 23 March 2006.

13 An example of this occurring in the 2002 Afghanistan conflict is described in Mark Bowden, 'The Kabul-ki Dance', *The Atlantic Monthly* (Boston) November 2002 <http://www.theatlantic.com/doc/prem/200211/bowden> at 2 March 2005.

14 The work in this chapter arose out of a series of questions and answer asked of the author in late 2002 and early 2003. I would like to acknowledge the assistance of Squadron Leader Pat Keane and the staff at the Australian Government Solicitor who were involved in refining the final wording and number of steps in the IHL targeting process. Subsequently it has come to my attention that Rogers has summarised an attacker's obligations into eight points, and further re-expressed those obligations into a seven point "offensive operations checklist"—Rogers, *Law on the Battlefield*, above n 84 (chapter 1), 113–7. While there are some similarities, the purpose behind Roger's summary appears to be for military manuals, whereas the IHL 6-Step Targeting Process is aimed at the tactical level. Rogers's summary does not have anything similar to steps 1 and 5 in the IHL 6-Step Targeting Process. These steps are important to one of the purposes behind the IHL 6-Step Targeting Process, which is to assist with allocating or ascertaining responsibility for various aspects of a targeting decision.

15 The tactical situation encompasses both the threat to the attacker as well as the likelihood of causing collateral damage by an inaccurate attack.

16 Step 6 can occur at anytime and can be undertaken either by planning staff, a commander, or the person executing the attack (eg, the pilot of a strike aircraft).

The above process was adopted by Australia during the 2003 Gulf War pursuant to a targeting directive issued by the Chief of the Defence Force.[17]

The intent behind this IHL 6-step targeting process is not to set out additional obligations to those already found in IHL. Rather, the process is meant as a way of conveniently expressing some of those obligations for the purpose of determining and allocating responsibility for compliance. Also, the process does not purport to be a complete statement of all IHL obligations. For example, it does not address the lawfulness of using a particular weapon. It could be easily modified to cover additional issues but that would be at the expense of simplicity. As the process is primarily aimed at the tactical level, it can normally be assumed that only lawful weapons will be available for use. As currently expressed, the IHL 6-step targeting process can be reduced to a card or other aide-memoire. The importance of this point will be explored further later in this chapter.

Having set out the IHL 6-step targeting process, it is useful to look at how it can be used in practice.

9.3 Specific examples

There is an interesting quote from the 1999 NATO air campaign in Kosovo.

> General Marani answered press questions about attacks from an altitude of 15,000 feet. He said that target identification was more complex and was carried out correlating more information, not only what the pilot could see but other information he had before leaving and before arriving in the area, which he received from other aircraft, from other weapons systems not necessarily on board his aircraft. In other words, it was, he said, very much a team effort and not a case of a single pilot acting on his own initiative.[18]

This is an example of the sharing of responsibility for step 1—locating and observing the potential target and its surrounding area. However, based on this quote alone, the pilot remains responsible for steps 2 through to 6. But, this would not always be the case. Fenrick has stated:

> It is probable that, in all but the most blatant cases of indiscriminate attack, subordinates would be entitled to assume that their superiors had carried out the attack precautions specified in Article 57 of Protocol I and, as a result, they could not be held personally liable for any violations which occurred as a result of superior orders.[19]

---

17 Houston, above n 4 (chapter 1). Step 5 has been slightly re-worded based on further discussions with Pat Keane (see footnote 14). The original wording was: 'Release (or fire) the weapon to achieve the best possible chance of impacting the selected aim point commensurate with the tactical situation.'

18 Rogers, 'Zero-casualty warfare', above n 94 (chapter 3).

19 Fenrick, 'The Rule of Proportionality and Protocol I in Conventional Warfare', above n 9 (chapter 7), 115.

When looked at it terms of the IHL 6-step targeting process, this statement can be interpreted as meaning that where procedures are in place for superiors (or a superior headquarters) to conduct steps 1 to 4 then the member carrying out the attack is responsible for only steps 5 and 6. This would occur with pre-planned strike missions on fixed targets, often called deliberate targeting. Deliberate targeting is where a target is planned well prior to the attack. This may be weeks, months or even longer before a likely attack. Indeed, there may never be an attack on that target as target development may occur in peacetime as well as armed conflict.

For example, a usual process for managing fixed targets (eg, buildings, bridges and other non-movable objects) is a deliberate and lengthy process. First, a target folder will be produced. This target folder may be produced long before a likely attack. For present purposes, this part of the process can be summarised as involving the collection of information on potential targets, assessing whether the proposed target is a military objective, identifying any collateral damage concerns, and assessing and recommending ways of attacking the target. These steps will be done by planning staff and will have only the most general input from commanders. A commander will not have 'approved' any of the targets at this stage, so it could be argued that the assessment as a military objective is perhaps better thought of as tentative classification subject to confirmation by a commander (a step discussed below).[20] At this time, collateral damage concerns are identified but proportionality is not yet assessed.

During Operation FALCONER, the deliberate targeting process involved each target being reviewed by a team comprising an intelligence officer, an imagery analyst and a legal officer (ie, a military lawyer).[21] Under a deliberate targeting process, if a target is subsequently identified for attack, a commander will be briefed and the commander will determine or approve the broad outline of how the attack is to be conducted, will approve a certain level of collateral damage, and, of course, will confirm that the object is a military objective at that stage of the armed conflict. In an air force context, that target might then appear on an ATO for attack. By that time the aircraft type and weapon load may have also be determined. Assuming that there are policies and procedures in place to support the above, the aircrew executing the attack can then rely upon the work already done to be satisfied that steps

20 As an object is legally either a military objective or not a military objective, if insufficient information is available to confirm a classification then the object should be classified not as a 'possible military objective' but rather as 'not a military objective'. Of course, in these circumstances, and for a sufficiently important enough target, further intelligence gathering would be warranted. Accordingly, the classification scheme should also identify those objects that warrant further intelligence gathering and analysis. Despite the views just expressed, we should be careful not to quibble. The application of IHL is inherently practical. The real issue is to avoid attacks on non-military objectives, and as long a military planning process achieves this, it is not important whether the use of language is 'pure'. However, it is my view that the correct use of terms can assist with ensuring that a correct process is adopted. In any event, the classification would have to be subject to review closer to the time of a proposed attack as whether there is a military advantage to be gained from attacking the object can only be determined in the circumstances ruling at the time—API, above n 2 (chapter 1), art 52(2).

21 Houston, above n 4 (chapter 1).

1 to 4 of the IHL 6-step targeting process have been complied with. Accordingly, if the aircrew comply with steps 5 and 6 then they would not be legally responsible if they accurately hit a target that was not a military objective but had been assigned to them incorrectly.[22]

One further point should be made before leaving this example. Fenrick refers to subordinates being "entitled to assume that their *superiors* had carried out the attack precautions".[23] If the IHL 6-step targeting process is adopted, it is not just a question of following superior orders (that are not manifestly unlawful). Rather, it is matter of a division of responsibility for complying with IHL in the targeting process. Looked at in that way, a superior officer could rely on the advice of a subordinate. For example, a commissioned officer could rely upon the advice from a non-commissioned officer (who might be in a better viewing position) that the object being observed was an enemy truck or that the target area was clear of civilians.

Deliberate targeting is not the only time when some or all of steps 1 to 4 might be completed by a third party. For example, there are cases in the 2001–3 Afghanistan conflict where a Forward Air Controller ('FAC')[24] identified and assessed the target. The pilot then dropped laser-guided bombs blind through clouds. The FAC was lasing the target, so that when the bomb came through the cloud cover the bomb tracked to the identified target.[25] In this case, the FAC would be responsible for steps 1 to 4. However, the aircrew still have the obligations for steps 5 and 6 (with step 6 being shared concurrently with the FAC). This example provides an interesting case of how step 5 is important in its own right. With a laser-guided bomb, the bomb must be released within a launch envelope to ensure that the guidance system can track the reflected laser energy (sometimes termed the 'basket' into which the weapon must be dropped).[26] In the example referred to above, the aircrew needed to determine the launch envelope. But, to complicate matters, the FAC was providing latitude and longitude coordinates in degrees, minutes and seconds. However, the United States Air Force uses degrees, minutes and thousandths of a minute. The weapon system operator in the aircraft had to convert the coordinates with a pencil, a piece of paper and the calculator on his watch in order to determine the correct launch envelope.[27]

In the above example of the FAC lasing a target under cloud cover, I said the FAC would be responsible for steps 1 to 4. This is because based on the material available in the article, it appeared as though the aircrew did not complete any of those steps. It would have been, of course, impossible for the aircrew to complete step 1 and impractical for them to complete step 2. While they could partly contrib-

22 See *OTP Report*, above n 90 (chapter 1), [85].

23 Fenrick, 'The Rule of Proportionality and Protocol I in Conventional Warfare', above n 9 (chapter 7), 115 (my emphasis).

24 Another term is use to describe a similar role is 'terminal attack controller', often preceded with either 'ground' or 'joint', and then abbreviated as GTAC or JTAC. The forward air controller may also be airborne, and is then termed FAC(A).

25 Bowden, above n 13 (chapter 9). See also Dunlap, 'America's asymmetric advantage', above n 2 (chapter 9), 24.

26 See generally *Laser Guided Bombs*, above n 12 (chapter 9).

27 Bowden, above n 13 (chapter 9).

ute to step 3, the prime responsibility rested with the FAC. Technically, the aircrew could have completed step 4 if enough information was relayed to them but this would have been impractical. However, it cannot be assumed that merely because a FAC is present that the aircrew are absolved of steps 1 to 4. For example, the standard "9-line brief"[28] used by many Western militaries only explicitly mentions that the FAC will, relevantly, identify the target and determine the presence of "friendlies".[29] It is not immediately apparent that friendlies extends beyond meaning friendly forces to include collateral damage. In such a case, the FAC may not be completing steps 3 and 4. Accordingly, policies and procedures must be confirmed to ensure that each group in a targeting process is aware of their responsibilities and, equally importantly, that each group is aware of what the other group believes to be its responsibilities.

9.4 IHL 6-step targeting process—aide-memoire

The advantage of reducing the IHL 6-step process to an aide-memoire is that in a complex and varied targeting environment, the responsibilities of the various groups can be outlined on the aide-memoire. For example, an aide-memoire card may indicate that:

(a) for fixed targets on an air task order, the aircrew are responsible for steps 5 and 6;

(b) for targets assigned by a qualified FAC, the aircrew are responsible for steps 3 to 6; and

(c) for targets assigned by a person who is not a qualified FAC (or similar), the aircrew are responsible for steps 2 to 6.

These three sub-paragraphs are only examples, and the exact responsibility for the various steps may vary in different circumstances. For example, in a large coalition a combatant from Australia may be authorized to accept the designation of an object as a military objective and not otherwise protected under IHL (ie, the completion of step 2) only from allies with the same IHL obligations as Australia. In that case, FAC from one of those allied countries could complete step 2. However, if operating with a FAC from one of the allied countries with different IHL obligations, then the aircrew would retain final responsibility for step 2. Alternatively, the Australian combatant may be authorized to accept designation from an ally with different IHL obligations (the United States of America is an obvious example). This may occur because even though IHL obligations may differ, the rules of engagement of the ally may be sufficiently prescriptive as to limit the ally from determining that an object is a military objective except in circumstances that equate to Australia's legal obligations. To give a partial example, the rules of engagement of a military belonging to a State not a party to API may include a rule stating that notwithstanding not being party to API, "works and installations containing dangerous

28 The 9-line brief is given by a FAC to provide the aircrew with essential information for execution of the mission.

29 See *Tactics, Techniques, and Procedures for the Strike / Recon Platoon (Striker)*, above n 11 (chapter 9). In particular, see figure 7-9, Example of 9-Line Brief.

forces" as defined in article 56 API are not to be attacked except in accordance with the requirements of API.

The IHL 6-step targeting process is not intended as a replacement for existing targeting process and methodologies. It is, rather, more of an overlay by which other process can be checked to ensure that all legal obligations are being fulfilled. It also provides a mechanism by which responsibility for particular legal obligations can be identified and assigned. In other words, the IHL 6-step targeting process provides a means to determine who owns the bomb, and has that owner fulfilled his or her obligations. By analysing a targeting decision through the lens of IHL 6-step targeting process, it is possible to determine who had, or should have had, responsibility for what. It is hoped that this may improve targeting outcomes and compliance with IHL.

Chapter 10

Conclusions and implications

> Here seems to be the proper place to bring this work to a conclusion, without in the least presuming that every thing has been said, which might be said on the subject: but sufficient has been produced to lay a foundation, on which another, if he pleases, may raise a more noble and extensive edifice, an addition and improvement that will provoke no jealousy, but rather be entitled to thanks.[1]

10.1 Introduction

Armed conflict is inherently about using force to achieve desired goals. As IHL regulates the means and methods that a belligerent may adopt to achieve its desired goals, there will inevitably be disagreements over the interpretation of the relevant IHL rules. When it comes to the rules that regulate targeting, the main difficulties that arise are over what is a lawful target and what is proportional collateral damage when compared to the military advantage to be gained from the attack. In this study, I have endeavoured to provide a detailed analysis of these issues.

10.2 Conclusions about the research problem

The sources of law that regulate targeting during armed conflict are uncontroversial. For the purposes of this study, I limited myself to reviewing the law that would be applicable to Australia. It is not difficult to identify the treaty law that applies to target selection and the concept of proportionality. However, issues arise when that law is applied to particular scenarios. Essentially, this is because the applicable law is stated in broad terms. It is generally recognised that broad terms are adopted in multi-lateral IHL treaties with a view to finding wide acceptance in the international community.[2] However, this approach poses difficulties when the articles of treaties need to be applied. In this respect, I refer to the opening remarks of Schachter when in 1992 he chaired a panel of distinguished practitioners and academics[3] gathered to discuss proportionality and necessity:

1 Grotius, above n 1 (chapter 1).

2 Boivin, above n 19 (chapter 1), i.

3 The panel was composed of Oscar Schachter, Frits Kalshoven, Francoise Hampson, Yoram Dinstein, Ruth Wedgwood and Fred Green.

> centuries of discussion by philosophers and jurists about the meanings of necessity and proportionality in human affairs do not seem to have produced general definitions capable of answering concrete issues.[4]

Mindful of Schachter's remarks, I looked at not only the words of individual articles of treaties but also the context of those words and the general principles of IHL. In my study, I discussed two broad areas of targeting law under IHL. Those areas are what are lawful targets and the law concerning proportional collateral damage. I also looked at two particular issues of the application of targeting law. First, I considered how sanctioning of participation in an armed conflict by the UN Security Council might affect the range of lawful military objectives available to a belligerent. Second, I set out a process by which legal responsibility for targeting decisions can be assessed in a complex decision making environment.

Lawful targets can be split into two groups. The first group comprises human targets, the second group all other targets. Different rules apply to each group for the purpose of determining whether someone or something is a lawful target. However, while the specific rules are different, in each case those rules are governed by the general principle of military necessity. In the context of targeting, this principle is expressed in the preamble to the *St Petersburg Declaration*: "The only legitimate object which States should endeavour to accomplish during war is to weaken the military forces of the enemy".[5] Reference back to this guiding principle is useful when trying to resolve disputed interpretations of specific rules concerning lawful targets.

By virtue of military necessity, combatants are lawful targets under IHL. I argue that the only exception to this is when a combatant is *hors de combat*. Other than when *hors de combat*, a combatant is subject to lawful attack at all times; this is regardless of whether the combatant is at that time posing a threat to the attacker or other belligerents associated with the attacker.

Unless by their actions they have become lawful combatants,[6] civilians enjoy general protection from direct attack. Civilians lose this protection in only one circumstance—by taking a direct part in hostilities. The test under article 52(2) API for objects becoming military objectives is not applicable to civilians becoming targets. When considering the meaning of taking a direct part in hostilities as used in API, it seems clear that taking a direct part in hostilities involves more than mere participation in the war effort. Accordingly, the mere fact that a civilian contributes to the military action of one party and an attack on whom would offer a military advantage to the attacker, does not make the civilian a lawful target. I argue for a conservative view of what amounts to taking a direct part in hostilities. It is my view that taking a direct part in hostilities is limited to actions that "by their nature or purpose are likely to cause actual harm to the personnel or materiel of the enemy armed forces"[7] or actions that are intimately linked to such actions. This latter group of actions would include tactical intelligence gathering and delivering ammunition

4 Schachter, above n 1 (chapter 7), 39.

5 *St Petersburg Declaration*, above n 64 (chapter 1).

6 For example, by joining a recognized militia or taking part in a *levee en masse*.

7 *Prosecutor v Galic, (Trial Chamber)* Case No IT-98-29-T (5 December 2003) [48].

to the very point at which it will be used but would not include strategic intelligence gathering (or analysis) or general distribution of munitions in a rear area.

An object becomes a military objective only where the attack offers a military advantage. The test set out in article 52(2) API does not allow for an object to be 'deemed' a military objective. So, there are no classes of objects that are ipso facto military objectives. Rather, each object must be assessed against the two-pronged test set out in article 52(2) API.[8] Consistent with the principle of military necessity, I argue that military advantage does not extend to the political or strategic goals of the armed conflict but is limited to actions that directly or indirectly weaken the military capability of the enemy. An aspect of this is that defending one's own combatants is a military advantage as weakening the enemy is not possible if all of one's own combatants are disabled first. Similar reasoning applies to protecting military equipment from destruction. This can be expressed as a test of general application as follows: the defensive range of activities that amount to a military advantage are those that preserve the capability to conduct military operations. As these points are fundamental to decisions as to what are lawful targets, they are extremely important points when considering the law that applies to targeting. Finally, when determining whether an object is a military objective, it is my conclusion that a commander is required to take all practicable steps to obtain information to enable the making of a good-faith assessment. What steps are considered practical will depend upon the difficulty in obtaining the necessary information. The level of verification required to reduce doubt, and the degree of acceptable doubt, will vary depending upon the likely adverse consequences of a wrong decision. Taking all of the above into consideration, a commander is then required to come to a *reasonable belief* about whether the object meets the criteria for being a military objective.

While there is little disagreement that IHL applies with equal force to a belligerent operating in a UN sanctioned armed conflict, it is my argument that the nature of the armed conflict may have an impact on the application of individual laws. In particular, where a UNSCR sets out the goals of a military operation, the range of military objectives may be constrained by the UNSCR. Primarily, it would not be lawful to attack a target if an attack on that target did not contribute in some way to achieving the goals of the UNSCR. However, the reverse is not true and targets cannot be attacked to achieve UNSCR goals unless that target is also a lawful target under IHL.

The concept of lawfully causing expected injury or damage to third parties and their property is a unique feature of IHL. Not unsurprisingly, the rule generates extensive discussion. It is not possible to produce an equation that will give an objective answer to whether any given level of collateral damage is or is not proportional to the military advantage of an attack. The answer to each scenario is ultimately a good faith, subjective decision to be made by the commander authorising the attack. The most that can be done is to set out clearly the legal issues involved. Perhaps the single most useful point to keep in mind is that the nationality of the civilians affected by an attack is irrelevant when assessing proportionality. When

8 In summary, the two prongs are whether makes an effective contribution to military action of the defender *and* whether an attack on the object will, in the circumstances ruling at the time, offer a definite military advantage to the attacker.

determining whether the amount of expected collateral damage from an attack is proportional to the anticipated military advantage from that attack, a commander should ask whether he or she would authorise the attack over his or her own territory.

When considering the military advantage to be gained from an attack, a commander is entitled to consider how the individual attack fits into the broader operation as a whole. However, in my view this does not extend to considering the overall campaign or the reason for the armed conflict. There remains disagreement as to how to classify the security of the attacking force. Is it part of the military advantage to be gained from the attack? I argue that the security of the attacking force is a lawful consideration and forms part of the military advantage to be gained from an attack. Accordingly, the security of the attacking force is an aspect of the proportionality equation. However, there may be a point where steps taken to protect the attacking force so increase the expected collateral damage that the only options that can be considered are to accept more risk to the attacking force or cancel the attack.

With the exception of civilians taking a direct part in hostilities, all civilians are counted as collateral damage. As I argue that a civilian working in a school, working in a munitions factory, or acting as a human shield is not taking a direct part in hostilities, it is my conclusion that these categories of civilians are counted as collateral damage.[9] Related to the previous point, I conclude that there is no graduation in the 'worth' of human life and, therefore, each civilian is worth as much as any other in the collateral damage equation. However, the same is not true of buildings and other objects—objects do have different values in the proportionality equation. How, or even whether, to consider indirect harm arising from an attack (ie, consequential or second tier effects) in the proportionality equation remains a debated point in IHL discussions. I reach the conclusion that indirect harm must be considered, but only where those consequences are an expected result of the attack.

Legal responsibility for IHL decisions exists at both the State and individual level. Targeting decisions in a modern conflict range from the factually very simple to extremely complex, and individual decisions might be shared across personnel. When planning and executing an attack, there is an obligation to assess the target as a military objective, determine the proportionality of the attack, and then execute the attack. To determine individual responsibility in a complex targeting situation, I have devised and set out the main legal obligations in an IHL 6-step targeting process. This process encompasses four steps that comprise the planning phase of an attack, and two steps that comprise the execute phase of an attack. Those steps are as follows:

1. Locate and observe the potential target and its surrounding area.
2. Assess whether the target is a valid military objective and that it is otherwise unprotected from attack by IHL.
3. Take all feasible precautions to minimise collateral damage.

---

9 The one exception to this is where acting as a human shield so impedes military operations as to amount to taking a direct part in hostilities.

4. Assess whether any expected collateral damage is proportional (ie, not excessive) to the anticipated military advantage to be gained from the attack.
5. Take such care as is appropriate in the tactical situation to release or fire the weapon to achieve the best possible chance of hitting the selected aim point.
6. Cancel or suspend the attack should it become apparent that any one of the assessments made under steps 2 or 4 is no longer valid.

This IHL 6-step targeting process is not in addition to the obligations of IHL but rather is a means of conveniently expressing some of those obligations. The process is not a complete statement of all IHL obligations. For example, weapon selection and the giving of warnings are not addressed. The reasons for this is that these issues will often be conducted separately and as currently expressed the IHL 6-step targeting process can be reduced to a card or other aide-memoire for use in the field. The advantage of reducing the IHL 6-step targeting process to an aide-memoire is that in a complex and varied targeting environment, the responsibilities of the various groups can be outlined on the aide-memoire. The IHL 6-step targeting process is not a replacement for existing targeting process and methodologies. Rather, it is an overlay by which other processes can be checked to ensure that all legal obligations are being fulfilled. It also provides a mechanism by which responsibility for particular legal obligations can be identified and assigned.

10.3 Further research

While I have discussed some aspects of the law concerning proportionality, and in particular what can and cannot be considered on each side of the equation, the fundamental issue remains that it is difficult to determine exactly what is *excessive* in any given case. It would be useful to undertake comparative research across various legal regimes to see how similar issues have been dealt with in either domestic law or other areas of international law.

A very interesting issue is how is legal responsibility attributed in a coalition environment? At the strategic level, does each coalition partner share responsibility for the decisions of other coalition partners? At the operational and tactical level, can decision-making be shared? In particular, how, if at all, might the steps in the IHL 6-step targeting process be performed in a coalition operation?

10.4 Final words

Despite the long history of IHL and the fundamental importance of the topics, it was only with the adoption of API that some of the most fundamental concepts were codified. Those concepts are what is a military objective, when does a civilian lose protection from direct attack, what level of incidental damage is lawful when conducting an attack, and what other precautions must be taken when conducting an attack? Notwithstanding this codification, further work is still required to provide clear and authorative interpretation of many of these rules. The purpose of this work has been to assist Australian military commanders with the application of these concepts and the codified rules.

The importance of IHL cannot be overstated. Civilians and civilian property have few protections when the guns roar. To the extent that commanders and soldiers of good conscience wish to reduce the impact of military operations on civilians, they should be assisted with clear rules and practical legal advice on how to apply those rules in an armed conflict; and for those who do not or choose not to act honourably, then the rules of IHL should be clearly ascertainable by courts and military tribunals to facilitate prosecutions. I hope that this book will contribute to those goals.

Bibliography

1. Articles/Books/Reports

af Jochnick, Chris and Normand, Roger, 'The Legitimation of Violence: A Critical History of the Laws of War' (1994) 35 *Harvard International Law Journal* 49

Air Power Development Centre, Royal Australian Air Force AAP 1003, *Operations Law for RAAF Commanders* (2nd edition, 2004)

ASIL Proceedings, *Implementing Limitations on the Use of Force: The Doctrine of Proportionality and Necessity* (1992)

Barber, Peter, 'Scuds, Shelters and Retreating soldiers: The Laws of Aerial Bombardment and the Gulf War' (1993) XXXI No.4 *Alberta Law Review* 662

Benvenuti, Paolo, 'The ICTY Prosecutor and the Review of the NATO Bombing Campaign against the Federal Republic of Yugoslavia' (2001) Vol 12 No 3 *European Journal of International Law* 503

Bialke, Joseph, 'Al-Qaeda & Taliban unlawful combatant detainees, unlawful belligerency, and the international laws of armed conflict' (2004) 55 *Air Force Law Review* 1

Bialke, Joseph, 'United Nations Peace Operations: Applicable Norms and the Application of the Law of Armed Conflict' (2000) 50 *Air Force Law Review* 1

Bothe, Michael, 'The Protection of the Civilian Population and NATO Bombing on Yugoslavia: Comments on a Report to the Prosecutor of the ICTY' (2001) Vol 12 No 3 *European Journal of International Law* 531

Bothe, Michael, Partsch, Karl and Solf, Waldemar, *New Rules for Victims of Armed Conflicts: Commentary on the two 1977 Protocols Additional to the Geneva Conventions of 1949* (1982)

Brown, Bernard, 'The Proportionality Principle in the Humanitarian Law of Warfare: Recent Efforts at Codification' (1976) 10 *Cornell International Law Journal* 134

Brownlie, Ian, *Principles of Public International Law* (6th ed, 2003)

Canestaro, Nathan, 'Legal and Policy Constraints on the conduct of Aerial Precision Warfare' (2004) 37 *Vanderbilt Journal of Transnational Law* 431

Cassese, Antonio, *International Law* (2001)

Cassese, Antonio, 'The Martens Clause: Half a Loaf or simply Pie in the Sky' (2000) 11 *European Journal of International Law* 187

Chetail, Vincent, 'The contribution of the International Court of Justice to international humanitarian law' (2003) 850 *International Review of the Red Cross* 235

Clark, Wesley, *Waging Modern War: Bosnia, Kosovo, and the Future of Combat* (2001)

Delissen, Astrid and Tanja, Gerard (eds), *Humanitarian law of armed conflict: Challenges ahead: Essays in honour of Frits Kalshoven* (1991)

de Lupis, Ingrid, *The Law of War* (1987)

Dinstein, Yoram, *The Conduct of Hostilities under the Law of International Armed Conflict* (2004)

Dinstein, Yoram, 'The Thirteenth Waldemar A. Solf Lecture in International Law' (2000) 166 *Military Law Review* 93

Dinstein, Yoram, *War, Aggression and Self-Defence* (4th ed, 2005)

Dunlap, Jr, Charles, 'America's asymmetric advantage' (2006) September *Armed Forces Journal* 20

Dunlap, Jr, Charles, 'The End of Innocence: Rethinking Noncombatancy in the Post-Kosovo Era' (2000) Vol XXXVIII:3 *Strategic Review* 9

Dunlap, Jr, Charles, 'The Revolution in Military Legal Affairs: Air Force Legal Professionals in 21st Century Conflicts' (2001) 51 *Air Force Law Review* 293

Eade, Charles, *The Dawn of Liberation: War Speeches by the Right Honourable Winston S. Churchill 1944* (1945)

Faite, Alexandre and Grenier, Jeremie (eds), *Report of the Expert Meeting on Multinational Peace Operations: Issues Relating to the Application of International Law* (2004) International Committee of the Red Cross <http://www.icrc.org/web/eng/siteengo.nsf/htmlall/5upd5e?opendocument> at 28 January 2007

Fleck, Dieter (ed), *The Handbook of Humanitarian Law in Armed Conflicts* (1995)

Fenrick, William, 'Attacking the Enemy Civilian as a Punishable Offense' (1997) 7:2 *Duke Journal of Comparative and International Law* 539

Fenrick, William, 'Targeting and Proportionality during the NATO Bombing Campaign against Yugoslavia' (2001) 12:3 *European Journal of International Law* 489

Fenrick, William, 'The Rule of Proportionality and Protocol I in Conventional Warfare' (1982) 98 *Military Law Review* 91

Gardam, Judith, *Non-combatant Immunity as a Norm of International Humanitarian Law* (1993)

Gardam, Judith, 'Proportionality and Force in International Law' (1993) 87 *American Journal of International Law* 391

Gomez, Javier, 'The Law of Air Warfare' (1998) 323 *International Review of the Red Cross* <http://www.icrc.org/Web/eng/siteengo.nsf/iwpList167/42F64C9A4212EA07C1256B66005C0BF1> at 4 June 2006

Gray, Christine, *International Law and the Use of Force* (2nd ed, 2004)

Green, Leslie, *The Contemporary Law of Armed Conflict* (2nd ed, 2000)

Greenwood, Christopher, 'International Humanitarian Law and United Nations Military Operations' (1998) 1 *Yearbook of International Humanitarian Law* 3

Greenwood, Christopher, 'International law and the United States' air operation against Libya' (1987) 89 *West Virginia Law Review* 933

Greenwood, Christopher, 'The Advisory Opinion on nuclear weapons and the contribution of the International Court to international humanitarian law' (1997) 316 *International Review of the Red Cross* <http://www.icrc.org/Web/eng/siteengo.nsf/iwpList159/C724E78E1FDDD9F5C1256B66005A623C> at 4 June 2006

Greenwood, Christopher, 'The twilight of the law of belligerent reprisals' (1989) 20 *Netherlands Year Book of International Law* 35

Grotius, Hugo, *On the Law of War and Peace* (A. Campbell trans, 1814) [trans of: *De Jure Belli ac Pacis*]

Heerey, Peter, 'Storytelling: Postmodernism and the law' (2000) 74 *Australian Law Journal* 681

Heintze, Hans-Joachim, 'On the relationship between human rights law protection and international humanitarian law' (2004) 856 *International Review of the Red Cross* 789

Henckaerts, Jean-Marie and Doswald-Beck, Louise (eds), *Customary International Humanitarian Law* (2005)

Henry Dunant Institute and UNESCO (eds), *International Dimensions of Humanitarian Law* (1988)

International Committee of the Red Cross, *Conference of Government Experts on the Reaffirmation and Development of International Humanitarian Law Applicable in Armed Conflicts*, Volume I, *Introduction* (1971)

International Committee of the Red Cross, *Conference of Government Experts on the Reaffirmation and Development of International Humanitarian Law Applicable in Armed Conflicts*, Volume III, *Protection of the civilian population against dangers of hostilities* (1971)

International Committee of the Red Cross, *Conference of Government Experts on the Reaffirmation and Development of International Humanitarian Law Applicable in Armed Conflicts*, Volume IV, *Rules Relative to the Behaviour of Combatants* (1971)

International Committee of the Red Cross, *Conference of Government Experts on the Reaffirmation and Development of International Humanitarian Law Applicable in Armed Conflicts*, Volume I, *Report on the Work of the Conference* (1972)

International Committee of the Red Cross, *Conference of Government Experts on the Reaffirmation and Development of International Humanitarian Law Applicable in Armed Conflicts*, Volume II, *Report on the Work of the Conference (Annexes)* (1972)

International Committee of the Red Cross, *Official Records of the Diplomatic Conference on the Reaffirmation and Development of International Humanitarian Law Applicable in Armed Conflicts* (1974–1977)

International Committee of the Red Cross, *Report of the Work of the Conference of Government Experts for the Study of the Conventions for the Protection of War Victims* (1947)

Kan, Paul, 'What Should We Bomb? Axiological Targeting and the Abiding Limits of Airpower Theory' (2004) XVIII:1 *Air & Space Power Journal* 25

Kaye, Stuart and Piotrowicz, Ryszard, *Human Rights in International and Australian Law* (2000)

Kelly, Justin and Kilcullen, David, 'Chaos Versus Predictability: A critique of Effects-Based Operations' (2004) Volume II(1) *Australian Army Journal* 87

Kendall III, Walter, 'Killing non-combatants in war: A critique of the justification and excuses' (2000) *Australian International Law Journal* 99

Kolb, Robert 'Origin of the twin terms jus ad bellum/jus in bello' (1997) 320 *International Review of the Red Cross* 553

Laursen, Andreas, 'NATO, the War Over Kosovo, and the ICTY Investigation' (2002) 17 *American University International Law Review* 765

McNeil, John, 'The International Court of Justice Advisory Opinion in the Nuclear Weapons Case—A first appraisal' (1997) 316 *International Review of the Red Cross* <http://www.icrc.org/Web/eng/siteengo.nsf/iwpList159/177FA9E94321B0DFC1256B66005A6346> at 4 June 2006

Macquarie Dictionary (3rd revised ed, 2001)

Maley, William (ed), *Shelters from the Storm: Developments in International Humanitarian Law* (1995)

Mani, V S, 'International humanitarian law: an Indo-Asian perspective' (2001) 841 *International Review of the Red Cross* <http://www.icrc.org/Web/eng/siteengo.nsf/iwpList182/FD9E38D48A5BAE3DC1256B66005FA894> at 4 June 2006

Matte, Nicolas (ed), *Annals of Air and Space Law*, Volume 4 (1979)

Maxwell, Mark, 'The Law of War and Civilians on the Battlefield: Are We Undermining Civilian Protections?' (2004) September-October *Military Review* 17, <http://usacac.

leavenworth.army.mil/cac/milreview/download/English/SepOct04/maxm.pdf> at 8 March 2007

Meyer, Jeanne, 'Tearing down the facade: A critical look at the current law on targeting the will of the enemy and air force doctrine' (2001) 51 *Air Force Law Review* 143

Meyer, Michael (ed), *Armed Conflict and the New Law: Aspects of the 1977 Geneva Protocols and the 1981 Weapons Convention* (1989)

Murphy, Ray, 'International humanitarian law training for multinational peace support operations—lessons from experience' (2000) 840 *International Review of the Red Cross* <http://www.icrc.org/Web/eng/siteengo.nsf/iwpList180/C8F44398050AEB52C1256B66005F39DD> at 4 June 2006

Ogren, Kenneth, 'Humanitarian law in the Articles of War decreed in 1621 by King Gustavus II Adolphus of Sweden' (1996) 313 *International Review of the Red Cross* 438

Palwankar, Umesh, 'Applicability of International Humanitarian Law to United Nations Peace-Keeping Forces' (1993) 294 *International Review of the Red Cross* 227

Parks, W. Hays, 'Air War and the Law of War' (1990) 32 *Air Force Law Review* 1

Pictet, Jean, *The Geneva Conventions of 12 August 1949: Commentary* (1952) vol I

Provost, Rene, *International Human Rights and Humanitarian Law* (2002)

Pustogarov, Vladimir, 'Fyodor Fyodorovich Martens (1845–1909)—a humanist of modern times' (1996) 312 *International Review of the Red Cross* <http://www.icrc.org/Web/eng/siteengo.nsf/iwpList153/80D55047E77CCE46C1256B66005A0861> at 4 June 2006

Shraga, Daphna, 'The United Nations as an Actor Bound by International Humanitarian Law' (1998) 5:2 *International Peacekeeping* 64

Roberts, Adam and Guelff, Richard, *Documents on the Laws of War* (3rd ed, 2000)

Robertson Jr, Horace, 'The Principle of the Military Objective in the Law of Armed Conflict' (1997–98) 8 *United States Air Force Journal of Legal Studies* 35

Rogers, Anthony, *Law on the Battlefield* (2nd ed, 2004)

Rogers, Anthony, 'Zero-casualty warfare' (2000) 837 *International Review of the Red Cross* <http://www.icrc.org/Web/eng/siteengo.nsf/iwpList177/A41F49D9F3CE3756C1256B66005E3594> at 4 June 2006

Ronzitti, Natalino, 'Is the non liquet of the Final Report by the Committee Established to Review the NATO Bombing Campaign Against the Federal Republic of Yugoslavia Acceptable?' (2000) 840 *International Review of the Red Cross* <http://www.icrc.org/Web/eng/siteengo.nsf/iwpList180/73C2B0D8BBFE408CC1256B66005F37FE> at 4 June 2006

Rowe, Peter, 'Kosovo 1999: The Air Campaign—Have the Provisions of Additional Protocol I Withstood the Test?' (2000) 837 *International Review of the Red Cross* <http://www.icrc.org/Web/eng/siteengo.nsf/iwpList177/B98F42CBD37BB2D3C1256B66005E3504 > at 4 June 2006

Rowe, Peter, *The Impact of Human Rights Law on Armed Forces* (2006)

Sandoz, Yves, Swinarski, Christophe and Zimmerman, Bruno (eds), *Commentary on the Additional Protocols of 8 June 1977 to the Geneva Conventions of 12 August 1949* (1987)

Sassoli, Marco and Bouvier, Antoine, *How Does Law Protect in War?* (1999)

Schmitt, Michael, 'Humanitarian Law and Direct Participation in Hostilities by Private Contractors or Civilian Employees' (2004) 5 *Chicago Journal of International Law* 511

Schmitt Michael (ed), *International Law Across the Spectrum of Conflict: Essays in Honour of Professor L.C. Green on the Occasion of his Eightieth Birthday* (2000)

Schmitt, Michael, *Precision Attack and International Humanitarian Law* (2005) 859 International Review of the Red Cross 445

Schmitt, Michael, 'Targeting and Humanitarian Law: Current Issues' (2004) 34 *Israel Yearbook on Human Rights* 59

Schmitt, Michael, 'The Principle of Discrimination in 21st Century Warfare' (1999) 2 *Yale Human Rights & Development Law Journal* 143

Schmitt, Michael, 'The Sixteenth Waldemar A. Solf Lecture in International Law' (2003) 176 *Military Law Review* 365

Sinclair, Ian, *The Vienna Convention on the Law of Treaties* (2nd ed, 1984)

Slomanson, William, *Fundamental Perspectives on International Law* (5th ed, 2007)

Smith, Hugh (ed), *The Force of Law: International Law and the Land Commander* (1994)

Solf, Waldemar, 'Protection of Civilians Against the Effects of Hostilities under Customary International Law and under Protocol I' (1986) 1 *American University Journal of International Law and Policy* 117

Spaight, J.M., *Air Power and War Rights* (1924)

Stone, Julius, *Legal Controls of International Conflict: A Treatise on the Dynamics of Disputes and War Law* (1954)

Ticehurst, Rupert, 'The Martens Clause and the Laws of Armed Conflict' (1997) 317 *International Review of the Red Cross* <http://www.icrc.org/Web/eng/siteengo.nsf/iwpList160/32AEA038821EA35EC1256B66005A747C> at 4 June 2006

UK Ministry of Defence, *The Manual of the Law of Armed Conflict* (2004)

US Department of the Navy, *Annotated Supplement to the Commander's Handbook on the Law of Naval Operations* (1997)

von Clausewitz, Carl, *On War* (8th revised ed, 1984)

Voon, Tania, 'Pointing the Finger: Civilian Casualties of NATO Bombing in the Kosovo Conflict' (2001) 16:4 *American University International Law Review* 1083

'What's up with our power supply?' (March 2005) *Choice* 26

2. Case Law

Legal Consequences of the Construction of a Wall in the Occupied Palestinian Territory (Advisory Opinion) [2004] ICJ Rep 131

Legality of the Threat or Use of Nuclear Weapons (Advisory Opinion) [1996] ICJ Rep 226

Military and Paramilitary Activities in and against Nicaragua (Nicaragua v United States of America) (Merits) [1986] ICJ Rep 14

Prosecutor v Erdemovic, (Appeals Chamber) Case No IT-96-22 (7 October 1997)

Prosecutor v Galic, (Trial Chamber) Case No IT-98-29-T (5 December 2003)

Prosecutor v Kordic & Cerkez, (Appeals Chamber) Case No IT-95-14/2-A (17 December 2004)

Prosecutor v Kunarac, Kovac and Vukovic, (Appeals Chamber) Case No IT-96-23&23/1 (12 June 2002)

Prosecutor v Nahimana, Barayagwiza and Ngeze, (Trial Chamber) Case No ICTR-99-52-T (3 December 2003)

Prosecutor v Rutaganda, (Trial Chamber) Case No ICTR-96-3-T (6 December 1999)

Prosecutor v Semanza, (Trial Chamber) Case No ICTR-97-20-T (15 May 2003)

Prosecutor v. Tadic, (*Trial Chamber*) Case No IT-94–1 (7 May 1997)

The Public Committee against Torture in Israel v The Government of Israel, HCJ 769/02 (13 December 2006) (available at <http://elyon1.court.gov.il/Files_ENG/02/690/007/a34/02007690.a34.pdf> at 09 January 2007)

United States of America v Krupp von Bohlen und Halbach in Hersch Lauterpacht (ed), *Annual Digest and Reports of Public International Law Cases: Being a Selection from the Decisions of International Courts and Tribunals and Military Courts given during the year 1948* (1953), 620

United States v Lindh, 212 F Supp 2d 541 (ED Va, 2002)

United States v List in Hersch Lauterpacht (ed), *Annual Digest and Reports of Public International Law Cases: Being a Selection from the Decisions of International Courts and Tribunals and Military Courts given during the year 1948* (1953), 632

3. Legislation

Criminal Code Act 1995 (Cth)

4. Treaties

Convention for the Protection of Cultural Property in the Event of Armed Conflict, opened for signature 14 May 1954, 249 UNTS 240 (entered into force 7 August 1956)

Convention for the Protection of Human Rights and Fundamental Freedoms, opened for signature on 4 November 1950, 213 UNTS 222 (entered into force 3 September 1953) (also known as the *European Convention on Human Rights*)

Convention on the Prohibition of the Use, Stockpiling, Production and Transfer of Anti-Personnel Mines and on Their Destruction, opened for signature on 3 December 1997, 2056 UNTS 211 (entered into force 1 March 1999)

Convention (IV) Respecting the Laws and Customs of War on Land, signed at The Hague 18 October 1907, 3 Martens Nouveau Recueil (ser. 3) 461 (entered into force 26 January 1910)

Declaration Renouncing the Use, in Time of War, of Explosive Projectiles Under 400 Grammes Weight, 18 Martens Nouveau Recueil (ser. 1) 474, 138 Consol. TS 297, (entered into force 11 December 1868 (29 November 1868 by the Julian calendar))

Geneva Convention for the Amelioration of the Condition of the Wounded and Sick in Armed Forces in the Field, opened for signature 12 August 1949, 75 UNTS 31 (entered into force 21 October 1950)

Geneva Convention for the Amelioration of the Condition of the Wounded, Sick and Shipwrecked Members of the Armed Forces at Sea, opened for signature 12 August 1949, 75 UNTS 85 (entered into force 21 October 1950)

Geneva Convention Relative to the Treatment of Prisoners of War, opened for signature 12 August 949, 75 UNTS 287 (entered into force 21 October 1950)

Geneva Convention relative to the Protection of Civilian Persons in Time of War, opened for signature 12 August 1949, 75 UNTS 135 (entered into force 21 October 1950)

Protocol Additional to the Geneva Conventions of 12 August 1949, and Relating to the Protection of Victims of International Armed Conflicts, opened for signature 12 December 1977, 1125 UNTS 3 (entered into force 7 December 1978)

Protocol Additional to the Geneva Conventions of 12 August 1949, and relating to the Protection of Victims of Non-International Armed Conflicts, opened for signature 12 December 1977, 1125 UNTS 609 (entered into force 7 December 1978)

Rome Statute of the International Criminal Court, opened for signature 17 July 1998, 2187 UNTS 90 (entered into force 1 July 2002)

5. Other Sources

12th/16th Hunter River Lancers, Department of Defence <http://www.defence.gov.au/army/12_16hrl/index.htm> at 3 December 2006

A Guide to the Legal Review of New Weapons, Means and Methods of Warfare: Measures to Implement Article 36 of Additional Protocol I of 1977 (2006) International Committee of the Red Cross <http://www.icrc.org/web/eng/siteengo.nsf/html/new-weapons-publication-190106> at 5 May 2007

Air Force Pamphlet 14-210 Intelligence, 'USAF Intelligence Targeting Guide' (1998) <http://www.e-publishing.af.mil/pubfiles/af/14/afpam14-210/afpam14-210.pdf> at 1 March 2005

Air Force Pamphlet No. 110-31, *International Law—The Conduct of Armed Conflict and Air Operations*, (1976)

Allard, Tom, 'Hill Credits ADF for Lower Civilian Toll', *The Age* (Melbourne), 24 April 2003

Amnesty International's initial comments on the review by the International Criminal Tribunal for the Former Yugoslavia of NATO's Operation Allied Force (2000) Amnesty International <http://web.amnesty.org/library/index/ENGEUR700302000> at 26 May 2006

Anderson, Kenneth, et al, *A Public Call For International Attention to Legal Obligations of Defending Forces As Well As Attacking Forces to Protect Civilians in Armed Conflict* (2003) Crimes of War Project <http://www.crimesofwar.org/print/onnews/iraq3-print.html> at 4 March 2005

Blake, Duncan, *Coalition Bombardment: Legal problems arising from aerial bombardment in a coalition context* (Masters Paper, University of Melbourne, 2004)

Block, Robert, *Shields*, Crimes of War Project <http://www.crimesofwar.org/thebook/shields.html> at 26 May 2006

Boivin, Alexandra, 'The Legal Regime Applicable to Targeting Military Objectives in the Context of Contemporary Warfare' (Research Paper Series No 2/2006, University Centre for International Humanitarian Law, 2006) <www.ucihl.org/research/legal_regime_applicable_to_targeting_military_objectives.pdf> at 24 May 2006

Bowden, Mark, 'The Kabul-ki Dance', *The Atlantic Monthly* (Boston) November 2002 <http://www.theatlantic.com/doc/prem/200211/bowden> at 2 March 2005

Briefing by the International Development Secretary, Ms Clare Short, and the Chief of Joint Operations, Admiral Sir Ian Garnett on 23 April 1999 (1999) <www.kosovo.mod.uk/brief230499.htm> at 26 December 2005

Brown, Gary, 'Proportionality for Military Leaders' (2000) *Air Command and Staff College, Air University* <http://www.au.af.mil/au/awc/awcgate/acsc/00-208.pdf> at 26 May 2006

'"Bugsplat" computer program aims to limit civilian deaths at targets', *The Seattle Times* (Seattle), 26 February 2003

Burger, James, 'International humanitarian law and the Kosovo crisis: Lessons learned or to be learned' (2000) 837 *International Review of the Red Cross* <http://www.icrc.org/Web/eng/siteengo.nsf/iwpList177/1A257FE6E1DC3A57C1256B66005E3484> at 4 June 2006

Bush, George W., *Operation Iraqi Freedom* (2003) The White House <http://www.whitehouse.gov/news/releases/2003/04/20030405.html> at 27 December 2005

Bush, George W. and Putin, Vladimir, *Joint Statement on Afghanistan* (2001) The White House <http://www.whitehouse.gov/news/releases/2001/11/20011113-9.html> at 27 December 2005

Civilian Deaths in the NATO Air Campaign (2000) Human Rights Watch <http://www.hrw.org/reports/2000/nato> at 25 May 2006

Civilians Must Not Be Used to Shield Homes Against Military Attacks (2006) Human Rights Watch <http://hrw.org/english/docs/2006/11/22/isrlpa14652_txt.htm> at 16 December 2006

Civilians under Assault: Hezbollah's Rocket Attacks on Israel in the 2006 War (2007) Human Rights Watch <http://hrw.org/reports/2007/iopt0807/iopt0807webwcover.pdf> at 19 September 2007

"Collateral damage" or Unlawful Killings?: Violations of the Laws of War by NATO during Operation Allied Force (2000) Amnesty International <http://web.amnesty.org/library/index/ENGEUR700182000> at 26 May 2006

Conditions of Application of Humanitarian Rules of Armed Conflict to Hostilities in which United Nations Forces May be Engaged (1971) Institute of International Law <http://www.idi-iil.org/idiE/resolutionsE/1971_zag_03_en.pdf> at 1 March 2005

Cordesman, Anthony, *The Lessons and Non-Lessons of the Air and Missile Campaign in Kosovo* (2003) Center for Strategic and International Studies <http://www.csis.org/media/csis/pubs/kosovolessons-full.pdf> at 25 May 2006

Cordone, Claudio, and Gidron, Avner, *The Kosovo conflict: NATO on trial* (2000) Le Monde diplomatique <http://mondediplo.com/2000/07/02kosovo> at 26 May 2006

Crawford, III, J.W., *The Law of Noncombatant Immunity and the Targeting of National Electric Power Systems* (1996) Defense Technical Information Centre <http://stinet.dtic.mil/cgi-bin/GetTRDoc?AD=ADA312110&Location=U2&doc=GetTRDoc.pdf> at 26 November 2007

Das, Balaram, *Effects-Based Operations: Simulations with Cellular Automata* (2004) DSTO <http://www.dsto.defence.gov.au/publications/2677/DSTO-RR-0275.pdf> at 24 December 2005

Department of Defense, Office of General Counsel, *An Assessment of International Legal Issues in Information Operations* (1999) Maxwell-Gunter AFB <http://www.au.af.mil/au/awc/awcgate/dod-io-legal/dod-io-legal.pdf> at 27 November 2007

DeSaussure, Hamilton, *Military Objectives*, Crimes of War Project <http://www.crimesofwar.org/thebook/military-objective.html> at 26 May 2006

Direct Participation in Hostilities under International Humanitarian Law (2003) International Committee of the Red Cross <http://www.icrc.org/Web/Eng/siteengo.nsf/iwpList74/459B0FF70176F4E5C1256DDE00572DAA> at 10 April 2006

Draft Rules for the Limitation of the Dangers incurred by the Civilian Population in Time of War (2005) International Committee of the Red Cross <http://www.icrc.org/ihl.nsf/FULL/420?OpenDocument> at 24 May 2006

Dunlap, Jr, Charles, *Law and Military Interventions: Preserving Humanitarian Values in 21st Conflicts* (2001) Duke University <http://www.duke.edu/~pfeaver/dunlap.pdf> at 27 November 2007

Dworkin, Anthony, *Iraqi Television: A Legitimate Target?* (2003) Crimes of War Project <http://www.crimesofwar.org/print/onnews/Brief-tv-print.html> at 2 April 2006

Dworkin, Anthony, *The Iraq War in Retrospect* (2003) Crimes of War Project <http://www.crimesofwar.org/print/onnews/iraq33-print.html> at 4 March 2005

Expert Meeting: "Targeting Military Objectives" (2005) University Centre for International Humanitarian Law <http://www.ucihl.org/research/military_objective_symposium_report.pdf> at 4 November 2007

Final Report to the Prosecutor by the Committee Established to Review the NATO Bombing Campaign Against the Federal Republic of Yugoslavia (2000) <http://www.un.org/icty/pressreal/nato061300.htm> at 2 April 2006

Fischer, Horst, *Proportionality, Principle of*, Crimes of War Project <http://www.crimesofwar.org/thebook/proportion-principle.html> at 26 May 2006

Forbes, Mark, 'Saddam a Legal Target for our Troops', *The Age* (Melbourne), 22 March 2003

Friedman, Herbert, *Psychological Operations in Iraq: No-Fly Zone Warning Leaflets to Iraq, 2002–2003* (2003) *psywar.org* <http://www.psywar.org/noflyzone.php> at 26 May 2006

Fusco, Paolo, *Legal status of human shields* (2003) Centro Studi per la Pace <http://www.studiperlapace.it/view_news_html?news_id=20050125105209> at 12 June 2005

Grant, Rebecca, *Altitude* (2001) Air Force Magazine Online <http://www.afa.org/magazine/oct2001/1001altitude.asp> at 23 May 2006

Grant, Rebecca, *Gulf War II: Air and Space Power Led the Way* (2003) Air Force Association <http://www.afa.org/media/reports/GulfWar.pdf> at 1 May 2005

Gutman, Roy and Kuttab, Daoud, *Indiscriminate Attack*, Crimes of War Project <http://www.crimesofwar.org/thebook/indiscriminate-attack.html> at 26 May 2006

Hackett, Bob, Kingsepp, Sander, and Cundall, Peter, *IJN AWA MARU: Tabular Record of Movement* (1985–2005) Imperial Japanese Navy Page <http://www.combinedfleet.com/Awa_t.htm> at 12 February 2006

Hampson, Francoise, *Military Necessity*, Crimes of War Project <http://www.crimesofwar.org/thebook/military-necessity.html> at 25 May 2006

Hate Radio: Europe (2002) Radio Netherlands <http://www2.rnw.nl/rnw/en/features/media/dossiers/hateradioeur.html> at 26 December 2005

History, Institute of International Law <http://www.idi-iil.org/idiE/navig_history.html> at 2 March 2005

Hosmer, Stephen, *Operations Against Enemy Leaders* (2001) RAND <http://www.rand.org/publications/MR/MR1385/> at 1 May 2005

Houston, Angus, 'The Law of Armed Conflict and Contemporary Air Operations—the ADF Approach' (Speech Delivered at the Solferino Seminar, Weston Creek, 11 May 2004) <http://www.defence.gov.au/raaf/corporate/leaders/Solferino%20Seminar.pdf> at 23 March 2006

IHL in Air and Missile Warfare, International Humanitarian Law Research Initiative <http://www.ihlresearch.org/amw/> at 6 March 2007

In America's Sights: Targeting Decisions in a War with Iraq (2003) Crimes of War Project <http://www.crimesofwar.org/print/onnews/iraq-print.html> at 4 March 2005

Israel destroys the highest bridge in Lebanon (2006) Ya Libnan <http://yalibnan.com/site/archives/2006/07/israel_destroys.php> at 6 November 2007

Israel/Lebanon: Deliberate destruction or "collateral damage"? Israeli attacks on civilian infrastructure (2006) Amnesty International <http://web.amnesty.org/library/pdf/MDE180072006ENGLISH/$File/MDE1800706.pdf> at 19 September 2007

Iyer, Pico, The Unknown Rebel (1998) Time <http://www.time.com/time/time100/leaders/profile/rebel.html> at 16 January 2007

Kehl, Robert, *The Time is Ripe for a More Effective International Law* <http://users.westnet.gr/~cgian/rkehl.htm> at 25 May 2006

Kellenberger, Jacob, *International Humanitarian Law at the Beginning of the 21st Century* (2002) International Committee of the Red Cross <http://www.icrc.org.web.eng/siteeng0.nsf/iwplist99/efc5a1c8d8dd70b9c1256c3600> at 25 May 2006.

Kitcher, Michael, email to Ian Henderson, 4 December 2003

Laser Guided Bombs (2000) Federation of American Scientists <http://www.fas.org/man/dod-101/sys/smart/lgb.htm> at 23 March 2006

Legal Issues Arising from the War in Afghanistan and Related Anti-Terrorism Efforts (2002) Human Rights Watch <http://www.hrw.org/campaigns/september11/ihlqna.htm> at 2 March 2005

Marine Judge Advocate Newsletter, Volume IV, Issue 6, (June 1999) Staff Judge Advocate to the Commandant of the Marine Corps <http://sja.hqmc.usmc.mil/newsletter/1999/6_99/june.htm> at 25 May 2006

Marjanovic, Biljana, *Collateral Damage*: A View Into the Daily Lives of Yugoslavs Under the Bombs <http://www.thing.net/~oliveworks/marjanovic.html> at 26 May 2006

Meilinger, Phillip, *Precision Aerospace Power: Discrimination, and the Future of War* (2001) Air & Space Power Chronicles <http://www.airpower.maxwell.af.mil/airchronicles/apj/apj01/fal01/meilinger.html> at 30 December 2005

Meron, Theodor, *Customary Law*, Crimes of War Project <http://www.crimesofwar.org/thebook/customary-law.html> at 25 May 2006

Mooney, Chris, *Did the United Nations Authorize 'No-Fly' Zones Over Iraq?* (2002) Slate <http://slate.msn.com/id/2074302> at 2 March 2005

Nabulsi, Karma, *Jus ad Bellum/Jus in Bello*, Crimes of War Project <http://www.crimesofwar.org/thebook/jus-ad-bellum.html> at 25 May 2006.

Nazi Conspiracy and Aggression Volume IV—Document No. 1800-PS (2005) The Avalon Project <http://www.yale.edu/lawweb/avalon/imt/document/nca_vol4/1800-ps.htm> at 10 September 2005

Needless deaths in the Gulf War: Civilian Casualties During the Air Campaign and Violations of the Laws of War (1991) Human Rights Watch <http://www.hrw.org/reports/1991/gulfwar/> at 2 March 2005

News Letter, No. 03-27 (2003) Center for Army Lessons Learned <http://call.army.mil> at 15 May 2003

Off Target: The Conduct of the War and Civilian Casualties in Iraq (2003) Human Rights Watch <http://www.hrw.org/reports/2003/usa1203/usa1203.pdf> at 4 November 2007

Parks, W. Hays, 'Rules of Conduct during Operations Other Than War: The Law of War Does Apply' (2001) *The University of North Carolina at Chapel Hill—American Diplomacy* <http://www.unc.edu/depts/diplomat/archives_roll/2001_07-09/hum_intervention/hum_08_parks.html> at 28 February 2005

Pfaff, Tony, Non-*combatant Immunity and the War on Terrorism* (2003) United States Air Force Academy <http://www.usafa.af.mil/jscope/JSCOPE03/Pfaff03.html> at 26 May 2006

Pickrell, John, *Dolphins Deployed as Undersea Agents in Iraq* (2003) National Geographic News <http://news.nationalgeographic.com/news/2003/03/0328_030328_wardolphins.html> at 7 August 2005

Popp, Carlo, *Desert Storm: Precision Guided Munitions* (2005) Air Power Australia <http://www.ausairpower.net/TE-PGM-ODS-92.html> at 29 December 2005

Preserving Humanitarian Principles While Combating Terrorism: Israel's Struggle with Hizbullah in the Lebanon War (2007) Israel Ministry of Foreign Affairs <http://www.mfa.gov.il/NR/rdonlyres/74D04C9D-FA73-4A54-8CBA-DBCB1152C82E/0/DiplomaticNotes01.pdf> at 4 November 2007

psywar.org <http://www.psywar.org> at 26 May 2006

Radio 2BL, 'Senator the Hon. Robert Hill, Minister for Defence, Leader of the Government in the Senate, interview with Richard Glover' 18 March 2003 <http://www.minister.defence.gov.au/HillTranscripttpl.cfm?CurrentId=2442> at 5 March 2007

Rado, Gaby, *Legitimate Military Targets*, Crimes of War Project <http://www.crimesofwar.org/thebook/legit-military-target.html> at 26 May 2006

Report of the Secretary-General on the Protection of Civilians in Armed Conflict, UN Doc S/2005/740 (2005)

Report on the work of its fifty-eighth session, International Law Commission, UN Doc A/61/10 (2006) (available at <http://untreaty.un.org/ilc/reports/2006/2006report.htm> at 11 January 2007)

Robertson, George, *Kosovo—An account of the crisis: NATO Air strikes* <http://www.kosovo.mod.uk/account/nato.htm> at 30 December 2005

Rogers, Anthony, *Combatant Status*, Crimes of War Project <http://www.crimesofwar.org/thebook/combatant-status.html> at 27 April 2006

Roth, Kenneth, *International Humanitarian Law Issues and the Afghan Conflict: Open Letter to North Atlantic Treaty Organization (NATO) Defense Ministers* (2001) Human Rights Watch <http://www.hrw.org/press/2001/10/nato1017-ltr.htm> at 28 February 2005

Rowe, Peter, *Soldiers, Rights of*, Crimes of War Project <http://www.crimesofwar.org/thebook/soldiers-rights-of.html> at 26 May 2006

Rowe, Peter, *Total W*ar, Crimes of War Project <http://www.crimesofwar.org/thebook/total-war.html> at 26 May 2006

San Remo Manual on International Law Applicable to Armed Conflicts at Sea (1994) International Committee of the Red Cross <http://www.icrc.org/Web/Eng/siteengo.nsf/iwpList375/966627225C719EDCC1256B6600598E0> at 25 May 2006

Sassoli, Marco, *Legitimate Targets of Attacks under International Humanitarian Law* (2003) Harvard Program on Humanitarian Policy and Conflict Research <http://www.ihlresearch.org/ihl/pdfs/Session1.pdf> at 2 March 2005

Schmitt, Michael, '"Direct participation in hostilities" and 21st century armed conflict' (2004) <http://www.michaelschmitt.org/images/ Directparticipationpageproofs.pdf> at 12 June 2005

Second Expert Meeting—Direct Participation in Hostilities under International Humanitarian Law: Summary Report (2004) International Committee of the Red Cross, <http://www.icrc.org/Web/Eng/siteengo.nsf/iwpList74/459B0FF70176F4E5C1256DDE00572DAA> at 10 April 2006

Shearer, Ivan, *Rules of Conduct during Humanitarian Interventions*, The University of North Carolina at Chapel Hill—American Diplomacy <http://www.unc.edu/depts/diplomat/archives_roll/2001_07-09/hum_intervention/hum_06_shearer.html> at 25 May 2006

Smyth, Frank, *Gulf W*ar, Crimes of War Project <http://www.crimesofwar.org/thebook/gulf-war.html> at 25 May 2006

States party to the Geneva Conventions and their Additional Protocols (2005) International Committee of the Red Cross <http://www.icrc.org/Web/eng/siteengo.nsf/htmlall/party_gc/$File/Conventions%20de%20Geneve%20et%20Protocoles%20additionnels%20ENG.pdf> at 28 August 2005

Tactics, Techniques, and Procedures for the Strike / Recon Platoon (Striker), US Army Field Artillery School <http://sill-www.army.mil/fdic/doctrine/task%20force%202000/striker/chap7.htm#c7_2> at 23 March 2006

'Target scope extended in no-fly zones', *Gulf News Online Edition* (Dubai) 3 March 2003 <http://www.gulf-news.com/Articles/news.asp?ArticleID=79241> at 9 September 2003

The ICRC's Mission Statement (2005) International Committee of the Red Cross <http://www.icrc.org/Web/Eng/siteengo.nsf/htmlall/68EE39?OpenDocument> at 3 December 2006

The War in Iraq: ADF Operations in the Middle East in 2003 (2004) Department of Defence <http://www.defence.gov.au/publications/lessons.pdf> at 27 March 2005

Third Expert Meeting on the Notion of Direct Participation in Hostilities: Summary Report (2005) International Committee of the Red Cross <http://www.icrc.org/Web/eng/siteengo.nsf/htmlall/participation-hostilities-ihl-311205/$File/Direct_participation_in_hostilities_2005_eng.pdf> at 20 December 2006

Tiananmen revisited (2001) CNN.COM <http://edition.cnn.com/SPECIALS/2001/tiananmen/> at 16 January 2007

Tran, Tini, '"Chemical Ali" reported killed in Basra', *The Age* (Melbourne), 8 April 2003

UK Government, *Defeating International Terrorism: Campaign Objectives* (2001) Global Security <http://www.globalsecurity.org/military/library/news/2001/10/uk-011016-terror-objectives.htm> at 27 December 2005

Understanding collateral damage workshop (2002) Carr Center for Human Rights Policy—Project on the Means of Intervention <http://www.ksg.harvard.edu/cchrp/Web%20Working%20Papers/WebJuneReport.pdf> at 15 May 2005

US Air Force grapples with continuous target identification (2002) International Defense Review <http://idr.janes.com/public/idr/index.shtml> at 15 May 2005

US Department of Defense, *Conduct of the Persian Gulf War: Final Report to Congress* (1992) National Defense University <http://www.ndu.edu/library/epubs/cpgw.pdf> at 25 May 2006

Walker, Paul, *U.S. Bombing: The myth of Surgical Bombing in the Gulf War* (1992) <http://deoxy.org/wc/wc-myth.htm> at 11 August 2003

Waxman, Matthew, *International Law and the Politics of Urban Air Operations* (2000) RAND Corporation <http://www.rand.org/publications/MR/MR1175> at 28 February 2005

What is international humanitarian law? (2004) International Committee of the Red Cross <http://www.icrc.org/Web/eng/siteeng0.nsf/htmlall/humanitarian-law-factsheet/$File/What_is_IHL.pdf> at 25 May 2006

Why They Died: Civilian Casualties in Lebanon during the 2006 War (2007) Human Rights Watch <hrw.org/reports/2007/lebanon0907/lebanon0907web.pdf> at 4 November 2007

Wyman, Richard, 'The First Rules of Air Warfare' (1984) *Air & Space Power Chronicles* <http://www.airpower.au.af.mil/airchronicles/aureview/1984/mar-apr/wyman.html> at 19 November 2005

Index

Q

R

S

T

U

W

International Humanitarian Law Series

1 Michael J. Kelly, *Restoring and Maintaining Order in Complex Peace Operations: The Search for a Legal Framework*, 1999 ISBN 90 411 1179 4
2 Helen Durham and Timothy L.H. McCormack (eds.), *The Changing Face of Conflict and the Efficacy of International Humanitarian Law*, 1999 ISBN 90 411 1180 8
3 Richard May, David Tolbert, John Hocking, Ken Roberts, Bing Bing Jia, Daryl Mundis and Gabriël Oosthuizen (eds.), *Essays on ICTY Procedure and Evidence in Honour of Gabrielle Kirk McDonald*, 2001 ISBN 90 411 1482 3
4 Elizabeth Chadwick, *Traditional Neutrality Revisited: Law, Theory and Case Studies*, 2002 ISBN 90 411 1787 3
5 Lal Chand Vohrah, Fausto Pocar, Yvonne Featherstone, Olivier Fourmy, Christine Graham, John Hocking and Nicholas Robson (eds.), *Man's Inhumanity to Man: Essays on International Law in Honour of Antonio Cassese*, 2003 ISBN 90 411 1986 8
6 Gideon Boas and William A. Schabas (eds.), *International Criminal Law Developments in the Case Law of the ICTY*, 2003 ISBN 90 411 1987 6
7* Karen Hulme, *War Torn Environment: Interpreting the Legal Threshold*, 2004 ISBN 90 04 13848 x
8 Helen Durham and Tracey Gurd (eds.), *Listening to the Silences: Women and War*, 2005 ISBN 90 04 14365 3
9* ** Marten Zwanenburg, *Accountability of Peace Support Operations*, 2005 ISBN 90 04 14350 5
10 Hirad Abtahi and Gideon Boas (eds.), *The Dynamics of International Criminal Law*, 2006 ISBN 90 04 14587 7
11 Frits Kalshoven, *Belligerent Reprisals*, 2005 ISBN 90 04 14386 6
12 Pablo Antonio Fernández-Sánchez (ed.), *The New Challenges of Humanitarian Law in Armed Conflicts: In Honour of Professor Juan Antonio Carrillo-Salcedo*, 2005 ISBN 90 04 14830 2
13 Ustinia Dolgopol and Judith Gardam (eds.), *The Challenge of Conflict: International Law Responds*, 2006 ISBN 90 04 14599 0
14* Laura Perna, *The Formation of the Treaty Law of Non-International Armed Conflicts*, 2006 ISBN 90 04 14924 4
15 Michael Schmitt and Jelena Pejic (eds.), *International Law and Armed Conflict: Exploring the Faultlines, Essays in Honour of Yoram Dinstein*, 2007 ISBN 978 9004154 28 5
16 Ola Engdahl, *Protection of Personnel in Peace Operations: The Role of the 'Safety Convention' against the Background of General International Law*, 2007 ISBN 978 9004154 66 7
17 Frits Kalshoven, *Reflections on the Law of War: Collected Essays*, 2007 ISBN 978 90 04 15825 2
18 Héctor Olásolo, *Unlawful Attacks in Combat Situations: From the ICTY's Case Law to the Rome Statute*, 2007 ISBN 978 90 04 15466 7
19 José Doria, Hans-Peter Gasser and M. Cherif Bassiouni (eds.), *The Legal Regime of the International Criminal Court: Essays in Honour of Professor Igor Blishchenko*, 2008 ISBN 978 90 04 16308 9
20 David A. Blumenthal and Timothy L.H. McCormack (eds.), *The Legacy of Nuremberg: Civilising Influence or Institutionalised Vengeance?*, 2008 ISBN 978 90 04 15691 3
21 Omar Abdulle Alasow, *Violations of the Rules Applicable in Non-International Armed Conflicts and Their Possible Causes: The Case of Somalia*, 2008 ISBN 978 90 04 16475 8
22 Ola Engdahl and Pål Wrange (eds.), *Law at War: The Law as it Was and the Law as it Should Be – Liber Amicorum Ove Bring*, 2008 ISBN 978 90 04 17016 2
23 Pablo Antonio Fernández-Sánchez (ed.), *International Legal Dimension of Terrorism*, 2009 ISBN 978 90 04 17053 7
24 Rob McLaughlin, *United Nations Naval Peace Operations in the Territorial Sea*, 2009 ISBN 978 90 04 17479 5
25 Ian Henderson, *The Contemporary Law of Targeting*, 2009 ISBN 978 90 04 17480 1
26 Cecilia M. Bailliet (ed.), *Security: A Multidisciplinary Normative Approach*, 2009 ISBN 978 90 04 17296 8
27 Kristen Eichensehr and W. Michael Reisman (eds.), *Stopping Wars and Making Peace: Studies in International Intervention*, 2009 ISBN 978 90 04 17855 7
28 Noelle Higgins, *Regulating the Use of Force in Wars of National Liberation – The Need for a New Regime: A Study of the South Moluccas and Aceh*, 2009 ISBN 978 90 04 17287 6

---

* Winner of the ASIL Francis Lieber Prize.

** Winner of the 2006 Paul Reuter Prize.

www.ingramcontent.com/pod-product-compliance
Lightning Source LLC
LaVergne TN
LVHW010632300926
849162LV00001B/132